Motivational Interviewing With Couples

Motivational Interviewing With Couples

A Framework for Behavior Change Developed With Sexual Minority Men

TYREL J. STARKS

OXFORD
UNIVERSITY PRESS

Oxford University Press is a department of the University of Oxford. It furthers
the University's objective of excellence in research, scholarship, and education
by publishing worldwide. Oxford is a registered trade mark of Oxford University
Press in the UK and certain other countries.

Published in the United States of America by Oxford University Press
198 Madison Avenue, New York, NY 10016, United States of America.

© Oxford University Press 2022

CIP data is on file at the Library of Congress
ISBN 978-0-19-754964-3

DOI: 10.1093/med-psych/9780197549643.001.0001

9 8 7 6 5 4 3 2 1

Printed by Marquis, Canada

CONTENTS

LIST OF FIGURES

Trey V. Dellucci, MS
Department of Psychology
Hunter College of the City University
   of New York
New York, NY, USA
Doctoral Program in Health
   Psychology and Clinical Science
Graduate Center of the City University
   of New York
New York, NY, USA

Kendell M. Doyle, MA
Department of Psychology
Hunter College of the City University
   of New York
New York, NY, USA

Doctoral Program in Health
   Psychology and Clinical Science
Graduate Center of the City University
   of New York
New York, NY, USA

Daniel Sauermilch, MA
Department of Psychology
Long Island University (Brooklyn)
Brooklyn, NY, USA

Tyrel J. Starks, PhD
Associate Professor
Department of Psychology
Hunter College of the City University
   of New York
New York, NY, USA

Introduction: Background, Terminology, and the Structure of this Volume

Interpersonal relationships are a central element of human existence. While cultures vary with respect to their individual versus collectivistic orientation (Triandis, 2018), even in the most individualistic of cultures people are to some extent embedded in networks of relationships. Individual experience is situated within a context that involves some combination of family, friends, community, and society. We feel the presence—or for some the absence—of these social forces. That does not mean relationships are uniformly sources of tremendous joy—they can also inspire indifference or become sources of pain. I mean to suggest only that the bonds we form to other people, or the absence of such bonds, are powerful influences on our behavior.

To the extent that I am inspired by something in psychology, it is the idea that we move each other around as we move through the world. I am fascinated by the impact interpersonal relationships have on personal behavior. I have been exceedingly lucky in this sense. I arrived at my early career as a clinical psychologist just in time to see something of a "relationship renaissance" in research on HIV prevention and treatment. What vision I had for my career was reshaped by the 2009 publication of Sullivan and colleagues' influential paper indicating that as many as 68% of new HIV infections among sexual minority men (a group that includes gay, bisexual, and other men who have sex with men) in the United States were transmitted between main or primary relationship partners. Reading it was the first time I recall being really excited about what I could potentially do as a behavioral scientist. This book represents the culmination of just over a decade of work that followed that realization.

NOTES ON LANGUAGE

This text specifically focuses on *couples*. It is worth taking a moment, to clarify what "couple" means in the context of this book. As Kelley (1979) pointed out, humans form a range of *close personal relationships*. Lovers, spouses, best friends, coworkers, siblings, parents and their children for example—when comprising two people, all of these relationships (and many more besides) might technically be considered couples of some form. All of them are characterized by some degree of commitment; shared interests (in the form of time, activities, or material resources); and the sharing of personal information and feelings. In all of them, there is "the likelihood that people see themselves as part of a unit and are seen that way by others" (Kelley, 1979, p. 1).

It is certainly plausible that the principles and techniques in this text are relevant to at least some of these diverse relationship contexts. Chapter 11, in fact, discusses this possibility in its section on future directions. Aside from that content, however, **this text is concerned specifically with couples that are characterized by a close personal relationship that is also sexual in nature.** Sexual relationships that otherwise lack the characteristics of close personal relationships (e.g., casual or anonymous sex partners) fall outside the scope of what my coauthors and I mean to imply by the term *couple*. As we have used the term, a couple is also distinct from close personal relationships that lack a sexual component (e.g., best friends, siblings, coworkers, or parent and child).

This relatively narrow definition of a couple as a close personal relationship that is sexual in nature reflects the emphasis on sexual health—and in particular human immunodeficiency virus (HIV)—in my research. As described in Chapter 1, my research team and I have been primarily interested in developing applications of Motivational Interviewing that address the intersection of drug use and sexual health in couples at high risk for HIV infection through sexual transmission. Fortunately, the kind of couple we have been considering is also in many ways the prototype client in the majority of couples and sex therapy interventions. We are therefore able to situate our work within these larger research and counseling traditions.

The subjectively meaningful terms that two people in a couple might use to refer to one another are extremely diverse and in many cases vary by cultural context. A "boyfriend" to one person might be "beau" or "boo" to another. While some might favor terms like "husband/wife" or "lover," others may be more comfortable with "spouse" or "partner." My coauthors and I use the term *partner* to refer to the individuals in a couple. This was done to achieve consistency across the text and is not intended as a specific recommendation for how counselors should refer to clients in session. Our general stance is that counselors should use language that is culturally appropriate and relevant to the clients they serve.

Motivational Interviewing texts vary in how they refer to the person conducting the interview (as an interviewer, provider, practitioner, counselor, group leader, etc.). My coauthors and I routinely use the term *counselor*. While not all providers who might utilize the concepts discussed in this text may identify with that professional label, the title is relevant in the context of drug use and sexual risk reduction intervention and allowed for consistency across the text and narrative examples.

Substance use is discussed widely throughout this text. Typically, my coauthors and I use the term *substance use* when making general references that encompass both drug and alcohol use. When used generally, the term *drug use* is meant to imply the use of any illicit substance, the misuse of prescription drugs, and the use of cannabis (regardless of whether it is legal in a particular local jurisdiction). When referring to specific substances by name, we have used the term *cannabis* to refer to marijuana and other products that contain tetrahydrocannabinol. We reserve the term *illicit drug use* or *other illicit drugs* to collectively refer to the use of any illicit drug (including the misuse of prescription drugs) excluding cannabis products.

Finally, this text also gives extensive attention to male couples' sexual behavior. Our language reflects relatively recent developments in nomenclature. Until 2014, it was common to refer to *condomless sex* (penetrative anal or vaginal sex that occurred without a condom being used) as *unprotected sex*. In a January 2014 conference call with HIV care providers, the Centers for Disease Control and Prevention officially acknowledged the need to stop treating condomless sex as synonymous with unprotected sex (Fleming, 2014). The shift was prompted by the emergence of biomedical HIV prevention options. Pre-exposure prophylaxis (PrEP) and postexposure prophylaxis (PEP) have made it possible for condomless sex to be protected with respect to HIV infection in at least some ways.

Until December 2021, PrEP options were limited to oral medication—antiretroviral drugs used to treat HIV infection among people living with HIV. If taken by an HIV-negative person prior to exposure, PrEP is capable of dramatically reducing the risk of acquiring HIV. Currently, the U.S. Food and Drug Administration has approved two drug options for use as PrEP. Both are single pills containing two different antiretroviral medications. Truvada[*] combines emtricitabine and tenofovir disoproxil fumarate (Dyer, 2019; Thorley et al., 2016; Yoshimura, 2017); meanwhile, Descovy[*] combines emtricitabine and tenofovir alafenamide (Krakower et al., 2020).

Pre-exposure prophylaxis is recommended for those who may be at increased risk of HIV infection (e.g., those in serodiscordant relationships, those who report inconsistent condom use) (Centers for Disease Control and Prevention, 2021c). Among sexual minority men, PrEP is 99% effective in the prevention of HIV when taken daily, and comparable benefits are achieved as long as at least four out of seven doses are taken as prescribed (P. L. Anderson et al., 2012). More recently, the World Health Organization has endorsed the use of "on-demand" or "event-driven" PrEP dosing among sexual minority men. Sometimes referred to as 2 + 1 + 1 (two-one-one), event-driven PrEP dosing involves taking 2 pills the day before a given sexual encounter, one the day of the encounter, and one the following day (World Health Organization, 2019).

One of the challenges of oral PrEP is that protection is contingent on adherence (Anderson et al., 2012). While on-demand dosing reduces this burden in some ways, people still need to take PrEP at least the day before engaging in condomless sex in order to achieve optimal protection (World Health Organization, 2019). In December 2021, the first alternative to oral PrEP medication received approval from the U.S. Food and Drug Administration (U.S. Department of Health and Human Services, 2021b). Cabotegrevir is a long-acting antiretroviral medication injected every 2 months. In two clinical trials, cabotegrevir was more effective at preventing HIV acquisition than oral PrEP medication taken daily (National Institute of Allergy and Infectious Disease, 2020a, 2020b).

In contrast to PrEP, PEP is the use of oral antiretroviral medications (typically for 28 days) to prevent seroconversion after an actual or potential exposure to HIV (Pett, 2019; U.S. Department of Health and Human Services, 2021a). PEP was used initially with medical professionals potentially exposed to HIV in the course of their work (Cardo et al., 1997; Kalichman, 1998). The U.S. Food and Drug Administration approved PEP to treat sexual and nonoccupational exposures to HIV in 2005 (U.S. Department of Health and Human Services, 2005). The efficacy of PEP to prevent HIV declines with the amount of time that elapses after exposure. If initiated immediately, PEP may be as much as 96% effective at preventing seroconversion (Sultan et al., 2014). Research suggested it is at least 80% effective if initiated within 72 hours (Roland et al., 2005); however, after 72 hours PEP provides little or no protection against seroconversion (U.S. Department of Health and Human Services, 2021).

A BRIEF REVIEW OF MOTIVATIONAL INTERVIEWING PRINCIPLES, PROCESSES, AND TECHNIQUES

In thinking about the application of Motivational Interviewing to couples, my aim has always been to extend the existing paradigm and not to create something entirely different. Those already familiar with Motivational Interviewing will recognize a continuation of the principles and practices they know. My goal in this text is to explain and demonstrate (through example interview transcripts) how W. R. Miller and Rollnick's (2013, p. 12) "collaborative conversation style for strengthening a person's motivation and commitment to change" might be expanded to encompass a couple's motivation and commitment to change.

Because my aim was to enhance the existing practice, this text is written with the assumption that the reader has a working understanding of Motivational Interviewing with individuals as outlined by W. R. Miller and Rollnick (2013). While it may be possible to learn Motivational Interviewing with couples without ever knowing anything about Motivational Interviewing with individuals first—I would not recommend it. In my own development as a counselor, I had years of practice conducting Motivational Interviews with individuals before I began to explore adaptations with couples. In my studies testing Motivational Interviewing interventions with couples, I always train counselors to conduct a Motivational Interview with an individual before they learn to do so with couples.

To any reader who is completely new to Motivational Interviewing, I would recommend familiarizing yourself with W. R. Miller and Rollnick's (2013) paradigm before proceeding into this text. For readers who have some experience with Motivational Interviewing, I offer here a brief review of the fundamental principles, core concepts, and basic technical terms you will need to understand the following chapters (see Box I.1). This is not an exhaustive summary of W. R. Miller and Rollnick's (2013) ideas. It is intended only to serve as a refresher for readers who are familiar with Motivational Interviewing but perhaps have not thought about specific terms and definitions in a while.

As suggested in the definition, **Motivational Interviewing is a way of talking to people**—"a conversational style" (W. R. Miller & Rollnick, 2013, p. 12). When I first learned Motivational Interviewing as a postdoctoral fellow in 2009, I thought myself a relatively advanced psychotherapy trainee. I had by that point spent 6 years providing counseling services in a variety of settings under skilled supervisors. Nevertheless, it was only in learning Motivational Interviewing that I finally had a framework for understanding clearly why I might choose to say some words and not others when speaking to my client. For the first time, I had a way of thinking explicitly about the connection between the language used in counseling and client behavior in the world.

The Spirit of Motivational Interviewing

In articulating their framework, W. R. Miller and Rollnick (2013) have given considerable attention not just to technique, but to the underlying assumptions held by the counselor. These represent the principles that guide their practice. This stance—"the mind-set and heart-set" (W. R. Miller & Rollnick, 2013, p. 14) of the counselor—is known as Motivational Interviewing Spirit. The expression of this spirit involves the counselor's ongoing attention to four components throughout the interview: partnership, acceptance, evocation, and compassion.

Partnership refers to a stance of collaboration. "A Motivational Interview is something done 'for' or 'with' a person"—rather than to them (W. R. Miller & Rollnick, 2013, p. 15). In enacting this element of Motivational Interviewing Spirit, counselors acknowledge the reality that change is something they cannot make happen to their client. They accept that they are witnessing and participating in the client's process and find ways to share power in session where possible.

Acceptance is itself multifaceted. Drawing on the work of Carl Rogers (1949), W. R. Miller and Rollnick (2013) suggested that acceptance encompasses the expression of accurate empathy and a belief in the absolute worth of the client. The critical element is that these sentiments must be communicated and not merely felt. The counselor must act and speak in ways that convey their effort to understand the client's perspective and their belief in the client's inherent value. This does not mean they need to approve of all the client's actions; rather, they must suspend such judgments, accept the client as they are—good or bad, wise or foolish—and focus on understanding them.

MOTIVATIONAL INTERVIEWING: KEY TERMS AND DEFINITIONS

All definitions are based on W. R. Miller and Rollnick (2013).

The Spirit of Motivational Interviewing
- Partnership—Functioning as a partner or companion, collaborating with the client
- Acceptance—Communicating absolute worth, accurate empathy, affirmation, and autonomy support
- Evocation—Eliciting the client's perspectives and motivation about the target behavior
- Compassion—Acting benevolently to promote the client's welfare, prioritizing client needs

The Processes of Motivational Interviewing
- Engaging—Establishing a mutually trusting and respectful relationship
- Focusing—Clarifying a goal or direction for change
- Evoking—Eliciting the client's own motivation for change
- Planning—Developing a specific change plan that the client is willing to implement

Additional Technical Language
- Empathy—Communicating accurate understanding of the client's perspectives and experience
- Discord—interactions that indicate a breach in working alliance between counselor and client (e.g., arguing, interrupting, discounting, or ignoring).
- Basic counseling skills
  - Open questions—Offer broad latitude and choice to the client in how to respond
  - Affirmations—Express value for a positive client attribute or behavior
  - Reflections—Statements that mirror the meaning (implicit or explicit) in preceding client speech
  - Summary statements—Reflections that draw together content from two or more client statements
- Forms of client speech
  - Change talk—favors movement toward a change goal.
  - Sustain talk—favors the status quo over movement toward a change goal.

Alongside empathy and belief in the client's absolute worth—W. R. Miller and Rollnick (2013) suggested two additional elements comprise acceptance: affirmation and support for client autonomy. In affirming clients, counselors acknowledge the client's strengths and effort. The counselor must seek to actively draw out and acknowledge client potential. Autonomy support involves respecting the client's right to self-determination. The counselor must eschew actions that would coerce or control their client and instead act in ways that validate the client's autonomy, emphasize their capacity to make choices, and draw out evidence of self-efficacy.

Evocation is a stance of curiosity (W. R. Miller & Rollnick, 2013). The counselor focuses on eliciting the client's perspectives and motivation rather than educating the client or proscribing change. In keeping with this element of Motivational Interviewing Spirit, the practice tends to deemphasize providing information in favor of drawing out the client's understanding and perspective. The goal is to explore the client's own reasons for change rather than educating them about why they should change and to invite the client to consider how they might go about changing (if they decide to) instead of instructing them on a plan for change. Note, the provision of information is not forbidden in Motivational Interviewing; however, strategies for providing information involve first exploring the client's understanding and afterward inviting the client to share their perspective on or reaction to the information provided (W. R. Miller & Rollnick, 2013). In this way, psychoeducation and attention to the client's perspective are complementary and not competing priorities.

Compassion refers to benevolence or the promotion of client welfare (W. R. Miller & Rollnick, 2013). The counselor must act in ways that prioritize the client's needs rather than their own vested interests. In introducing compassion to Motivational Interviewing Spirit, W. R. Miller and Rollnick (2013) acknowledged that Motivational Interviewing shares at least some techniques of persuasion with fields like advertising. The ethical use of these techniques in a helping profession requires that the counselor consciously center their decision-making in the client's best interest in order to avoid actual or perceived coercion. In this way, compassion is aligned with the concept of benevolence as articulated in the ethical code of the American Psychological Association (2017).

The Four Processes of Motivational Interviewing

W. R. Miller and Rollnick (2013) suggested that the interaction between client and counselor during a Motivational Interview can be understood in terms of four processes. **Engaging** refers to the establishment of rapport or working alliance— the development of a "mutually trusting and respectful relationship" (p. 408). **Focusing** involves agreeing on the subject matter of interest in the interview— "clarifying a goal or direction for change" (p. 409) with the client. In **evoking**, the counselor actively seeks to draw out or "elicit the client's own motivation for change" (p. 408). Finally, **planning** entails the "developing of a specific change plan that the client is willing to implement" (p. 411).

In outlining their processes, W. R. Miller and Rollnick (2013) emphasized that they are ongoing and co-occurring. In other words, these are not stages through which the client and counselor progress sequentially and then leave behind. Ongoing attention to engaging, focusing, evoking, and planning is necessary throughout the entire course of a Motivational Interview. That said, processes do tend to vary in their salience. Early in an interview, when the client and counselor are new to one another, the engaging and focusing processes are often particularly salient. Once a working alliance is established and some consensus about how they will use their time together has been achieved, the emphasis likely shifts to evoking and planning processes. Even as such a shift occurs, engaging and focusing remain active and relevant processes. The counselor must notice and attend to discord—"signals of disharmony" (W. R. Miller & Rollnick, 2013, p. 204) or breaches in rapport between client and counselor—and strive to maintain the working alliance even as they seek to evoke motivation or plan for change. The focus of an interview may shift and evolve as client's share more information and their perspective on the original focus is elaborated.

Additional Technical Language

This text also assumes readers are familiar with a handful of additional terms common in the Motivational Interviewing lexicon. These are particularly relevant to discussions of technique. They provide a vocabulary essential to organizing the language used by counselors and clients.

W. R. Miller and Rollnick (2013) have provided a particularly succinct and accessible formulation of microcounseling skills. Their system comprises four skills: open questions, affirmations, reflections, and summary statements. The acronym OARS then serves as a mnemonic device for counselors.

Open questions are formulated to give the client space to provide an elaborated response (W. R. Miller & Rollnick, 2013). Examples might include "How do you two manage HIV risk?" or "What rules or agreements do you have around sex with people outside of your relationship?" They contrast with close questions that are framed to elicit a yes or no answer or a response that is a single fact. Examples of closed questions might include "Are you currently on PrEP?" or "Have you agreed to be monogamous?"

Affirmations are counselor statements recognizing a positive attribute or behavior of the client (W. R. Miller & Rollnick, 2013). They serve as one tool to express acceptance—a willingness to value the client just as they are. They may also serve as a tool to support client autonomy by emphasizing the client's strengths, effort, or potential. Example affirmations might include statements such as "I respect your willingness to share so much about yourself in these sessions" or "You are clearly someone who is willing to work really hard for the things you care about."

Reflections are statements (never questions) that encapsulate or mirror the content and meaning in previous client speech (W. R. Miller & Rollnick, 2013).

Reflections exist on a continuum. On the one hand, simple reflections merely re-state or paraphrase content the client has stated.

> CLIENT: I am tired of using drugs. It's actually exhausting to live like this.
> COUNSELOR: Drug use has worn you out.

The counselor's utterance here echoes the client's idea in different words, but the meaning is largely unaltered in the counselor's reflection. In contrast, complex reflections go further. They extend the client's thought, explicitly name an emotion the client has hinted at, expand meaning through the use of metaphor, or make connections among content the client has expressed without linking together for themselves (W. R. Miller & Rollnick, 2013).

> CLIENT: I am tired of using drugs. It's actually exhausting to live like this.
> COUNSELOR: You don't want to keep going on like this. It's making you unhappy.

Unlike the prior example, the counselor utterance here both extends the client's thought ("You don't want to keep going on like this.") and alludes more directly to a feeling ("It's making you unhappy."). It goes beyond restating what the client has said and voices the counselor's impression of what the client meant but may not have explicitly stated.

Summary statements are reflections that draw together content from two or more client statements (W. R. Miller & Rollnick, 2013). While they might be used at any point, summaries may be particularly useful to conclude an inter-view, to facilitate transitions, and to open subsequent interviews in multisession interventions. When used to conclude an interview, summaries serve to capture and preserve the most important ideas covered in the time spent together. As transitions, they pull together what has been discussed and end by pointing to new content. After the initial interview in a multisession intervention, the coun-selor might open subsequent sessions by summarizing what has been discussed previously.

W. R. Miller and Rollnick (2013) also provided a framework for conceptualizing client speech. **Sustain talk** is any speech that favors the status quo. In contrast, **change talk** is speech in favor of a change goal. By actively listening for these two forms of client speech, counselors can adjust their approach in an interview. Sustain talk serves as an indicator that the current approach may not be the most effective strategy to elicit motivation for change, whereas change talk serves to in-dicate that a technique may be relatively more effective.

Sustain talk might include instances in which clients explain why they do not need to change, what they like about their current behavior, or why change is not possible. W. R. Miller and Rollnick (2013) emphasized the distinction between sustain talk and discord. The latter represents some breakdown in rapport, what they term "disharmony" in the working alliance. The presence of sustain talk in session does not inherently mean there is a problem within the counselor–client relationship. Rather, the two forms of client speech call for different counselor responses. Sustain talk might be addressed by adjusting strategy with a goal of eliciting change talk—more aligned with the evoking process. In contrast, discord calls for an emphasis on the engagement process—rebuilding trust and reestablishing mutual respect.

Change talk can manifest in myriad ways. W. R. Miller and Rollnick (2013) distinguished between preparatory and mobilizing statements. Preparatory change talk manifests as expressions of desire, ability, reasons, and need for change. These kinds of statements indicate the client "wants" change, "could" accomplish change if they decided to, sees potentially compelling reasons for change, and has some sense that they "have" or "must" accomplish change. As preparatory change talk increases, mobilizing change talk tends to emerge (W. R. Miller & Rollnick, 2013). Mobilizing change talk encompasses statements of commitment (indicating the client will, or intends to, change), activation (statements indicating a willingness to act but stopping short of express commitment), and taking steps (statements indicating that the client has already done something to move in the direction of change). For those who appreciate a mnemonic device, the acronyms DARN and CAT can be used for preparatory and mobilizing change talk respectively (W. R. Miller & Rollnick, 2013).

AN OVERVIEW OF THIS TEXT

Through a combination of theoretical and empirical rationale, this text argues that Motivational Interviewing with couples can meaningfully enhance the repertoire of intervention options available to counselors. Chapter 1 begins by explaining the premise for the approach my team and I developed for conducting a Motivational Interview with couples. It situates this work in the context of existing Motivational Interviewing and couples therapy practice.

Our work has been heavily influenced by interdependence theory (e.g., Kelley & Thibaut, 1978; Rusbult & Van Lange, 2003). Chapter 2 provides an introduction to the theory and defines principles that are essential for understanding the content in subsequent chapters. The chapter establishes the rationale for considering the couple as the client and dyadic functioning as a determinant of a couple's ability to work together toward change. Concepts introduced in this chapter are extensively referenced throughout the remainder of the text, for example, transformation of motivation (i.e., the process whereby individuals consider the consequences of their actions not only for themselves but also for their partner and their relationship); accommodation (i.e., how partners respond in moments of potential conflict when their interests are incongruent); and joint effort (i.e., wherein partners collaborate to achieve a goal they are both invested in).

In conceptualizing the Spirit of Motivational Interviewing, W. R. Miller and Rollnick (2013) drew heavily from humanistic psychology and the work of Carl Rogers. Chapter 3 revisits the concept of Motivational Interviewing Spirit with couples. In keeping with the humanistic zeitgeist, the chapter integrates concepts from person-centered couples therapy practice (e.g., O'Leary, 2012, 2015) to articulate how the Spirit of Motivational Interviewing might be expressed with couples. The counselor's role is conceptualized in terms of two dialectics. The first requires the counselor to balance attention to the couple as well as the individual partners in the couple. The second requires the counselor to balance their participation in dialogue—moving between a stance of observing the couple's communication and one of actively moderating the discourse between partners.

Chapters 4 through 8 are organized around the processes of Motivational Interviewing as they are enacted with couples. Chapters 4, 6, 7, and 8 revisit W. R. Miller and Rollnick's (2013) existing processes (engaging, focusing, evoking, and planning). Through the integration of interdependence theory and related research on relationships and health, these chapters describe and demonstrate how established Motivational Interviewing processes are enacted in session with couples. Chapter 4 examines the pathways of communication involved in engaging with couples and discusses how information about relationship functioning may emerge in session content and be inferred from partners' pronoun use. It also introduces new counseling skills in the form of utterances directed toward the couple as a whole (e.g., dyadic reflections and relationship affirmations). Chapter 6 gives substantial attention to developing consensus about the focus of a Motivational Interview. It also provides a novel structure for elaborating on a particular focus with a couple once it has been established. Chapter 7 addresses the challenges of evoking change talk with couples while also responding to dyadic ambivalence. It gives attention to counselor strategies relevant to responding to discord—or conflict—between partners that may emerge in session. Finally, Chapter 8 examines joint goal formation and the development of dyadic change plans. Goal-setting theory (e.g., Locke & Latham, 2006) is used to conceptualize the roles that partners might play in one another's change process.

Chapter 5 introduces a novel process specifically relevant to Motivational Interviewing with couples—facilitating dyadic functioning—sometimes referred to just as facilitating. The chapter begins with a general overview of how relationships and relationship quality are associated with individual health and well-being. It then details three aspects of relationship functioning that are particularly salient in interdependence theory—satisfaction, emotional investment, and commitment. Each of these is discussed in terms of how they might manifest in session—behaviors the counselor might observe in the interaction between partners that could signal the degree to which these elements of relationship quality are present versus absent. They are also discussed in terms of the impact they might have on partners' motivation for change. The chapter culminates with a review of strategies counselors can use to draw out, highlight, and develop these aspects of relationship quality.

Chapter 9 can, in many ways, be understood as an extension the work begun in Chapters 2 and 6. Communication, trust, and power are aspects of dyadic functioning that are potentially highly relevant to understanding interactions between partners; however, they are in many respects implicit in the larger context of interdependence theory. Chapter 9 explicitly defines these dimensions of dyadic functioning and describes how each might manifest in a Motivational Interview with a couple. The chapter also draws on existing couples therapy practice to outline strategies counselors might use to cultivate more adaptive communication between partners, enhance trust, and increase equity.

Chapter 10 takes on the challenge of integrating attention to sex into Motivational Interviewing practice more broadly. The chapter begins with a general introduction to sexual development. It then examines the intersection of drug use and sexual behavior. Specifically, it considers the ways in which sex may serve as both a motivation for drug use and a context in which use occurs. It goes on to consider how concepts from sexual health intervention research and more general sex therapy might be used to engage couples whose behavioral goals include making changes in the nature or amount of sex they have.

Finally, Chapter 11 is focused on the consideration of future directions. Motivational Interviewing has a strong tradition of practice integration—particularly with cognitive behavioral interventions (e.g., Naar & Safren, 2017). We provide several emerging examples of this kind of integration in Motivational Interviewing practice with couples and thoughts on future directions for such work. Acknowledging that my team's work has had a relatively narrow focus on male couples, drug use, and sexual health, the chapter also considers how the concepts described in this text might be extended to encompass more diverse couples and a wider range of health behavior change.

There is presently no extant text that defines a comprehensive theoretical framework to guide the application of Motivational Interviewing with couples or provides specific counseling techniques relevant to this practice. Notably, the second edition of W. R. Miller and Rollnick's (2002) foundational text on Motivational Interviewing included a chapter on Motivational Interviewing with couples. This chapter was omitted from the third edition (W. R. Miller & Rollnick, 2013). My coauthors and I hope this book may serve as the foundation for further research and also as a guide for clinical work using techniques that have, until now, been discussed only in journal publications (Starks, Millar, et al., 2018; Starks, Robles, et al., 2020) or consolidated in the intervention manuals used in our study trials (Starks, Adebayo, et al., 2022; Starks, Dellucci, et al., 2019; Starks, Feldstein Ewing, et al., 2019; Starks, Kyre, et al., 2021).

The Case for Motivational Interviewing With Couples

TYREL J. STARKS AND DANIEL SAUERMILCH ■

Motivational interviewing has a robust evidence base and a dedicated, enthusiastic, and talented group of counselors and trainers around the globe. Although it was initially developed in the area of substance use, a considerable amount of research has demonstrated the efficacy of Motivational Interviewing across a wide array of health conditions, including the treatment of chronic conditions, patients coping with recovery challenges postsurgery as well as with physical disability, and in recent years, the treatment of emerging problematic health behaviors (DiClemente et al., 2017; Hunt, 2011; Mirkarimi et al., 2017; Scheffel et al., 2019; Verma, 2019; Watkins et al., 2011; Yakovenko et al., 2015). Motivational Interviewing therefore occupies a unique space as a counseling approach; its application may be broad, yet its techniques aim to undergird an individual's motivation for change with respect to a specific, targeted health behavior.

Despite a remarkable track record of success with individuals as well as groups, the use of Motivational Interviewing with couples—including married couples as well as unmarried romantic and sexual partners—has been mixed (e.g., Anton et al., 2006; Apodaca et al., 2013; Babor & Del Boca, 2003; Manuel et al., 2012; Martín-Pérez et al., 2019; Miller-Matero & Cano, 2015; Monti et al., 2014; Navidian et al., 2016; Ukatt Research Team, 2005). In some prior studies, involving relationship partners in Motivational Interviews was associated with long-term, positive outcomes, including decreased substance use (e.g., Monti et al., 2014); meanwhile, others have failed to find such benefits (e.g., Bourke et al., 2016). Still others have found that the presence of relationship partners in session may result in worse outcomes for identified clients, particularly when partners argue for the status quo or in favor of sustained substance use (Manuel et al., 2012).

These initial interventions were largely conceived for couples consisting of one partner—the identified client or patient—who had been diagnosed with a given health condition (e.g., chronic pain) or engaged in a particular behavior (e.g., problematic drinking) and another who had not (Manuel et al., 2012; Miller-Matero & Cano, 2015). Within this context, researchers and clinicians have discussed the phenomenon of a relationship partner's involvement in a Motivational Interviewing session at length (Magill et al., 2010; W. R. Miller & Rose, 2010; Monti et al., 2014). During the course of an interview, relationship partners ideally enhance motivation for change by describing the consequences of the client's behavior, providing support for client change, or commenting in ways that reinforce counselor feedback. The premise is that relationship partners may "contribute opinions that may be more positively received by the [client] than if delivered by the [counselor]" (Monti et al., 2014, p. 937).

This discourse articulated a dilemma. What should a counselor do when one partner argues against change during the session? The framework outlined in this book was developed first and foremost to address this central and pernicious challenge. Our approach deviated markedly in two ways from previous efforts to test Motivational Interviewing with couples. First, we viewed the couple in toto—rather than one partner within the couple—as the client. Second, we conceptualized components of dyadic functioning—satisfaction, commitment, and emotional investment—as providing a foundation for change rather than separate goals unto themselves.

Building on these ideas, our initial qualitative analyses of intervention session content suggested that counselors need to be prepared to engage in a process of facilitating dyadic functioning in order to support couples in the resolution of dyadic ambivalence and the formation of joint goals before proceeding to change planning (Starks, Millar, et al., 2018). From this and our subsequent qualitative work, we derived counselor skills and strategies that contribute to achieving these ends (Starks, Doyle, Stewart, et al., 2022; Starks, Robles, et al., 2020). The principles outlined in these articles have informed two different interventions that demonstrated promise in initial randomized controlled trials: *We Test* (Starks, Dellucci, et al., 2019) and *The Couples Health Project* (Starks, Adebayo, et al., 2022).

We Test: Capitalizing on couples' HIV testing and counseling (CHTC). Our initial attempt to realize a couples Motivational Interviewing intervention was centered on CHTC. CHTC was initially developed for heterosexual couples and primarily in the African context (Painter, 2001). More recently, it has been tailored for use with male couples in the United States (e.g., Stephenson et al., 2016; Sullivan et al., 2014) and has become a mainstay in the care of sexual minority men in relationships (World Health Organization, 2012a). During CHTC, counselors facilitate a discussion about the couples' strengths, their current HIV prevention strategy, as well as their sexual agreement. Partners then learn their respective HIV statuses together and discuss a shared HIV prevention plan informed by these results.

In this first study (Starks, Dellucci, et al., 2019 [National Clinical Trial (NCT)03125915]), we developed brief adjunct components to CHTC intended to enhance dyadic functioning and address drug use. These included a communication skills training video as well as a motivational enhancement activity. Both were designed to be delivered by routine HIV testers without advanced training in mental health or substance use treatment. The video component was intended to enhance dyadic functioning by modeling common communication errors and adaptive communication alternatives in the context of discussions about drug use and sexual risk reduction between partners in male couples. The motivational enhancement activity included the creation of a calendar detailing both partners' recent substance use. Counselors utilized this as a source of immediate feedback to evoke a discussion of substance use that encompassed the establishment of shared limits and the creation of a shared plan to maintain use within these limits.

We conducted a pilot randomized controlled trial involving 70 New York City–based male couples who had been together at least 3 months. In each couple, at least one partner was 18 to 29 years old, was HIV negative, and reported recent drug use. Couples were randomized to one of four conditions: CHTC as usual, CHTC plus the communication skills training video, CHTC plus the motivational enhancement activity, or CHTC plus both adjunct components. Completion of the motivational enhancement activity resulted in significant decreases in the odds of drug use and the number of related problems 1 month later. Those participants who viewed the communication skills training video benefitted more from the motivational enhancement component over time. At 3- and 6-month follow-ups, completion of the motivational enhancement component was associated with significant decreases in the odds of drug use and drug use–related problems only among those participants who watched the video.

The Couples Health Project: multisession substance use and HIV prevention intervention. Our second application of couples Motivational Interviewing was a three-session protocol: the *Couples Health Project* (Starks, Adebayo, et al., 2022 [NCT03386110]). Unlike We Test, which was intended for delivery by routine HIV testing staff, this protocol was developed as a framework for mental health and substance use counselors to engage male couples around drug use and HIV risk reduction.

The Couples Health Project trial involved 50 New York City–based male couples who were together for at least 3 months. In each couple, one partner was 18 to 29 years old, was HIV negative, and had reported recent drug use. Unlike We Test, at least one partner in each couple reported sexual HIV transmission risk, defined as condomless anal sex with a casual partner, a nonmonogamous main partner, or a serodiscordant main partner. Couples were randomized to complete either the three-session Motivational Interviewing intervention or an attention-matched (dyadically delivered) psychoeducation condition in which the couple received information about sexual health, the prevention of sexually transmitted infections, and the risks associated with drug use.

Overall differences between the Motivational Interviewing and psychoeducation condition were nonsignificant; however, moderation analyses indicated that Motivational Interviewing significantly reduced illicit drug use (excluding cannabis) and condomless sex with casual partners for those men at highest risk. Illicit drug use declined significantly among those participants in couples where at least one partner reported high-frequency use of illicit drugs at baseline. Condomless sex with casual partners was reduced among those participants in couples where both partners reported high baseline frequency.

The remainder of this chapter positions our framework for couples Motivational Interviewing in the context of existing research and practice. We begin by illustrating how the challenges and opportunities inherent in couples Motivational Interviewing diverge from Motivational Interviewing with individuals and groups. We then summarize the formative research on drug use and sexual health among male couples. This body of work provided the rationale for developing an approach to couples Motivational Interviewing specifically in this population. Finally, we situate couples Motivational Interviewing in the larger context of existing couples therapy and substance use treatment alternatives.

WHEN PARTNERS ARGUE AGAINST CHANGE

The central challenge of Motivational Interviewing with couples can perhaps most easily be seen in the following fictional session transcript: Jarred and Alex are discussing possible HIV prevention options with a counselor. This is the sort of exchange that might occur as part of an HIV testing session when discussing prevention planning or after delivering the results of other sexually transmitted infection tests. Jarred and Alex have been together for 5 years and have an "open" sexual agreement, which permits them both to have sex with outside partners independently of one another. Note that the session transcript includes reference to pre-exposure prophylaxis (PrEP)—a biomedical option for HIV prevention that is highly effective in oral and injectable forms. See the Introduction for more information.

* * *

COUNSELOR: It's clear that you both want to reduce your HIV risk. How do you imagine going about that?

JARRED: I'd like to see us start using condoms when we play with other people.

ALEX: No way that's happening. Nice idea, but we both know it won't happen.

JARRED: Why not?

ALEX: I've always hated condoms.

JARRED: That's ridiculous.

COUNSELOR: Jarred, help me understand why you see condoms as a good solution here.

ALEX: He's saying that because it sounds nice here. We've never been good about using condoms.

JARRED: But that doesn't mean we shouldn't try. I mean, it's not like we don't know how to use condoms. We just aren't consistent.

COUNSELOR: So, Jarred, you see this as something you could do with some additional effort.

JARRED: Exactly.

ALEX: But if we can't be consistent about it, what's the point? You'd have to use them every time.

COUNSELOR: So for you, Jarred, condoms might work. But for you, Alex, we would need another option.

ALEX: Yes. Well—honestly, I think we both need another option, but whatever.

COUNSELOR: Would you mind if I told you a little bit about PrEP?

ALEX: Sure, though I think I probably know what you're gonna say.

JARRED: We've been over this so many times. It doesn't make any sense to put a pill in your body every day for nothing.

COUNSELOR: There are more PrEP options now than ever before. You guys are right that one of those options is a daily pill. It dramatically reduces your risk of HIV infection. It makes it basically zero, as long as you are consistent about taking the medication. PrEP also offers similar levels of protection if you take it "as needed." That means instead of taking it every single day, you take two pills the day before sex, one the day you have sex, and another the day after. Finally, we now have an injectable form of PrEP that you only take once every 2 months. So PrEP is not just pills any more. What are your thoughts on that?

JARRED: I still feel like you have to worry about being consistent with all those options.

ALEX: It's a lot easier for me to remember to take a pill every morning than to use a condom all the time.

COUNSELOR: So for you, Alex, PrEP might be an option.

JARRED: I just don't see why you want to do that to your body.

ALEX: It's just way easier. And then you get to have sex without a condom.

JARRED: Condoms would be just as good if you'd just use them.

* * *

Both Jarred and Alex are on board with the idea of reducing HIV risk. Each of the counselor's individual utterances is a reasonably proficient example of Motivational Interviewing skill. The counselor is using accurate reflections and asking open-ended questions that invite Alex and Jarred to give detailed responses. Despite this, the couple remains stuck. Why do tried-and-true interviewing skills, which are known to work reliably with individual clients, sometimes fail with couples? The quandary has led some to speculate that perhaps there are some couples who are simply not appropriate for Motivational Interviewing, while others are ready (Manuel et al., 2012; W. R. Miller & Rose, 2010; Monti et al., 2014).

Why not just separate the partners and work individually with each of them? The fact that Jarred and Alex favor different HIV risk reduction strategies, and each opposes the other's preference, places the counselor in a bind. Utterances that elicit change talk from one of them automatically elicit sustain talk—or the counterargument—from the other. It is tempting to suggest that the counselor should separate the couple. By themselves, it is easy to see that Jarred might readily formulate a plan to use condoms, and Alex might be interested in a referral for PrEP.

While it would solve the challenge in session, separating the partners does not change the fact that their sexual health remains linked to one another's choices. Jarred and Alex have been together for years. They see each other on most days. The conversation they are having in session is just one of dozens they will have today. While the counselor could escape the challenge of grappling with their disagreement about HIV prevention in this specific session by separating them, its reality will shape their behavior nonetheless.

Right now, their lack of consensus diminishes HIV prevention motivation for both men. Separating Jarred and Alex and elaborating individual change plans embraces that lack of consensus and makes it easy for each of them to undercut the other's efforts outside of session. What the counselor needs is a strategy to help them recognize common ground, negotiate a shared goal for their sexual health, and support one another's change efforts.

Motivational Interviewing with a couple is more than just an individual Motivational Interview with two people. One potential reason why Motivational Interviewing with couples has been challenging is that most efforts have attempted to extend the theory and practice of individual Motivational Interviewing to instances where two people in a relationship are in the room. Individual Motivational Interviewing provides a framework for conceptualizing client readiness for change, and strategically responding to change and sustain talk, in instances where one person may be ambivalent about change (W. R. Miller & Rollnick, 2013; W. R. Miller & Rose, 2009). While immensely useful, the individual Motivational Interviewing framework falls short in two ways. First, it is difficult to employ in situations where two people feel differently about change. Second, it does not account for the interdependence of partners' behavior and the influence they have on one another.

Unfortunately, individual Motivational Interviewing was never developed to account for the possibility that the interviewer may be speaking simultaneously to two people who feel differently about a behavior. This challenge, depicted in Jarred and Alex's narrative, has also been explicitly documented in research on the effect of relationship partner involvement in Motivational Interviewing sessions among those with alcohol use disorders. Clients whose significant others offered supportive or encouraging statements regarding alcohol cessation in session were more successful at abstaining from drinking after the intervention compared to those whose partners' statements undermined their efforts to abstain from drinking (Manuel et al., 2012). Motivational Interviewing, in its current form, does not have a framework for guiding counselor responses when a partner argues against change.

Just devising techniques for speaking to two people simultaneously about change is not sufficient to achieve a robust framework for Motivational Interviewing practice with couples. Speaking to two unrelated people is not the same as speaking to two partners in a relationship. In many instances, relationship partners have a vested interest in one another's choices. They rely on one another, and their choices impact each other in myriad ways. To guide practice with couples, counselors need a framework that accounts for the ways in which partners influence one another's personal behavior.

Motivational Interviewing with a couple presents challenges and opportunities different from Motivational Interviewing with groups. Principles for conducting Motivational Interviewing with groups have been well articulated; however, these principles generally assume that group members are not dependent on one another outside of the group. Rather, Motivational Interviewing with groups is largely based on the notion that individuals reap psychological and somatic health benefits through belonging to a collective (Wagner & Ingersoll, 2012). Group membership, in this context, staves off feelings of isolation that an individual Motivational Interviewing session may engender in some treatment seekers (Wagner & Ingersoll, 2012).

As group allegiance develops, group members may become committed to outcomes that would affect the group as a whole (Wagner & Ingersoll, 2012). By virtue of becoming invested in the outcome of other members—and the group more broadly—group members may also experience perceived task interdependence, whereby engaging with other group members regarding their goals makes one's own seem more attainable as well (Wagner & Ingersoll, 2012). While these phenomena could be understood in terms of interdependence theory, the degree of dependence among group members still remains quite modest in comparison to relationship partners. Partners in a relationship have a vested interest in many of each other's choices within and beyond a session. If Jarred contracts HIV, Alex's life is also changed.

Relationship partners have motivation and mechanisms to influence each other's behavior that extend far beyond the influence group therapy members are typically able to exert on each other. This means that, when relationship partners feel differently about change, progression toward behavioral goals may be stymied for one or both. Chapters 7 and 8 discuss this phenomenon and associated counselor strategies for responding to it in detail. Work on Motivational Interviewing with groups makes little mention of group-level or interpersonal ambivalence toward change. This may be because, although group members may experience some interdependence with one another, one member's reluctance to change is not necessarily a direct logistical impediment to another member enacting change outside the context of the therapy room (Wagner & Ingersoll, 2012). In most instances, group members do not require the cooperation of the other members to bring about change in their personal lives. In contrast, relationship partners may in many instances be reliant on one another to enact change (or maintain the status quo).

Furthermore, group counselors often strategically select or assign members of Motivational Interviewing groups. This may be done to achieve homogeneity with respect to stage of change and health condition (Wagner & Ingersoll, 2012). Even when heterogeneous groups are selected (perhaps to allow people at various stages of change to interact with and learn from one another), they are often, to an extent, still curated to develop group cohesion (Wagner & Ingersoll, 2012). Obviously a Motivational Interviewing counselor does not match the partners in a given couple. They therefore need a framework that can guide practice when partners may feel differently about change. This apparent challenge, however, is one that is not insurmountable, as made evident by work on Motivational Interviewing among heterogeneous groups (Caponnetto et al., 2020; Santa Ana et al., 2016; Wagner & Ingersoll, 2012).

Dyadic participation in counseling presents challenges for some couples. It is certainly possible that some couples may not be in a place where they can productively engage in a counseling interaction together. In any dyadic intervention, both partners in a relationship must give informed consent. After that, they have to coordinate schedules and other logistics in order to participate in sessions together. Couples with sufficiently poor relationship functioning may find the notion of joint participation in a counseling session to be prohibitive in and of itself (Hoff & Beougher, 2010; Starks, Millar, & Parsons, 2015). Ironically, those in relationships that may stand to benefit most from a couples intervention may be the least likely to seek counseling together. Therefore, Chapter 11 speaks more directly to the development of individual interventions for those in relationships who may not be willing or able to engage in counseling that requires dyadic participation for this very reason.

No counseling technique exists that can work infallibly with all clients, and it would be naïve to expect that a couples Motivational Interviewing strategy could be developed that would work for all couples irrespective of circumstance. At the same time, to attribute the mixed performance of couples Motivational Interviewing to client readiness is to overlook an opportunity to examine the ways the technique could evolve to work more effectively. This text is founded on the premise that Motivational Interviewing with couples, in fact, holds substantial promise. The approach described is predicated on the idea that knowledge drawn from the fields of relationship science and dyadic coping can inform Motivational Interviewing practice with couples and enhance counseling efficacy.

WHY FOCUS ON SEXUAL HEALTH AND SUBSTANCE USE?

The intervention principles and strategies described in this text have potentially broad applications. Why then focus on sexual health—particularly HIV infection—and substance use? Why focus on sexual minority men or male couples specifically? The answer is that work in this area has been driven by urgent need for novel intervention.

Since the beginning of the epidemic, sexual minority men—including gay, bisexual, and other men who have sex with men—have been at elevated risk for HIV infection. Sexual minority men accounted for 69% of new HIV infections in the United States in 2019 (Centers for Disease Control and Prevention, 2021b). Despite the emergence of biomedical HIV prevention options, the number of new HIV infections among sexual minority men has been relatively stable over the past decade. An estimated 23,100 sexual minority men were diagnosed with HIV in 2019. This overall number did not differ significantly from the 25,100 diagnosed in 2010 (Pitasi et al., 2021).

There are also significant racial and ethnic health disparities among sexual minority men. In 2019, majority White sexual minority men accounted for only 25% of new HIV infections; meanwhile, Black or African American sexual minority men accounted for 37%, and those sexual minority men who identified as Hispanic or Latino accounted for 32% (Centers for Disease Control and Prevention, 2021b). Longitudinal analyses suggested that racial and ethnic disparities in HIV infection rates have widened in recent years. Between 2015 and 2019, new HIV infections fell 17% among majority White sexual minority men and 18% among those who identify as Asian. In contrast, the rate of new infections was unchanged among Black or African American, Hispanic or Latino, and Native Hawaiian or other Pacific Islander sexual minority men. More alarming, infections rose 31% among those who identify as American Indian or Alaskan Native (Centers for Disease Control and Prevention, 2021b).

HIV incidence is also highest among sexual minority men under the age of 35. Collectively, sexual minority men between the ages of 13 and 34 have accounted for roughly two thirds of new HIV infections among sexual minority men over the past decade (Pitasi et al., 2021), making the periods of adolescence and emerging adulthood a time of particularly high HIV infection risk. In 2010, sexual minority men aged 13 to 24 accounted for 10,400 (41%) of the estimated 25,100 new infections. Those 25 to 34 years old accounted for an additional 6,700 (27%) new infections that year. These proportions reversed by 2019. Rates among those aged 13 to 24 fell significantly to an estimated 5,700 (25%) of the 23,100 new infections that year; meanwhile, rates rose significantly among those 25 to 34 to an estimated 10,000 (43%) new infections (Pitasi et al., 2021).

For decades, HIV prevention either implicitly or explicitly focused on risky sexual behaviors with casual—rather than main or primary relationship—partners. In 2009, epidemiological data from the United States emerged indicating that between one and two thirds of new infections occur between main—rather than casual—partners (Goodreau et al., 2012, 2013; Sullivan et al., 2009). Comparatively quickly, relationship research—and relationship-focused interventions—garnered increasing attention in HIV prevention and care research. In the decade that followed, research revealed that characteristics of relationships (e.g., the agreements couples form, concerns about rejection from romantic partners, individual perceptions of the relationship, and the quality of interactions between partners) predict sexual behavior (e.g., Hoff et al., 2012; Martinez et al., 2017; Rios-Spicer et al., 2019) as well as perceptions of condom use (e.g., Starks, Gamarel, et al., 2014; Starks, Robles, Bosco, Dellucci, et al., 2019) and biomedical HIV prevention (e.g., Gamarel & Golub, 2015; John et al., 2018; Kahle et al., 2020; Mimiaga et al., 2014; Starks, Doyle, et al., 2019). Work with HIV-positive men suggested that relationship factors are associated with medication adherence, viral load, and sexual behavior (e.g., Gamarel, Neilands, et al., 2014; Gamarel, Starks, et al., 2014; Goldenberg et al., 2013).

Today, it is evident that attention to relationships and the health of sexual minority men in relationships is essential to a comprehensive HIV prevention strategy. This centrality is embodied in medical guidelines. Guidance from the World Health Organization recommended CHTC as a standard of care for sexual minority men in relationships (World Health Organization, 2012a). Guidance for PrEP to prevent HIV indicates that sexual minority men in nonmonogamous relationships and those with serodiscordant partners are high-priority candidates for PrEP dissemination (Centers for Disease Control and Prevention, 2019).

Sexual agreements have been an early and ongoing focus in research on male couples HIV prevention. Sexual agreements—the rules and boundaries couples form related to sex with partners outside their relationship—are common among sexual minority men (e.g., Davidovich et al., 2000; Hoff & Beougher, 2010). While proportions vary widely across samples, research suggested that 24.7% to 64.8% of male couples have a monogamous sexual agreement, which prohibits sex with outside partners (e.g., Mitchell et al., 2012; Parsons et al., 2013; Sharma et al., 2019, 2021; Starks, Jones, et al., 2020; Starks, Robles, Bosco, Dellucci, et al., 2019).

Some work has examined subtypes of nonmonogamy in male couples. In these studies, the most common form of nonmonogamy is an *open* agreement, meaning partners in the relationship may have sex with casual partners independently or together. Between 22.4% and 65.2% of male couples have such an agreement (e.g., Mitchell & Petroll, 2013; Parsons et al., 2013; Starks, Jones, et al., 2020; Starks, Robles, Bosco, Dellucci, et al., 2019). Somewhat less common, between 10.2% and 44% of male couples have an agreement (termed *monogamish* by some) that permits sex with outside partners only when both main partners are present (e.g., Mitchell et al., 2012; Parsons et al., 2013; Starks, Jones, et al., 2020; Starks, Robles, Bosco, Dellucci, et al., 2019).

The general consensus has been that sexual minority men are capable of enacting a diverse range of sexual agreements successfully as long as partners concur about what their agreement is (e.g., Grov et al., 2014; Mitchell, 2014; Parsons et al., 2012; Sharma et al., 2019). When partners are aligned about having a specific sexual agreement and they adhere to it, irrespective of type, they are more likely to be satisfied with their relationship, engage in HIV testing more frequently, and engage in less condomless anal sex with outside partners than those in relationships who have no sexual agreement or who hold discrepant perceptions of their agreement (Mitchell et al., 2012). Further, couples that are satisfied with their sexual agreement are less likely to engage in condomless anal sex with main as well as casual partners (Mitchell & Petroll, 2013; Neilands et al., 2009).

Despite their apparent benefits, sexual agreements are imperfect. Estimates suggest that 12% to 20% of sexual minority men in relationships have violated their sexual agreement at some point (Mitchell et al., 2012; Sharma et al., 2021). While sexual minority men in monogamous relationships are less likely to have sex with partners outside their relationship (e.g., Dellucci et al., 2020; Starks, Jones, et al., 2020; Starks, Robles, Bosco, Dellucci, et al., 2019), 15% to 27% report having concurrent sexual partners presumably in violation of their agreement (Blashill et al., 2014; Feinstein, Dellucci, et al., 2018). Moreover, when sexual minority men in monogamous relationships do violate their agreement, there are indications they are actually sexually riskier than single and nonmonogamous men (e.g., Blashill et al., 2014; Feinstein, Dellucci, et al., 2018; Starks, Jones, et al., 2020). Starks, Jones, et al. (2020) specifically found that those sexual minority men in monogamous relationships who reported condomless sex with casual partners actually had condomless sex with casual partners more frequently than men in nonmonogamous relationships.

This formative work on sexual agreements provided evidence that sexual minority men in relationships engage in some amount of collaborative decision-making with their partners. It demonstrated that couple-level agreements are relevant to individual health behavior. This notion, that the formation of agreements may serve as a mechanism to promote individual behavior change, provided a critical point of intersection between Motivational Interviewing and relationship theory that is explored in greater detail in the following chapters. The imperfections of sexual agreements—the fact that sometimes individuals violate their agreements in ways that increase health-related risk—also highlighted the need to look beyond agreement formation and consider adherence.

The development of intervention strategies that can address the intersection of drug use and sexual risk-taking has particular urgency for sexual minority men. Rates of drug use among sexual minority men are consistently higher than those observed among heterosexual men. These disparities emerge in adolescence and continue through adulthood (e.g., Jones et al., 2020; Medley et al., 2016; Starks, Cabral, et al., 2020). Data from the 2015–2016 National Survey on Drug Use and Health (NSDUH; Medley et al., 2016) indicated as many as 36.3% of sexual minority men used cannabis or other illicit drugs. In contrast, the rate among heterosexual men was estimated at 20.4% (Medley et al., 2016). Disparities in substance use disorders mirror those observed in drug use (Krueger et al., 2020). Upward of 16.7% of sexual minority men met the criteria for a substance use disorder, compared with 10.6% of their heterosexual counterparts (Medley et al., 2016).

When thinking about drug use and HIV risk, it may be tempting to focus largely on intravenous drug use and the transmission of HIV through shared needles or works. While the rate of HIV diagnoses among those who use intravenous drugs has remained a consistent contributor to HIV incidence nationwide, intravenous drug use accounts for only about 7% of new HIV infections in the United States (Centers for Disease Control and Prevention, 2021b). In contrast, sexual HIV transmission accounts for the other 93% of infections. To the extent that drug use (intravenous or otherwise) catalyzes or occurs in conjunction with risky sexual behavior, its association with HIV infection risk is far greater than would be inferred from intravenous drug use transmission alone.

The relevance of drug use to sexual HIV transmission risk is extensively documented among sexual minority men. Sexual minority men frequently combine drug use with sex. In fact, 27.2% of sexual minority men reported using cannabis; 5.6% reported the use of stimulants (e.g., cocaine and crack, amphetamines); and 4.1% reported the use of other illicit drugs (excluding cannabis and stimulants) with sex (Feinstein et al., 2018). Sexual minority men who use drugs are more likely to be sexually risky compared to those who do not (e.g., Cain et al., 2021; Loza et al., 2020; Starks, Jones, et al., 2020). Even at the event level, sex that occurs on days sexual minority men use drugs is more likely to be risky than when drug use and sex do not co-occur (e.g., Halkitis et al., 2016; McCarty-Caplan et al., 2014; Rendina et al., 2015; Vosburgh et al., 2012).

Concerns about drug use—and associated sexual risk-taking—extend to sexual minority men in relationships. Rates of drug use varied between 12.5% (for illicit drugs) and 33% (for cannabis) among partnered sexual minority men (Mitchell, 2016). Interestingly, drug use varied consistently with sexual agreements. Men in monogamous relationships were less likely than single men and their nonmonogamous counterparts to use drugs, including cannabis (e.g., Mitchell et al., 2014; Parsons & Starks, 2014; Starks, Jones, et al., 2020). Specifically, while 8.8% of sexual minority men in monogamous relationships may use both cannabis and illicit drugs, 15.4% of men in open relationships reported the use of such substances (Starks, Jones, et al., 2020). Further, partners in monogamous relationships tend to be more similar to one another in their drug use than those in nonmonogamous relationships (Parsons & Starks, 2014). Meanwhile, the use of drugs specifically during sex with outside partners has varied between 10.6% (for illicit drugs) to 31% (for cannabis) among partnered sexual minority men (Mitchell et al., 2016).

Regardless of sexual agreement, the use of illicit drugs other than cannabis has been associated with both the occurrence and the frequency of sexual risk-taking (condomless sex with casual partners) among sexual minority men in relationships. While the effects were somewhat smaller among men in monogamous versus nonmonogamous relationships, they were uniformly statistically significant (Starks, Jones, et al., 2020). In contrast, the association between cannabis use and sexual risk-taking was both smaller in magnitude and more restricted in relevance than other illicit drug use. Cannabis use was associated with a modest but statistically significant increase in the odds of having condomless anal sex with casual partners among monogamous men. It was not associated with the odds of condomless sex with casual partners among nonmonogamous men, and it was not associated with the frequency of sexual risk-taking among any partnered sexual minority men (Starks, Jones, et al., 2020).

One study examined day-level associations between drug use and sexual risk-taking using dyadic data from nonmonogamous and serodiscordant male couples. Starks, Sauermilch, et al. (2021) found that associations between drug use and sexual behavior were a function of day-level similarity in main partners' use. Main partners were more likely to have condomless sex with each other on days they used similar drugs. Cannabis was significantly associated with the occurrence of condomless sex between main partners only on days both partners reported cannabis use. The same pattern was observed for other illicit drug use. It was significantly associated with condomless sex between main partners only on days both main partners reported other illicit drug use. In turn, on the days main partners had condomless sex together they were more likely to also have condomless sex with partners outside their relationship. Both cannabis and other illicit drug use predicted condomless sex with casual partners above and beyond condomless sex with main partners; however, these associations were significantly diminished on days partners used different drugs (Starks, Sauermilch, et al., 2021). In our conclusions, we put forward the hypothesis that the use of similar drugs on a given day may indicate that main partners are engaged in shared activities that are characterized by opportunities to have sex. In contrast, we speculated that days on which partners use different drugs, use may be occurring in contexts where sex is less likely (Starks, Sauermilch, et al., 2021).

In addition to being associated with HIV infection risk, drug use is associated with the health of individuals living with HIV. In fact, sexual minority men living with HIV use illicit drugs at higher rates than sexual minority men who are HIV negative (e.g., Mimiaga et al., 2013; Parsons et al., 2005). The use of such drugs—especially opiates and cocaine—has been linked to suboptimal antiretroviral therapy adherence (e.g., Cepeda et al., 2017; Nolan et al., 2017). Further, problematic alcohol use has been linked to increased viral load (Starks, Skeen, Jones, Millar, et al., 2022) suboptimal treatment adherence as well as lower rates of medical appointment attendance (e.g., González-Álvarez et al., 2019; Howe et al., 2014; Tran et al., 2014).

WHAT CAN MOTIVATIONAL INTERVIEWING OFFER COUPLES THERAPY?

There is a robust and varied body of scholarship and research on couples therapy. Work spans theoretical orientations, including psychoanalytic (notably object relations and attachment-oriented approaches; Scharff & Scharff, 1997); interpersonal; and cognitive behavioral perspectives. Many of these approaches, in particular emotion-focused couples therapy (an approach grounded in attachment theory), integrative behavioral couples therapy, and cognitive behavioral couples therapy, have a substantive evidence base and a community of practitioners dedicated to the dissemination of expertise (e.g., D. H. Baucom et al., 2008; Jacobson et al., 2000; S. M. Johnson, 2020).

Motivational Interviewing with couples and other couples therapies have a number of points in common. Both Motivational Interviewing and couples therapies more broadly incorporate attention to relationship functioning. For the most part, couples therapies like those enumerated above generally view relationship functioning (i.e., indicators of relationship quality, e.g., satisfaction, commitment, emotional investment, communication skills, or trust) as an end unto itself (e.g., Jacobson et al., 2000). These interventions are formulated with the assumption that the presenting problem is a relational problem (i.e., partners are unhappy and the couple may separate), and the explicit treatment goal is to improve the relationship. This is not inherently a shortcoming. Many couples may seek therapy in order to improve their relationship, and in these instances, these interventions may effectively address the couple's concerns.

Just as with Motivational Interviewing with couples, applications of these other kinds of interventions have been developed for sexual minority couples. Gottman method couples therapy, for example, has been found to improve relationship satisfaction among sexual minority couples specifically (Garanzini et al., 2017). See Chapter 9 for additional discussion of this approach. Research on the Strengthening Same-Sex Relationships program—an adapted relationship education approach—has indicated it improves communication and relationship satisfaction for sexual minority men in relationships (Whitton et al., 2016). In fact, the Strengthening Same-Sex Relationships program for sexual minority men in particular borrows from Motivational Interviewing techniques to facilitate adaptive forms of communication (Scott et al., 2018). Extensive work has also been done on the adaptation of structural family and attachment-oriented approaches for sexual minority men in relationships (e.g., Greenan & Tunnell, 2003; Tunnell, 2012). Finally, preliminary research on cognitive behavioral couples therapy among couples of sexual minority women has also shown potential benefits regarding relationship functioning (Pentel, 2020).

These interventions for sexual minority couples all aim to enhance partners' empathy for one another, foster adaptive communication, engender emotional acceptance of one's partner, and—in some of these interventions—provide couples the opportunity to discuss and define their sexual agreement (e.g., D. H. Baucom et al., 2008; Jacobson et al., 2000; Scott et al., 2018). Motivational Interviewing with sexual minority couples shares these aims. It differs in that the couples therapy options previously described provide less guidance on how to address individual behavior change in a relationship context.

Additionally, attention to substance use and sexual health specifically in these contexts is limited—particularly for sexual minority populations. While some sex therapies for male couples incorporate attention to HIV risk behavior and drug use, these are generally framed as ancillary concerns (Rutter, 2012). The framework articulated here can be applied to situations where these behaviors are addressed as specific targets. Motivational Interviewing engages with sexual risk behavior and drug use as central—not peripheral—concerns and views sexual satisfaction specifically (and relationship functioning generally) as context essential to understanding decisions partners make about drug use and sexual behavior. See Chapter 10 for more detail.

Motivational Interviewing with couples diverges from other forms of couples therapy in a foundational way. It views relationship functioning as a

mechanism to achieve individual behavior change. Motivational Interviewing (whether for individuals, groups, or couples) has a focus on a specific target behavior. Rather than viewing it as an end unto itself, the Motivational Interviewing counselor views relationship functioning as a foundation on which individual behavior change is built. It catalyzes the formation of shared goals and motivates partners to support one another in their accomplishment. Facilitating dyadic functioning is one way in which Motivational Interviewing achieves treatment goals, rather than being the goal of treatment in and of itself.

Similar to other couples therapies, the Motivational Interviewing counselor seeks to draw out and highlight the couple's strengths and may deliberately engage in relationship skill building in order to enhance dyadic functioning. The difference is that the purpose of relationship facilitation in Motivational Interviewing with couples is to help the couple tolerate difficult conversations about behavior change when they emerge in session and to lay the foundation for partners to support one another in the change process (in the case of our research, reducing substance use or mitigating sexual HIV risk-taking). Facilitating dyadic functioning will therefore be a recurring theme throughout this text; however, it will generally be treated as a formative process that underlies behavior change and not as the final goal of treatment itself.

WHAT CAN COUPLES MOTIVATIONAL INTERVIEWING OFFER COUPLES SUBSTANCE USE TREATMENT?

Because our work on Motivational Interviewing with couples has centered on drug use and sexual risk-taking among sexual minority male couples, it sits at the intersection of two bodies of existing literature. One has examined substance use treatment with couples. The other has developed substance use interventions for sexual minority populations. The overlap between these two areas of work is surprisingly modest. By and large, couples substance use treatment has focused primarily on heterosexual couples and given relatively limited attention to the intersection of drug use and sexual behavior. At the same time, substance use interventions for sexual minority populations have largely overlooked couples and given relatively little attention to the role of relationship partners in the regulation of health behavior.

While there are noteworthy exceptions (e.g., Fals-Stewart et al., 2004; McCrady, 2012; McCrady et al., 1991; Powers et al., 2008), scholarship and research on couples substance use treatment specifically is somewhat more limited than the body of literature focused on couples therapy more generally. In some instances, books on family therapy and addiction address couples as a topic of special interest (e.g., Bacon, 2019). Inclusion of sexual minority populations in studies of couples substance use treatment is particularly scant.

In contrast to the relatively robust literature on individual substance use treatment with sexual minority clients (Pantalone et al., 2020), only a few published studies of couples interventions have examined effects on substance use (e.g., Fals-Stewart et al., 2009; Newcomb et al., 2017; Wu et al., 2011) outside of our own work on couples Motivational Interviewing. Behavioral couples therapy for alcoholism and drug abuse (O'Farrell & Fals-Stewart, 2006) is a notable exception, and there is modest evidence that the intervention, which involves 32 sessions, is effective with sexual minority couples (Fals-Stewart et al., 2009). The *2GETHER* intervention (Newcomb et al., 2017), a four-session intervention comprising group sessions with multiple couples and couple-specific sessions, examined alcohol use as a secondary outcome. Effects on alcohol use were marginally significant, and there was no evidence of effects on drug use (Newcomb et al., 2017). Notably, *Connect With Pride*, a seven-session cognitive behavioral treatment, has shown promise in reducing methamphetamine use specifically among partnered Black sexual minority men (Wu et al., 2010, 2011).

In bridging these areas of research, Motivational Interviewing with couples substantially enhances the intervention options available to substance use counselors working with sexual minority men in relationships. Similar to the small number of interventions that have addressed drug use in ways tailored for sexual minority male couples (e.g., Newcomb et al., 2017; Wu et al., 2010, 2011), Motivational Interviewing with couples provides a framework for integrating attention to the intersection of drug use and sexual behavior largely absent from the existing couples drug treatment literature even when sexual minority couples have been included in intervention testing (e.g., Fals-Stewart et al., 2009). It also provides an alternative to the identified client paradigm that underlies most of the existing research in this area (e.g., Fals-Stewart et al., 2009; McGeough, 2021). In doing so, it provides a wider array of counselor strategies for responding to circumstances in which partners disagree about drug use–related change.

Meanwhile, existing intervention options developed for male couples tend to be time intensive, highly structured, and relatively complex; emphasize psychoeducation; and—in the case of Connect With Pride—tailored for a highly specific population and substance of choice. In contrast, couples Motivational Interviewing has demonstrated promise in brief doses of one to three sessions (Starks, Adebayo, et al., 2022; Starks, Dellucci, et al., 2019). The Couples Health Project used an attention-matched control condition that included psychoeducation sessions with the couple and CHTC in the final session. Results therefore provided some indication that Motivational Interviewing with couples might be associated with some benefit above and beyond interventions that rely primarily on these components. Taken together, there is reason to believe that Motivational Interviewing with couples might prove applicable across a wide range of substances and offer flexibility in the course of treatment similar to Motivational Interviewing with individuals (Branscum & Sharma, 2010; DiClemente et al., 2017; Polcin et al., 2014; Stotts et al., 2001).

WHAT CAN COUPLES MOTIVATIONAL INTERVIEWING OFFER COUPLES HIV RISK REDUCTION INTERVENTIONS?

As previously mentioned, a number of HIV risk reduction interventions have been developed for male couples. 2GETHER (Newcomb et al., 2017); *Project Nexus* (Stephenson, Freeland, et al., 2017); CHTC (Sullivan et al., 2014); project *Stronger Together* (Stephenson, Suarez, et al., 2017); and *We Prevent* (Gamarel et al., 2019) are a few such interventions that have been tested in recent years. Many of these are informed by interdependence theory and, like Motivational Interviewing with couples, assume that the formation of and adherence to sexual agreements is a mechanism to achieve risk reduction.

Also aligned with interdependence theory, these interventions largely conceptualize relationship functioning as a mechanism for behavior change. In standard CHTC protocols (Stephenson et al., 2016; Sullivan et al., 2014), the HIV testing counselor elicits the couple's strengths before entering into the potentially more challenging discussion of HIV prevention and the establishment of a sexual agreement. Some interventions (e.g., Gamarel et al., 2019; Newcomb et al., 2017) go even further and incorporate relationship skill building. They not only draw out the couple's strengths but also seek to actively coach couples in more adaptive interactions.

Motivational Interviewing with couples extends this work. Motivational Interviewing with couples was developed to address the intersection of drug use and sexual risk-taking. Most of these existing sexual health interventions for couples do not address drug use explicitly (Gamarel et al., 2019; Stephenson, Freeland, et al., 2017; Stephenson, Suarez, et al., 2017; Sullivan et al., 2014). Those that do (Newcomb et al., 2017), address it as a secondary concern. Building on models of individual interventions for sexual minority men that integrated a focus on drug use and sexual health (reviewed in Pantalone et al., 2020), Motivational Interviewing with couples provides a framework that is sufficiently flexible to accommodate a focus on both of these target behaviors.

In addition, these existing sexual health interventions for male couples provide limited guidance about how to navigate situations in which partners disagree about change. These interventions may improve relationship skills, but managing disagreement or conflict in session is not an element that is extensively addressed in their application. In contrast, couples Motivational Interviewing anticipates this phenomenon and has developed techniques for responding to such discord between partners.

CONCLUSIONS AND KEY POINTS

Sexual minority men account for the majority of new HIV infections in the United States. Many, perhaps most, of these HIV infections are transmitted between main or primary relationship partners rather than casual or anonymous partners. At the same time, sexual minority men are also at elevated risk for drug use and dependence compared to heterosexual men. Those sexual minority men who use drugs are more likely to engage in the kinds of sexual behaviors that readily transmit HIV.

The intersection of drug use and sexual risk-taking among sexual minority men in relationships presents challenges for counselors and an ideal opportunity to meet those challenges through a renewed exploration of the potential for couples Motivational Interviewing. The approach outlined in this text deviates from previous iterations of Motivational Interviewing with couples in two ways. First, we viewed the couple in toto—rather than one partner within the couple—as the client. Second, we conceptualized components of dyadic functioning—satisfaction, commitment, and emotional investment—as providing a foundation for individual behavior change rather than being separate goals unto themselves.

Although a variety of existing interventions in some way address drug use or sexual risk-taking in this population, few integrate attention to these two behaviors and provide guidance for counselors working with couples. Broadly speaking, individual Motivational Interviewing interventions were not intended for use in a situation where a counselor might be talking to two people simultaneously. Group-based approaches to Motivational Interviewing do not consider the factors unique to relationship partners. General couples therapy approaches typically view the enhancement of relationship functioning as the end goal or target of intervention—providing limited guidance for applications to partners' individual health behavior change. Couples drug treatment options are largely conceptualized from an identified-client perspective, complicating application with couples where both partners may use drugs. In addition, they often give scant attention to sexual behavior. Most existing sexual risk reduction interventions, even those developed for male couples, give limited attention to drug use or provide limited guidance for counselors on how to respond in situations involving conflict and disagreement in session. Couples Motivational Interviewing therefore shares some common features with all of these existing intervention paradigms and also occupies a unique space at their intersection.

The Couple as "Client"

It is not particularly unusual for counselors—even those who work primarily with individuals—to sometimes have sessions in which their client may bring in an adjunct participant (e.g., a spouse, family member, or close friend). In this paradigm, the counselor's primary alliance typically remains with their identified client, and the additional participants are viewed largely in terms of their potentially meaningful role in the identified client's treatment process. Models for this kind of work have been developed for couples substance use treatment specifically (e.g., McCrady, 2012; O'Farrell & Schein, 2000), and the paradigm has generally organized previous applications of Motivational Interviewing with couples (Manuel et al., 2012; Martín-Pérez et al., 2019; Miller-Matero & Cano, 2015; Monti et al., 2014; Navidian et al., 2016).

The approach to Motivational Interviewing with a couple that is detailed in the chapters that follow was developed from a different conceptual stance—one wherein the couple, rather than one of the partners, is the client. The session transcript that follows illustrates the transformative impact of this paradigm shift on the counseling dialogue. This transcript returns to the (fictional) case of Jarred and Alex introduced in Chapter 1. Here, it illustrates how that session might have played out if the counselor had done more to engage them as a couple—rather than focusing on their separate, individual concerns.

* * *

COUNSELOR: It's clear that you both want to reduce your HIV risk. How do you imagine going about that?

JARRED: I'd like to see us start using condoms when we play with other people.

ALEX: No way that's happening. Nice idea, but we both know it won't happen.

JARRED: Why not?

ALEX: I've always hated condoms.

JARRED: That's ridiculous.

COUNSELOR: So you two disagree about the best way to prevent HIV, and it's clear that you both feel strongly about prevention.

JARRED: This always comes up. It's always a fight.

ALEX: Ever since PrEP [pre-exposure prophylaxis].

COUNSELOR: It's interesting because not only do you both agree about HIV prevention, but also you both agree that condoms and PrEP are effective. The only thing you disagree about is which you prefer.

ALEX: I guess that's true. I mean, I don't think condoms are like a hoax or something. I just don't like them.

COUNSELOR: And Jarred, you are not crazy about the idea of PrEP, and you think PrEP might be effective at reducing HIV risk.

JARRED: Right. It probably does reduce HIV risk. I just don't like the side effects.

COUNSELOR: So, I'm wondering, given that you both more or less want the same outcome—HIV prevention—and given that you both think condoms and PrEP work, I am wondering how possible it might be for the two of you to find a plan that would allow some flexibility for each of you to use your preferred strategy. For example, what would it be like if you [JARRED] used condoms and you [ALEX] tried PrEP?

ALEX: I would be fine with that, but I don't think you [JARRED] would be.

JARRED: We've been over this so many times. It doesn't make any sense to put a pill in your body every day for nothing.

COUNSELOR: I have the sense that everyone hears you on that Jarred. PrEP is not something you see as worth the risk. And similarly, condoms are not something Alex sees as a realistic goal either. And yet, both of you would like to see one another reduce your HIV risk. You guys generally work together really well. This one issue is sort of a stumper. What makes this issue so much tougher than the other things you've tackled together?

JARRED: I want to do it my way, and he wants to do it his way.

COUNSELOR: Got it. It's hard for you to imagine supporting Alex trying PrEP when it isn't something you want. And Jarred, it's hard for you to imagine supporting Alex using condoms because you find it challenging yourself.

JARRED: Yeah.

ALEX: I mean, when you say it that way, it does feel sort of stupid. Like, I don't actually need you to be on PrEP in order for me to do it. I do want to be able to take it without feeling judged.

JARRED: Okay. Yeah. And I don't want to feel like I'm ruining sex just because I want to use condoms.

COUNSELOR: So if you guys felt like the other was not going to judge you, was accepting and supportive of you, it could potentially work out for you guys.

* * *

The dialogue above plays out quite differently from the narrative that began Chapter 1. Alex and Jarred continue to have different ideas about the best way to reduce HIV risk, but they express a willingness to support each other's choices. Neither of them loves the strategy the other wants to implement, but they are able to see each other as "working toward" the same larger goal.

The difference in this dialogue is due, at least in part, to strategic changes in the counselor's technique. In the opening of Chapter 1, the counselor utilized Motivational Interviewing strategies proficiently; however, they primarily spoke to each of the partners in turn. Questions and reflections were directed at one partner at a time. In doing this, strategies that activated change talk from one partner routinely activated sustain talk from the other. In contrast, the counselor in the example above speaks "to the couple" much of the time. Before exploring the theoretical rationale for this shift, let us first consider the general impact of the strategy of "speaking to the couple."

THE IMPACT OF SPEAKING TO THE COUPLE

Couple-level utterances are diverse. They include reflections (e.g., "So you two disagree about the best way to prevent HIV, and yet it is clear that you both feel strongly about prevention.") and questions (e.g., What makes this issue so much tougher than the other things you guys have tackled together?"). The counselor also uses a couple-level utterance to affirm the couples' general ability to cope (e.g., "You guys generally work together really well.").

While the content of couple-level utterances may vary widely, there are two common features that distinguish them. **First, couple-level utterances are always directed "to the couple."** This means the statement or question must be phrased to encompass both partners. Any use of "you" must imply "you two" rather than "you personally." It also means that the counselor's nonverbal behavior must convey attention to both partners when speaking—a feature that cannot be represented fully in a written transcript. **Second, couple-level utterances convey or inquire about information that is relevant to both partners.** "What HIV prevention measures does Alex take?" is functionally an individual-level question about Alex even though it is worded in such a way that it could be directed to the couple. "How do you two manage HIV risk?" and "How do Alex's decisions about HIV prevention impact the two of you?" are couple-level questions.

Couple-level utterances are a way of sharing power in the session. When counselor statements are uniformly directed toward one of the individuals in the couple, the counselor implicitly conveys whose turn it is to talk throughout the session. Without a doubt, there are moments where it is strategic to activate one partner in the relationship and ensure that they have adequate time and space to express their response; however, it may not be strategic to exercise that level of control routinely throughout the entire session. Doing so may induce passivity in the couple. It diminishes the need for the partners to negotiate with one another in the exchange and limits the opportunities for them to speak directly to one another.

When a statement or question is directed to the couple, the partners in the relationship are then free to determine for themselves how to organize their reply. In some couples, partners may speak equally and take turns; others may talk over each other. In some couples, one partner may serve as the "spokesperson" in most circumstances, with the other providing input only as a follow-up. Counselor-imposed expectations about who should be talking may at times conflict with a couples' natural style or pattern of talking together. While there are times when it is strategic and effective for the counselor to disrupt a couples' habitual exchanges (see Chapter 9 for a detailed review of couples communication research and related interventions), doing so all the time and from the outset might diminish rapport and implicitly position the counselor as the expert in "who should be talking now."

Couple-level utterances create an opportunity to observe communication. Because couple-level utterances leave the couple free to organize their response with less direction from the counselor, they create an opportunity in session for the counselor to observe how the partners relate to one another. By giving the couple control over how to respond, the counselor gains invaluable observational data about how the partners interact. This includes things like how the partners share talking time, whether they tend to confirm or contradict one another, the content they agree on, areas of disagreement, and the manner in which agreements and disagreements are expressed. From this, the counselor may formulate hypotheses about the couple's strengths and challenges. Chapter 9 specifically examines how aspects of a relationship like trust and power are manifest in partners' communication. The counselor can then utilize statements directed to each of the individual's strategically in conjunction with couple-level utterances to mitigate conflict and enhance effective exchanges.

Couple-level utterances may capture common ground and strengths perceived by both partners. Many of the counselor's utterances draw on content from both partners. In doing so, the counselor is able to counterbalance areas of disagreement by reminding the partners of where they agree. Struggles can be offset by a reminder that partners share a common perception of at least some strengths and resources in their relationship. This does not negate the reality of challenges and disagreements. The truth is Alex and Jarred do see some things differently: They do not have the same preferred approach to HIV prevention. Reminding the couple of what they agree on gives them a goal that they can share even as they navigate these points of disagreement. Reminding them of their shared belief in their ability to work together enhances their collective self-efficacy for coping with the present challenge.

Couple-level utterances facilitate partners' collaborative problem-solving and enhance motivation to achieve a common goal. The counselor utilizes couple-level utterances to invite the couple to think about what will work "for them." This also allows the counselor to recast personal preferences—which may appear contradictory—as contributing to the accomplishment of a shared goal. The exchange between Alex and Jarred demonstrates that partners have the potential to be an impediment to change. By conceptualizing their behavior as part of a shared plan for change, they are motivated not only to enact their respective plans but also to support one another's actions. The counselor's aim is to identify a consensus goal—shared by both partners—that the behavior of both men can contribute to.

INTERDEPENDENCE THEORY: IMPLICATIONS FOR PRACTICE WITH COUPLES

Interdependence Theory can help explain why the dialogue in the beginning of this chapter is so different from the one that began Chapter 1. The theory was first developed as an extension of social exchange theory (Kelley & Thibaut, 1978; Thibaut & Kelley, 1959). Sometimes "winning as a team" requires sacrificing personal success in favor of the overall good of the group. This means shifting away from "maximizing your own gains" or "minimizing your own costs" to focus on "maximizing someone else's outcome" or "maximizing the collective good." One simple example might be that a basketball team often does better if its star player is willing to pass the ball and allow someone else to also score points. If the star player focuses only on making as many points as they can without allowing others to score, the team's overall outcome is likely diminished.

Interdependence theory has a lot to say about motivation. What incentive does the star player have to give up the ball? Why would anyone forfeit the chance to score—and the rewards and recognition that come with it—just so that their team member can take a shot? Why would someone sacrifice their own immediate gains for those of a fellow player or the good of the team?

In recent decades, Rusbult's *investment model* has expanded interdependence theory to elaborate the cognitive, emotional, and developmental mechanisms through which partners influence one another's decisions (e.g., Lewis, McBride, et al., 2006; Rusbult & Buunk, 1993; Rusbult & Van Lange, 2003). It has been used specifically to study substance use and HIV risk outcomes in sexual minority male couples (Lewis, Gladstone, et al., 2006). It is particularly useful here as a framework for thinking about how partners work together (or against each other) in a change process, conceptualizing partners' behavior toward one another in session, and formulating strategic counselor responses.

When applied to understand the process of change relevant to a Motivational Interview, the target behavior that is the focus of the interview can be thought of as the outcome of an interdependent process. In other words, the target behavior is equivalent to the final score in that basketball game. The partners are players on the same team. The counselor works a bit like the coach in this analogy. Their goal is to facilitate not only individual motivation for change, but also the partners' ability to work together toward change. Just like the players on a basketball team, sometimes achieving success together requires partners to think about supporting one another for the good of the team (i.e., their relationship). When partners focus solely on their own needs or desires—maximizing personal gains—they can sometimes hold one another back. One partner's progress potentially comes at a cost to the other or their relationship overall.

How do partners get to a point where they can work together toward a shared goal? How do they come together as a team, achieve consensus, and coordinate their efforts in ways that allow compromise to feel like a sacrifice that allows shared success? Interdependence theory and the investment model would suggest that partners either succeed or fail in working together as the result of a series of interpersonal and intra-individual events depicted in Figure 2.1, and definitions of key terms are summarized in Box 2.1.

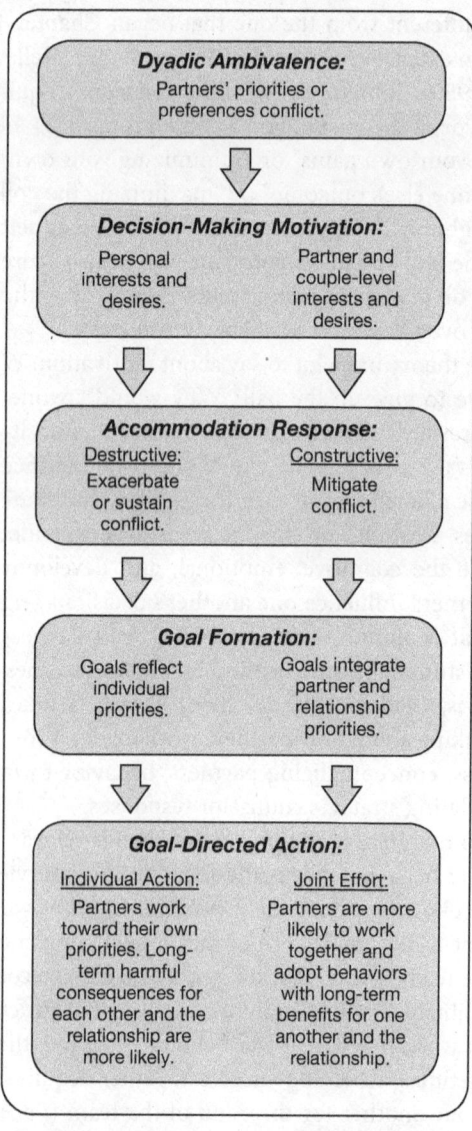

Figure 2.1 The process of interdependent decision-making. Figure by Stephen Sullivan.

Box 2.1

(See additional references in text.)

Accommodation—The way partners respond to one another when faced with dyadic ambivalence. Sometimes used specifically to refer to adaptive accommodation or "the tendency to react to a partner's potentially destructive act by inhibiting destructive impulses, instead responding constructively" (Yovetich & Rusbult, 1994, p. 139; also see Rusbult et al., 1991).

Accommodation response types (examples drawn from Rusbult et al., 1982, 1986)

- **Voice**—**Active and constructive** responses such as discussing a problem, negotiating compromise, sharing information about goals and priorities, or proposing solutions.
- **Loyalty**—**Passive and constructive** responses that avoid conflict in the hope that things will get better on their own. Sometimes characterized as "waiting and hoping" or "giving things time."
- **Neglect**—**Passive and destructive** responses such as spending less time with or ignoring a partner, refusing to discuss a topic, as well as insulting or becoming generally critical of a partner.
- **Exit**—**Active and destructive** responses decrease dependence on the relationship. May include separating or ending the relationship, decreasing investment (e.g., moving out of a shared residence), or deciding to "just be friends."

Dependence—The degree to which an individual relies on their relationship partner. Reliance here implies that one partner's outcomes are influenced by the other partner's actions. Alternatively, it represents the degree to which partners need their relationship or the extent to which their personal well-being rests on involvement in the relationship (Drigotas et al., 1999; Rusbult & Van Lange, 2003).

Dyadic ambivalence—A circumstance in which the partners' interests, preferences, or goals diverge. Sometimes described as a circumstance in which one partner behaves destructively or wherein partners have conflicting interests, discordant preferences, or incongruent goals.

Investment—The extent to which important resources, such as time, money, possessions, and social network, are shared (e.g., Rusbult, 1983).

Joint goal—A goal in which both partners feel some investment in accomplishing. Also referred to as a shared goal.

Relationship discord—Conflict between partners. A condition that may arise when partners respond destructively to dyadic ambivalence.

Transformation of motivation—Partners shift their focus away from a primary emphasis on maximizing personal gains to consider the impact of their behavior on their partner and the relationship as a whole. Also described as the "tendency to pause and take account of broader considerations such as the long-term consequences of one's actions for a relationship" (Yovetich & Rusbult, 1994, p. 138).

The sequence of events in Figure 2.1 begins with *dyadic ambivalence*—a circumstance in which the partners' interests, preferences, or goals conflict. They see things differently. One partner may desire something the other does not. Partners may prefer different things. One partner may want something that presents a threat to the relationship itself. Confronted with this disagreement, partners must make a decision about what to prioritize. Will they consider making some sacrifice to achieve compromise that might benefit their partner and the relationship overall? Will they instead focus on achieving their preferred outcome regardless of the cost?

This decision—to consider some compromise or prioritize personal interests and goals at all costs—influences subsequent steps in the exchange pictured in Figure 2.1. A willingness to consider one another's goals increases the likelihood that partners respond constructively to one another when communicating about the disagreement. In contrast, a focus on personal interests increases the likelihood the partners respond to one another in destructive or counterproductive ways. When partners respond constructively, it increases the likelihood that consensus is ultimately achieved, and they are then able to work together toward a shared goal. When partners respond destructively in moments of conflict, compromiseis less likely, often leaving partners to work independently on their individual goals. This decreases the likelihood of goal attainment and increases the chance of continued conflict.

The term *dyadic ambivalence* is used throughout this text to refer to situations where partners have divergent interests, preferences, or goals because it aligns with the existing concept of ambivalence in Motivational Interviewing. The phenomenon has been discussed in terms of the degree of *concordance* in partner's preferred outcomes (Kelley & Thibaut, 1978) or the *covariation of interests* (Rusbult & Van Lange, 1996) in much of the literature on interdependence theory. Some have termed it a *diagnostic situation* because motivational tendencies can be deduced from partners' behavior in these moments (e.g., Holmes & Rempel, 1989; Rusbult & Van Lange, 2003). Others have talked about it in terms of a problem faced by the couple (Rusbult et al., 1986); a point of relationship dissatisfaction (Rusbult, Zembrodt, & Gunn, 1982); or a situation in which one partner behaves destructively (Yovetich & Rusbult, 1994). All of these terms refer in some way to a moment—a situation—in which partners are at odds with one another or present some threat to the interests of the couple as a whole. The partners may want different things or view some aspect of one another's behavior as unacceptable or aversive.

As discussed in greater detail in Chapter 7, the term *dyadic ambivalence* here is an extension of how ambivalence has traditionally been understood in Motivational Interviewing (W. R. Miller & Rollnick, 2013; W. R. Miller & Rose, 2009). In their foundational text, W. R. Miller and Rollnick (2013, p. 157) suggested ambivalence was characterized by "simultaneous conflicting emotions and can thus be an uncomfortable place to be." Their focus was on the phenomenon wherein one person feels two ways about something, or someone is torn between two options that are both in some way desirable. Dyadic ambivalence refers to a state in which the partners in a relationship feel differently about something, or they are divided in their preferences. Even though the ambivalence in this case arises between people—rather than within a person—the state can be no less uncomfortable.

The more interdependent partners are the less dyadic ambivalence can be ignored. *Dependence* generally refers to "the degree to which an individual relies on an interaction partner, in that [their] outcomes are influenced by [their] partner's action" (Rusbult & Van Lange, 2003, p. 355). Applied more directly to a close personal relationship, dependence has also been defined as "the degree to which an individual relies uniquely on a relationship for attaining good outcomes" (Drigotas et al., 1999, p. 390) or alternatively as "the degree to which each of two interacting individuals needs their relationship, or the extent to which each individual's personal well-being rests on involvement in the relationship" (Agnew et al., 1998, p. 940).

Building on interdependence theory, Rusbult's investment model suggested that dependence is the product of high satisfaction with the relationship, the perception that available alternatives would be less good than the current relationship, and a high degree of investment in the relationship (Agnew et al., 1998; Rusbult, 1983; Rusbult & Buunk, 1993; Rusbult, Martz, et al., 1998). Investment in this sense is the extent to which important resources (e.g., time, money, possessions, and social network) are shared. Dependence emerges over time. As the partners' reliance on one another increases—as their relationship becomes more central to their own identity and investment increases—the salience of a disagreement and the way partners respond to one another during periods of potential conflict both evolve.

My favorite example of this is my cat. I have believed pretty strongly my entire life that house pets are anathema. People live in houses; animals should live outside. The evening I first met my husband, there was a lot of mutual interest and attraction. On our second date, I learned he had a cat. At the time, I did not think much of it. It certainly was not a barrier to continuing to date someone who I otherwise enjoyed a great deal. Fast forward a year and half and we were considering moving in with one another. Suddenly, the need to resolve our difference of opinions about house pets was unavoidable. Fortunately for us, the cat turned out to be terrifically endearing, and I was ultimately invested enough in the relationship to agree to have him around—after we established some expectations about the scope of my role regarding his litter box.

How partners respond to one another when faced with nonignorable dyadic ambivalence depends in part on which motivations they experience as salient. On the one hand, partners might focus on their own immediate needs, desires, and benefits in the given situation. Alternatively, partners may shift their focus to consider the impact of their behavior on their partner and the relationship as a whole (Kelley & Thibaut, 1978; Thibaut & Kelley, 1959). This shift in perspective, or the "tendency to pause and take account of broader considerations such as the long-term consequences of one's actions for a relationship" (Yovetich & Rusbult, 1994, p. 138) is referred to as a *transformation of motivation* (Kelley & Thibaut, 1978; Rusbult & Van Lange, 1996, 2003; Yovetich & Rusbult, 1994).

The reason why the transformation of motivation is so critical is that it facilitates adaptive *accommodation* (e.g., Rusbult et al., 1982, 1991, 1996;Rusbult & Van Lange, 2003), which is defined as "the tendency to react to a partner's potentially destructive act by inhibiting destructive impulses, instead responding constructively" (Rusbult et al., 1991; Yovetich & Rusbult, 1994, p. 139). Arriving at a compromise—achieving consensus when sacrifice is required—is extremely difficult when partners respond to one another in ways that exacerbate conflict. In contrast, when partners accommodate adaptively, they respond to potential conflict with constructive and assertive words and actions that minimize conflict and increase the likelihood of compromise. Accommodation, then, is not the achievement of consensus. Rather, it is an initial response to conflict that creates the opportunity for consensus to emerge.

Through this book, the term "accommodation" will often be used to connote successful or adaptive accommodation, consistent with others (e.g., Rusbult et al., 1991; Yovetich & Rusbult, 1994). Destructive responses to dyadic ambivalence are instead referred to as *relationship discord*. As with ambivalence, the use of the term *discord* here is an extension of its typical use in the Motivational Interviewing literature. W. R. Miller and Rollnick (2013, p. 204) defined discord as "signals of disharmony" in the collaborative relationship between the counselor and client. They suggested that discord is indicated sometimes by blaming or oppositional exchanges. It might also manifest as problems in the flow of conversation, wherein client and counselor interrupt one another or disengage from the dialogue. Discord signals that something has gone amiss in the working alliance between the counselor and client. Their goals, interests, values, and attitudes are not aligned. Failure to adequately address discord has been linked to poor treatment outcomes (e.g., W. R. Miller et al., 1993; Patterson & Chamberlain, 1994).

In the same way that discord in the alliance between counselor and client can signal challenges in working together toward change, relationship discord is a potential signal that partners are struggling to work together. The topic of relationship discord receives considerable attention throughout this text. Many of the strategies discussed in the chapters that follow are intended to diminish the occurrence of discord between partners and to mitigate the severity of conflict when relationship discord emerges. Chapter 7 specifically reviews research on common manifestations of relationship discord that emerged in Motivational Interviewing sessions with couples and identified counselor strategies that mitigate conflict and help partners work together in session (Starks, Robles, et al., 2020).

The consensus itself—the formation of a joint goal—opens the door to the creation of a shared plan to accomplish that goal. This process has sometimes been termed communal coping (Lewis, McBride, et al., 2006). Partners may contributions to goal attainment in different ways, based in part on the mutuality of dependence present in the situation (Rusbult & Van Lange, 2008). Sometimes in order to achieve a goal, both partners have to work together in some way. One partner may simply not have the ability to achieve the goal on their own without the support of the other. The goal may rest largely in the partner's hands (e.g., a person might need their partner to cover the cost of going to school), or it may require collaborative effort (perhaps both partners need to share responsibilities to successfully care for a pet). Even in situations where one person could independently achieve a goal through their personal effort, the presence of a supportive partner who promotes their success increases its likelihood (Righetti et al., 2016; Rusbult & Van Lange, 2008). In the absence of achieving consensus around a joint goal, partners are left to pursue their individual priorities. It is more likely that individuals will persist in behaviors that have long-term negative consequences for their partners and their relationships. It also increases the likelihood that partners will present barriers to the achievement of each other's individually identified goals.

We can now understand the counselor's role in instances where partners disagree about change as a manifestation of dyadic ambivalence and the subsequent interactions between partners in terms of an interdependent process. Counselors need to create a space where partners can explore their divergent perspectives on the target behavior productively—minimizing the likelihood or intensity of relationship discord. This means counselors need to support couples in achieving adaptive accommodation. Partners need to respond to one another in session in ways that minimize unnecessary conflict and emotional pain and maximize the likelihood that they are able to listen, express themselves, and find common ground. Then, within this atmosphere of emotional safety, the counselor can begin to explore how the partners' views of the target behavior might contrast with their broader goals and values, their own individual needs, and the needs of their relationship.

In order for counselors to do this, they must first be able to distinguish between relatively adaptive manifestations of accommodation and those that are more likely to be problematic. Counselors must also understand how relationship functioning is related to the accommodation process. This knowledge base is essential to understand and apply the processes and techniques described in the chapters that follow.

A taxonomy of accommodation responses. Researchers have given substantial consideration to the range of potential reactions partners might have to dyadic ambivalence (i.e., in moments of dissatisfaction with one another) (e.g., Hirschman, 1970, 1974; Rusbult et al., 1982, 1986; Yovetich & Rusbult, 1994). The more recent work in this area, by Rusbult and colleagues, suggested that accommodation responses can be organized along two dimensions. The first dimension characterizes the effect of the response on the relationship and ranges from constructive to destructive. The second characterizes the response as active versus passive in nature (Rusbult et al., 1982; Rusbult & Zembrodt, 1983; Yovetich & Rusbult, 1994).

In conceptualizing the effect of a response on the relationship, Rusbult et al. (1982, p. 1231) suggested that constructive responses "maintain or revive the relationship." In contrast, destructive responses are those that either end the relationship or diminish its quality. It is worth noting that the terms "constructive" and "destructive" here are defined with respect to the impact of a partner's actions on the relationship—and not on their own individual well-being. It is possible to imagine a situation in which it might be in an individual's best interest to terminate a relationship and separate completely from a partner. One example might be a situation in which an individual experiences physical, mental, or emotional abuse perpetrated by their partner. While the decision to end the relationship might very well be "constructive" with regard to the overall mental and physical health of the individual, it is in the strictest sense a "destructive" accommodation response in that it involves dissolution of the relationship.

In addition, responses vary in the degree to which they are active versus passive in promoting problem resolution. Active responses in some way seek to "do something about the relationship" (Rusbult et al., 1982, p. 1231). In other words, they aim to address the problem at hand or resolve the dissatisfaction. In contrast, passive responses leave the initiation of a resolution up to the partner. A prototypical example of passive responses might be ignoring a problem in the hope that it improves on its own or refusing to discuss a topic with a partner. Note, Rusbult et al. (1982, p. 1231) specified: "Passive refers to the impact of the behavior on the problem at hand and may not necessarily be descriptive of the behavior itself." Responses that involve insults (e.g., "You are so stupid") or criticism unrelated to the actual problem may, on the surface, appear to be quite "active" behaviors; however, their actual impact on problem resolution is minimal. They are therefore characterized as passive accommodation responses because they do not directly initiate problem resolution.

These two dimensions—constructive versus destructive and active versus passive—are orthogonal. Constructive responses can take an active or a passive form, as can destructive responses. This produces four subtypes of accommodation responses (Rusbult et al., 1982, 1986; Yovetich & Rusbult, 1994). On the adaptive end of the spectrum, active responses—termed **voice**—involve instances when partners discuss a problem, share information about their goals and priorities, propose solutions, or attempt to negotiate compromise. **Loyalty** responses are characterized by one partner passively tolerating or acquiescing to the other's preferences for the shared good. They avoid conflict in the hopes that things will improve or get better on their own if given sufficient time. On the destructive end of the spectrum, **exit** responses seek to address dissatisfaction by actively diminishing dependence on the relationship. A partner may threaten to leave the relationship in response to disagreement. They may take steps to decrease relationship investment (e.g., moving out of a shared living space or separating finances). They may opt to "just be friends" or to end the relationship altogether. **Neglect** responses are destructive to the relationship; they diminish relationship quality, but are passive with respect to problem resolution. Some neglect responses, such as ignoring a partner or refusing to discuss a problem, may look behaviorally similar to loyalty responses to an outside observer. They differ with respect to motivation. Loyalty responses are undertaken in the hope that the situation will improve. Neglect responses are motivated by self-interest and to escape from conflict. As suggested previously, behaviors such as insulting or criticizing a partner fall under the category of neglect behaviors because they are destructive but ultimately passive in nature (Rusbult et al., 1982, 1986; Yovetich & Rusbult, 1994).

Overall relationship functioning matters. Belonging to a team, being a member or a part of a social group that is larger than oneself, is a potent and meaningful experience. Even if the team does not always win, merely belonging is potentially valuable. When we struggle, team members pick us up. When we doubt we can go on, team members pull us through. When we cannot see hope, they keep us going. In moments where we cannot imagine doing something for ourselves, we might just hang in there and "do it for them." In the same way, the support of a partner, the emotional and logistical resources that come from being part of a successful couple, are some of the most powerful things about being in a relationship.

The benefits of group membership come with a trade-off. To be a good team player, some compromise is inevitably required. Relationships are no exception. When partners disagree about what they should do, when interests conflict, they have to find a consensus solution to maintain cohesion. Compromise inherently requires sacrifice (Rusbult & Van Lange, 2003). Partners must give something up in order to achieve consensus and work together.

Partners are more willing to make sacrifices when relationship functioning is strong (Rusbult & Van Lange, 2003). Chapter 5 provides an extended discussion of key elements of relationship functioning. The concept that is important presently is that people who are satisfied with, invested in, and committed to their relationships are more likely to listen openly and respond constructively when faced with dyadic ambivalence (Rusbult et al., 1986; Rusbult & Van Lange, 2003). This assertion is supported by related research on partners' social control strategies. Substantial research with heterosexual and same-sex couples has indicated that partners in relationships try to exert social control—or influence over—one another's health behavior (e.g., Bui et al., 1994; Howard et al., 1986; Lewis, Gladstone, et al., 2006). Among male couples specifically, there is evidence that partners commonly try to influence one another's substance use and HIV risk–related behaviors (Lewis, Gladstone, et al., 2006).

Some forms of social control are more aversive than others. Negative, or aversive, social control strategies include behaviors such as nagging, yelling, invoking obligation, or making someone feel guilty. These attempts to influence a partner's concerning health behavior are largely aligned with neglect accommodation responses. In contrast, positive social control strategies are aimed at supporting a partner's health behavior through assertive negotiation, providing information, engagement in the behavior together, or offers of help or support—strategies largely aligned with voice or loyalty accommodation responses. Research consistently indicated that partners in better functioning relationships—those who are more satisfied, invested, and committed to their relationship—are more likely to select positive social control strategies that support one another's health behavior change while minimizing conflict (Bui et al., 1994; Lewis, Gladstone, et al., 2006).

There are several reasons why relationship functioning may contribute to adaptive accommodation. People in better functioning relationships have more incentive to avoid conflict and inflicting unnecessary harm or discomfort on their partner. If someone values their relationship a great deal, then by extension they have more to lose if they act in ways that harm their partner or the relationship. People who are highly satisfied in their relationship may simply be more likely to experience rewards that offset the sacrifices involved in compromise (Rusbult & Van Lange, 2003). In contrast, when couples are already struggling and partners see little merit in continuing the relationship, they have less to lose by responding to disagreements by prioritizing their own needs and goals or responding to conflict in ways that are harsh and critical of their partner.

Given the influence of overall relationship functioning on accommodation and social control, the chapters that follow—and Chapter 5 in particular—devote considerable attention to counselor strategies that draw out the couple's strengths. These strategies are intended to identify and make explicit what works and what is valued about the relationship. Their presence is an essential ingredient of Motivational Interviewing with couples because building strong and rewarding relationships generally lays the foundation for partners to negotiate shared goals and work together toward change.

When it comes to accommodation, success may beget success. Exploring past successes is a common strategy familiar to many Motivational Interviewing counselors (W. R. Miller & Rollnick, 2013). When it comes to supporting adaptive accommodation in session, it is particularly useful to keep in mind that a history of successful accommodation makes dealing with a present conflict easier (Rusbult & Van Lange, 2003). This may arise partly as a result of practice. Any difficult negotiation affords partners an opportunity to learn more about how to effectively express their preferences to one another. Couples who find a way to listen to each other once have a potential road map for success in future conversations. In addition, successful accommodation in one instance may accrue goodwill that facilitates accommodation in future instances (Rusbult & Van Lange, 2003). Over time, as partners engage in more acts of accommodation, partners learn to trust or anticipate that even if they do not agree, they will be kind to one another and seek to understand each other's perspective. That anticipation has the potential to be a self-fulfilling prophecy. When partners expect conflict, they may approach a conversation "on their guard" or "prepared to fight" in ways that actually activate or exacerbate conflict. When partners anticipate a thoughtful and respectful dialogue about differences, they may initiate conversations in ways that help to bring that about.

HOW MOTIVATIONAL INTERVIEWING WITH COUPLES EXPANDS THE EXISTING MOTIVATIONAL INTERVIEWING PARADIGM

Motivational Interviewing has already demonstrated success in reducing substance use and sexual HIV transmission risk behavior among sexual minority men specifically (e.g., Chen et al., 2016; Kahler et al., 2018; Parsons et al., 2014;

Z. Wang et al., 2018). Similar interventions addressing substance use and HIV medication adherence have also received support (e.g., Naar et al., 2020; Naar-King et al., 2009). All of these are individually delivered. As Chapter 1 illustrated, applying the techniques from an individual intervention to a session with a couple presents challenges. Tools effective during a one-on-one session may become less reliable when working with both partners in a couple. There is also some indication that these individually focused interventions may be most effective for single clients. The *Young Men's Health Project*—a four-session Motivational Interviewing intervention—significantly reduced drug use and sexual HIV transmission risk behavior in an initial efficacy trial (Parsons et al., 2014); however, follow-up analyses suggested that participants who were in relationships at the time they received the intervention benefitted less than their single counterparts (Starks & Parsons, 2018). One potential reason is that the intervention does not address relationship factors relevant to the target behavior.

As mentioned in Chapter 1, partners may play a number of productive roles during a Motivational Interviewing session. They may provide feedback, affirm the skills of the identified client, facilitate goal setting, and provide ongoing support for behavior change (Monti et al., 2014). Unfortunately, evidence suggests that when partners step outside of these productive roles in session, their presence may not be helpful. This may happen when partners actively argue against change. Results from Project MATCH (Matching Alcoholism Treatment to Client Heterogeneity) indicated that a partner's sustain talk predicted worse drinking outcomes from identified clients (Manuel et al., 2012). Partners may also detract from the session by shifting the focus to themselves even if they are not arguing directly against change. In Project MATCH, change talk from identified clients decreased when relationship partners shifted the focus of the session to their own experiences or personal feelings (Manuel et al., 2012).

Interdependence theory now provides a framework for understanding the challenges faced in conducting a Motivational Interview with couples and a road map to inform and guide counselors. Partners can encourage and support change; however, the strategies they use—and the way those efforts are perceived by their partner—depends on whether or not the partners have arrived at a shared goal and how well the overall relationship is functioning. Partners can detract from conversations about change if they focus on their own personal interests and goals, but counselors who are able to balance a focus on couple-level and individual-level interests can help clients think about how their individual behavior impacts one another and their relationship.

Facilitating dyadic functioning emerges as a unique process. Chapter 5 is devoted exclusively to the introduction of a novel Motivational Interviewing process unique to couples—*facilitating dyadic functioning*. Sometimes referred to as simply *facilitating*, this process was first conceptualized by Starks, Millar, et al. (2018) based on an analysis of content drawn from Motivational Interviewing sessions with couples. We suggested that prior to focusing in on the target behavior, counselors should explore the couple's strengths. This involves asking partners to describe what they value about the relationship, what they appreciate

about each other, and the ways in which they work and communicate well together. Facilitating dyadic functioning can also involve some exploration of where
"things get hard." This might include areas of common disagreement and communication weaknesses. In instances where weaknesses are explored, it is also
common to troubleshoot identified challenges using a strengths-based approach.
The possibilities of integrating adjunct intervention components drawn from
cognitive and behavioral skill building to improve dyadic communication, and
problem-solving is explored further in Chapters 9 and 11.

Being perfectly happy with a relationship is not a prerequisite to working together toward change. Couples do not need to solve every problem before they
can tackle the challenge of behavior change together. The goal in facilitating dyadic functioning is to ensure that the couple has at least some foundation to build
on—to focus on the two of them as a team before turning the focus to their views
on the target behavior. Chapter 5 illustrates this exploration of couples' strengths.
In addition, it outlines counselor strategies that can enhance dyadic functioning
and improve the quality of communication between partners.

**Attention to relationship functioning is ongoing throughout the course
of a Motivational Interview with a couple.** We have typically found that the
facilitating process emerges as particularly salient after the engaging process in our
interventions; however, in keeping with W. R. Miller and Rollnick's (2013) overall
concept of processes as ongoing, attention to facilitating dyadic functioning is
relevant throughout the entire interview (Starks, Miller, et al., 2018). In this way,
engaging, focusing, evoking, and planning with a couple involve consistent and
sustained attention to the couple as a whole as well as to the individual partners.
During initial engagement, partners must agree to participate in the session together. This initial willingness to attend the session and speak with the counselor
is—in and of itself—joint effort or shared action. When focusing the session, partners must achieve some consensus about a productive topic of conversation. Even
if they feel very differently about the topic, even if they have very divergent ideas
about change, partners must arrive at some understanding about what they will
discuss. This is easier when partners have a shared sense of what they value about
their relationship. When evoking change talk, counselors must facilitate adaptive
accommodation responses and mitigate the emergence of relationship discord in
session and help couples find a shared vision for change. Only then can partners think about planning together toward change in ways that generate mutual
investment.

New dimensions are added to traditional counselor skills. Most all counselors
acquainted with Motivational Interviewing will be familiar with the foundational
engaging techniques of open questions, affirmations, reflections, and summary
statements (OARS; W. R. Miller & Rollnick, 2013). Conducting a Motivational
Interview with a couple involves the added dimensions of speaking to the couple
as a whole as well as each of the partners in the couple. Throughout the coming
chapters, narrative examples and discussions of relevant counselor strategies
demonstrate approaches to balancing attention across these dimensions. The
core skills of Motivational Interviewing remain the same, but now counselors

can employ them along a wider range of communication pathways to flexibly direct attention to the couple as a whole or to one of the partners as the situation demands. See Chapter 4 and Figure 4.2.

These dimensions also give rise to novel counselor utterances that are not ordinarily applicable to an individual Motivational Interviewing session. The universe of OARS gets bigger. Specifically, Chapter 4 introduces the techniques of dyadic reflections and relationship affirmations—utterances commonly directed at the couple. Dyadic reflections serve to pull together content from both partners, to capture common ground, or to reflect on shared values, attitudes and ideas. Relationship affirmations are a tool for explicitly identifying couple-level strengths and areas of successful dyadic functioning. These novel OARS feature prominently throughout all of the chapters that follow as core components of proficient Motivational Interviewing practice with couples.

CONCLUSIONS AND KEY POINTS

Interdependence theory provides a framework for thinking about Motivational Interviewing with couples in a novel way. It suggests, first and foremost, that counselors should consider a paradigm in which the couple—rather than an individual partner—is their client. Seen through this lens, disagreements between partners about whether change should happen or how it should proceed can be understood as dyadic ambivalence. The counselor's role is to help mitigate the occurrence of relationship discord so that dyadic ambivalence can be explored and resolved. Only then can partners plan for change successfully together.

Drawing on the concepts of interdependence theory, this book introduces a novel process to Motivational Interviewing—facilitating dyadic functioning. This process emphasizes eliciting the couple's strengths, developing relationship skills, and cultivating the couple's capacity to work together by highlighting satisfaction, commitment, and emotional investment. In addition to this novel process, unique counselor skills, in particular the use of dyadic reflections and relationship affirmations, expand the repertoire of OARS.

3

The Spirit of Motivational Interviewing With Couples

Motivational Interviewing has deep roots in person-centered or client-centered therapy (W. R. Miller & Rollnick, 2013). Beyond the technique or content of an interview, Motivational Interviewing has placed a strong emphasis on the importance of "how" the interview is conducted. The counselor's mindset, attitude, or stance toward the client is an essential component of delivery. This acknowledges that no technique—no tool—is inherently effective. The effectiveness of a tool is determined at least in part by the intention of the person using it. Hammers build, and they also knock things down.

FOUNDATIONS OF CLIENT-CENTERED COUNSELING

In his formative writing on client-centered therapy, Rogers (1949) highlighted the central importance of the counselor's own philosophical stance—their attitudes, beliefs, or worldview "towards the worth and significance of the individual" (p. 82). Rogers referred to this stance as the counselor's "basic operational philosophy" (p. 82) and suggested it was a primary determinant of how long it would take the counselor to become proficient. Rogers saw client-centered therapy techniques as a mechanism to genuinely express respect for the person of the client; that is possible only insofar as the counselor enters into the counseling process with a basic operational philosophy that is characterized by a belief in the significance and worth of each person.

Rogers (1949) suggested that, in order to enact their respect for people, counselors must strive to express "moment-to-moment empathy." The function of the counselor during the therapeutic process is to "assume, in so far as [they] are able, the internal frame of reference of the client, to perceive the world as the client sees it, to perceive the client as [they] are seen by [themselves], and to lay aside all perceptions from the external frame of reference while doing so" (p. 86). The expression of empathy then arises from an active listening process, one in which the counselor not only gathers information, but also objectively demonstrates or conveys in ways that are detectible to the client that they are actively trying to understand the client's experience from the client's own perspective—just as they are without bias or judgment.

There are two essential elements to Rogers's (1949) concept of empathy. Together, these can be understood as *active listening*. **First, empathy is active**—it must be implemented. It is a thing the counselor does—not merely a passive or subjective emotional experience. Counselor utterances like affirming the client, reflecting back their feelings and ideas, and summarizing the information they provide are all examples of strategies or techniques that serve to enact or implement empathy by directly conveying the counselor's ongoing attempts to glean meaning from information the client has provided. **Second, empathy requires listening.** In order for the counselor to understand the client as they are, the counselor must be curious and willing to learn about the client's experience. The counselor must set aside the expert role and allow the client to tell their story—to explain their unique and subjective experience. The use of open questions (which invite a robust client response) and reflections (which amplify and continue a client's thoughts) are good examples of counselor techniques that serve this purpose. The key is that these techniques are not used to gather information for its own sake. The end goal is not the counselor's understanding, but rather the expression of that understanding to the client.

Rogers's writing reflects a deep conviction about the posture of empathic, active listening. He saw it as one of three components essential to the creation of a climate that will facilitate the realization of the client's potential, or self-actualization (Rogers, 1946, 1979). The other two components are the expression of acceptance and genuineness.

The concept of acceptance has often been linked to the idea of suspending judgment. Linehan (2015) characterized a nonjudgmental stance as the radical acceptance of what is, letting go of one's beliefs about what should or ought to be happening. It is the acknowledgment of facts without evaluating them as "good" or "bad"; the separation of ongoing events from one's opinion about them. This concept—that acceptance and the suspension of judgment are related to one another—is syntonic with Rogers's thinking. It is embodied in his concept of unconditional positive regard—an attitude of caring for or prizing the client for whatever they are in the moment (Rogers, 1979).

Note, the suspension of judgment—the unconditional acceptance of the client as they are in the moment—is not the same as universal approval for the client's actions. It is possible to acknowledge the effects of one's actions (both adverse and enjoyable) without reacting to them with disapproval or approval. In fact, the act of approving of an action is—in and of itself—a judgment. Rogers's point was that regardless of whether clients succeed or fail, whether their actions are noble or nefarious, the client remains a human being possessed of an inherent worth and a capacity for growth toward an ideal self. Acceptance or unconditional positive regard means expressing a nonpossessive love for the person of the client without limits, qualifications, or conditions (Rogers, 1979).

The ongoing or moment-to-moment expression of empathy and acceptance requires that counselors not merely say anything that comes to mind, but that they say something that conveys in a compelling way they are actively trying to understand and unconditionally accept the client just as they are. For those statements to be effective, the counselor must be credible. The client must come to believe that the counselor's statements are genuine and authentic. It may be for this reason that Rogers (1949, 1979) placed a strong emphasis on the counselor's capacity for congruence, or the match between their thoughts and feelings about the client and what they express to the client in session. Here, we see a return of the importance of Rogers's basic operational philosophy. Counselors who enter into therapy with a core belief in the worth of the individual are freed to transparently act as their authentic selves in session. In doing so, their respect for the person of the client will be credibly enacted in their expression of empathy and acceptance.

The counselor's expression of empathy becomes the mechanism of therapeutic change. Rogers (1946, 1949, 1979) believed that by demonstrating their active attempts to understand the client just as they are, counselors offer clients the opportunity to see themselves through the counselor's eyes. The counselor's effort to take on the client's point of view affords the client a new perspective on their own experience. This allows them to understand and (re)organize their experiences in ways that facilitate growth and change or self-actualization.

THE SPIRIT OF MOTIVATIONAL INTERVIEWING: AN EXTENSION OF CLIENT-CENTERED CARE

Wholly consistent with Rogers, W. R. Miller and Rollnick (2013) articulated four concepts that comprise the Spirit of Motivational Interviewing. These can be thought of collectively as the articulation of a basic operational philosophy for counselors providing Motivational Interviewing. **Collaboration** or partnership represents a commitment to power sharing. A Motivational Interview is done "with" or "for" not "to" the client (p. 15). **Evocation** indicates counselors should take a stance of curiosity about the client and seek to draw out their goals, rationale, and plans for change. **Acceptance** addresses that counselors must be willing to set aside their judgments about what a client "should" do, think, or feel in order to learn about the client as they are now. **Compassion** indicates counselors must act with the best interests of their clients in mind. (See the Introduction for more detail.)

The elements of Motivational Interviewing Spirit are as critical to a couple's interview as they are with an individual; however, implementing them looks somewhat different. Returning to Rogers's source material serves as a foundation for considering how the Spirit of Motivational Interviewing is realized with a couple. How can the counselor be person centered when there are two people in the room—and also while thinking of the couple in toto as the client? How does the counselor balance their belief in the absolute worth of the two people they are serving, and what should their stance be toward the relationship overall? Finally, to what extent can the counselor's behavior facilitate partners' credible expression of empathy and acceptance toward each other? The pages and chapters that follow explore these questions.

One of the ways to recognize the enactment of Motivational Interviewing Spirit is to notice its absence. The narrative that follows is an antithetical example session. It illustrates the importance of Motivational Interviewing Spirit by demonstrating the impact of partial lapses or the uneven expression of Spirit. In other words, this is an example of what we might hope does *not* happen in a Motivational Interview with a couple. Readers who are at all familiar with Motivational Interviewing will likely notice the counselor say things that are not aligned with proficient delivery. After the example, we consider what went awry in those moments.

This example introduces the second of our (fictional) couples, Darin and Simon. The excerpt comes from a portion of their first session with this counselor. The transcript begins as the counselor has focused on the target behavior of substance use and related sexual risk-taking. In the discussion that follows, the couple describes their current substance use and the rationale for some changes that they have recently made. Darin has stopped using cocaine, and the couple has changed their sexual agreement from one that was open (they were able to have sex with partners outside the relationship) to one that is now monogamous.

* * *

COUNSELOR: What kinds of decisions do you two make about drugs and alcohol?

DARIN: Well, right now we just drink. And we smoke weed. But that's it. We're taking a break from everything else.

COUNSELOR: Got it. You have stepped back from other drugs you used to do. Sounds like you had a problem.

SIMON: Do you want to tell him?

DARIN: Well, not really, but—

COUNSELOR: It's probably best if we just get it out there.

DARIN: Oh fine. So, I used to also be into cocaine. Nothing too crazy. I just used to go clubbing with friends and we'd, you know, typically do a bump or two.

SIMON: Or three or four.

DARIN: Sure. Whatever. Anyway. About a month ago I was out and one thing led to another and I ended up having sex with one of the guys I was out with. Not my best move.

COUNSELOR: Yikes. You cheated.

SIMON: No. We were open at the time. He hasn't explained what happened.

COUNSELOR: There is more to this story.

DARIN: Well, we didn't use a condom. It was stupid, I know. I apologized. But I did at least know the guy. So I was pretty sure it would be fine, but it was stupid.

SIMON: And he kept it from me. That's the part he's not saying.

COUNSELOR: I see. And that's the part you really struggle with Simon. The lie.

SIMON: Exactly.

COUNSELOR: It's not so much that he had sex with another person. Keeping it from you, especially when there was some potential for risk, was the issue.

DARIN: Look, it's not like I lied about it. I didn't deny it. I just didn't want to talk about it because it felt like such a stupid thing to do. And I knew you'd be angry.

COUNSELOR: Simon, it sounds like that actually might have made it worse for you.

SIMON: It did. If he had just said something right away, we could have dealt with it—

COUNSELOR: Right, because now you have doubts about whether he is being honest with you.

SIMON: I do, which is why closing the relationship and just focusing on us has also been important. I just don't think we are at a place where there's enough trust to have that freedom.

COUNSELOR: It sounds like you needed that. It doesn't have to be permanent you know. You can always revisit your agreement down the road when Simon is ready. For now, it will remove some uncertainty for you, which sounds like a challenge.

SIMON: Yeah.

DARIN: Yeah? But how does this get fixed? Like at what point are you gonna decide you reached a point where there's that trust again?

COUNSELOR: I think that is something that Simon will need to determine. Trust takes time to develop and he needs to give himself that time.

SIMON: See, this is what I was trying to say.

* * *

Regardless of experience level, most Motivational Interviewing counselors could probably find a reason (or three or four) to cringe while reading that example. It is possible to imagine that the counselor's intentions are good. The counselor is, after all, trying to understand a challenge this couple faced. That challenge is relevant to the target behavior, and the counselor may even believe that they have useful information about how best to recover from such a challenge. Despite this, the exchange is undermined by the uneven and inconsistent implementation of Motivational Interviewing Spirit.

The counselor's expressions of empathy and acceptance are uneven. There is quite a good chance that Darin and Simon experienced their exchange with the counselor very differently. Consider for a moment the extent to which each of them likely felt understood, accepted, and valued. To what extent might they feel their autonomy was respected and their self-efficacy affirmed?

One reason why the exchange above falls short is that the counselor's expressions of empathy and acceptance are directed primarily toward Simon. Reflections that convey the counselor's understanding of client emotions and concerns are uniformly directed at Simon and largely contain only content expressed by him. In an individual session with Simon alone, these utterances might be effective; however, in the context of a couple's session, they have the effect of simultaneously expressing judgment toward Darin. The same statement that affirms Simon's autonomy to take the time he needs undermines Darin's efficacy and agency in the relationship.

The counselor's evocation is uneven and inconsistent. Not only is the counselor more empathic and accepting toward Simon, the counselor is also more curious about Simon's perspective. Questions and reflections intended to draw out the client's perspective on the challenge and how to proceed are consistently directed toward Simon. There is little or no attention given to Darin's perspective on the challenge or his view on how the couple should move forward together. This inhibits the couple's potential to work together toward a solution. Simon's goals, ideas, values, and preferences are—by default—given preeminence in the session by virtue of how the counselor is eliciting, attending, and elaborating on information. It is challenging for a couple to work together to make things better if the counselor is more interested or invested in the perspective of one partner more than the other.

The counselor's expression of evocation is not only uneven across partners, but also inconsistent over the session. Near the end, the counselor steps into the expert role and provides direction about when the couple should revisit their sexual agreement as well as an unsolicited opinion about the benefits of a monogamous sexual agreement at this time. As a result, the counselor learns less than they otherwise might about why Darin and Simon chose this option, what they need to do for one another to rebuild trust, and steps they see as important to take in their relationship. This misstep—telling rather than asking—is not unique to couples work; however, the effect on the session is equally problematic.

The counselor's collaboration is uneven. It is possible to get the impression that Darin is largely witnessing a conversation that Simon and the counselor are having about him. To the extent that the counselor is collaborating in determining the direction of the session, identifying a focus, and developing a perspective on change it is with Simon. The counselor and Simon determined that Darin's sexual behavior should be disclosed. They decided how the couple should proceed to rebuild from that challenge. Darin's influence on the content of the session and the proposed plan for change is minimal. If the ultimate goal is for Darin and Simon to work together toward some shared goal they are both invested in, this imbalance in partnership is counterproductive.

The counselor's compassion is uneven. Whose best interests are guiding the session? One of the problems with uneven expressions of empathy, evocation, and collaboration is that collectively they convey that the counselor is more attuned to the interests of one partner over the other. This has the potential to create the perception of an alliance that pits the counselor and one partner against the other.

A basic operational philosophy for Motivational Interviewing with couples. In truth, Motivational Interviewing with couples does not need a wholly new basic operational philosophy. Rogers's general premise will serve very well with only modest modification. To be client centered, counselors must begin with a core belief in the inherent worth of the individual—a respect for persons. The application of this premise to a couples Motivational Interview requires that the counselor at all times maintain a posture of respect—of unconditional positive regard—toward both partners and their relationship. O'Leary (2008, p. 298) expressed something similar in his assertion that therapists should "actively seek to understand and show acceptance of each person present."

The uneven expression of the Spirit of Motivational Interviewing connotes an implicit judgment. The expression of empathy toward one partner, creating space for one partner to articulate their experience in ways that allow the counselor (and the other partner in the relationship) to understand their perspective is not inherently bad. It becomes problematic when the counselor's attention is biased toward one partner. Providing moment-to-moment empathy, actively listening, and expressing understanding and acceptance toward one person in the relationship while relatively neglecting the other means that the worth of one of the people in the room is being undervalued. Counselors must therefore strive at all times to convey the Spirit of Motivational Interviewing to both partners in equitable ways.

The counselor's beliefs about relationships can be a particularly poignant source of judgment. Most of us have opinions about what "good" relationships look like and when relationships should be terminated. We have ideas about how "good partners" should behave toward one another and when a partner's behavior is unacceptable. When client circumstances activate these personal beliefs, it can be particularly tempting to view the partners and the relationship through the lens of our own beliefs and preferences.

This phenomenon is not unique to couples work and has been well described in the psychodynamic literature as countertransference (e.g., Freud, 1993; J. A. Hayes et al., 2018). Counselors—across a wide range of established orientations—are generally trained from early on about the importance of recognizing personal biases in session and mitigating their effect on treatment (e.g., Enns, 1993; Hays & Iwamasa, 2006). What is unique in a couple's session is that the relationship activating the counselor's biases is there in the room. It is one thing to hear an individual client describe a fight with their partner; it is quite another to witness a confrontation in session.

The issue of counselor bias in couples therapy has received considerable attention particularly with respect to gender-related attributions, expectancies, and biases (e.g., Guanipa & Woolley, 2000; Stabb et al., 1997); however, the concept that counselor beliefs about relationships may influence their interactions with a couple is not restricted to the heterosexual context. Counselor beliefs about the acceptability of sexual and gender minority people and the unique characteristics of their relationships have the potential to shape the way they understand interactions between partners and respond to couples in session. Concerns that counselors may deem sexual or gender diverse couples as "deviant" by virtue of comparing them to heterosexual norms are long-standing (e.g., Eldridge, 1987; LaSala, 2001; Spitalnick & McNair, 2005), as are concerns that counselors may fail to consider the impact of societal acceptance, bias, and discrimination on relationship functioning (e.g., LaSala, 2000; Neilands et al., 2020; Rosenthal et al., 2019; Spitalnick & McNair, 2005). Fortunately, current resources are available describing affirmative counseling and assessment or diagnostic practices with sexual and gender-diverse couples (e.g., DeBord et al., 2017; Rothblum, 2020). Guidelines for psychotherapy practice with lesbian, gay, and bisexual clients issued by the American Psychological Association specifically addressed issues of relationships and families (American Psychological Association, 2012) as did the practice guidelines for transgender and gender-nonconforming clients (American Psychological Association, 2015).

Implementing acceptance and empathy in a couples Motivational Interview therefore requires the counselor to maintain a stance of nonjudgmental acceptance toward the relationship as a whole. The counselor not only must try to understand each person in the relationship as an individual, but also must strive to understand the couple as they are together. This involves a nonjudgmental curiosity about what works and what does not in this relationship and a willingness to accept the fact that no matter how beautiful or horrible the relationship might be, the partners are choosing to remain in it and might also chose to end it.

So, we have now extended Roger's basic operational philosophy to work with two people. The counselor must genuinely implement acceptance and empathy toward two individuals and the couple they comprise. We might then extend Rogers's ideas about the mechanisms of therapeutic change and surmise that in striving to implement their genuine understanding and acceptance of both partners and their relationship, counselors afford both individuals a new perspective on their own experience as well as their partner's. In trying to understand the couple—just as they are—counselors offer both partners a chance to (re)organize their understandings of who they are individually and together.

THE ROLE OF THE COUNSELOR IN A MOTIVATIONAL INTERVIEW WITH COUPLES

The question of how a counselor should implement their respect for both persons and the couple in session has been explored extensively by O'Leary (e.g., 2008, 2012, 2015) in his writing on client-centered couples therapy. This work has the potential to provide a framework for the implementation of Motivational Interviewing Spirit with a couple. Before discussing the implementation of Spirit specifically, it may be helpful to briefly consider the overall role of the counselor during a Motivational Interview.

Ironically, enacting a client-centered stance toward a couple may sometimes require the counselor to actively interrupt the flow of the couple's typical dialogue. O'Leary (2015, p. 240) suggested that counseling should be "a place in which persons may have a different experience than they have at home." In training and supervision, I have at times suggested that "watching a couple have the same argument in session that they could have on their own is not helpful." While my sentiment is admittedly less artful than O'Leary's, we share the basic idea—Part of the counselor's role is to support the couple in having a conversation that is different in some way from the ones they typically have. We aim to support couples in the constructive discussion of issues that commonly produce conflict, or we seek the explicit discussion of topics that the couple typically avoids. O'Leary (2015) suggested that to achieve this the counselor must step into a role as *host* to the couple. Much like the host of a party or gathering, the counselor as host plays a structuring role in social interactions. They introduce novel topics and establish new norms. In doing so, the counselor facilitates a conversation that the couple might not be able to sustain on their own.

O'Leary (2015) suggested that in fulfilling the role of host, counselors must at times take on two other roles—*translator* and *moderator*. The counselor fulfills the role of translator by actively listening—and reflecting back their understanding—of each partner's perspective. Because both partners are in the room, they witness one another's disclosures. This potentially achieves several useful counseling functions simultaneously. The counselor serves as a model for active listening behaviors that partners might adopt when speaking to each other. The partner speaking is able to share their experience in an atmosphere of acceptance and support. The partner listening has the opportunity to hear from their partner directly and also to witness the meaning the counselor extracts and reflects back about their partner's experience. Effective translation can help to clarify intentions, correct misperceptions, and prevent miscommunication from unnecessarily sustaining conflict. In their role as Moderator, counselors actively structure the counseling dialogue to ensure that both partners have space to speak and be heard. They disrupt patterns of communication that tend to exacerbate conflict. They introduce communication norms, practices, or activities that facilitate partners' understanding of one another and their relationship.

The contrast between the relatively more observational role of translator and the relatively more active role of moderator has some similarities to W. R. Miller and Rollnick's (2013, p. 4) conceptualization of counseling styles along a continuum of activity from "following" to "directing." Ideally, the counselor seeks a position in between these two extremes, resolving the dialectic by assuming a "guiding" stance. From this position, the counselor exerts an influence on the direction of the session and the content discussed while also being open and responsive to the client's agenda.

For the purposes of conducting a Motivational Interview with a couple then, it may be most useful to consider a continuum of counselor activity that ranges from "reflective observing" to "moderating." The stance of reflective observer encompasses O'Leary's concept of the translator role. As a reflective observer, the counselor is an active listener intent on understanding each partner's perspective as well as the experience of the couple as a whole. They seek to articulate empathy and acceptance in an ongoing way. The concept of reflective observation also acknowledges that some portion of the counselor's role is to create space and opportunity for partners to speak directly to one another. The stance of moderator here is highly akin to O'Leary's concept of the role, wherein the counselor at times structures or interrupts the flow of clients' conversation.

The overall result is a sense of fluidly "stepping in and stepping back." Counselors observe and also direct who is speaking. Effective Motivational Interviewing with couples is characterized by fluid movement along this spectrum of counselor activity. Counselors should not strive to be either reflective observers or directive moderators exclusively. In fact, a number of the interviewing strategies and techniques discussed in the coming chapters involve the counselor moving quickly along this continuum. At times they may step in, disrupt the flow of ongoing conversation with a key question or clarifying reflection, and then step back—resuming an observer stance while the partners talk to one another. Effective counselors balance this tension throughout the session and seek to achieve a stance from which they can have a meaningful impact on the couple's communication in strategic ways while also allowing partners to communicate with one another freely.

A two-dimensional understanding of the counselor's role in Motivational Interviewing with couples. The task of expressing Motivational Interviewing Spirit toward both partners in the relationship as well as toward the couple as a whole introduces a second dialectic to the role of the Motivational Interviewing counselor. There is a tension along a continuum of focusing on the individual(s) versus the couple. O'Leary (2015) captured this in his enumeration of counselor activities in session. He suggested that one of the key things a counselor does is to create space for both partners to communicate. Counselors "slow the process down" and create opportunities for partners to "think effectively or listen to the thinking of others" (O'Leary, 2015, p. 238)—activities with a relative focus on each individual partner. O'Leary (2015, p. 239) also asserted that counselors push couples to "think meta" or understand the bigger picture of their interaction— an activity that could be seen as emphasizing a focus on the couple. The ideal counselor stance is not to achieve one exclusive focus or the other, but to flexibly occupy a middle space in which both individual perspectives and the couple's collective needs receive attention.

In the chapters that follow, we can now conceptualize the role of the counselor using these two dimensions. We can think about the counselor's level of activity— ranging from reflective observer to moderator—and the counselor's relative focus on individual versus couple-level perspectives. This does not mean that every moment of each interview needs to be perfectly balanced. But awareness of these dialectics may help counselors notice when sessions drift toward a focus on one partner to the exclusion of the other or when they are exerting too much or too little influence on the conversation.

EXPRESSING THE SPIRIT OF MOTIVATIONAL INTERVIEWING WITH A COUPLE

This chapter began with an antithetical example. We can now advance a framework for how counselors might understand and enact Motivational Interviewing Spirit with couples. To do this, let us consider how the exchange between Darin and Simon might have gone if the counselor had been more aligned with the Spirit of Motivational Interviewing with a couple. In this alternative example, annotations are provided in the column on the right to clarify the function of specific counselor utterances.

* * *

COUNSELOR: What kinds of decisions do you two make about drugs and alcohol?

DARIN: Well, right now we just drink. And we smoke weed. But that's it. We're taking a break from everything else.

COUNSELOR: Got it. Things have changed for you guys recently.

[Nonjudgmental reflection directed to the couple.]

SIMON: Yes. Do you want to explain this one?

DARIN: Well, not really, but I guess . . .

COUNSELOR: No pressure. Whether we talk about it or not is up to you two.

[Emphasizing autonomy directed to the couple.]

DARIN: Oh fine. So, I used to also be into cocaine. Nothing too crazy. I just used to go clubbing with friends and we'd, you know, typically do a bump or two.

SIMON: Or three or four.

DARIN: Sure. Whatever. Anyway. About a month ago I was out and one thing led to another and I ended up having sex with one of the guys I was out with. Not my best move.

COUNSELOR: That is not how you wanted things to go.

[Empathic reflection directed to Darin.]

DARIN: No.

COUNSELOR: What was it about that set of events that felt off? What is the part that bugs you?

[Evoking Darin's perspective.]

DARIN: So, we didn't use a condom. It was stupid, I know, and I felt terrible about it. I did at least know the guy. So I was pretty sure it would be fine, but still it was stupid.

SIMON: And, he kept it from me. That's the other part.

COUNSELOR: I see. And that is part of why things felt so off for you Simon. Something about that doesn't feel right.

[Empathic reflection directed to Simon.]

SIMON: Exactly.

COUNSELOR: How well does that fit for you Darin?

[Evoking Darin's perspective.]

DARIN: Yeah, I have to admit that didn't help. Look, it's not like I lied about it. I just didn't want to talk about it because it felt like such a stupid thing to do. [to SIMON] And I knew you'd be angry.

COUNSELOR: You felt really bad. That is not the person you want to be, and it was hard to come out and own that initially.

[Empathic reflection directed to Darin.]

SIMON: If he had just said something right away, I wouldn't have been happy, but we could have dealt with it.

COUNSELOR: This situation hurts. Looking back, you really wish it had played out differently.

[Empathic reflection directed to Simon.]

SIMONE: Right.

COUNSELOR: In a lot of ways, you guys see this situation similarly. This is not something you want to have happen again. And part of what brings you here actually is that you are really focused on finding a way to work together so that it doesn't.

[Empathic reflection directed to the couple.]

SIMON: Right. Like, I'd really like to make this work and not put each other through this again. I think you probably do too, right?

DARIN: Definitely, but like, how does that get fixed? Like at what point are we gonna decide that we have reached a point where there's that trust again?

COUNSELOR: You guys are suggesting something that [Collaborative
might be a good use of our time for the next few weeks. statement directed
You want to find a way to rebuild, and you are not quite to the couple.]
sure how to do that. If you wanted to, one thing we could
do here is talk about what you guys both need in this
relationship and perhaps consider some plans for how to
get there together.

* * *

Much like we were able to derive a basic operational philosophy for Motivational
Interviewing with couples by a modest modification of Rogers's original, the
essential aspects of Motivational Interviewing Spirit are the same in a couples
session as they are in an individual interview. Enacting them successfully just
requires some additional considerations. The unique challenges of expressing the
Spirit of Motivational Interviewing toward a couple can be understood in terms
of the counselor's two-dimensional role (depicted in Figure 3.1) and the basic
operational philosophy of couples Motivational Interviewing—which is that the

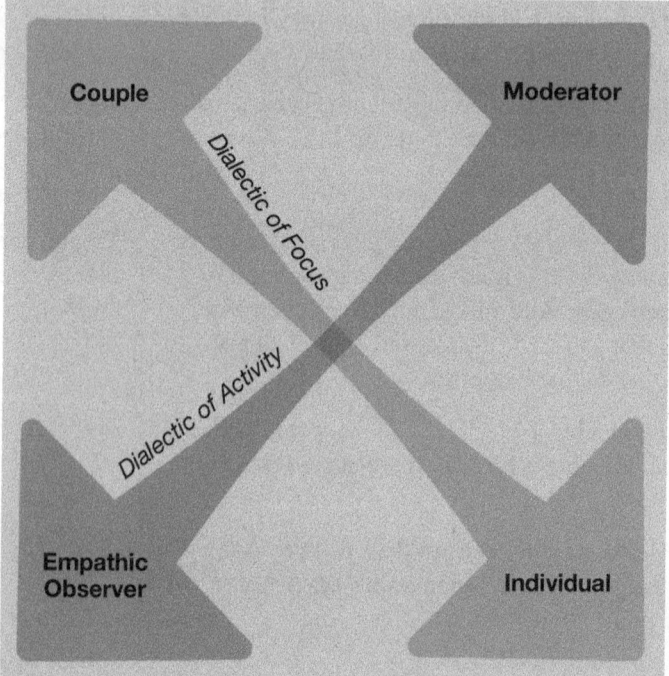

Figure 3.1 Dialectics that define the counselor role. Figure by Stephen Sullivan.

counselor must genuinely implement acceptance and empathy toward both partners and the couple they comprise.

Acceptance With Couples

W. R. Miller and Rollnick (2013) conceptualized acceptance as multifaceted. It encompassed not only a belief in the client's absolute worth and the expression of accurate empathy, but also a willingness to affirm the client's strengths and support for client autonomy. With a couple, counselors must attend to these four facets at both the individual and the couple levels. They must assume a stance of acceptance toward the couple as well as both of the individual partners.

Relationships themselves have an absolute worth—even when they are imperfect and do not endure. Time is a precious commodity, and even if relationships go badly, the people in them give something of themselves and their time. Part of expressing respect and a belief in clients' absolute worth during a couple's session involves maintaining a stance or mindset that relationships themselves have some inherent value and meaning.

Believing in the inherent worth of the relationship does not mean the counselor has to approve of how the partners behave toward one another. Instead, it means the counselor must always hold on to the idea that there is something about the relationship that may be valued by the people in it. A willingness to believe in this potential value and actively look for those facets of the relationship that are meaningful simultaneously expresses respect toward each of the partners in the relationship. This positions the counselor to explore how the partners work together from a neutral and nonjudgmental stance. Even in the worst-looking relationships, the partners have found something sufficiently motivating to bring them to counseling together.

The expression of empathy then becomes evidence of the counselor's belief in the absolute worth of the couple as well as the worth of each of the partners. The counselor's willingness to state aloud the couple's strengths and challenges attests to their desire to understand the couple as they are. The counselor's ability to verbalize what the partners value about the relationship, and perhaps also what the partners wish could be different, testifies to the counselor's genuine wish to understand this relationship and the individuals in it—just as they are.

Ongoing attention to acceptance is important throughout a Motivational Interview, but it may be particularly helpful when counselors are faced with a couple that is making decisions about whether they should remain together or end the relationship. The dialectic between an emphasis on the individual partners and the couple becomes particularly pointed in this kind of moment. The fact that the relationship has inherent worth does not mean that the partners are obligated to maintain it at all costs. Respect for individual autonomy does not end simply because respect for the couple is present.

Evocation With Couples

In Chapter 2, we spent substantial time illustrating the importance of speaking "to the couple." Effective Motivational Interviewing with couples requires balancing this new stance of speaking to the couple with the need to draw out the individual perspectives of both partners in the relationship. Therefore, one important element of successful evocation with couples is balancing attention to individual perspectives and the relationship overall. The counselor must move fluidly along the dialectic of focus. Doing so can help identify areas of consensus and clarify points of disagreement.

Successful evocation with a couple also involves fluid "stepping in and stepping back." By strategically moving along the dialectic of activity—skillfully varying the use of reflective observation and moderating strategies—counselors can draw out individual perspectives in ways that enhance partners' understandings of one another. This has the potential to facilitate the partners' expression of empathy toward one another, similar to empathy induction activities used in other forms of couples therapy (e.g., Christensen et al., 1995). Partners can then provide feedback about the accuracy of one another's hunches.

Collaboration With Couples

W. R. Miller and Rollnick (2013) accurately pointed out that Motivational Interviewing requires balancing multiple agendas. The client comes to the interview with a perspective on what would be worthwhile to focus on, what changes are possible, and how change might occur. The counselor may also have an assessment of what content would be useful for the client to focus on and what strategies for change might be most successful. There may also be agendas from third parties, such as insurance companies, treatment agencies, or legal entities that place mandates or restrictions on what is addressed in the interview. The guiding stance in Motivational Interviewing is that the counselor should share power with the client. The client's priorities are respected, and their perspective is valued; meanwhile, the counselor's expertise and professional limitations are also relevant.

A couple's session requires balancing multiple agendas as well—except there are even more of them. Each of the partners may have their own goals, there may be things they wish to achieve as a couple, and the counselor may have opinions about what would be best to focus on for each of the partners individually and also for them together as a couple. When those preferences all align, collaboration may be relatively easy. Maintaining a collaborative stance with a couple becomes challenging as those agendas diverge. Part of balancing these agendas is balancing attention to the multiple relationships in the room—maintaining attention to that dialectic of focus on the individual partners and the couple. Chapter 6 dedicates considerable attention to navigating such challenges in the focusing process.

There is a range of practice conventions in couples therapy, some of which incorporate sessions with individual partners in the relationship (see Chapter 11). The framework for Motivational Interviewing with couples was derived from sessions in which counselors largely restricted themselves to working only with the couple as a whole. My working hypothesis was that this would facilitate more equitable collaboration. It helps the counselor maintain attention to the dialectic of focus—consistent awareness of both partners and the couple. In addition, it signals that both partners have a voice in decisions about whether and how counseling will proceed. Working consistently with the couple together serves to underscore the shared nature of activity.

As discussed in Chapter 1, counselors may be tempted to work with each partner separately, particularly when disagreements emerge in session. This strategy comes with several risks. First, it potentially opens the counselor up to being a holder of secrets in the relationship. If one partner discloses information to the counselor in an individual session but then asks that this information be kept secret from the other partner, there is a danger that the counselor becomes a coconspirator. This has the potential to diminish the counselor's ability to see the couple as a whole. It may also shape the counselor's perception of the other partner in ways that the counselor cannot disclose. Even if secrets are not shared and the content of individual sessions is unremarkable, conducting them sends the implicit message that partners may be keeping secrets from one another. This, and the related issue of informed consent, are discussed in greater detail in Chapter 11.

This is one way in which couples Motivational Interviewing diverges markedly from significant-other involvement in the ongoing treatment of an identified patient. When a client is being seen in individual therapy and they subsequently bring their partner in, the counselor's primary alliance typically remains centered on the identified client. The involved partner enters the room as an adjunct participant lacking the same rapport with the counselor and with less knowledge about the content of the interaction up to that point. It is a very different paradigm from one in which the partners enter the relationship with the counselor together and engage collaboratively throughout the course of treatment.

Compassion With a Couple

Expressing compassion toward a couple requires ongoing attention to the dialectic of focus—attending to both partners and the couple. When the best interests of the couple and both partners are all aligned, then expressing compassion may be relatively straightforward. Expressing compassion becomes relatively more challenging when partners have substantially different interests and when the needs of the couple require substantial sacrifice on the part of one or both partners.

In these situations—where the counselor is faced with a couple that is making difficult choices about sacrifice because the partners see things differently—the concept of counselor equipoise may be particularly relevant. Zuckoff and Dew (2012, p. 39) cogently articulated the stance of equipoise in their work with living organ donors as one that is "equally welcoming of strengthened resolve to donate or the decision not to do so." Some target behaviors, like whether to donate an organ such as a kidney or part of the liver, have complex costs and benefits that make either choice deeply personal. There is not a clear best choice that can be determined in any objective sense—and certainly not one that could be dictated by the counselor. The best choice is the one the client resolves is right for them. Any attempt by the counselor to influence the client's decision toward a particular outcome would represent a lapse in both compassion and respect for autonomy.

Zuckoff and Dew (2012) articulated three pathways through interviews requiring equipoise. When clients are acutely ambivalent—meaning they genuinely have not made up their mind about what to do, the counselor should remain in equipoise and give equal attention to evaluating both sides (the risks and benefits or pros and cons) of the decision. When it becomes clear that the client has resolved themselves to move forward with the target behavior and residual doubt is lingering ambivalence that continues to accompany an otherwise clarified goal, the counselor steps out of equipoise and conducts a Motivational Interview from the ordinary stance—focused on facilitating client progress toward their identified goal. Similarly, when it becomes clear that the client has resolved not to engage in the target behavior, the counselor assumes a stance consistent with the ordinary delivery of Motivational Interviewing.

As couples weigh the sacrifices involved in the formation and pursuit of a shared goal, it is important that counselors maintain a stance of equipoise until it becomes clear that the partners have resolved themselves to a goal. Doing so is consistent with the conceptualization of nondirectivity in client-centered couples therapy more generally (e.g., O'Leary, 2008). This is particularly true in moments where partners question whether they should continue in the relationship. That question, much like organ donation, is complex, deeply personal, and often without an objective best answer. The counselor can help partners to explore why they might consider a sacrifice—the risks and benefits or pros and cons of a particular compromise. The counselor can help to ensure both partners have space to share their perspective on the compromise and understand one another's reasoning; however, the final decision about any shared goal ultimately resides with the partners. Maintaining equipoise in a couples Motivational Interview then means the counselor must give balanced attention to the consideration of such compromises until partners have resolved themselves to a goal or it becomes clear that the couple must cope with the circumstance of being unable to achieve a compromise.

CONSIDERING RELATIONSHIP MAINTENANCE AND TERMINATION IN THE SPIRIT OF MOTIVATIONAL INTERVIEWING

It is extremely likely that counselors who work for any extended time with couples will encounter those who are considering ending their relationship. A stance of equipoise is useful in most situations where partners are negotiating a shared goal. It is particularly important when couples are making decisions about whether or not to continue in the relationship overall.

It is not the counselor's role to make a relationship last. Motivational Interviewing with couples may improve relationship functioning. In fact, facilitating dyadic functioning (see Chapter 5) is now put forth as an essential process; however, relationship maintenance is not, in and of itself, an indicator of treatment success. It is possible for a counselor to conduct a high-quality Motivational Interview and for one or both of the partners to decide that continuing the relationship is not something they are invested in any longer.

It is not the counselor's job to break up a couple. It can be painful to watch a couple struggle. This might be particularly true when it seems obvious, from the counselor's point of view, that the partners would each be happier if they separated and moved on independently. No matter how convinced the counselor might be that it would be in the couple's best interest to separate, that decision lies with the partners, not the counselor.

Counselors should not be afraid to explore the possibility that a relationship could dissolve. In assuming a stance of partnership, counselors acknowledge that they are participating in the client's process and cannot proscribe change (W. R. Miller & Rollnick, 2013). Analogously, counselors must also acknowledge the reality that both partners have the ability to decide they no longer want to continue the relationship. Doing so demonstrates recognition and acceptance of partners' individual autonomy. The counselor cannot—and should not—try to force or coerce the partners to "make the relationship work."

Ironically, it is at least possible that acknowledging that the relationship could end might elicit a paradoxical response from one or both partners. Motivational Interviewing counselors may be familiar with *emphasizing autonomy* as a strategy to evoke change talk (W. R. Miller & Rollnick, 2013, p. 201). Sometimes acknowledging the reality that a client does not have to change actually makes it easier for them to discuss the possibility of change. Similarly, it is possible that acknowledging the reality that partners do not "have" to continue their relationship might make it easier for them to consider what they would need to maintain it. Even if partners decide they must end their relationship, an openness to talking about that separation affords the counselor the opportunity to invite them to think about how they might minimize unnecessary emotional pain and logistical hardship in that process. See Chapters 8 and 11 for additional discussion of issues involved in planning for relationship separation.

CONCLUSIONS AND KEY POINTS

The established components of the Spirit of Motivational Interviewing—acceptance, collaboration, evocation, and compassion—generalize to motivational interviewing with couples. The essential difference in a couples Motivational Interview is that the counselor must express the Spirit of Motivational Interviewing toward both partners and toward the couple as a whole. The counselor must actively express their genuine belief in the inherent worth of both individuals in the relationship and toward the relationship itself.

To do this, the counselor must balance two dialectics as they navigate the session. The dialectic of activity represents the degree to which the counselor acts as a reflective observer of the couple's interaction versus serving as a moderator of their exchanges. The dialectic of focus refers to the degree to which the counselor directs their attention and their utterances to the individual partners versus to the couple as a whole. Ideal performance is characterized by flexibility along these dimensions. Effective counselors are able to shift between reflective observation and serving as a moderator—sometimes stepping into the couple's interactions and other times stepping back to allow those interactions to play out. The counselor is also able to shift between the activation of individual partners and the couple in order to balance their expression of Spirit across all the working alliances in the room.

4

Engaging With Couples

One of the most challenging things about training people to conduct a Motivational Interview with a couple is giving them a chance to practice. The use of role-play practice is a common element in Motivational Interviewing training (Madson et al., 2009); however, it is surprisingly hard for many people to play a mock couple. The counselor skills can be practiced readily enough. The struggle comes in large part from the fact that everyone—the counselor, the people playing the couple, and the supervisor giving feedback—can readily detect that the mock couple is inauthentic. There are times when the people playing the couple know each other well, and they manage to achieve a credible approximation of a couple; however, quite often the conversation simply does not flow in a way that feels genuine. Somehow the challenge feels very different from anything encountered in an individual role-play practice.

The reason, I suspect, it is so hard to play a mock couple is that real couples have a shared story and a way of telling it. In a mock individual session, an actor–client can ad lib that story on the spot and tell it at whatever pace they like. But to play a credible couple, the mock partners must have a pool of shared knowledge about each other and their time together. In addition, real couples are practiced at speaking together to others and to each other. They have habits of communication that are enacted automatically. That familiarity and flow is difficult for mock partners to reproduce.

The features that make it challenging to role-play with a mock couple throw into relief some of the essential elements of the engaging process in couples Motivational Interviewing. The counselor must learn about the shared story of the couple as well as the individual stories of the partners. Part of establishing rapport with a couple is learning about how the couple communicates. Who speaks? How much do they say? How—if at all—do partners respond to each other during conversation?

The purpose of this chapter is to examine elements of the engaging process that are unique to couples Motivational Interviewing. This provides the rationale for proposing an expansion to the typical reflective listening skills (open questions, affirmations, reflections, and summary statements; OARS) that Motivational Interviewing counselors are likely familiar with. Balancing attention along the dialectic of focus (from the couple as a whole to each of the individual partners) looks different depending on the extent to which the partners' lives are shared. In some couples, partners share almost everything. They may have common friends, interests, work, and sense of family. In others, partners' lives may be much more separate and distinct. Regardless of how much the partners in the relationship share, the challenge for counselors is to form a working alliance with "both of them" and "each of them"—to balance the dialect of focus. Doing so provides a foundation for later understanding how the couple views the target behavior and the manner in which they might work together toward possible change.

RELATIONAL ORIENTATION: INDICATIONS AND IMPLICATIONS FOR ENGAGING WITH COUPLES

It is common for counselors to begin a course of treatment with a general question. Some version of "Tell me a little bit about yourself" has launched a lot of counseling sessions. In a couple's session, that question could be directed to one of two individuals, or it could be directed to the couple. The answer to that question could be a personal story about either one of the partners or a shared story about the two of them together. Engaging successfully with a couple during a Motivational Interview requires some attention to all of these possible stories. The counselor is meeting—and establishing rapport—with not two but three entities.

Therefore, one unique aspect of engaging with a couple is to evaluate the extent to which being a part of the couple is central to the individual identity—or the self-concept—of each of the partners. One way to imagine the development of shared identity is to think of a Venn diagram. This conceptualization is embodied in the Inclusion of Self in Other scale (Aron et al., 1992). Early in relationships, the circles overlap very little or not at all. Each partner has a distinct personal identity and development of little or no shared or relational identity has yet occurred. As time passes, shared experiences accrue and partners' investments in the relationship typically increase. The partners in most cases become increasingly involved in meaningful ways in one another's lives. The two circles in our Venn diagram begin to merge with one another. The couple develops an identity—a sense of "we"—a way of thinking about the "two of them together" that becomes a meaningful component of the partners' individual identities.

This idea—that a couple-level identity emerges over time—has been examined in research on *cognitive interdependence* (Agnew et al., 1998). In couples that have a high degree of cognitive interdependence, the partners have a strong relational orientation. They come to think of themselves as members of a collective unit— the couple. Participating in their relationship becomes integrated into personal identity. This reorganization of the individual's self-schema is a component of the transformation of motivation described in Chapter 2. When an individual comes to consider membership in their relationship as an aspect of who they are, it changes the way they think about "personal" gains. There is a cognitive shift toward consideration of the partner's well-being and the good of the relationship overall because these things are aspects of oneself. The boundary between personal gains and partner or relationship gains is diminished.

In her investment model (Figure 4.1), Rusbult (1980, 1983) articulated the distinctions and connections among *dependence, commitment, cognitive interdependence,* and *relationship maintenance.* Dependence arises from satisfaction with the relationship, the perception that the relationship is superior to available alternatives, and investment (shared resources). These elements of dependence engender commitment. The more committed an individual is, the more they intend to persist in the relationship. In other words, they develop a long-term orientation toward the relationship. Commitment also involves psychological attachment; one's emotional well-being is influenced by their partner and the relationship. Cognitive interdependence emerges from commitment (Agnew et al., 1998). As the relationship becomes a component of an individual's imagined future and the affective connection between partners grows, the self is redefined to encompass the relationship. This motivates partners to engage in *relationship maintenance* behavior. They tend to drive away, avoid, or devalue potential alternative relationships that might overshadow their satisfaction with the current one (D. J. Johnson & Rusbult, 1989). They are more willing to accommodate—or respond constructively in times of conflict—and to make sacrifices to achieve consensus and work toward shared goals (Rusbult, 1983).

The development of cognitive interdependence is directly related to health outcomes for people in relationships. Studies in heterosexual couples have shown that relationship orientation predicts better outcomes for individuals with heart disease (Rohrbaugh et al., 2008) and cancer (Badr et al., 2008). Among sexual

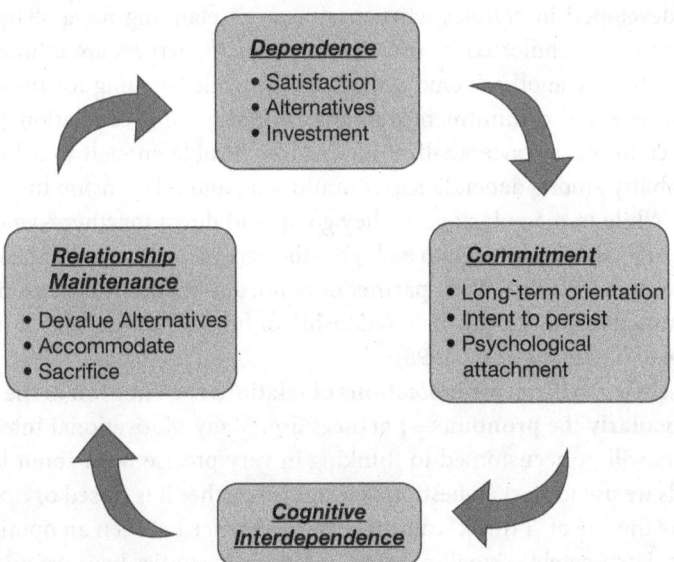

Figure 4.1 The investment model of relationship functioning. Figure by Stephen Sullivan.

minority men specifically, research on couples where partners have different HIV statuses (i.e., serodiscordant couples) has indicated that a relational orientation predicts decreased HIV viral load among HIV-positive partners (Gamarel, Neilands, et al., 2014) and decreased sexual HIV transmission risk to negative partners (Gamarel, Starks, et al., 2014).

Relational orientation can serve as one indicator of the couple's capacity to work together toward change and how they may respond to one another during moments of conflict. It therefore becomes an informative component of the counselor's early and ongoing conceptualization of the couple. Partners with a strong relational orientation tend to be more dependent on their relationships, more committed to them, and more willing to maintain them. When partners' relational orientation is low, partners' investment in the relationship may be modest; conflict in response to disagreements may be more likely; and the partners may be less likely to sacrifice and support one another in the change process. Gaining an initial sense of the centrality of the relationship to partners' personal identity can help the Motivational Interviewing counselor consider how much emphasis to place on the facilitating processes described in the following chapter.

Counselors can listen for indications of relational orientation in the content of partners' disclosures about themselves. One way a counselor can begin to gauge the extent to which a couple-level identity or relationship orientation may have developed is by listening for its precursors in partners' speech—indications of dependence and commitment. Client utterances that indicate satisfaction with the relationship, a preference for the relationship over available alternatives, and resource sharing between partners may serve as an indicator of greater potential for relationship orientation. Similarly, a relational orientation is more likely to have developed in couples when partners are planning for a shared future together. It is also indicated by the extent to which partners are attuned to and influenced by one another's emotions. Notably, while listening for these aspects of dependence and commitment may inform perceptions of relational orientation, the counselor's conceptualization must be flexible enough to acknowledge that variability among dependence, commitment, and relationship orientation is possible. While in many instances, they go up and down together—when any of them are high all of them tend to be high—they are distinct factors. The mere fact that someone is reliant on their partner does not automatically always mean they are committed to continuing the relationship or have a strong sense of subjective allegiance to it (Agnew et al., 1998).

Counselors can listen for indications of relational orientation in the words— and particularly the pronouns—partners use. Many Motivational Interviewing counselors will be accustomed to thinking in very precise ways about language. The words we use to start a question determine whether it is closed or open. Little things like the use of "I think" can make the difference between an opinion and a reflection. Fortunately, a small number of linguistic studies have examined relational orientation and the pronouns people use when talking about themselves. This kind of subtlety in language fits with the way Motivational Interviewing counselors have often practiced attending to the "language of change" (W. R. Miller & Rollnick, 2013, p. 29).

As Fitzsimons and Kay (2004) cogently explained, language can have subtle but powerful effects on the way we perceive social interactions. The difference between "I wish you and I could spend more time together" and "I wish we could spend more time together" may seem minor; however, that switch from singular (e.g., "I" and "you") to plural (e.g., "we" and "us") pronouns is a powerful predictor. Among heterosexual couples, plural pronoun use during cognitive behavioral and family systems treatment for alcohol use was associated with successful outcomes, while individual pronoun use predicted unsuccessful ones (Rentscher et al., 2017). Plural pronoun use has been directly correlated with measures of relational orientation (Aron et al., 1992); commitment and closeness (Agnew et al., 1998); and communal coping with chronic illness (Rohrbaugh et al., 2008). Analysis of qualitative interviews conducted with male couples discussing HIV risk and prevention found that plural pronoun use was associated with higher levels of constructive communication and lower levels of avoidant communication (Cortopassi et al., 2018).

In the engaging process, counselors may be particularly likely to ask couples to share their story in order to develop familiarity and rapport. These are questions like "How did you two meet?" or "What do you like to do together?" There are indications that the predictive power of pronoun use may emerge even as couples respond to these kinds of questions. Buehlman et al. (1992) studied the content of oral history interviews. Couples responded to a number of open-ended questions covering content that might be commonly seen in the engaging process, particularly in early sessions (e.g., how the couple met, courted, and decided to get married; the good and bad times in their relationship; how their marriage has changed over time). Objective raters listened to these and evaluated the extent of spouses' relational orientation versus individual identity ("we-ness versus separateness"). Couples who were rated high on we-ness scored better on a range of relationship functioning measures and had lower rates of divorce over a 3-year follow-up period.

"I" is not the enemy—there is still a place for singular pronoun use in couples counseling. While there is substantial evidence that plural pronoun use is a positive indicator, there is also reason to retain a place for "I-talk" during counseling sessions. Simmons et al. (2005) found that the use of first-person pronouns during a problem-solving task was associated with marital satisfaction and more effective problem-solving. In contrast, the use of second-person pronouns was associated with lower satisfaction and poorer performance. Singular pronouns are essential in moments where partners need to clarify their individual thoughts, feelings, and goals for one another. The use of "I-statements" to achieve this purpose is a component of a number of well-established couples or family therapy techniques (e.g., Farmer & Geller, 2005; Garfield, 2010; Haefner, 2014; Hendrix et al., 2015). In short, the use of I is not something to be universally avoided or actively discouraged. Such an exclusion would make exploration of individual perspectives complicated. At the same time, the prevalence of third-person pronouns can substantially inform the counselor's conceptualization of couples' functioning. Furthermore, as discussed further in this chapter as well as Chapter 5, use of plural pronouns may even induce a sense of closeness between partners (Fitzsimons & Kay, 2004).

SOCIAL NETWORK INTEGRATION AND SOCIAL SUPPORT

Counselors often inquire about client's social networks or assess sources of social support (Pearson, 1990). There is good reason for doing this. The presence of strong ties to family, supportive friends, and a connection to a larger community have been linked to positive mental and physical health outcomes generally (B. C. Feeney & Collins, 2015) and more successful treatment outcomes in psychotherapy specifically (Asay & Lambert, 1999; Leibert et al., 2011). Assessing social support is particularly relevant when working with sexual and gender minority participants, who may be more likely to experience stigma, discrimination, and rejection as a result of their sexual or gender minority identity (e.g., Lick et al., 2013).

When thinking about the social network of an individual, studies often focus on size (the number of relationships in a network); composition (e.g., friends, family, romantic partners, coworkers); and quality (the degree of support vs. strain experienced in relationships) (e.g., Due et al., 1999; Meltzer et al., 2010; Wrzus et al., 2013). These network characteristics are relevant in work with couples as well; however, there are several features of social networks that are unique when engaging with a couple. Specifically, counselors can glean important information relevant to their conceptualization of the couple by attending to the degree of overlap in the partners' social network as well as the extent to which each partner's social network is accepting and supportive of the other partner and of the couple as a whole (Sprecher & Felmlee, 2000).

The general notion that partners' dependence increases as important resources are shared—the concept of investment—has been discussed at length in the context of interdependence theory (e.g., Rusbult, 1983). Research on social network overlap in heterosexual couples suggests that counselors can in some ways think about social relationships as one kind of shared resource. When partners' social networks have a high degree of overlap, they have more common friends, they know one another's family members better, and they have more community ties in common. In contrast, when partners' social networks have limited overlap, acquaintances with one another's' friends or family may be relatively limited, and partners may have very different community connections.

Network overlap has been associated with better relationship outcomes in heterosexual couples. People whose partners have relatively more contact with their social networks overall report more positive perceptions of their partner and better relationship communication. In addition, they are more likely to discuss health concerns with their partner (Cornwell, 2012). Cornwell suggested this arises because having access to a partner's social network helps someone understand the amount and nature of support their partner receives from that network. It affords them opportunities to learn about their partner's social support needs and increases their capacity to empathize with their partner.

Overlap alone is not the only determinant of how social networks shape relationships. The extent to which a network is supportive and accepting of one's partner and one's relationship also matters. Research among heterosexual couples has indicated that partners' perceptions of social network approval are associated with advancement in relationship milestones (progressions to engagement and marriage) and a reduced likelihood of breakup (Felmlee, 2001; Sprecher & Felmlee, 2000).

Sexual and gender minority couples may face unique challenges when making decisions about integrating their social networks. The extent to which couples are able to integrate their social lives may be limited by the partners' individual degree of "outness"—or their degree of identity disclosure. For individual sexual and gender minority people, concerns about rejection because of one's identity—and the effort to keep that identity secret from important social others—comes at a psychological cost (Pachankis, 2007). Identity concealment is associated with increased drug use, mental health problems, poorer physical health, and greater sexual risk-taking (Pachankis et al., 2008, 2014; K. Wang & Pachankis, 2016).

Identity concealment may also impact relationship quality. If either person in the relationship needs to maintain secrecy about their sexual or gender identity, there may be people who cannot know their partner or that they cannot meet "as a couple." There may be places, events, and circumstances in which they cannot be openly "together." This is one way in which identity concealment may impede relationship investment. It presents a challenge to partners sharing important aspects of one another's lives. It also diminishes the extent to which couples are able to benefit from social support. Research on sexual minority couples suggested that, among those who had lower levels of outness, partner stress on a given day was associated with lower commitment to the relationship on that day. When people had higher levels of outness, daily partner stress was unrelated to relationship commitment (Totenhagen et al., 2018).

Couples can also experience a form of discrimination directed specifically at the relationship. This is distinct from discrimination directed at the partners individually. In some instances, friends, family, and communities may be able to tolerate the idea that someone has a sexual or gender minority identity provided that they "keep it to themselves." Presenting as a couple becomes a visible embodiment of their identity, and people who might otherwise be accepting of the partners as individuals may struggle to accept the couple. The phenomenon goes something like the following: "I like you, and he is nice enough. I just don't like the two of you being together."

This form of stigma has been studied initially as relationship marginalization (e.g., Gamarel, Reisner, et al., 2014; Lehmiller, 2012; Rosenthal & Starks, 2015)—the extent to which individuals perceive their family, friends, and community to be accepting and supportive of their relationship. Relationship marginalization has been linked to poorer individual mental health in partnered sexual minority men, heterosexual people in interracial relationships, and relationships in which one person identifies as transgender (Gamarel, Reisner, et al., 2014; Lehmiller, 2012; Rosenthal et al., 2019). Among sexual minority men, the association between relationship marginalization and mental health holds even after controlling for discrimination experienced by the individual partners (G. Robles et al., 2022). Some evidence suggested relationship functioning generally (G. Robles et al., 2022) and specifically egalitarianism and dyadic coping (Rosenthal et al., 2019) tend to buffer against these effects; however, relationship marginalization has also been linked to diminished relationship functioning—potentially undermining this key source of resilience (Gamarel, Reisner, et al., 2014; Lehmiller & Agnew, 2006, 2007). Partners in same-sex and interracial (heterosexual) relationships who reported higher levels of relationship marginalization reported lower commitment, love, and trust as well as higher rates of intimate partner violence (Rosenthal & Starks, 2015).

Relationship marginalization is directed at the couple, but it is not necessarily experienced during a shared event in which the relationship partners are together. At the most basic level, items on scales used to assess relationship marginalization utilize singular pronouns (e.g., "My relationship has general support from my friends."). Recently, a coherent framework for conceptualizing couple-level minority stress has been introduced along with a novel assessment measure (Neilands et al., 2020). Couple-level minority stress encompasses stigma and discrimination experienced by the couple, as well as dyadic coping strategies (i.e., seeking safety and managing stereotypes) and social engagement (i.e., couple-level visibility, integration with families of origin and social support networks). Couple-level minority stress is conceptualized as a shared experience unique from individual-level stigma and discrimination. Assessment items are generally worded with plural pronouns and intended to capture the couple's shared experience. The construct is therefore complementary to relationship marginalization, and together these two concepts highlight a range of ways in which stigma may be direct at relationships.

Implications for Motivational Interviewing practice. The overarching theme of attending to both partners individually and the couple as a whole emerges as particularly salient when assessing and conceptualizing couples' social support. Counselors must be prepared to assess and recognize network overlap as well as network support and acceptance of the partner and the relationship. These factors can inform the counselor's conceptualization of relationship functioning as well as readiness for change. Network integration, support, and acceptance serve as indicators of relationship investment and assets that couples may draw on in support of change.

COUPLES HAVE A WAY OF SPEAKING

Navigating the dialectic of focus in the counseling role, balancing attention to individual partners and the couple as a whole, has been an ongoing theme since Chapter 3. Successful engagement requires the counselor not only to understand this conceptually, but also to enact this behaviorally. In their development of couples' HIV testing and counseling (CHTC), Grabbe et al. (2014) clearly articulated the possible pathways for communication during a couples intervention session. These are depicted in Figure 4.2. Three of these pathways are dyadic—exchanges that involve two people. Communication may flow between the counselor and either one of the partners individually (Pathways A and B). The partners may also direct communication toward one another (Pathway D). The fourth pathway connects the counselor to the couple in toto (Pathway C). This pathway is active when the counselor directs communication toward the couple as a whole, and the couple coordinates a response.

Counselors have the potential to activate these various pathways selectively by strategically directing their speech toward the individual partners or the couple. This strategic activation is the foundational skill for navigating the tension between a focus on the individual and on the couple. When the focus drifts too much toward each person's story, the counselor can shift back to a focus on the couple's shared interests and investment. When one partner takes up too much space in the conversation, the counselor might create space for the other partner to speak.

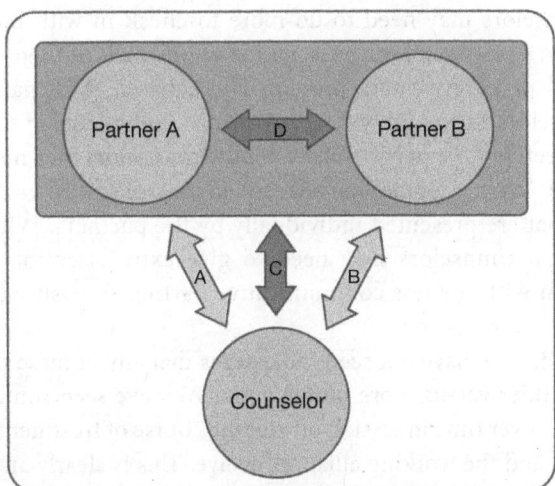

Figure 4.2 Communication pathways in couples interventions (based on Grabbe et al., 2014). Figure by Stephen Sullivan.

While a number of theories have been articulated describing typologies of couples' communication (e.g., Christensen, 1987, 1988; J. M. Gottman, 1999; J. M. Gottman & Gottman, 2008), they focus primarily on how the partners in the relationship speak to each other. Chapter 9 dedicates considerable attention to reviewing these theories and their implications for Motivational Interviewing with couples. Substantially less work has been done to describe the way a couple speaks to a third person. What research exists has focused primarily on pronoun use, as reviewed previously in this chapter.

In our clinical work with couples, we have informally identified three prototype styles of speaking in session. There are couples who truly co-speak. They tend to tell a story together. Both partners contribute to a single narrative. Other couples tend to speak in parallel. One partner tells their version of a story, followed by a telling from the second partner. Finally, some couples have a spokesperson. One person is the default respondent, and the other partner tends to chime in only to correct, amend, or add content as needed.

It is important to acknowledge that these styles are not yet something we have examined in a systematic or empirical way. Our acknowledgment of them has arisen during session review in the context of clinical supervision. Research on the expression of power in couples' communication (see Chapter 9) hints at the possibility that these styles of speaking in session may be indicative of the degree to which power is equitably distributed in the couple; however, that work has not examined the way couples speak in a counseling session specifically. Thus far, these prototype styles have proved a useful heuristic tool in case conceptualization, and counselors have at times found them helpful when thinking about when and how to direct their attention in session.

These styles call for slightly different responses from counselors in order to effectively engage both partners and the couple as a whole. With couples who co-speak, counselors may need to do more to check in with individual partners in order to gather relevant information about each of them and to ensure that individual perspectives are presented in session. With parallel-speaking couples, counselors may simply need to ensure that adequate time is allotted for both perspectives to emerge. Subsequently, counselors may need to do more reflections back "to the couple" in order to emphasize shared goals, values, and perspectives that are presented individually by the partners. With designated-speaker couples, counselors may need to give extra attention to individual communication with the less communicative partner to ensure that their perspective is present in session.

At least thus far, we have not seen indications that any of these three styles are inherently healthier versus more problematic. We have seen some potential for style to fluctuate over time in session or over the course of treatment as the subject matter changes and the working alliances evolve. This is clearly an area in which future research in both qualitative and quantitative domains could substantially hone and inform clinical decision-making.

THE ENGAGING PROCESS IN COUPLES MOTIVATIONAL INTERVIEWING

The tools and techniques most relevant to the engaging process in a couples Motivational Interview are demonstrated in the following transcript of an initial session with the third of our fictional couples, Otto and Rafael. The opening portion of a first session is used here in order to demonstrate relatively broad use of engaging skills, which are particularly salient in such initial exchanges. As in the previous example, annotations in the column on the right label specific counselor skills that are discussed in greater detail following the transcript. In addition to attending to these skills, it may be useful to notice what the transcript reveals about how Otto and Rafael are functioning as a couple. What indications of dependence and investment are present? What strengths do Otto and Rafael perceive in their relationship? How does their relationship stack up against alternative options? How much have they put into making this relationship work? What indications are there of a relationship orientation or couple-level identity in the way they talk about themselves?

* * *

COUNSELOR: Welcome you two. Thanks for coming in.

OTTO: No problem.

COUNSELOR: If it's ok, there are a few things I typically want all of my clients to know before we get started. Would you mind if I told you a little bit about this process? [Collaboration directed to the couple.]

OTTO: That's fine.

COUNSELOR. Great. In some ways, couples counseling works a little like individual counseling, and in other ways it is different. Like any individual counseling, what you say in here stays between you guys and myself—unless you tell me you are going to hurt yourself or someone else. In which case, I would need to break confidentiality to make sure everyone is safe. The thing that is a little unique about couples counseling is that these sessions happen with the two of you together, so you will hear what one another say. Any questions about that? [Structuring opening statement directed to the couple.]

OTTO: No.

RAFAEL: Yeah. No. That makes sense.

COUNSELOR: There are a lot of different ways to do couples counseling, but in my practice, I generally do not meet with folks individually when I am seeing them as a couple. I have a few reasons for this. First, the most important conversations are typically the ones that happen between the two of you. My biggest goal here is to provide an opportunity for you both to talk about your relationship, identify any goals you may have individually or as a couple, and then think about how the two of you can work together toward those goals. Second, I want to avoid being a "go-between" or "messenger" between you two. My goal is to help you both discuss your relationship and your behavioral goals together—whatever those might be—not to speak "on behalf" of either of you. There may be some times when we are sorting out schedules and it is easier to just have one of you reach out to me to make an appointment. That is fine. But when we actually meet, my assumption is that it will be all of us together and if we cannot meet together with you as a couple, we will reschedule for a time that works.

[Continuation of structuring opening statement directed to the couple.]

What questions, if any, do you have for me?

RAFAEL: Nothing I can think of.

OTTO: Me either. That makes sense. This is something we more or less wanted to do together anyway.

COUNSELOR: Excellent. If you have questions as we go, it's totally OK to ask. Meanwhile, often because of the nature of my practice, I end up talking with guys about the decisions they are making around substance use and sex; however, I am also happy to talk about whatever goals and priorities you guys have.

[Emphasizing autonomy directed to the couple.]

I have worked with lots of different kinds of couples, some of whom are doing well, and some of whom are struggling. I don't come in here with any particular sense of what you guys' relationship *should* look like or what you *have* to say to one another. Ultimately, what we focus on is something I will work with you to determine. And what you guys do in your relationship is always going to be up to you. My goal is to create a space where the two of you can talk about those things and to perhaps prompt you to think through why a particular choice is the right fit, but I'm not here to tell you what to do or how to be together.

OTTO: Great.

RAFAEL: Makes sense.

COUNSELOR: It might be good if we start off with you just telling me a bit about yourselves first.

[Question directed to the couple.]

OTTO: [to RAFAEL] You want to go first?

RAFAEL: [to OTTO] Take it away.

OTTO: All right, well, I'm not sure what you want to know exactly, but I work in publishing. I mostly edit medical textbooks. It's sort of ironic because I literally hated biology, and now I spend most of my days reading over stuff doctors write. He is a bartender—but I'll let him tell you more about himself I guess. Umm . . . what else?

COUNSELOR: How did you guys meet?

[Question directed to the couple.]

OTTO: Ha! That's a fun story. We actually first met on an app. We talked for a bit there, just chatted or whatever for like a day.

RAFAEL: And then he came into my bar that evening.

RAFAEL: Well, I wanted to see him, and it seemed like an easy way to get a sense of whether he was who he said he was.

COUNSELOR: It was a way for you guys to check each other out in person.

[Dyadic reflection.]

RAFAEL: Right. I was a little nervous because like, what if he had turned out to be a crazy person, and then I'd have to throw him out of the bar?

OTTO: [laughing] Rude.

RAFAEL: But it actually was sweet. He came by, had a couple drinks, and then we ended up actually meeting the next night.

OTTO: Well, you can only talk so much with the bartender before you just look desperate.

COUNSELOR: Right, so it was a good way for you guys to meet, but not really a great first date setup since one of you was at work.

[Dyadic reflection.]

OTTO: Exactly, but the next night we went to dinner and then walked through the park at sunset and ended up back at my place, and—the rest is more or less history.

COUNSELOR: That's very sweet. When did all this happen? I don't have a good sense of how long you guys have been together.

[Question directed to the couple.]

RAFAEL: This was like 4 years ago now when we first met.

COUNSELOR: Cool. How did things evolve for you guys after that?

[Question directed to the couple.]

OTTO: Pretty normally I guess. We dated for a while before things got too serious. I was pretty sure early on that I was into him. [to RAFAEL] I feel like it took you longer.

RAFAEL: It did. That's fair. Well, I'd just seen a lot of relationships sort of flame out. So I think for a long time I kinda saw this as something that was fun while it lasted.

COUNSELOR: When did that change? When did you guys start to see this as more of "a thing"?

[Question directed to the couple.]

OTTO: [to RAFAEL] I'm really curious what your answer is to this.

RAFAEL: Ooh, I'm on the spot now. Ha! I think for me at least it was when we met your family for the first time.

OTTO: That makes sense. That was a whole production.

RAFAEL: The short version of the story is that his family had never met a boyfriend before.

OTTO: I came out to my family when I was at college. My mom has been pretty good about it. My dad is what he is. Neither of them has really ever wanted details. We kinda did a "don't ask, don't tell" thing.

COUNSELOR: And that changed when Rafael came over.

[Reflection directed to Otto.]

OTTO: Yeah, well, we had been together for a while at that point and—at least for me—I was pretty into him. I had really wanted to spend the holiday together, but I also didn't feel right trying to go and pretend like we were just friends or something.

COUNSELOR: You wanted to be honest with everyone.

[Reflection directed to Otto.]

OTTO: Yeah, that seemed only fair. So, I told my parents I was bringing Rafael, that he was my boyfriend, and that it was OK if they didn't want us to come, but that I was not gonna come without him.

RAFAEL: That sounds so harsh! It was really fine. His parents were very nice to me. Whatever may have been going on for them personally, at least while I was around, they were very chill.

OTTO: We also kept ourselves in check and were like pretty modest about it. We weren't like kissing in the living room or anything.

COUNSELOR: So you guys kinda met them halfway.

[Dyadic reflection.]

RAFAEL: Yeah, but I also knew it was a big deal for him to have brought me. And I guess that was the point where I was like: "If it's this important to him, I should probably take this seriously."

COUNSELOR: That really signaled to you that this was a big deal for him.

[Reflection directed to Rafael.]

RAFAEL: Yeah, I guess I didn't really realize until we were there, but that whole week with them it was really clear that like, this was not something you had done with other guys before.

OTTO: And that's true. I definitely had never had anyone meet my family in that way.

COUNSELOR: You were invested in this.

[Reflection directed to Otto.]

OTTO: Definitely.

COUNSELOR: Rafael, what is family like on your side?

RAFAEL: Well, that's maybe not such a heartwarming story. My mom and I were superclose. She was like my best friend. But she died of brain cancer like 6 years ago, just before I moved here. My dad has not been in the picture since I was a kid, so he's doing whatever he's doing. I have two sisters back home still. They're nice and very supporting. They always ask about Otto and stuff. But we don't really go back and see them that much. They don't really come here. I talk to them now and then, and that's cool. But we are not involved with them like we are with his family.

COUNSELOR: Got it. So they are there, and those relationships with your sisters are meaningful, but you guys are closer to Otto's folks.

OTTO: Yeah, like if we are gonna go for a holiday or something, we probably go to my family and more or less never his. I think that's OK; I hope that's OK. It's seemed OK.

RAFAEL: It's fine. It is what it is. If my mom was alive, it would be really different. But, as it is, I actually would rather go visit your folks.

COUNSELOR: So what does social life look like for you guys here then?

OTTO: Well, I feel like the social thing is all him.

RAFAEL: So much pressure. It's true though; I am the one who sort of knows everyone. It goes with being a bartender.

OTTO: It's also why he's so good at it though. We say he's a bartender, but the truth is, he is actually also like the general manager of the bar.

RAFAEL: It wasn't always my plan to do this, but I sort of ended up evolving into the role, and now the owner basically trusts me to run the place. I've gotten to know party planners and stuff really well, and I do a lot of our special event organizing and staff management. The owner makes final hiring decisions, but he lets me do a lot to run the place.

OTTO: He's very good at it. The bar has grown like crazy over the last few years, and I think it's a big part driven by the work he has done to bring in events and like performers and stuff. Would you say?

RAFAEL: Well, who knows. We have been really successful though. And it's been a lot of work, but when I think about it, I really like it. It would be amazing to actually own a bar or to be a professional event producer. I feel like it's something I sort of get.

COUNSELOR: So this isn't necessarily what you planned to do, but it's worked out really well for you.	[Reflection directed to Rafael.]

RAFAEL: Yeah. I guess that's true.

COUNSELOR: [to OTTO] And you are really proud of what he's been able to accomplish.	[Reflection directed to Otto.]

OTTO: Yeah, it's true. I really admire that aspect of what he does. I feel like all my work is me alone at a computer typing diligently. He's like out there every day engaging people and making a business happen. Plus, it's also great because I get to go to the parties.

RAFAEL: Ahh—see there it is. He just likes to feel fancy.

OTTO: Editing is like the least sexy job ever. So it's fun for me.

COUNSELOR: You guys have very different work lives.	[Dyadic reflection.]

OTTO: Yes. Definitely. That's also one of the hard things though. We have really different schedules, and that's hard. I think it's kinda a part of our problem really.

RAFAEL: A lot of my work, because it is like parties and stuff, happens at night and on weekends.

OTTO: Which is exactly when I would be free. So we often struggle to find time to be together.

COUNSELOR: Got it. So it isn't always easy.	[Dyadic reflection.]

RAFAEL: It's not. I feel like it's harder for him than me. When he's at work, I'm often like sleeping or appreciate the downtime. Then when I'm at work, he's like off, and I feel like he wishes I was around to do stuff with more.

COUNSELOR: [to OTTO] How accurate is that?

[Question directed to Otto.]

OTTO: Sometimes that's true.

COUNSELOR: How do you spend that time? It sounds like Rafael has a lot going on. What do you do in those times when you are free and he's still busy?

[Question directed to Otto.]

OTTO: Well, I have a few friends from work that I hang out with sometimes. Just like happy hour after work or something. But a lot of nights I just go home and watch my shows or call family. Or I end up texting him incessantly.

RAFAEL: That. Is also a thing. But it's sweet though. Sometimes when I'm really busy, it's a lot. But it's at least one way to be in touch on those days when our schedules just don't work out.

COUNSELOR: So you guys make it work.

[Dyadic reflection.]

RAFAEL: I think so. It's not ideal, but we have lasted this long.

COUNSELOR: You definitely have. Four years is a meaningful amount of time. What's your living situation?

OTTO: Well, so that's kinda part of it, too. We don't live together yet.

RAFAEL: We've thought about it, and we are both totally willing to. But our schedules are so different, sometimes it's actually nice to have our own apartments.

OTTO: And yet it's also hard because it means that we don't see each other unless we like go out of our way.

RAFAEL: We are planning to finally bite the bullet and get a place together this year. It's time. But it's also a luxury on crazy days not to have to worry about someone else being in your space.

COUNSELOR: So right now you guys are not living together, but that is likely to change soon. It's a step you both feel ready for.

[Dyadic reflection.]

RAFAEL; Yeah. That's where we're headed.

OTTO: And I think some of why we're here is to work a few things out before we move in.

* * *

In this initial session content, the counselor has drawn out a number of indicators of dependence and investment. In introducing themselves and telling their story, Otto and Rafael use third-person pronouns with reasonable consistency. While some aspects of their lives are not shared (e.g., work and living arrangement), a sense of shared story is present and hints at a more developed relationship orientation. This is further underscored by the discussion of their social network. Where possible, given family attitudes and constellation, the partners have integrated into one another's family network.

In this excerpt, the counselor is working toward a number of goals. First, the counselor is seeking to explicitly and implicitly establish norms for the therapeutic interaction. Second, they are working to establish an alliance with both partners individually and the couple as a whole. Third, in exploring the couple's psychosocial history, they are gathering information about the couple's degree of interdependence, level of investment, and social integration—all of which are relevant to the couple's eventual capacity to work together toward change.

Establishing norms and opening the session. Opening statements are a well-established component of a number of Motivational Interviewing intervention protocols (e.g., Naar et al., 2020; Parsons et al., 2014). Their purpose fits with the counselor's role as a host (O'Leary, 2015) in the interaction. The counselor begins by introducing themself and explicitly establishing some of the key norms and expectations of the session. Consistent with the Spirit of Motivational Interviewing, the opening statement also includes an explicit invitation to collaborate in determining the direction of the session and an acknowledgment of clients' autonomy.

In addition to establishing norms and expectations around confidentiality and the counseling process as it would in an individual session, the opening statement also provides the couple with initial information about how they can expect to work together in session. Even clients who are familiar with the norms of psychotherapy more generally may be unsure what to expect with regard to a couples session. Will they be seen separately or together? What degree of confidentiality can they expect in either case? In a clear opening statement, the counselor can help set expectations around these issues and provide a rationale for clients who may have questions about the format. More information on considerations in the informed consent process is provided in Chapter 11.

Notably, the example here illustrates an opening statement assuming a course of treatment where the couple will be seen together. This is consistent with the paradigm utilized in our work with couples, and for various reasons (see discussion of collaboration with couples in Chapter 3), we believe it may be an optimal default. That said, counselors who wish to utilize a mixture of individual and dyadic sessions could easily modify this sort of opening statement for that paradigm. They might benefit from then incorporating some information about the number and timing of individual sessions and the expectations each partner should have about confidentiality of content expressed in individual sessions.

Establishing alliance—balancing attention through the use of OARS (open questions, affirmations, reflections, and summary statements) in couples sessions. Experienced counselors will likely recognize basic active listening techniques at work in the transcript provided above. In many respects, the counselor is utilizing OARS in ways that should be familiar (W. R. Miller & Rollnick, 2013). The difference in the application of these strategies lies in the variation in where they are directed. The counselor moves flexibly along the dialectic of focus—varying attention to each of the partners and the couple as a whole. When focused on individual partners, the counselor shifts attention from one partner to another, alternating between the activation of Paths A and B in Figure 4.2. Consistent with the counselor's role as a moderator during the session (O'Leary, 2015), this variation serves to ensure that each partner has adequate space and opportunity to describe their perspective.

The counselor opens with a question directed to the couple. The majority of counselor utterances maintain that stance of speaking to the couple (or using Path C in Figure 4.2); however, there are several key points where the counselor strategically directs a question or reflection to one specific partner. For example, the counselor utilizes individually directed utterances to ensure that Rafael's family circumstances are elaborated after the couple had more spontaneously discussed Otto's family. This can also be seen when the counselor inserts themself into the couple's dialogue to give Otto an opportunity to verify or react to Rafael's assumptions about how he feels about the amount of time they spend together.

In this way, counselors should be prepared to spend perhaps somewhat more time allowing the engaging process to be salient with a couple than they might with an individual client. There are two people's stories to hear and also a shared story that must be elaborated. The counselor alternates between hearing about the couple's experience of work, family, and so on and then the details of each individual's experience as well. This does not mean that all dyadic interventions have to be lengthy, multisession encounters. Our brief, single-session motivational enhancement intervention demonstrated preliminary efficacy (Starks, Dellucci, et al., 2019); however, it does mean that working with a couple may take relatively more time to cover an equivalent amount of content compared to speaking only to one person.

Acknowledging interdependence: Dyadic reflections and affirmations. The transcript above illustrates two engaging strategies that are unique to couples work. The first is a dyadic reflection (Starks, Robles, et al., 2020). These utterances pull together content that has been shared by both partners. They capture "common ground" or "shared goals and values." In our work, we have begun to think of dyadic reflections as a unique and distinct form of complex reflections. There is evidence to suggest that coders using the Motivational Interviewing Treatment Integrity system (Moyers et al., 2014) are capable of differentiating between simple and complex reflections directed at individuals—and containing content primarily from that individual—versus reflections directed to the couple that emphasize common ground, integrating content that has come from both partners (Starks, Doyle, Stewart, et al., 2022).

Simple and complex reflections are an essential mechanism to demonstrate empathy (W. R. Miller & Rollnick, 2013). Dyadic reflections serve a similar purpose; however, they go one step further and serve to underscore shared resources, experiences, values, and beliefs. In this way, they are often reflections of the couple's level of dependence and investment (Starks, Robles, et al., 2020). Their identification at this early stage in the counseling process serves to lay a foundation for potentially more difficult conversations that may come later. The counselor is not only conveying a willingness to actively understand the couple's shared perspective, but also identifying past successes and resources the couple might draw on should more difficult conversations or conflict arise.

Some of the counselor's utterances explicitly name the couple's strengths, identify potential, and recognize efforts they have made to sustain the relationship. These utterances—termed relationship affirmations (Starks, Doyle, Stewart, et al., 2022; Starks, Robles, et al., 2020)—are similar to affirmations that might be directed at individuals in a typical Motivational Interviewing session (W. R. Miller & Rollnick, 2013); however, they are capturing strengths inherent in the relationship the partners share. Emphasizing elements of satisfaction, emotional connection, and commitment to the relationship underscores partners' interdependence. Similar to dyadic reflections, these affirmations of dyadic functioning clarify the relational foundation on which future change planning can build.

Counselor pronoun use. It is notable that in using dyadic reflections and affirmations, the counselor regularly speaks to the couple using plural pronouns (e.g., "you guys," "the two of you," or "you together"). Not only is pronoun use reflective of relationship orientation, but also the use of relational pronouns can actually shape people's perceptions of closeness (Fitzsimons & Kay, 2004). There is a recursive association between the language partners use to talk about themselves and their perceptions of the relationship. The more partners identify with the relationship—the more they have a relationship orientation—the more they tend to use third-person pronouns. The more partners tend to speak about themselves in the third person, the more closeness and connection they perceive in the relationship. To the extent that counselor pronoun use catalyzes or emphasizes partners' use of third-person pronouns, this may serve as one mechanism for actively enhancing the working alliance between partners early in the session.

CONCLUSIONS AND KEY POINTS

While many elements of the engaging process with couples are similar to individual Motivational Interviewing, several unique factors are relevant. Counselors must balance attention along the dialectic of focus—attending to both individuals and the couple. They are forming collaborative relationships with both partners and the couple as a whole. Attention to pronoun use takes on new salience as third-person or plural pronoun use serves as one potential signal of relational orientation or the extent to which membership in the couple has become integrated into each partner's sense of self.

Several unique features of practice are evident in the engaging process with couples. Counselors can begin to gather information about dyadic functioning by listening for indications of dependence and investment in session content. Opening statements clarify norms and expectations about the structure of counseling—and in particular expectations about individual versus dyadic interaction with the counselor. Two novel active listening skills are also relevant. Dyadic reflections are directed specifically to the couple and capture common ground. They provide a counseling tool to synthesize content shared by both partners. Relationship affirmations are acknowledgments of the couple's strengths and the counselor's respect for the relationships as a whole. Similar to affirmations of an individual, they provide a mechanism for the counselor to convey positive regard and highlight assets the couple may draw on in later conversations about change.

5

Facilitating Dyadic Functioning

Dyadic functioning has been a recurrent but underlying theme in theoretical discussions thus far. In applying interdependence theory (Kelley & Thibaut, 1978; Rusbult & Van Lange, 2003) to Motivational Interviewing with couples, the previous chapters have illustrated that partners' thoughts and feelings about their relationship—and one another—shape their degree of dependence on and investment in their relationship. By extension, dyadic functioning undergirds the way partners respond to one another in moments of conflict and their willingness to make sacrifices for the sake of the relationship.

Across the broad area of relationship research, there is considerable variability in the terminology used to refer to dyadic functioning. The terms "dyadic functioning," "relationship functioning," and "relationship quality" are used throughout this text and treated as essentially synonymous. In their overview of the emerging area of research on adolescent relationships, W. A. Collins (2003, p. 11) suggested relationship quality was one of five content areas that warrant research attention. They defined it as "the degree to which the relationship provides generally beneficent experiences." They went on to characterize high-quality relationships as "those in which the partners manifest intimacy, affection, and nurturance."

While W. A. Collins (2003) offered a unified definition of relationship quality, the assessment of the construct has varied considerably across studies. Researchers have focused on diverse aspects or indicators of relationship quality (e.g., satisfaction, commitment, egalitarianism, communication, trust, or conflict). Some studies have examined individual dimensions of relationship quality, while others have tested models incorporating multiple components. Despite this heterogeneity, substantial evidence has amassed indicating that being in a high-quality relationship is associated with mental and physical health benefits (e.g., Braithwaite & Holt-Lunstad, 2017; Davila et al., 2014; Loving & Slatcher, 2013; Rauer et al., 2008; T. F. Robles et al., 2014). Partnered people live longer, healthier, and happier; however, not every person in a relationship benefits equally. The quality of relationship functioning is a powerful determinant of the benefits—and also the risks—of being partnered (e.g., Braithwaite & Holt-Lunstad, 2017; Rauer et al., 2008; T. F. Robles et al., 2014). This chapter culminates in a discussion of how counselors might facilitate growth in relationship quality during a Motivational Interview with a couple. Before focusing on intervention application, it is potentially useful for counselors to have some theoretical framework for conceptualizing why relationships would be linked to health outcomes as well as a general understanding of the domains of relationship functioning commonly studied.

RELATIONSHIPS AND HEALTH

High-quality relationships are an asset to individuals' health and well-being. There is a substantial body of evidence from heterosexual samples indicating that people in relationships have better physical (Loving & Slatcher, 2013; T. F. Robles et al., 2014) and mental (Braithwaite & Holt-Lunstad, 2017) health outcomes compared to those who are single. As evident in reviews of this literature (Braithwaite & Holt-Lunstad, 2017; Loving & Slatcher, 2013; T. F. Robles et al., 2014), outcomes associated with relationship status are broad, ranging from decreased probability of hospitalization and readmission, lower rates of cardiovascular disease and diabetes, and lower levels of depression. Of particular relevance, research also indicates that heterosexual people in relationships are less likely to use drugs and engage in problematic alcohol use compared to those who are single (Austin & Bozick, 2012; Schulenberg et al., 2005).

A small body of literature has examined the effects of being partnered on sexual minority individuals. Much of this work has focused on substance use and mental health outcomes. Results are more mixed than those from heterosexual samples. For example, Whitton and colleagues (2018b) examined longitudinal data from a sample of sexual minority youth aged 1620 and found that Black-identified participants and those who identified as gay or lesbian reported lower psychological distress when they were partnered compared to periods when they were single. In contrast, being partnered predicted greater psychological distress for bisexual participants and was not a significant predictor of psychological distress among White participants. Similarly, there is equivocal evidence about whether the prevalence of drug use is comparable among partnered versus single sexual minority men. While Austin and Bozick (2012) found that relationship status was unrelated to use among sexual minority respondents, Whitton and colleagues (2018a) noted that being partnered was associated with decreased drinking. For gay- and lesbian-identified participants, being partnered was also associated with decreases in illicit drug use; however, among bisexual-identified participants, being partnered was associated with increased use of cannabis and other illicit drug use.

Investigations incorporating attention to relationship functioning may provide some insight into why studies comparing partnered people to those who are single would produce variable results. Not everyone who is partnered experiences comparable benefits. Relationship quality matters. In their meta-analysis of 126 studies conducted over 50 years, T. F. Robles et al. (2014) found that relationship quality had small but robust associations with a range of health outcomes.

Effect sizes ranged from .07 to .21. Across studies, relationship conflict was a consistent predictor of negative health outcomes, while indicators of relationship quality were protective. This pattern is consistent with the observations of others. Relationship conflict has been associated with diverse indicators of psychological stress (Loving & Slatcher, 2013; Wright & Loving, 2011), particularly when partners respond to one another negatively with reactions such as scorn or hurt (Bierstetel & Slatcher, 2020). Complementary research on positive aspects of relationship quality have found that relationship commitment (Braithwaite et al., 2010; Braithwaite & Holt-Lunstad, 2017) and relationship satisfaction (Rauer et al., 2008; Stanton & Campbell, 2014; Whitton & Kuryluk, 2012) are robust predictors of positive physical and mental health outcomes for heterosexual people in relationships.

Mirroring the trend in relationship research overall, most investigations have focused on heterosexual samples; however, a small but growing number of studies indicated similar trends among sexual minority individuals. Relationship quality has been linked to lower levels of depression (Whitton & Kuryluk, 2014) among sexual minority individuals generally and sexual minority men specifically (Starks, Doyle, et al., 2017). Relationship formalization—a potential indicator of commitment—has been associated with decreased psychological distress, particularly for adults younger than age 40 (Bariola et al., 2015). Starks, Robles, Bosco, Doyle, et al. (2019) examined associations between relationship functioning and substance use in a sample of sexual minority male couples. Problematic drinking was negatively associated with respondents' relationship satisfaction and also their partners' commitment to the relationship. In contrast, the use of illicit drugs (excluding cannabis) was predicted by a pattern of associations with relationship functioning indicative of ambivalence. For example, both the rewards and the perceived costs of the relationship were positively associated with illicit drug use.

Three primary explanations have been put forward for why partnered people would have better health outcomes than those who are single (Braithwaite & Holt-Lunstad, 2017). The selection model suggests that the apparent health benefits of relationships arise simply because people with better mental and physical health are more likely to enter and maintain relationships. Here, better health is posited as the cause of being partnered, rather than being partnered resulting in better health. Experience models suggest that health and relationship quality exert recursive influences on one another. Braithwaite and Holt-Lunstad (2017) illustrated this in their discussion of stress generation (Davila et al., 1997) and marital discord (Beach et al., 1990) models of depression and relationship functioning. The former posits that depression is the cause of marital discord, while the latter posits that marital discord increases depression.

Not all experience models have viewed the association between relationship functioning and mental health through the lens of risk. Relationships also provide a source of resilience in the form of social support (Stanton & Campbell, 2014). Research on diverse couples, including sexual minority couples, indicated that social support provided by partners directly predicted better mental health outcomes and also buffered against the negative effects of other sources of stress (e.g., Graham & Barnow, 2013).

Facilitating dyadic functioning in a Motivational Interview with couples. One of the core assumptions of Motivational Interviewing generally is that counselors have the potential to foster behavior change through their communication with clients. Definitions of Motivational Interviewing propose that counselors can enhance personal motivation by attending to the "language of change" (W. R. Miller & Rollnick, 2013, p. 29). Extending this logic from individual Motivational Interviewing yields two fundamental assumptions applicable to Motivational Interviewing with couples. **The first assumption is that counselors have the potential to facilitate—to foster or enhance—dyadic functioning.** In much the same way counselors evoke and attend to the language of change, they can evoke and attend to language that highlights what the partners value about their relationship, what they mean to one another, and their strengths as a couple. They can also help couples generate plans to change or optimize their behavior together and reactions to one another in times of conflict. **The second assumption is that facilitating dyadic functioning directly enhances the partners' capacity to work together toward change.** While improving relationship functioning is not—in and of itself—the target of intervention, it is a posited mechanism that increases the potential for change (Starks, Millar, et al., 2018).

Counselor behavior can facilitate dyadic functioning. The premise that what counselors do and say in session may improve relationship functioning is in many respects shared with a range of couples therapies. While specific techniques and theoretical rationale may differ, the general idea that counselors can intervene with couples in ways that help partners understand one another's perspectives and respond more effectively to one another is inherent in most all of the couples approaches to counseling discussed in Chapter 1.

Cordova et al. (2001) specifically examined the premise that Motivational Interviewing with couples could enhance relationship functioning in a pilot study with heterosexual couples at high risk of relationship dissolution. All couples reported poor relationship functioning in the form of low levels of satisfaction or high relationship conflict at baseline. Relationship satisfaction improved significantly from pre- to postintervention, and improvements were maintained at 1-month follow-up. The authors subsequently speculated that brief Motivational Interviewing may be sufficient to catalyze change because "once the initial move towards change had begun, naturally occurring contingencies . . . [would] maintain partners' momentum towards action and maintenance" (Cordova et al., 2001, p. 317).

While promising, Cordova et al. (2001) provided limited theoretical rationale for the mechanisms in their intervention that would produce changes in relationship functioning. They also did not expand on whether or how changes in relationship functioning might then be leveraged to support change in a target behavior such as substance use. These elements are necessary in order to situate the process of facilitating dyadic functioning within the larger framework of Motivational Interviewing practice.

Facilitating dyadic functioning enhances the potential for change. The premise that improvements in relationship quality would facilitate health behavior change flows directly from two sources of evidence already reviewed. First, relationship functioning is a consistent predictor of health outcomes generally and substance use specifically. It therefore follows that reducing relationship conflict and facilitating high-quality relationship functioning might potentially improve health outcomes for partners in the couple. Second, interdependence theory (Kelley & Thibaut, 1978; Rusbult & Van Lange, 2003) positions aspects of relationship quality as determinants of key interpersonal processes. Relationship satisfaction predicts dependence; relationship commitment is a determinant of investment; and by extension these factors therefore predict whether partners will respond to conflict adaptively and engage in behaviors that maintain the relationship. It therefore follows that improving relationship functioning might enhance partners' willingness and ability to work together toward change.

Integrating facilitating dyadic functioning into the existing framework of Motivational Interviewing processes. The decision to introduce facilitating dyadic functioning prior to focusing was informed directly by interdependence theory. Focusing involves arriving at a shared understanding of the direction or goal of the Motivational Interview. W. R. Miller and Rollnick (2013, p. 94) suggested that it is formed through "a purposeful conversation that has change at its heart." As the focusing process becomes salient, the couple must decide together what they want to accomplish in the counseling experience. This represents a point where dyadic ambivalence may emerge in the form of partners' conflicting priorities or perceptions of what the purpose of counseling might be. In instances where partners do not agree on what the focus of the Motivational Interview should be, strong dyadic functioning can provide a foundation for negotiating a consensus focus and mitigating conflict around what will happen in session.

One feature of couples Motivational Interviewing then is a delay of the focusing process. Moving too soon to identify "the problem" or explore potential change can result in challenges. When partners lose sight of what they value in one another and why their relationship is important, they may struggle to arrive at a shared goal. Facilitating dyadic functioning can be thought of as preparing the couple to work together toward change.

DOMAINS OF DYADIC FUNCTIONING

The field of relationship science is well evolved, and multiple models of relationship functioning have been articulated. The universe of potentially meaningful domains of dyadic functioning is not necessarily limited to those described in this section, which focuses on three dimensions of dyadic functioning that feature prominently in interdependence theory: satisfaction, commitment, and emotional investment (Rusbult, 1980). The goal of this section is to acquaint readers with these theoretically salient dimensions of dyadic functioning and provide an overview of how they might emerge as relevant to motivation for change in session. Other aspects of relationship functioning, including communication, power, and trust, are discussed in Chapter 9. Readers may also wish to review content on cognitive interdependence and relationship orientation in Chapter 4.

Satisfaction

Relationship satisfaction is perhaps the most commonly studied component of dyadic functioning. As a consequence, it is perhaps also the most variously defined. Broadly, a distinction could be made between dimensional and comparative approaches to conceptualizing satisfaction. Dimensional approaches assume one's happiness or contentment with a relationship varies along one or more continua. In contrast, comparative approaches conceptualize satisfaction as the extent to which one's relationship approximates their ideal.

Dimensional conceptualizations of satisfaction. A number of multi-item measures assess relationship satisfaction as a unidimensional construct (e.g., Funk & Rogge, 2007; Hendrick, 1988; Norton, 1983; Schumm et al., 1983). Satisfaction is also included as a unidimensional subscale in commonly used multidimensional measures of relationship functioning such as the Dyadic Adjustment Scale (Spanier, 1976) and the Perceived Relationship Quality Component scale (Fletcher et al., 2000). While all of these measures vary in the exact number and content of items, they all capture the extent to which one is happy with, content in, or rewarded by their relationship.

One of the drawbacks of unidimensional measures is that they assume that satisfaction exists along a single continuum. This necessarily assumes that the more satisfied someone is with their relationship the less dissatisfied they are. But what happens when someone is ambivalent about their relationship? In her writing on interdependence theory, Rusbult (1980) argued that satisfaction arises in part from one's comparison level. Relationships that have high "costs" may still be satisfying as long as the "rewards" offset those costs. We will work at a relationship if it is worth it. In contrast, relationships that have modest rewards may be viewed as satisfactory if they are also associated with sufficiently low costs. Things maybe do not have to be great if the relationship is sufficiently easy to be in.

Unidimensional scales are not well equipped to capture the experience of someone who is happy with their relationship in some respects but also unhappy with it in others. For example, the satisfaction subscale of the Dyadic Adjustment Scale (Spanier, 1976) includes the item, "In general, how often do you think that things between you and your partner are going well?" and also the reverse-scored item, "How often do you and your partner quarrel?" The scoring of the scale implicitly assumes that people who endorse the first item highly will endorse the second one less so and vice versa.

There are examples of dimensional measures that assess satisfaction in terms of perceived rewards and costs separately (e.g., Kurdek, 1995). These align directly with Rusbult's conceptualization of satisfaction. Perhaps the most useful artifact of this multidimensional conceptualization of satisfaction is that it illustrates the potential for people to feel ambivalent. The fact that there are things someone likes about a relationship does not mean that there cannot also be a lot of things they dislike as well. Counselors who are able to listen for this kind of ambivalence may be successful in helping clients identify the aspects of their relationship that are working well and areas where growth and change would be welcome or necessary.

Comparative conceptualizations of satisfaction. How rewarding does a relationship have to be in order to be satisfying? What costs will someone tolerate while still feeling satisfied with a relationship? Comparative metrics of satisfaction address this question to some extent. Interdependence theory scholars have suggested that individuals evaluate their degree of satisfaction with the rewards and costs experienced in their relationship by comparing them to their expected or ideal relationship (Kurdek, 1995; Rusbult, 1980, 1983; Thibaut & Kelley, 1959). The assumption here is that people have a concept of what their relationship "ought to be," and they are satisfied to the extent that their current relationship approximates that ideal. Subsequent work on relationship development (Soller, 2014) and closeness (Frost & Forrester, 2013) suggested such comparisons are not restricted only to the dimensions of rewards and costs most commonly associated with satisfaction. When people consider whether their relationship is "moving fast enough" or whether they are "as close to their partner as they should be," part of how that question is answered involves comparing their relationship to what they imagine it "should" or "ought" to be.

Discussing satisfaction in terms of approximation to an imagined ideal has the potential to draw out clients' beliefs about how relationships should be, the kind of relationship they think that they deserve, and the kind that they imagine is possible. It is noteworthy that this sort of discussion may be particularly meaningful for gender and sexual minority clients. There are relatively fewer visible models of successful sexual and gender minority couples. It may be more challenging for these minority couples to consolidate information from heterosexual models into a coherent idea about what their relationship "could be." Experiences of stigma and shame around sexuality and same-gender attraction may influence people's thoughts about interpersonal relationships (Pachankis, 2007; Pachankis et al., 2008). For at least some, this may translate to a diminished vision of what is possible in a relationship and what sexual and gender minority people deserve from or are capable of giving to their partners.

The expression of satisfaction in a Motivational Interview. These diverse conceptualizations of satisfaction give the counselor multiple indicators to listen for. Clients vary in how they make meaning of their relationships. Some may talk about global happiness and contentment with their partners, while others think more in terms of how well their lives match up with what they imagined they would be. Counselors who are able to recognize these various manifestations of satisfaction can draw out and elaborate the couple's strengths in whatever form they are expressed.

Satisfied partners may see fewer reasons to change. There is no inherent guarantee that satisfied partners are proponents of behavior change. In fact, it is plausible that a partner who is very happy with a relationship is also quite happy with things just as they are. Counselors in such cases may need to be alert to acknowledging what the satisfied partner values about the relationship. What things is this person afraid they might lose if change happened? What are the essential components of the relationship that this person values, and how can anxiety about losing those elements be mitigated and tolerated if change were to happen?

Satisfied partners may see more reasons to make sacrifices. As already discussed (see Chapter 2), interdependence theory would suggest that partners who are highly satisfied with their relationship may be more likely to respond constructively in moments of conflict. Partners who value their relationships a great deal may be more likely to perceive any sacrifices involved in achieving consensus around a shared goal as "worth it." Their satisfaction with the relationship may serve as a motivation to make behavior change—or to support their partner's behavior change—even if they do not personally see the change as particularly necessary.

Unsatisfied partners might provide the motivation for change. It is sometimes possible that identifying areas of dissatisfaction—costs, challenges, or areas of desired growth in the relationship—will elicit change talk. Sometimes exploring the aspects of a relationship someone is unhappy with can help to clarify where change is needed for things to "get better." Individuals who are generally invested in the relationship and concerned for their partner's happiness may be distressed to learn that their behavior has a negative impact on their partner's satisfaction with the relationship. The trade-off is that unsatisfied partners may also have relatively less motivation to make compromises or sacrifices in order to achieve that change.

Commitment

How do partners express or manifest their degree of investment in or attachment to the long-term durability or sustainment of their relationship? It seems intuitively clear that relationships may vary in their levels of commitment. Some relationships are intended to be passing, transient exchanges, while others are seen as constant features with pervasive influence across substantial portions of the lifespan. Similar to satisfaction, commitment has been operationalized in varying ways. Some relationship research has conceptualized commitment as a structural feature of relationships (e.g., Braithwaite et al., 2010)—the achievement of a particular milestone like marriage—while other work has suggested it is a multifaceted psychological construct (e.g., Agnew et al., 1998; Rusbult, Martz, et al., 1998). Both of these approaches likely provide Motivational Interviewing counselors with content that may inform their conceptualization of a couple's dyadic functioning.

Commitment as structural milestone attainment. Studies that have taken a structural view of commitment have largely examined relationship formalization. Through this lens, distinctions between committed and noncommitted couples are commonly made based on whether some formal step or relationship milestone has occurred, such as marriage (Loving & Slatcher, 2013); marital engagement or other subjective labeling of the relationship as "committed" (Braithwaite et al., 2010); or cohabitation (Poortman & Mills, 2012). The assumption here is that formalization signals the partners' intention to maintain the relationship in the long term.

Based on interdependence theory and more specifically on assumptions of the investment model (Rusbult, 1980, 1983), it is reasonable that these structural indicators of commitment would provide meaningful information about relationship functioning. Transitions such as marriage or cohabitation often signal increases in investment (Poortman & Mills, 2012). More resources are shared between the partners, and legal commitments that are relevant to resource sharing are made. Entering into a legally binding commitment to one's partner also potentially increases the social and logistical consequences of leaving the relationship. This may diminish the appeal of alternatives and enhance motivation to maintain the relationship.

One of the shortcomings of structural conceptualizations is that they often imply an "all-or-none" view of commitment. For example, couples are either "married or not" and therefore grouped as either "committed or not." While from a logistical perspective this distinction may sometimes make sense—couples either do or do not have access to the set of legal benefits and recognition associated with being married—it overlooks the potential for partners to experience varying degrees of commitment within these categories. A couple's marital status, living situation, or other formal indicators of relationship establishment may inform a counselor's conceptualization; however, viewing commitment solely through this lens may underestimate commitment in couples who have not yet met particular relationship milestones. Likewise, it may overestimate commitment in couples who have reached such milestones—ignoring the potential that these couples may be wavering in their commitment and considering separation.

A note of caution about language—for at least some people, the term "commitment" may be treated not only as synonymous with marriage but also as synonymous with having a monogamous sexual agreement. This is a particularly dangerous default for counselors working with at least some sexual and gender minority couples. Chapter 1 introduces sexual agreements in detail. There it was pointed out that roughly half of male couples have nonmonogamous sexual agreements, and similar findings are seen among transgender women and their relationship partners (Gamarel et al., 2016; Skeen et al., 2021). There is little evidence suggesting that monogamous relationships have inherently superior dyadic functioning (e.g., Grov et al., 2014; Mitchell, 2014; Parsons et al., 2012; Sharma et al., 2019; Starks, Robles, Bosco, Doyle, et al., 2019). In fact, some evidence suggests that nonmonogamous agreements are actually more likely among couples that have been together longer (e.g., Parsons et al., 2013; Starks, Robles, Bosco, Doyle, et al., 2019). Counselors working with sexual and gender minority couples should explore and clarify relationship functioning and sexual agreements; however, in doing so, they must be careful to guard against interpreting nonmonogamy as an indicator of diminished commitment or other deficits in relationship quality.

Commitment as a psychological construct. The investment model (Agnew et al., 1998; Rusbult & Buunk, 1993) offered a multifaceted psychological conceptualization of commitment encompassing intentions and expectancies. High levels of relationship commitment are characterized by an intention to persist or a motivation to engage in behaviors that will preserve, maintain, and perpetuate the relationship. This is referred to as the *conative* component of commitment (Agnew et al., 1998). High commitment is also characterized by a *long-term orientation*, or the expectancy that the relationship will endure into the foreseeable future. This expectation is informed, at least in part, by experiences in prior relationships.

Scholars of interdependence theory posited that individuals evaluate the quality of their relationship in part by comparing the rewards and costs experienced in it to those they anticipate would be associated with available alternatives (Kurdek, 1995; Rusbult, 1980; Thibaut & Kelley, 1959). Here, alternatives encompass "all the forces pulling the individual away from the relationship" (Rusbult & Buunk, 1993, p. 182). This might include other potential relationship partners, the option of being single or unpartnered, as well as nonromantic social ties and other valued activities. When plausible alternatives are perceived as having more rewards and fewer costs than the current relationship, commitment is diminished. Interestingly, Rusbult's investment model (D. J. Johnson & Rusbult, 1989; Rusbult, 1983) suggests that the devaluation of alternative relationships is one cognitive relationship-maintenance mechanism. When individuals are highly committed to their relationship, they are motivated to depreciate their estimation of the value associated with alternative relationships, thereby increasing their satisfaction with their current one.

Research on sexual minority adolescent relationships has sometimes assessed the construct of *seriousness* (e.g., Newcomb et al., 2014) using face-valid items, such as, "How serious is your relationship with this partner?" In this context, seriousness likely shares at least some features with elements of commitment. Recent quantitative evidence aligned with this and suggested that seriousness is highly correlated with comparable items assessing commitment (Starks, Dellucci, et al., 2021) and potentially represents a developmentally relevant formulation of the construct for this age group. Counselors working with relatively younger people in relationships may encounter this kind of language when discussing commitment. Adolescents have relatively less financial independence, and most are at a developmental stage where more elaborated forms of commitment are difficult to enact. The relatively simpler concept of a relationship being "serious" may simply fit better for this age group.

The expression of commitment in a Motivational Interview. As with satisfaction, diverse conceptualizations of commitment provide counselors with a wide range of potential indicators that might inform their conceptualization. Not all will be meaningful for every client. For some, formalizing the relationship may be a powerful expression of commitment. For others, intentions, expectations, and actions that maintain the relationship may be the most essential indicators of commitment, while legal formalization is viewed as unnecessary or unpalatable.

The essential thing is that counselors be prepared to recognize and reflect the couple's degree of commitment accurately regardless of how it is manifest.

Commitment and working together toward change. For a number of theoretically grounded reasons, commitment in most instances would be expected to increase a couple's capacity to work together toward change. Counselors might expect highly committed partners to be more willing to "work things out," respond constructively when faced with conflict, and make sacrifices for the sake of their partner and maintenance of the relationship. Actions that diminish a partner's happiness or jeopardize the relationship itself would be incongruent with the broader intentions and expectations that the relationship will endure into the future. In contrast, partners who are not particularly committed have fewer reasons to make such sacrifices and may be more likely to respond destructively when faced with conflicting priorities.

Commitment as a unique barrier to sexual risk reduction. Of particular relevance to the focus of this text, a substantial body of research has indicated that commitment is a specific barrier to implementing sexual risk reduction strategies for sexual minority men in relationships (e.g., Goldenberg et al., 2015, 2019). Across a range of prevention behaviors, including HIV testing (Starks, Lovejoy, et al., 2021), condom use (e.g., Davidovich et al., 2004; Golub et al., 2012; Starks, Pawson, et al., 2018; Starks, Payton, et al., 2014) as well as pre-exposure prophylaxis (PrEP) (e.g., Malone et al., 2018; Starks, Doyle, et al., 2019) and postexposure prophylaxis (PEP) to prevent HIV infection (Bosco et al., 2019), the concerns are similar. Participants worried that implementing these strategies, or in some instances even discussing them with a partner, would signal mistrust or a lack of commitment to the relationship. The context of a Motivational Interview may give counselors the opportunity to help couples discuss sexual risk reduction practices by removing the pressure on partners to "start the conversation." Research on couples' HIV testing and counseling has demonstrated that discussions of HIV prevention are sometimes easier for couples when the topic is raised as part of a routine service (Sullivan et al., 2014).

Emotional Investment

The concept of "emotional investment" is common across a number of theories of dyadic functioning and love. Though the construct is referred to by a wide range of terms, it typically captures the strength of emotional bonds between partners. Both Sternberg (1997) and Z. Rubin's (1970) conceptualizations of love involve elements of "intimacy" that encompass feelings of closeness and connectedness— an awareness of and caring concern for a partner's thoughts and feelings. The concept is also present in interdependence theory under the egis of *psychological attachment* (Agnew et al., 1998; Rusbult, Martz, et al., 1998). Partners' emotional well-being becomes interrelated with one another and the well-being of the relationship. In the investment model, this emotional interdependence is positioned as a subdomain of commitment and contributes to the promotion of relationship maintenance behaviors.

Emotional investment is incorporated into measures of relationship quality in diverse ways. Some measures include a specific subscale that directly assesses feelings of caring for, closeness to, or connection with one's partner (Fletcher et al., 2000; Sternberg, 1997). In other measures, items assessing elements of emotional investment are diffused across related subscales. For example, the Cohesion subscale of the Dyadic Adjustment Scale assesses how often partners share ideas and talk, laugh, or work together; however, an item assessing how often partners confide in one another contributes to the Satisfaction scale, and the extent to which partners agree on demonstrations of affection is a component of the Affective Expression subscale (Spanier, 1976). In Kurdek's (1995) Multiple Determinants of Relationship Commitment Inventory, feelings of companionship and being able to "count on" one's partner contribute to the Rewards subscale. Meanwhile, the Barriers to Leaving scale includes items assessing emotional pain and loss of attachment that would come with losing the relationship.

Discussing emotional investment in a Motivational Interview. As with satisfaction and commitment, diverse conceptualizations of emotional investment give counselors a range of indicators to listen for. In session, it might be signaled by verbal as well as nonverbal expressions of affection. Participants may verbalize what they "like," "appreciate," "respect," or "admire" about their partner. It can also be signaled by partners' awareness of one another's thoughts and feelings and the extent to which they communicate about these elements of their individual internal worlds. Drawing on patterns evident in the assessment of relationship quality, counselors might anticipate the potential for these expressions of emotional investment to emerge independently or in conjunction with expressions of relationship satisfaction or commitment.

The term "intimacy" is used so variously that it is almost impossible to know what it implies without probing. For some couples, "being intimate" means sharing feelings, communicating, and staying emotionally connected. For others, being intimate implies a physical sexual connection or may serve as a euphemism for the act of sex itself. Clarifying the use of the word "intimacy"—or avoiding it until clients provide such clarity spontaneously—is often helpful in preventing confusion. If counselors wish to initiate the use of this word in session, they may need to define what they intend to express by it. Otherwise, it is quite possible the term will connote something different for their clients.

As mentioned, the investment model (Agnew et al., 1998; Rusbult, Martz, et al., 1998) positions emotional investment—there called psychological attachment—as a subdomain of commitment. By extension, similar to other elements of commitment (i.e., conative intention to persist and long-term orientation), there are theoretical reasons to anticipate that emotional investment would be expected to signal the couples' capacity to work together toward change. In most instances, it would be expected that care and concern for one's partner would contribute to a willingness to make sacrifices to enhance a partner's happiness and motivation to avoid behaviors that are distressing to the partner or may harm the relationship.

Drug use and sexual risk-taking as catalysts for emotional connection. Emotional investment—while a potential catalyst for change in many instances—may present a specific barrier to reducing drug use or implementing HIV risk reduction practices for some sexual minority men. Research has indicated that sexual minority men who are concerned about potential rejection by relationship partners are more likely to believe that the use of drugs during sex will facilitate emotional connection and increase the likelihood that sex will lead to a relationship (Starks, Millar, Tuck, et al., 2015). For partners who use drugs as a way to connect, changes in drug use may diminish their emotional investment in one another unless they can find alternative strategies and mechanisms to achieve this connection. Analogous research has also indicated that that many sexual minority men perceive the use of condoms during sex as a barrier to emotional closeness (Golub et al., 2012; Starks et al., 2016). Some evidence suggests that sexual minority men who are concerned about condom use as a barrier to emotional closeness may find biomedical prevention options to be more appealing (Gamarel & Golub, 2015, 2019); however, these findings must also be weighed against evidence indicating that sexual minority men also worry about the emotional connotations of biomedical prevention options for their relationship (e.g., Bosco et al., 2019; Malone et al., 2018; Starks, Doyle, et al., 2019).

RECOGNIZING DYADIC FUNCTIONING IN SESSION

Counselors can begin to assess dyadic functioning early in the engaging process. Often just in introducing themselves, couples may signal their satisfaction, commitment, and emotional investment. For example, in their Chapter 4 session transcript Otto and Rafael provided several indications of high levels of commitment. Both viewed Otto's sexual identity disclosure and introduction of Rafael to his family as expressions of his intention-to-persist in the relationship. In addition, the example ended with the couple explaining that they are considering moving in together—a structural indicator of long-term orientation. Subtle indications of emotional investment were also evident in that transcript. Otto took pride in Rafael's work success. Rafael was appreciative of the connections to Otto's family.

This sort of progression, in which indicators of relationship functioning emerge over the engaging process, is relatively common in couples we have seen. In the example below, the session in Chapter 4 with Otto and Rafael continues. In this passage, the process of facilitating dyadic functioning moves into the foreground. The counselor transitions into a more focused exploration of relationship functioning, elaborating on and extending content that was initially introduced in the engagement process. Annotations indicate the skills used by the counselor to draw out and emphasize various domains of dyadic functioning.

* * *

COUNSELOR: With any of the couples I work with, I'm always curious what you appreciate about this relationship? What is important about it? [Question directed to the couple.]

OTTO: I think for me it's having someone to be with. Even if I don't get to see him as much as I would like, it means a lot to me that I know he's there.

COUNSELOR: There is a real comfort just from being in this relationship. [Individual reflection of emotional investment.]

OTTO: Right, which is why I end up feeling so annoyed by how hard it is for us to coordinate and spend time together. The truth is, when we met, I was honestly really lonely. Since we have been together, things have gotten a lot better for me.

RAFAEL: Some of that is also because work and stuff has gotten better for you though.

OTTO: True. This is not the only thing that has changed.

COUNSELOR: Got it. So having Rafael in your life gives you a sense of comfort and companionship. What else do you appreciate about the relationship? [Individual reflection of emotional investment followed by an open question directed to Otto.]

OTTO: Umm . . . I think we do a really good job of communicating.

RAFAEL: Most of the time anyway.

OTTO: Most of the time. Sometimes it's hard because we typically have a few days each week where we are only in touch through like text or social media. And that's fine when it's fine. But if a serious issue comes up or something, working it out over text doesn't always go well.

COUNSELOR: So what about communication works for you guys? What do you really get right. [Question directed to the couple.]

OTTO: I appreciate that, when we are able to talk face to face, we are really good at hearing each other out. Like we never end up screaming at each other. [to RAFAEL] And, I feel like you are just really good at getting when I need space and when it's actually important that we work something out.

RAFAEL: Aww . . . thanks. Well, we've had practice.

COUNSELOR: I want to come back to that actually, because knowing when to give each other space and when it's time to come together and talk is a huge advantage. That's a real strength for you guys.
But first, Rafael, I want to give you a chance to answer the same question. What's important to you about this relationship? What do you value?

[Relationship affirmation.]

RAFAEL: So, to understand my answer, you need to know that I am HIV positive, and he is not. [to OTTO.] I hope it's OK I just say that.

[Question directed to Rafael.]

OTTO: [to RAFAEL] I wasn't sure if you were gonna want to go there, but I'm good if you are.

RAFAEL: We might as well. I was diagnosed like a year and half before we met. How I got it is a story itself, but the point is that I really believed for a while after I was diagnosed that I was never gonna find someone. I tried dating a few guys and things always got messed up. Either I was weird or they got weird. I eventually just decided that I should quit trying. I was actually only on that app because my friend was so tired of me moping around that she was like: "Dammit, just see who is out there." She hung out with me one night, and we set up my profile together. The thing I liked about it was that I could just say on my profile that I was HIV positive, and then I didn't have to worry about figuring out how or when to tell someone. If they weren't going to be interested, then they didn't have to be interested.

COUNSELOR: So this relationship is something you had sort of stopped believing was possible for a minute.

[Reflection of satisfaction directed to Rafael. The relationship exceeds his ideal expectations.]

RAFAEL: Yeah. I know, I know, being HIV positive is not a death sentence. I'm really healthy. I'm in good shape. Blah. That's not a lie, but anyone who thinks that means it is "easy" to date when you're HIV positive should try it sometime. It's not.

COUNSELOR: And yet you guys have made this work.

[Dyadic reflection.]

OTTO: It was never an issue for me. It was just a part of who he was. We used condoms at first, which was fine. Then I was on PrEP for quite a while. Now we even sort of let that go because his viral load has been undetectable for so long. But it was never something that scared me or whatever. I think it helped actually knowing up front.

RAFAEL: Yeah, 'cause it was a while before we really talked about it. But at least I knew that he knew from the beginning and I didn't have to worry that he would find out and freak out.

COUNSELOR: So, in a way, you two both find a lot of comfort in this relationship. You both were at a place where you were kinda lonely when you met, and being part of this has given you a sense of family and belonging.

[Dyadic reflection of emotional investment.]

OTTO: Exactly.

COUNSELOR: So, in every relationship, there can be some bumps in the road. For you two, where do things get hard? What are the challenges, if any?

[Question directed to the couple.]

OTTO: I feel like I've kinda said this. It's just frustrating to me that it's so hard for us to coordinate our lives and schedules. Almost all of our "fights" end up coming back to that.

RAFAEL: Sort of, I feel like some of it is just straight up about sex as well.

OTTO: [to RAFAEL] You think?

RAFAEL: [to OTTO] Well, yeah. Because honestly I think some of the times you are upset about me not responding or being available or whatever, you are worried that I'm like out fooling around with someone.

OTTO: Ugh . . . well. Because sometimes you have been.

RAFAEL: Well, it's not like I've always been the only one.

COUNSELOR: If I could, I would pause you guys for a minute and ask what agreements or understandings you guys have about sex with people outside your relationship. I work with all kinds of couples, so I truly have no judgments about what your agreement should be. I'm curious where you guys are at right now with that.

[Question directed to the couple.]

RAFAEL: So, we are not monogamous. And I think that's more because I just have never really bought into monogamy. [to OTTO] I think if it were up to you we would be.

OTTO: Well, probably. It's not that I think monogamy is the only thing that works. It's not like a moral thing. I just think I'm less interested in the idea of having sex with other people.

COUNSELOR: So it sounds like there are two challenges here. One is that your work lives don't align very well. That means it's tough to find time to communicate and be together. A second challenge is that you guys have different perspectives on what your ideal sexual agreement would be. And those two things sometimes feed off each other a bit.

[Summary of challenges related to investment (spending time together) and satisfaction (the couple's sexual agreement falls short of Otto's ideal.]

OTTO: Exactly. That's the struggle.

RAFAEL: Most of the time, if we have a fight, or I feel like he's like nagging me or something, it happens over text. It's when we are not together. Once we are around each other, it all kind of works itself out usually.

COUNSELOR: Got it, so sometimes how you communicate contributes to a challenge. Texting about the tough stuff doesn't always work out the way you would like.

[Individual reflection directed to Rafael.]

RAFAEL: Right. Especially if one of us has had a drink or is using anything else.

OTTO: I know some couples talk it out over drinks. That does not end well for us.

COUNSELOR: Got it. So there are some things you guys would like to work out—this is not necessarily perfect—and that is part of why you are here. And there is a lot that works about this relationship. You guys mean a lot to each other. Over your time together, you have found ways to talk things out and work together successfully.

[Dyadic reflection that ends with an emphasis on strengths in dyadic functioning.]

* * *

STRATEGIES TO FACILITATE DYADIC FUNCTIONING

This narrative illustrates a number of essential aspects of the counselor's stance during the facilitating process. First and foremost, the counselor holds the focus on the strengths and weaknesses of the relationship. Some content has emerged that hints at where a focus on target behaviors like substance use and sexual risk reduction might develop, but the counselor has not yet moved to make that particularly salient. In addition, some may wonder why the counselor chose not to elaborate on Rafael's narrative about contracting HIV. The answer is primarily that, at this point in the session, that narrative is out of sync with an emphasis on facilitating dyadic functioning. It is meaningful to Rafael that Otto accepts and loves him even though he is HIV positive. The counselor holds on to that thread and sustains attention on understanding the couple's functioning rather than gathering history per se.

Begin with what works. The counselor sustains attention on what works before exploring challenges. This is true even as information about challenges is volunteered spontaneously early on in the passage. We have commonly seen this pattern in our work with couples. When asked, What works? couples may often volunteer information about relationship problems. The discussion of challenges has the potential to activate conflict in the room. By sustaining a focus on relationship strengths and temporarily delaying the discussion of where things get hard, the counselor is able to provide reflections that juxtapose dyadic strengths with these weaknesses when they emerge. Exploring strengths first allows the counselor to situate challenges in a broader relationship context. If challenges are discussed in detail before strengths are explored, the counselor has less information about relationship assets to draw on.

The concept of beginning with what works when facilitating dyadic functioning is aligned with the established Motivational Interviewing technique of reviewing past successes (W. R. Miller & Rollnick, 2013). By first inviting the couple to think about what is going well, the counselor affords Otto and Rafael the opportunity to reflect on times they supported one another or found ways to work together successfully. Such a discussion has the potential to draw out skills and strengths the couple already possess. Doing so may enhance Otto and Rafael's belief in their capacity to address some of the challenges that are later identified.

Avoiding the halo effect. The counselor also does an effective job of avoiding a halo effect (Thorndike, 1920). It may be tempting for clients and counselors alike to default to generalizing the relationship overall as either "good" or "bad," or "functional" or "dysfunctional." These global evaluations can make it difficult for struggling couples to see where things are working, and they can make it hard for successful couples to acknowledge where things get hard. The counselor's use of double-sided reflections and questions that balance attention to strengths and weaknesses helps to emphasize that relationships can be good *and* couples may want to change some things. Some things may be wrong *and* there may be things partners truly value about the relationship.

Relationship skill building—The potential for integrated practice. The example narrative in this chapter ends with the counselor and couple having established a sense of relationship functioning strengths and challenges. Had the transcript continued, it is possible to imagine the couple might have identified changing their communication habits as a goal or focus of counseling. If such a focus emerged, the counselor might then go on to invite Otto and Rafael to consider how their relationship strengths and previous successes—times when they did communicate productively—might inform the development of a plan to address their current challenges.

The topic of practice integration is discussed in greater detail in Chapter 11, and Chapter 9 takes on the topic of couples communication—and related skill-building interventions—in detail. The process of facilitating dyadic functioning represents a potentially fruitful domain to examine practice integration. While many couples may have sufficiently good dyadic functioning that a strengths-based exploration of relationship quality will be sufficient, in other instances, one or both partners may have knowledge gaps or deficits in their behavioral repertoire that impair the couple's functioning.

There are examples of relationship skill-building interventions that have shown efficacy in heterosexual samples (e.g., Davila et al., 2021). There are also examples of existing dyadic interventions focused on sexual health among sexual minority men that specifically integrate relationship skill building (e.g., Gamarel et al., 2019; Newcomb et al., 2017). The integration of these kinds of relationship skill-building activities into couples Motivational Interviewing may enhance the counselor's repertoire of strategies available for facilitating dyadic functioning. Our initial attempts at this have utilized video-based modeling as a precursor to engagement in a motivational enhancement activity (Starks, Dellucci, et al., 2019; Starks, Feldstein Ewing, et al., 2019; Starks, Kyre, et al., 2021); however, the potential for intervention development in this area is hardly limited to our relatively narrow initial application.

CONCLUSIONS AND KEY POINTS

Facilitating dyadic functioning is introduced here as a novel process unique to couples Motivational Interviewing. The emphasis in this process is on drawing out the couple's strengths and bolstering their ability to work together by supporting adaptive functioning. In keeping with the formulation of other Motivational Interviewing processes, attention to facilitating is ongoing throughout the session; however, it is introduced here after the engaging process and before the focusing process as a reflection of when it is perhaps most likely to emerge as salient.

This chapter focuses primarily on three elements of dyadic functioning particularly salient in interdependence theory: satisfaction, commitment, and emotional investment. All of these constructs have been assessed in various ways. Satisfaction has been evaluated in terms of the relative rewards and costs of a relationship. It has also been conceptualized as the extent to which the relationship approximates an ideal. Commitment has been operationalized as milestone attainment (e.g., marriage) and also as a multifaceted and dimensional psychological construct that captures the extent to which an individual intends to persist with their relationship. Finally, emotional investment refers to the strength of emotional bonds between partners or the extent to which one partner's emotional experiences are linked to the other's. From the prospective of a Motivational Interviewing counselor, all of these conceptualizations are potentially informative because they provide a wide range of indicators that counselors can listen for in session.

The skills used in facilitating dyadic functioning are similar in many ways to those relevant in the engaging process. Counselors use OARS (open questions, affirmations, reflections, and summary statements), including dyadic reflections and relationship affirmations new to couples Motivational Interviewing—to elicit partners' perspectives about what works and where challenges may lie in their relationship. Throughout, it is essential that they begin with what works and elicit the couple's strengths before examining challenges. It is also essential that counselors avoid the halo effect or global assessments of the relationship as uniformly good or bad. The potential to integrate relationship skill-building components into couples Motivational Interviewing during the facilitating process is discussed. Chapters 9 and 11 further discuss such potential for practice integration.

Focusing—Finding a Shared Goal

The content in the previous chapters has largely focused on what might be thought of as laying the foundation for change. The engaging process highlighted the development of a working alliance between the counselor and couple; meanwhile, the facilitating process emphasized the cultivation of the partner's relationship quality. This interpersonal foundation—the web of relationships between the counselor and couple, between the counselor and each individual partner, and between the partners themselves—is the groundwork for change.

The narratives in previous chapters have in various ways illustrated that the processes of engaging and facilitating dyadic functioning may organically elicit potential targets of intervention. Until this point, the counselors in our example narratives have largely chosen to prioritize gaining a general understanding of the couple, establishing rapport, and exploring strengths and weaknesses in the relationship. That was consistent with an emphasis on the engaging and facilitating processes and was appropriate for those particular points in the course of intervention. In this chapter, we examine the process of clarifying the target behavior and focusing the session on the discussion of potential change. The focusing process represents a transition in the counseling discourse. It narrows the conversation from the relatively broad domain of establishing and exploring relationships among the people in the room to the identification of how the time together will be used.

In couples Motivational Interviewing, focusing can be thought of as a two-stage process. In the first stage, a focus is identified. The partners and counselor establish a shared priority—the topic or topics they will discuss together. In the second stage, a dyadic focus is elaborated. This involves exploring each partner's perspective on the identified topic, their understanding of one another's perspective, and their beliefs about how their own position is perceived by their partner.

Before launching into the details of the focusing process, it is potentially useful to acknowledge the limits of its scope. The goal of the focusing process is for the counselor and partners in the couple to arrive at consensus about what they should talk about. Agreeing that a particular issue is worthy of attention in counseling is not the same thing as agreeing about whether change is necessary or how it should happen. Sometimes, the process of identifying and elaborating a focus actually reveals areas of disagreement that were previously implicit or unknown. Chapter 7 is dedicated to the exploration of disagreements about change and evoking motivation for change. The purpose of the focusing process here is to set the stage for that discussion to follow.

IDENTIFYING A FOCUS: FINDING SHARED PRIORITIES FOR THE SESSION

W. R. Miller and Rollnick (2013) characterized the focusing process as a balancing of priorities. In individual counseling, there are at least two sets of priorities to consider in session—potentially more. There are client priorities (the content they would prefer to focus on), counselor priorities (the content that in their clinical judgment would be most useful to discuss), and potentially a "third voice" in the room. This third voice might be the agenda of a service agency that has a specific focus, an insurance company that has particular billing restrictions, or some other person who has influenced the client to attend the session but is not participating as a client (e.g., a parent, spouse, or employer who has "mandated" or "demanded" the client attend the session).

Box 6.1 provides some examples of how counselors might introduce an emphasis on the focusing process based in part on the source of the agenda. Counselors might elicit the client's agenda simply by inquiring in some way about how they would like to use the time in session or what priorities motivated them to seek counseling services. Counselors might introduce their own ideas for a focus as well. Doing so effectively requires ongoing attention to the spirit of collaboration. Box 6.1 provides some examples of how this can be achieved. The counselor explicitly seeks collaboration with the client by asking permission to introduce their potential focus (e.g., "If it's OK with you . . .") and also by evoking the client's perspective on their focus once proposed (e.g., "What do you think of that as one option?") Finally, Box 6.1 also includes some examples of how counselors can acknowledge the need to accommodate third-party agendas in session in ways that seek to maintain a working alliance and a collaborative stance toward the client.

Focusing involves balancing these agendas in a manner that shares power with the client and respects their autonomy. Sometimes this process is easy and straightforward. Shared or agreed-on priorities are identified, and the client and counselor can move forward with an exploration of potential change. When client and counselor priorities diverge, focusing becomes more challenging. Imposing an agenda on an unwilling client runs contrary to the Spirit of Motivational Interviewing; however, third-party agendas or a counselor's own assessment may sometimes compel them to explore a potential focus even if clients are reticent to do so. It is not always possible for counselors to offer what clients are seeking, and sometimes providing a referral to an alternative provider or refusing to provide a desired service are the only ethical options logistically available.

W. R. Miller and Rollnick (2013) provided a cogent discussion of how counselors might balance the ethical principles of beneficence (to provide benefit

Box 6.1

STRATEGIES FOR INTRODUCING A FOCUS

Client driven
- What brought you in to see me?
- What do you two hope to achieve in these sessions?

Counselor driven
- If it's ok with you, I typically ask all of my clients about what is happening for them around drug use, just to evaluate if there is anything useful for us to talk about there. How would you feel if we talked about that a bit?
- Based on what I am hearing you say, it sounds like one thing we might spend some time talking about is the sex you guys have together. What do you think about that as one option?

Third-party driven
- Because of the nature of our funding sources, one topic I need to bring up with everyone is HIV prevention. That may or may not be a big issue for you guys, but I appreciate your patience with me in either case. What concerns if any do you have about that requirement?
- For billing purposes, I am indicating that our session is addressing a substance use disorder. That does not mean that is the only issue we are able to talk about here. But our work overall needs to be relevant to that somehow in order to bill your insurance. How does that seem to you?

---

to the client), nonmalfeasance (to do no harm), respect for client autonomy, and justice (equitable access to the benefits of treatment and fair distribution of risk) when making decisions about whether to pursue the exploration of a change goal their client does not share. They asserted that "Motivational Interviewing is not about persuading people to do something that is against their values, goals, or interests" (W. R. Miller & Rollnick, 2013, p. 125). While counselors may explore potential change goals that the client does not share, the power to make decisions about whether and how change occurs rests with the client.

The ethical decision-making inherent in establishing a counseling focus—and the principles proposed by W. R. Miller and Rollnick (2013) to guide that process—largely generalize to Motivational Interviewing with couples. Similar to an individual session, the counselor and the couple need to come to an agreement about how to use their time together. While that core element of balancing priorities is the same, focusing with a couple is potentially more complex because there are simply more people who have to reach consensus. Counselors must consider the ethical implications of decisions for both partners in the couple, rather than a single client.

A viable focus requires that everyone in the room is "at least willing" to tolerate participating in a conversation about a topic. Thinking about the establishment of a focus in a couples Motivational Interview is somewhat easier if we distinguish among topics that people "want" to discuss; those they are "willing" to discuss; and those they are "unwilling" to discuss. Topics people want to discuss are those they feel are most important—or most useful—to bring up in counseling. There is a desire to broach the subject. Topics people are willing to discuss are ones they are open to, but not necessarily issues they personally believe are particularly important, require immediate attention, or necessitate change. Topics people are unwilling to discuss are those that they would refuse to engage with. This might include content that one partner is (or both partners are) unwilling to share with the other or with the counselor. It might also include topics that one or both partners are willing to acknowledge, but unwilling to sustain a discussion about.

As with individual counseling, sometimes achieving consensus about a topic of focus is easy. Perhaps both partners see a particular issue as relevant or problematic; they seek a counselor who works in that area; and the agenda coalesces readily. In these instances, counselors can likely progress fairly quickly to elaborating the identified dyadic focus as described in the following section. Once partners in the couple are aligned on what to discuss in session, counselors can apply W. R. Miller and Rollnick's (2013) ethical decision-making framework to think about the alignment of the counselor's and the couple's agenda.

Negotiating a topic of focus when partners disagree. Unfortunately, consensus within the couple about a topic of focus is not always guaranteed. Partners may come to counseling with divergent views about what they hope to accomplish. One may be interested in reducing substance use, while the other wants to save their relationship. One might be most concerned about feeling depressed, while the other is upset about financial issues. These agendas could launch multiple different conversations. Without a shared vision of the purpose of the counseling process and how partners' priorities will be addressed, the processes of evoking and planning for change can be derailed by competing or contradictory agendas.

Drawing on interdependence theory (Kelley & Thibaut, 1978; Rusbult et al., 1996), Starks, Millar, et al. (2018) suggested that accommodation was a prerequisite to eliciting motivation for change. If partners respond to one another in destructive ways when a topic is introduced, they are less likely to be successful at negotiating a shared goal and supporting one another's goal-directed behavior. Specific strategies for managing conflict or responding to discord between partners are discussed in the following chapter. If the act of identifying a focus— merely agreeing on what should be discussed in counseling—elicits conflict between partners, counselors may need to utilize strategies discussed in Chapter 7 to mitigate conflict and support couples in identifying what they might address together in counseling. Assuming partners are able to give a constructive accommodation response when they disagree about session priorities, there are a number of ways in which consensus might ultimately arise. These can be understood in terms of accommodation processes (Rusbult, Bissonnette, et al., 1998).

Finding shared priorities through compromise. When partners are able to engage in productive and assertive conversations about their respective visions for what counseling can accomplish (i.e., voice-type accommodation responses), compromise priorities may emerge in one of three primary ways. Sometimes partners can come to understand one another's priorities as different components of the same overall goal. Alternatively, it may become clear that one partner's goal is a precursor, or a step along the way, to achieving the other partner's priority. In this case, the couple might agree to take on these priorities in sequence. Finally, it is possible that each partner has distinct priorities that are not meaningfully related to one another. In this case, a quid pro quo can sometimes be achieved in which partners agree to divide attention and give time to discussing each of their priorities in turn. This might involve dividing each session, or it may mean dedicating some sessions to one partner's priorities with the understanding that subsequent sessions will focus on the other's.

At other times, compromise may emerge when one partner simply agrees to discuss an issue because the other partner is concerned about it—this is akin to a loyalty-type accommodation response. In these instances, the partner may see acquiescing to discuss an issue as a way of demonstrating care, concern, and support for their partner and a general commitment to the relationship. The compromise may be expressed in utterances like: "I don't know that I necessarily am worried about that issue, but if it is important to my partner then we can talk about it."

Responding to a partner's refusal or rejection of a potential focus. When one partner refuses to discuss an issue that is a priority for the other, the counselor may consider several ways to proceed. If the refusing partner is able and willing to explain why they do not wish to focus on a particular issue, the counselor or partner for whom it is a priority may be able to offer assurances or negotiate boundaries that increase willingness to discuss the issue in some limited scope. The process for elaborating on a dyadic focus can provide one road map for such a discussion of each partner's perspective on the topic, even if their perspective is that the topic should not be a priority. Understanding why someone does not want to talk about something can provide valuable information about what would have to change to make the topic accessible. If the refusing partner is unable or unwilling to engage in a conversation about why they do not wish to discuss a topic, then the counselor and couple may have no choice but to find an alternative focus, at least initially. It is possible that, as the working alliance matures over time, topics that were initially inaccessible become available for discussion.

If one partner is insistent on the discussion of a topic while the other is unwilling to engage, the counselor may need to assist the couple in evaluating how useful counseling can be at this time. As W. R. Miller and Rollnick (2013) pointed out in their ethical framework, counselors cannot compel clients to change. In a couple's session, counselors must also be cognizant of the fact that they cannot compel one of the partners in a couple to discuss an issue with the other if they feel that doing so runs contrary to their personal goals and values. Counselors can help couples explore the implications of not being able to talk about the issue—but coercing a discussion runs counter to the Spirit of Motivational Interviewing.

Note, special issues related to informed consent in couples counseling are discussed in Chapter 11. Content in this chapter is written with the assumption that both partners have consented to participate in counseling—even if they disagree on what they should focus on together in session. If one of the partners is ultimately unwilling to engage in the counseling process itself, the issue of informed consent must be dealt with first.

Assuming both partners have consented, the counselor and couple will be faced with the task of identifying what they will accomplish together. Achieving an initial consensus to discuss a topic is only the first stage of the focusing process in a couples Motivational Interview. It defines the space where evoking could begin. It gives a domain for the target; however, just sorting out a topic of conversation that both partners are "at least willing" to discuss does not necessarily confer clarity about how the partners view the behavior. Investing some time in elaborating and aligning an initial focus before moving on to emphasize evoking change talk can help a counselor make more strategic decisions to support the couple later.

ESTABLISHING AND ELABORATING A FOCUS

Before discussing the research and theory that informed our conceptualization of a dyadic focus, it is potentially useful to see it in action. The example narrative here continues the session that began in Chapters 4 and 5 with Otto and Rafael. The transcript begins as the counselor shifts to make the focusing process salient and clarify goals for the session. The counselor then elaborates that focus with the couple, which reveals areas of convergence and divergence in their perspectives. In addition to labeling counselor skills, annotations label key elements of elaborating a dyadic focus that will be discussed in detail afterward.

* * *

COUNSELOR: Based on what you have told me, it sounds like there are a few concerns we could focus on. You mentioned some tension around spending enough time together, also around your sexual agreement— and what may be happening with other sexual partners, and also substance use seemed to complicate communication between you two. What specifically brings you guys in? What is important for us to address here, and where might we start?	[Summary transition directed to the couple makes the focusing process salient.]

RAFAEL: I guess we could start wherever, but I feel like it's gonna come back to sex at some point.

COUNSELOR: We probably cannot avoid that topic no matter where we start.

[Individual reflection to Rafael.]

OTTO: Yeah, I mean, we've had a pretty rocky month—some of our worst fights actually—over exactly this. For the first time, I've sort of doubted where we were headed.

COUNSELOR: There is some concern that if you don't sort this out, it could be a spoiler.

[Individual reflection to Otto.]

OTTO: Yeah.

COUNSELOR: One possibility then is that we start there. Rafael, how does that sit with you?

[Dyadic reflection followed by a question seeking collaboration with Rafael.]

RAFAEL: Well, this should be interesting.

OTTO: I mean, we do probably need to figure it out.

RAFAEL: I'm just afraid we end up back in the same spot every time.

COUNSELOR: I can't promise you we will find a perfect resolution here; however, if you guys are open to it, we could give it a go.

[Affirmation of autonomy directed to the couple.]

RAFAEL: I guess it is why we came.

OTTO: Agreed.

COUNSELOR: So, help me understand that spot where you guys get stuck. What do each of you want in your sexual agreement?

[Consensus on the focus is achieved. The counselor's question directed to the couple begins to elaborate the focus.]

RAFAEL: Well, I guess like I said, we are not monogamous. That seems fine a lot of the time, but I think he is not really OK with it. [to OTTO] Like it bugs you.

COUNSELOR: [to OTTO] How accurate is that?

[Rafael has expressed his belief about what Otto wants. This question invites Otto to agree or correct Rafael's assumption.]

OTTO: Pretty accurate I guess. I get why we are not monogamous. It's fine. But sometimes it does bug me, even though I understand his argument.

COUNSELOR: I have the sense that your agreement right now feels pretty OK to Rafael.
Otto, what ideally would you want your sexual agreement to be? How would you handle this if it were totally up to you?

[The counselor now elicits Otto's preference directly.]

OTTO: I don't know honestly. The thing is, being open is kind of nice. Sometimes it's fun to have the freedom. I don't use that freedom as much, but it has been nice now and again.

COUNSELOR: So there are some good things about it. You guys, at least in some ways, have a similar perspective on this. [to OTTO] And it sounds like there are things you do not like.

[Dyadic reflection of common ground before continuing to elicit Otto's concerns.]

OTTO: I think I just resent it because we don't get to see each other that much in the first place, and then, if he's with someone else, it takes that much more time away from us.

COUNSELOR: Got it. It isn't so much the idea of being open that bothers you. It's that it takes time away from the two of you being together.

[Individual reflection to Otto clarifying what he wants.]

OTTO: Right. I think if we didn't have to work so hard to coordinate, I don't honestly know that I'd have the same issue.

RAFAEL: Fair. If I—or you for that matter—were out with someone else instead of prioritizing us, that would be lame. But, are you sure that's it for you? Like if I told you that I'd be fine with the idea of only hooking up at times there was no way we'd be hanging out, it wouldn't still bother you?

OTTO: Umm . . . I want to say no. I mean, maybe I'm wrong and it actually would, but at least at the moment I don't think so.

COUNSELOR: OK. So, at least as far as we know now—you guys could get on board with the idea of figuring out how to make an open relationship work, as long as you could also work out how to prevent it from infringing on your time together.

[Dyadic reflection summarizing common ground]

OTTO: Yes.

RAFAEL: Yes. But I think it would help to know if that's actually possible.

COUNSELOR: Rafael, you have some doubts even though you guys, in theory, are on the same page.

[Individual reflection captures Rafael's doubt about Otto's stated preferences]

RAFAEL: I mean, it sounds nice. I'm just skeptical. We've been stuck on this for so long.

OTTO: I'll be honest, I would have said something like this a long time ago. I just always assumed you wanted like no limits. I didn't want you to think I was trying to force you to be monogamous in a back-handed way.

COUNSELOR: So, part of why it's been hard to talk about this is that you've both been kinda concerned about how the other views this. Rafael, you have been worried Otto might not really be OK with being open, and Otto, you have been worried that Rafael might be upset if you suggested any limits at all on sex.

[Dyadic reflection of common ground summarizes the partners' worry about being judged by one another.]

OTTO: Which I guess is not quite true.

RAFAEL: We've kinda been tiptoeing around the issue.

COUNSELOR: I really respect that you both put your perspectives out there. I want to continue that conversation, but, if it is OK with you, I want to check in on just a couple of other things before we sort of dig into that specifically.

[The focus on sexual agreements is now elaborated. The counselor introduces the idea of exploring a related focus on sexual health.]

OTTO: OK.

RAFAEL: Go for it.

COUNSELOR: I am curious how you guys handle sexual health decisions. What are your rules or understandings about STI [sexually transmitted infection] prevention, HIV prevention, and—for you Rafael—HIV care?

[Both partners have agreed to the counselor's proposed focus on sexual health. The counselor's question begins to elaborate that focus.]

RAFAEL: And . . . now it's gonna be his turn to be skeptical.
OTTO: Go on.

RAFAEL: So there are some people I play with who I don't use condoms with. But either they're also HIV positive or on PrEP [pre-exposure prophylaxis].

OTTO: Ah yes. I'm going to be skeptical. I don't love that. Me, condoms always.

RAFAEL: And . . . there we go.

COUNSELOR: Got it. So this is something you two feel somewhat differently about.

[Dyad reflection captures dyadic ambivalence.]

OTTO: Yeah. I mean, I know what you [Rafael] are gonna say. You are already HIV positive, and so it's fine. But I still think it's not OK, and this month proved that.

RAFAEL: Don't act like you always used condoms when you were on PrEP.

COUNSELOR: Rafael, I wonder if we could back up just a bit. Help us understand how you think about HIV and STIs when you are making decisions about sex.

[The counselor's question elicits information about what Rafael wants.]

RAFAEL: I guess I do feel like the big concern is HIV. If someone is positive or if they are on PrEP, I don't worry about it so much.

OTTO: [to RAFAEL] And you see where that got us.

RAFAEL: So, what he's getting at is 3 or 4 weeks ago, I got diagnosed with chlamydia. I'm pretty sure I know who I got it from. He was a nice guy, and I don't think he had a clue he had anything, but it was really lame.

COUNSELOR: And that has complicated things between the two of you.

[Dyadic reflection.]

RAFAEL: I had to tell him, and we had to take a break from sex because I didn't want him to get it, too.

OTTO: I do respect that he told me, but it is like a really big example of the things that also frustrate me about this relationship. It like plays to all our weaknesses.

COUNSELOR: Right. In some ways this is about sexual health. In other ways, it is a bit bigger because this takes away from the quality of your time together.

[Dyadic reflections links the counselor-driven agenda to discuss sexual health with the client-driven agenda on sexual agreements.]

OTTO: Exactly.

COUNSELOR: In some ways, preventing an STI—thinking about sexual health and safety—actually ends up being a way of taking care of your relationship. It's connected to how you feel about your sexual agreement and has some consequences for what you can do together sexually.

OTTO: Right. I think also I would feel better about what you're doing with other people if I knew you were being safe, which, right now, I don't always think you are.

RAFAEL: I mean, what you call "safe" is a matter of debate. But yes, I will admit that I guess it is something we need to work out.

COUNSELOR: OK, so this bigger goal of preserving and protecting time together means getting some clarity about your sexual agreement. Even though you guys are open, and in principle that's OK, decisions about what you do with other people can impact your time together. And that's the piece you don't want.

[Dyadic reflection emphasizing common ground and shared priorities.]

RAFAEL: Right.

OTTO: Yes. And also we don't want chlamydia.

COUNSELOR: Got it. Somewhat related to all of this, we have not really talked much about how you guys feel about sex between the two of you. Would it be OK if we talked briefly about how things are going there?

[The focus on sexual health is now elaborated. The counselor introduces one last potential focus on the sex Otto and Rafael have together.]

RAFAEL: What do you mean?

OTTO: Yeah, like, how often are we doing it or . . . ?

COUNSELOR: For some people how often they have sex is the important bit. For others it is less about how much sex they have and more about the kind or quality of sex they have. I am really just curious how happy you guys are with how sex is going for both of you together.

[The couple has implicitly agreed to discuss the focus and elaboration begins.]

OTTO: I think I would probably like to have sex together more often than we do, but I don't know that's true for you.

RAFAEL: Wait seriously? Because I totally assumed you are actually not super interested in sex.

OTTO: Ummm . . . nope. Not true.

RAFAEL: It is really hard to tell.

COUNSELOR: So it sounds like actually you guys might agree on this more than you suspected.

[Dyadic reflection highlights misaligned assumptions and the presence of common ground.]

* * *

DEVELOPING A DYADIC FOCUS

As illustrated in the example above, the heuristic structure of a dyadic focus serves several purposes. First, the structure provides a framework for counselors to determine if there is sufficient consensus about a particular focus to begin emphasizing the evoking processes. In addition, it helps the counselor conceptualize what might be happening in those instances when consensus is difficult or even impossible to achieve. Finally, it gives partners in the couple an opportunity to hear and respond to one another's perspectives in a detailed way. It therefore reduces the possibility that the appearance of agreement or disagreement about change arises from miscommunication between partners.

Three Intra-individual Elements of a Dyadic Focus

Ultimately, a dyadic focus—the agreed-on purpose of a couples Motivational Interview—is an interpersonal phenomenon. It arises from the priorities of both partners and whether or not it can be realized will also be determined, in part, by the counselor's professional expertise and limitations. Once an initial topic of focus has been identified, three intra-individual cognitive elements—the priorities, beliefs, and expectancies of each partner—serve as the building blocks of a dyadic focus. These elements are depicted in Figure 6.1. The essential feature of these intra-individual elements is that they can vary across partners. Each person in the relationship has their own priorities, beliefs, and expectancies—and partners may or may not be aligned or accurately aware of each other's positions. For this reason, Figure 6.1 is organized such that one partner's priorities, beliefs, and expectancies are positioned along the right side and the other's are positioned along the left.

Individual priorities. Once a general topic of focus has been established—once partners have agreed that they are at least willing to talk about an issue or area of potential change—the counselor can begin to draw out each partner's perspective or related priorities. These represent what each partner "wants" related to the topic of focus. For example, Rafael prefers an open sexual agreement. Otto generally shares that preference but in a qualified way. He also views spending time together

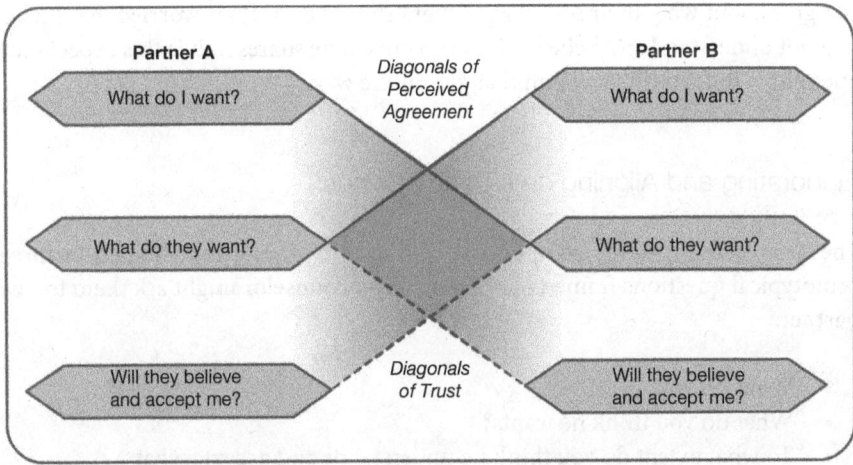

Figure 6.1 Elements of a dyadic focus. Figure by Stephen Sullivan.

with Rafael as a priority. Otto sees using condoms as an essential element of sexual risk reduction; Rafael does not have the same perspective on this priority.

Beliefs about partner preferences. Each partner also potentially has thoughts about what the other partner's priorities and preferences might be. These represent beliefs or hunches about what their partner will want related to a topic of focus. These beliefs also encompass expectations about whether the partners agree on a particular issue. We see this in the narrative between Otto and Rafael. Rafael begins the conversation with some assumptions about Otto's comfort with nonmonogamy and Otto's interest in having sex together. He is initially operating under the hypothesis that Otto largely does not share his perspective on these issues. In the process of elaborating a dyadic focus, Rafael learns new information from Otto that challenges his initial assumptions about what Otto wants and their level of agreement.

Expectancies about being believed and accepted. The third intra-individual element of a dyadic focus is perhaps the most complicated. Each person in the relationship has an expectation about whether their partner will understand, believe, and accept them if they express what they want. This idea is similar to the concept of the *introject*, a component that has been articulated as part of an interpersonal focus for individual psychotherapy (Henry et al., 1990; Strupp & Binder, 1984). The introject refers to an individual's belief about how they will be viewed by others. It is their inference about the inferences that other people make about them.

As outlined by Strupp and Binder (1984), these inferences about how other people think about us can have a powerful effect on our behavior. We see this manifest in Otto's statement to Rafael: "I didn't want you to think I was trying to force you to be monogamous in a back-handed way." Here Otto is worried that even if he expresses his preferences for a sexual agreement, Rafael will come to the wrong conclusion about his intentions: He doubts he will be accurately understood and believed. As a result, Otto has avoided bringing up the topic of their sexual agreement, which has contributed to the couple's ongoing frustration around the issue. Notably, Otto's concern here is not so much that he and Rafael disagree about what their sexual agreement should be. Otto is worried that Rafael will not understand and believe his perspective if he shares it. It is this expectancy about how Rafael will view him that gets in the way.

Elaborating and Aligning on a Dyadic Focus

These three intrapsychic components of a dyadic focus are embodied in three prototypical questions framed here in the way a counselor might ask them to one partner.

- "What do you want?"
- "What do you think he wants?"
- "To what extent do you think he understands and accepts what you want?"

The first step in elaborating a dyadic focus is to draw out the answers to these key questions from each partner. They do not necessarily need to be asked verbatim. There are lots of ways to get at the content implied by these questions. Counselors may utilize a range of active listening skills to explore these areas. It is also not necessary that these questions be answered in any specific order. Some sessions may proceed in a linear way, wherein each partner provides answers for all three questions in turn. Other sessions may proceed in a much less linear way, with partners actively exchanging ideas and their understandings of one another's preferences.

As the counselor draws out and explores the building blocks of a dyadic focus with each partner, the interpersonal dynamics of establishing a dyadic focus for the Motivational Interview are set in motion. This happens because each partner is not only sharing their answers to these three key questions, they are also hearing each other's answers. This provides an immediate opportunity to assess whether the assumptions they have made about one another's priories are accurate.

When a dyadic focus is aligned, each partner has an accurate understanding of the other's priorities, and each partner feels that their priorities are understood by the other. Alignment therefore is assessed by inviting the couple to consider two things. The first of these is whether partners have an accurate understanding of one another's priorities, and the second is whether the partners believe they are communicating in good faith. Good faith communication here refers to a situation where each partner believes the other is being genuine, and each partner also believes that what he is saying is being heard, understood, and accepted by the other.

In exploring these domains of alignment, the counselor is exploring congruence along the edges of the triangles in Figure 6.1. The counselor is not concerned here with whether partners have the same goal—whether their answers to the question "What do you want?" are the same. Rather, the counselor is concerned with whether the partners have an accurate and mutual understanding of one another's priorities. This is captured in the top edge of the triangles in Figure 6.1, referred to as the diagonals of perceived agreement. Misalignment along these diagonals will produce inaccurate conclusions about the presence or absence of agreement between partners. The counselor is also concerned with whether the partners believe in the authenticity of their communication exchange. This is captured in the bottom edge of the triangles in Figure 6.1, referred to as the diagonals of trust.

RATIONALE FOR THE COMPONENTS OF A DYADIC FOCUS

To understand the challenges most commonly encountered in exploring a dyadic focus—the forms of misalignment counselors are most likely to see—it is potentially useful to understand the research from which the concept of a dyadic focus was derived. The three building blocks—and the diagonals of alignment that are emphasized—emerged in part from research that has examined congruence in partners' perceptions of one another's behavior. Much of this work has focused on sexual behavior or substance use among sexual minority male couples specifically, and it has indirectly illustrated the potential for partners to have an inaccurate understanding of one another's behavior. In addition, it has provided an indication that concerns about being doubted or suspected by one's partner may inhibit disclosure.

Partners do not always agree on whether they have a sexual agreement. When studies of sexual agreements have access to data from both partners, there is a small but consistently observed subgroup of male couples in which partners have discrepant perceptions of their agreement. The number has ranged from 5% to 19.3% across samples of male couples (e.g., Dellucci et al., 2020; Hoff & Beougher, 2010; Mitchell, 2014; Parsons et al., 2012; Sharma et al., 2019, 2021). These studies have typically surveyed partners separately, and discrepancy has been identified by comparing partner's reports. This means that these studies are identifying couples in which partners have different beliefs about what their sexual agreement is and are potentially unaware that their impressions differ. Perhaps not surprisingly, partners in couples who have discrepant perspectives of their sexual agreement score lower on measures of satisfaction (Mitchell et al., 2012) and some measures of adaptive communication (Dellucci et al., 2020) compared to partners in couples who concur about what their sexual agreement is.

Having a sexual agreement does predict behavior, and partners do not always do what they say they will. As reviewed in Chapter 1, it is worth noting that sexual agreements do predict behavior. A number of studies indicated that, on average, sexual minority men who report monogamous agreements are less likely to have sex with casual partners compared to single men and those with nonmonogamous agreements (e.g., Starks, Jones, et al., 2020; Starks, Robles, Bosco, Dellucci, et al., 2019).

At the same time, agreements are not perfect representations of what people do. Studies of agreement violations have observed that 23% to 46% of sexual minority men reported breaking their agreement (e.g., Gomez et al., 2012; Mitchell, 2014). These investigations have highlighted the importance of relationship functioning yet again. Not only are partners in high-quality relationships more likely to concur about their agreement, but also they are more likely to adhere to the agreement they have formed (e.g., Davidovich et al., 2006; Gomez et al., 2012; Mitchell, 2014).

Partners may define "having sex" differently. Consider the case of Darin and Simon from the narrative example in Chapter 3. There we learned that the couple had recently closed their sexual agreement after an incident when Darin had sex with a casual partner and did not use a condom. They are currently monogamous. Now imagine a hypothetical situation in which Darin is at a bar with his friends and he kisses a casual acquaintance he met there. Has he broken his sexual agreement to be monogamous with Otto? What if oral sex (fellatio) occurred? Does it matter if oral sex stopped before orgasm was achieved? What if he ended up going back to the acquaintance's home and having anal sex? Which of these behaviors, if any, Darin believes would violate his sexual agreement is in part a function of how he defines having sex. Similarly, whether Simon feels Darin has broken their agreement is a function of how he defines having sex. This question of what people mean when they say they "had sex" or whether a particular behavior is perceived as meeting the threshold for having sex has been investigated in a number of studies. While this research is limited by an emphasis on college-age heterosexual folks, it effectively illustrates how much people vary in their perceptions of what constitutes sex.

The findings of Byers et al. (2009) are a good exemplar of trends generally observed (e.g., H. E. Randall & Byers, 2003; Sewell & Strassberg, 2015) in this area of research. In their sample of nearly 300 undergraduate students, the majority of men and women (approximately 83%) classified intimate behaviors that do not involve the genitals as consistent with sexual abstinence. This included behaviors like kissing, showering together, or caressing a female partner's breasts. In contrast, most (approximately 90%) classified penetrative sex (both penile–anal and penile–vaginal) as having sex. People are most variable in how they think about oral sex and behaviors that include fondling of the genitals. About half of respondents included these behaviors in their definitions of being sexually abstinent, and only about 18% included them in definitions of having sex. Notably, behaviors that stop before orgasm were less likely to be classified as having sex than behaviors that result in orgasm.

The situation is made more complex by two additional factors. **First, sometimes people consider a behavior an act of infidelity even when they do not classify it has having sex.** For example, H. E. Randall and Byers (2003) found that while only 20% of their respondents considered oral sex to constitute having sex, 97% considered a partner who had oral sex with someone else to be "unfaithful." **Second, people tend to evaluate a partner's behavior more stringently than their own** (Gute et al., 2008; Sewell & Strassberg, 2015). Other than penetrative sex, participants are more likely to consider a behavior having sex if their relationship partner does it than if they do it. This phenomenon has been labeled *definitional discontinuity* (Gute et al., 2008). Only penile–anal and penile–vaginal intercourse were evaluated equivalently for oneself and one's partner—perhaps due to the largely uniform consensus that this behavior meets criteria for having sex generally.

While most of this research has relied on samples of primarily heterosexual university students, some studies have investigated how sexual minority people define having sex (Sewell et al., 2017; Shick et al., 2016). Among sexual minority men, trends largely mirrored those observed in heterosexual samples (Sewell et al., 2017). There was general consensus that anal intercourse constituted having sex. Approximately 90% considered receptive or insertive penile–anal intercourse to constitute having sex. In contrast, consensus was lower for oral sex acts; between 50% and 63% of sexual minority male respondents considered this having sex. Consensus was lower still (varying between 41% and 43%) for various acts that involved nonoral genital touching. Also similar to heterosexual respondents, sexual minority men were more likely to classify a behavior as having sex if their partner engaged in it than when considering their own behavior.

Concerns about judgment, doubt, or mistrust complicate disclosure. All of this research on sex and sexual agreements collectively illustrates the potential for partners to misunderstand one another's preferences or to be unaware of one another's behavior. Even when partners believe they are aligned, misunderstandings may exist if the two people in a relationship do not share compatible perceptions of the behaviors or rules implied by an agreement. But why is it so easy for partners to get out of sync with one another? There are indications throughout the literature that concerns about doubt, suspicion, and mistrust are at least one part of what makes it hard for partners to get—and to stay—on the same page.

As mentioned in the previous chapter, research on HIV prevention has consistently demonstrated that sexual minority men worry that asking a partner to use a condom, bringing up pre-exposure prophylaxis, or discussing HIV testing will convey a lack of commitment, closeness, or trust in the relationship. For the purposes of considering our dyadic focus, these concerns can broadly be understood as worries about being judged, doubted, or misunderstood in some way. We can return to Darin and Simon for an example here. Imagine Darin is very committed to the relationship and also wants to renegotiate his sexual agreement with Simon to permit some sexual behavior with outside partners at some point. If Darin believes that broaching the topic of their sexual agreement will lead Simon to question—or doubt—his commitment, then avoiding the conversation altogether may be the easiest way to escape the danger of Simon's doubt.

While the components of our dyadic focus were derived from research on sexual behavior and agreements, the framework has potentially broad applications to other behaviors. In our own work, we have observed a similar phenomenon around substance use. If one partner is worried that the other would find his use of drugs or alcohol unacceptable or concerning, he may be motivated to avoid discussion or disclosure of substance use to avoid stigma, shame, and conflict in the relationship. This kind of motivation for avoiding a conversation that may invoke potential conflict can be understood as a neglect response in Rusbult, Zembrodt and Gunn (1982) accommodation framework. Following Rusbult's model, this kind of response is likely to inhibit the couple's ability to establish and work together toward shared goals. It therefore may ultimately have an adverse impact on relationship quality as well as individual health outcomes.

COMMON CHALLENGES IN ELABORATING A DYADIC FOCUS

As illustrated in the example of Otto and Rafael, elaborating a dyadic focus sometimes activates discord between the partners in the relationship. Sustaining a conversation about a topic typically avoided may elicit negative feelings partners have about one another's actions or areas of frustration with the relationship. Learning that a partner's priorities deviate from what one believed they were may lead people to question other aspects of the relationship. Learning a partner has concerns about being doubted or judged can produce guilt. While strategies for responding to discord are discussed in detail in Chapter 7, counselors may be more successful in employing those skills strategically if they are able to recognize some of the more common challenges they are likely to encounter during this stage of the focusing process.

Challenges Arising From Miscommunication

Two common challenges result from miscommunication. **In some instances, partners simply do not know that they do not agree.** These couples begin a conversation believing that they are in agreement; however, disclosure or clarification of their preferences reveals that they actually disagree about what they want to have happen. **In other instances, partners are not aware that they do agree.** These couples believe at the outset that they want different things; however, disclosure and clarification leads to the realization that they actually are in agreement.

The formation of a shared goal—one which both partners are invested in accomplishing—relies on a reasonably accurate understanding of one another's preferences. If partners misunderstand what one another wants, there is a chance that they make sacrifices unnecessarily out of respect for what they believe a partner's desires to be. There is also a chance that partners fail to make concessions they might otherwise be willing to make simply because they are unaware of the need for compromise. In both instances, the anodyne here is for the counselor to facilitate accurate communication between partners. If miscommunication is a barrier to adaptive accommodation or joint goal formation, then assertive and direct expression of preferences is the "cure" as it were.

Ongoing attention to facilitating dyadic functioning may be necessary in order to support couples through the revelation of miscommunication. Learning their ideas about what their partner is thinking or feeling are incorrect can elicit a range of emotions from clients. In some instances, one partner expressing a newly accurate understanding of the other partner's thoughts and feelings can lead to validation and relief. In other instances, partners may feel guilty, ashamed, frustrated, or betrayed by the fact that they weremisunderstood or that their perception was in some way inaccurate. In these moments, it may be helpful for counselors to return to an emphasis on the facilitating process (see Chapter 5). Reminding the couple of what they value about the relationship, their emotional investment in and commitment to one another, can help to reframe and contextualize miscommunication. Doing so can help partners obtain the benefits of clarifying and aligning their understandings even when initial reactions are adverse in some way.

The proposition that partners achieving and expressing an accurate understanding of one another's thoughts and feelings is shared by couples therapies broadly. A number of approaches emphasize partners' capacity for empathy as a mechanism of therapeutic change. Integrated behavioral couples therapy (IBCT) (e.g., B. R. Baucom et al., 2015; Christensen et al., 1995; Christensen & Jacobson, 2000; Dimidjian et al., 2008) facilitates more successful dyadic interaction, in part, through increasing partners' understandings of each other's behavioral goals and intentions. A central component of emotion-focused therapies (EFTs) (Garanzini et al., 2017; Wiebe & Johnson, 2016) is to enhance partners' awareness of one another's emotions during behavioral exchanges. The premise is that this leads to behavior change through improved understanding and compassion.

Challenges Arising From Doubt or Fear of Judgment

The communication essential to joint-goal formation is undermined when partners doubt or judge one another. Interestingly, it is also undermined by the anticipation of being doubted or judged—even when a partner might actually respond with acceptance. These two challenges must therefore be understood to have some degree of independence from one another. One partner may respond with doubt or judgment when the other anticipated they would be accepting. Conversely, one partner may respond with acceptance when the other anticipated doubt and judgment. Both the act of doubt and judgment and the anticipation of doubt and judgment can prevent partners from arriving at a place where they feel their perspectives have been heard and understood in a mutual way.

Responding to doubt and judgment in the focusing process has typically taken two forms in our work with couples. The selection of strategy is guided by the counselor's assessment of whether doubt and judgment are intended to convey negative affect toward the partner or whether they are the result of a lack of trust. In the former situation, facilitating dyadic functioning and partners' expression of accurate empathy toward one another are called for. In the latter, enhancing trust may actually become a goal for which the couple creates a change plan.

Doubt and mistrust as social punishment. Sometimes doubt or judgment is one partner's way of conveying that the other partner has not fully acknowledged or atoned for the impact of their actions. In these instances, trust is not the problem per se. Partners may very well believe one another's statements are credible. The doubt and mistrust is intended to make a partner "feel bad" for doing something that has been hurtful, upsetting, or frustrating. In these instances, an emphasis on rebuilding trust may not actually help to facilitate consensus. Instead, acknowledging the emotional impact partners are having on one another, catalyzing their expression of accurate empathy toward one another, while facilitating dyadic functioning is more likely to be successful in mitigating expressions of doubt and judgment.

In other instances, doubt or judgment may be the result of a true deficit in trust. Negotiations become increasingly challenging as doubt and judgment increase. If partners do not believe they are communicating honestly, then negotiations become perfunctory and engagement in the counseling process is undermined. At the same time, negotiations are also increasingly challenging when people do not believe they will be believed. If one partner thinks that even if he honestly expresses his preferences, his partner will doubt him, then he has relatively little motivation to state his beliefs. This situation can sometimes arise when partners are unwilling to modify their beliefs about one another's preferences even when presented with new information.

The topic of trust is discussed in greater detail in Chapter 9. In the narrow context of the focusing process, we have found it useful (if admittedly unromantic) to conceptualize trust in purely behavioral terms. From this perspective, **trust might be thought of as the expectancy that a partner's verbal behavior (i.e., "what they say") is a reasonably accurate predictor of what they have done or what they will do.** Can someone's words be used as a meaningful indicator of their actions, past or present? This does not mean that someone has to be 100% correct all of the time. Research on behavioral learning suggests that intermittent reinforcement schedules produce learning (Skinner, 1953), and a stimulus can elicit a response as long as it provides a meaningful amount of information about other events: Perfect accuracy is not required (Rescorla, 1988).

This very behavioral conceptualization of trust is clearly not the only potentially meaningful one. It is offered here because it implies a particular strategy for responding to a true lack of trust. One challenge with trust is the idea that "it has to be earned." While I have no objection to that general concept, it does not provide much information about how one goes about earning or accruing trust. **A behavioral conceptualization of trust, as the expectancy that someone's verbal behavior is a reasonably good indicator of their actions, means that trust might be enhanced by the accrual of evidence that people will "do what they say."** When a couple has struggled to align on a shared goal because partners simply do not believe one another, the rebuilding of trust has sometimes become a preparatory step in the change process. In these instances, couples actually adopt rebuilding trust as the immediate change goal and may develop a plan whereby partners communicate about and verify one another's behavior in a manner that begins to establish new expectancies. Specific strategies for enhancing trust and supporting couples in this goal are discussed further in Chapter 9.

CONCLUSIONS AND KEY POINTS

The end goal of elaborating a dyadic focus is to establish an intervention target and clarify each partner's perspective on change versus the status quo. This is achieved through a two-stage process in which partners first establish a general priority or target behavior and then subsequently elaborate that focus by sharing their perspective, their beliefs about one another's perspectives, and their expectancies about whether their perspective will be believed and accepted. These elements provide the foundation for the evoking process to emerge as salient and a conversation about the potential for behavior change to begin in earnest.

Reaching consensus about what will be discussed, and ensuring that the conversation begins with everyone holding a reasonably accurate understanding of one another's perspectives, increases the likelihood of success in the exploration of potential change.

Common challenges encountered in this process are described along the diagonals of perceived agreement and the diagonals of trust. Challenges involving the diagonal of perceived agreement are characterized by the revelation that partners have an inaccurate understanding of one another's priorities and preferences. Challenges along the diagonals of trust occur when the presence of doubt or judgment between partners precludes them from negotiating with one another in good faith.

While this process is arguably more complex than focusing in individual Motivational Interviewing—due to the presence of multiple people in the room and the interdependent nature of partners' participation in the counseling process—the same general ethical principles guide counselor decision-making. In ideal circumstances, partners successfully negotiate a mutually agreeable priority for counseling, which the counselor is professionally competent to address. When partners cannot agree on a focus, or when the partners align on an agenda that diverges from the counselor's priorities or is beyond the scope of their competence, focusing is more challenging. The counselor must navigate the negotiation of consensus goals or else help the couple evaluate how useful the counseling process can be in the absence of consensus about what they will do with their time together in session.

7

Evoking Change Talk From
a Couple

One of the most daunting challenges faced in the development of Motivational Interviewing with couples has been what to do when partners have divergent views about change. Everything discussed to this point has been in preparation for tackling this concern. Now we take this central conundrum head on. This chapter examines how counselors might go about cultivating change talk while mitigating discord between partners.

Experienced Motivational Interviewing counselors will likely recognize the presence of well-established techniques for evoking change talk in the narrative example and discussions in this chapter. In approaching the challenge of evoking change talk with couples, we did not focus on the development of novel evoking strategies per se. Instead, we focused on providing a framework for counselors to recognize and respond to situations where partners disagree about whether or how change should happen.

The reason for this approach is that, when partners have similar perspectives on change, evoking change talk is relatively straightforward. That does not mean it is easy; it just means that tried-and-true evoking skills that most Motivational Interviewing counselors will be familiar with (e.g., asking evocative questions, coming alongside, agreeing with a twist) (W. R. Miller & Rollnick, 2013) will likely work in the way counselors expect them to. It is in situations that involve dyadic ambivalence about change—instances where partners' perspectives on change conflict—that these well-established strategies are most likely to run amok. As we saw in the narrative example in Chapter 1, when partners have divergent perspectives about change, it becomes increasingly likely that counselor utterances that elicit change talk from one partner simultaneously elicit sustain talk from the other.

It is essential to say from the outset that dyadic ambivalence is not something that once resolved is gone forever. For a more general discussion of how dyadic ambivalence impacts couples' decision-making, readers may refer to Chapter 2. The sections that follow explore the concept of dyadic ambivalence in detail and introduce strategies for responding strategically in instances when partners react to dyadic ambivalence destructively—when relationship discord emerges. While these have proven essential in advancing this framework for couples Motivational Interviewing, no strategy guarantees that just because partners' perspectives on change are aligned at one point in the session they will remain in synchrony thereafter. For example, as counselors amplify change talk, one partner may move in the direction of change faster than the other. This actually produces dyadic ambivalence in session. When this happens, a singular focus on continued amplification of change talk can magnify the difference in partners' perspectives and lead the less motivated partner to argue against change.

Therefore, our premise is that attention to dyadic ambivalence and its successful resolution is an essential and ongoing component of the evoking process unique to Motivational Interviewing with couples. In order to successfully cultivate change talk, counselors must actively look for common ground—shared perspectives on change. To do this, counselors must be able to accurately recognize the emergence of divergent perspectives and help couples navigate discussion of these disagreements in ways that minimize relationship discord and facilitate dyadic functioning in an ongoing way.

DYADIC AMBIVALENCE: WHEN PARTNER PERSPECTIVES ON CHANGE DIVERGE

The concept that an individual can feel ambivalent about a decision—simultaneously aware of both positive and negative consequences of a particular behavioral goal—has been a central tenant of Motivational Interviewing from its outset (Miller & Rose, 2015). This conceptualization of ambivalence is consistent with a wide range of research on decision-making conflict or approach and avoidance across disciplines spanning psychology (e.g., Janis & Mann, 1977); phenomenology (e.g., Cartwright, 1952); behavioral economics (e.g., Noyes & Schlauch, 2018); public health (e.g., Wells et al., 2011); and neuropsychology (e.g., McNaughton et al., 2016). The transtheoretical model of change (Prochaska et al., 2008) acknowledges the potential for ambivalence explicitly in its contemplation stage, which is characterized by an individual's weighing of both the benefits and costs of change.

W. R. Miller and Rollnick (2013, p. 29) offered a practitioner's definition of Motivational Interviewing that highlights the centrality of ambivalence: "Motivational Interviewing is a person-centered counseling style for addressing the common problem of ambivalence about change." Notably, addressing ambivalence does not mean arguing for or proscribing change. Somewhat paradoxically, the conventions of Motivational Interviewing would suggest that the counselor should avoid making or taking on the argument for change (W. R. Miller & Rollnick, 2013; Miller & Rose, 2015). The rationale is that if the counselor makes the argument for change, the client will be motivated to make the counterargument. Instead, the Motivational Interviewing counselor focuses on drawing out or evoking the argument for change from the client (W.

R. Miller & Rollnick, 2013). Rather than providing reasons for change, the counselor might ask why the client would consider change. Rather than educating the client about change, the counselor might ask the client what they know about the benefits of change. Rather than telling a client they need to change, a counselor might amplify through reflections the client's own sense of why change is important.

Dyadic ambivalence represents the interpersonal extension of the concept of ambivalence. If one person can feel two ways about something, certainly two people could potentially feel differently from one another about whether or how change should happen. Ultimately, dyadic ambivalence presents challenges similar to intra-individual ambivalence. Because partners influence or exert social control over one another, their progress toward a goal may be impeded by a lack of consensus or agreement about the desired outcome or how it should be achieved (Lewis, Gladstone, et al., 2006; Lewis, McBride, et al., 2006).

This idea that dyadic ambivalence might inhibit health behavior or goal attainment is supported by research on congruence in dyadic coping with chronic illness and well-being (e.g., Badr, 2004; Bodenmann et al., 2011; Kraemer et al., 2011; Revenson, 1994). Research in this area has generally indicated that congruent coping—particularly similarity in instrumental or active coping that aims to mitigate the stressor—is associated with better psychological adjustment, improved health outcomes, and better dyadic functioning in heterosexual couples.

A smaller body of research has examined congruence and health behavior among sexual minority men specifically. Recently, Starks, Doyle, Bosco, et al. (2021) showed that partners' consensus about COVID-19 prevention was positively associated with relationship satisfaction. In addition, it predicted social distancing and the use of other COVID-19 prevention behaviors among sexual minority men in relationships. Similarly, Lewis, Gladstone, et al. (2006) found that when partners in male couples agreed about health-enhancing behaviors, they were more likely to jointly engage in them. Likewise, agreement about sexual health outcomes specifically has been linked to greater sexual risk reduction in male couples (Salazar et al., 2013).

In the most basic sense, then, dyadic ambivalence occurs as a disagreement in session. It is evidenced by partners voicing different points of view or pointing out the problems with one another's perspectives. As described in the discussion in Chapter 6 of identifying a focus, this might arise because partners have different goals or priorities. It might also arise because partners have divergent perspectives on how they should go about achieving a particular goal, even when they agree on what the end goal should be.

Whenever it emerges, dyadic ambivalence presents the counselor with the task of helping the couple navigate a discussion in which their disagreement is explored in productive ways. Doing so may create opportunities to identify common ground or points of agreement where partners might work together. This can be understood as the task of mitigating relationship discord (or destructive accommodation responses to the disagreement) while facilitating adaptive accommodation (e.g., Rusbult, Zembrodt, et al., 1982; Rusbult, Verette, et al., 1991;

Rusbult, Yovetich, & Verette, 1996; Rusbult, Bissonnette, et al., 1998; Rusbult & Van Lange, 2003). See Chapter 2 for an overview of accommodation and interdependent decision-making as well as a review of Rusbult's taxonomy of accommodation responses.

Notably, merely staving off conflict is not an end unto itself. The counselor must also help the couple capitalize on the opportunity to negotiate consensus that is afforded by adaptive accommodation. In the same way that intra-individual ambivalence has to be addressed before planning can become salient, dyadic—or interpersonal—ambivalence between the partners has to be resolved before they can work together or support one another in a change process. Starks, Millar, et al. (2018) suggested that identifying joint goals—or achieving consensus about whether and how change should happen—was a prerequisite to change planning. Consistent with this, Salazar et al. (2013) argued that dyadic interventions aimed at reducing HIV transmission risk need to facilitate attitude alignment between partners.

The following section describes specific strategies derived to help mitigate the occurrence and intensity of relationship discord and facilitate adaptive accommodation responses to dyadic ambivalence in session. Consistent with O'Leary's (2015) concept of the counselor's role as moderator described in Chapter 3, use of these strategies requires the counselor to recognize the occurrence of conflict and then engage with or disrupt the couple's typical conversational flow. The counselor does this by redirecting the conversation in various ways that not only diminish conflict but also help partners to clarify their perspectives and correct inaccuracies in their understandings of one another's behavior. In other words, these strategies blend elements of conflict mitigation and negotiation.

RESPONDING TO DYADIC AMBIVALENCE: RECOGNIZING AND REDUCING RELATIONSHIP DISCORD

One of the most common questions I am asked when training counselors to conduct Motivational Interviews with couples is: "What do you do when couples fight?" The question has many times led to discussions with trainees that have revealed their beliefs and biases about the necessity and merit of conflict in relationships—as well as my own. Opinions ranged. Some believed that conflict would be harmful and were anxious for strategies to prevent or mitigate it the moment it occurs. Some believed conflict was essential and should be encouraged rather than curtailed. My own stance was, and largely remains, that differences or disagreements are inevitable; however, conflict wherein partners do psychological or emotional harm to one another is not and can be mitigated. It was this question that launched a systematic study of counseling process to identify the most common forms of conflict encountered and effective counselor responses in session (Starks, Robles, et al., 2020).

It is worth noting that conflict here—relationship discord—is conceptualized as destructive accommodation responses to dyadic ambivalence. Strategies in this chapter largely deal with circumstances in which partners respond to one another in destructive ways when confronted with a situation where they feel differently about change. Conflict in this sense excludes arguments between partners that might be considered "off topic" or unrelated to the target behavior. Generalized conflict or chronic deficits in dyadic functioning are probably best responded to with renewed emphasis on the facilitating dyadic functioning process. If there is a global breach in the relationship between the partners that precludes them working together effectively, then that deficit in relationship functioning may need to be attended to before discussion of a specific change goal can proceed. In addition, Chapter 9 provides an overview of couples' communication research and generalized strategies for reducing conflict that apply in situations that may be unrelated to disagreements about a target behavior.

To introduce these manifestations of relationship discord and possible counselor responses, we return to the session with Otto and Rafael that has been ongoing in Chapters 4 through 6. The dialogue in most of this excerpt centers on the target behavior of sexual risk reduction. In the narrative from Chapter 6, it became clear that Otto and Rafael have substantial disagreements around this target behavior. Rafael does not use condoms consistently with casual sex partners, and Otto believes that he should. As the counselor evokes change talk around sexual risk reduction, Otto and Rafael experience some forms of relationship discord commonly seen in Motivational Interviews with couples (Starks, Robles, et al., 2020). Annotations label the counselor strategies used to evoke change talk and also to respond to conflict when it emerges.

* * *

COUNSELOR: OK, so we have this big goal of preserving and protecting the time you two have together. For you two, that means thinking about when it is OK to engage with partners outside your relationship, taking steps to minimize risk when you do that, and also finding ways to connect sexually with one another. You would both like to see that happening more often. [Summary transition begins the evoking process.]

OTTO: When you say it like that, it sounds simple enough, but I feel like it's been really hard to make all that happen.

RAFAEL: And so we end up just kind of not talking about it.

COUNSELOR: It's uncomfortable for you to not be on the same page about this stuff, and you'd like to clear it up. [Dyadic reflection.]

RAFAEL: Right. So you'll be doing that for us?

COUNSELOR: Well, let's see where we can get together. There are, I think, two issues here really to begin with. One has to do with clarifying when sex with other people can happen, and the other has to do with your expectations about sexual safety when things do happen. I am wondering which you guys think we should tackle first?

[Summary and collaboration in agenda setting for the evoking process.]

RAFAEL: So, I think the issue of "when" is handled. If Otto is really OK with whatever as long as we are not hooking up with guys when we could be hanging out, then I think that's that.

COUNSELOR: OK, so we have a clear goal there. Before we leave today, if it is helpful, we could consider a plan for how you might make that happen. But for the most part, we know where we are headed there.

[Summary captures the fact that planning for this focus could begin.]

RAFAEL: Yes.

COUNSELOR: So, that leaves us with sexual safety and STI [sexually transmitted infection] prevention.

[Dyadic reflection shifts attention to the focus where evoking change talk is most relevant.]

OTTO: Where we do not agree.

COUNSELOR: So, you guys have managed to agree on a lot of things in this relationship. You made it through meeting family and work stress. You are thinking about moving in together. What makes this issue so tough to sort out?

[Dyadic reflection emphasizes common ground and investment followed by a question exploring dyadic ambivalence.]

RAFAEL: Honestly, I think it's just different being HIV positive. [to OTTO] I'm just not worried about things in the same way you are.

OTTO: OK, I am sorry to say this, but I feel like that's an excuse. It's not like nothing else matters.

COUNSELOR: So, Otto—there are ways in which you still feel concerned for Rafael. Even though he has HIV, you still worry about what would happen if he encountered other STIs.

[Complex reflection explicitly labels Otto's concern and worry for Rafael.]

OTTO: Right. I feel like you are blowing off everything else.

COUNSELOR: And that is upsetting to you. That idea, that thought, that maybe he is not taking care of himself as well as he could, it makes you frustrated.

[Complex reflection labels Otto's emotion.]

OTTO: Yes.

COUNSELOR: Rafael, what do you make of that?

[Question elicits Rafael's perspective.]

RAFAEL: I mean, look, I appreciate that he is concerned. And I guess I probably should be too. This past month, the chlamydia thing, has not been fun. On some level, I know he's right. I have HIV. I don't also need hepatitis or herpes or whatever. I just hate having to think about one more thing related to sex. Like, I spend so much time thinking about HIV—or wishing I wasn't thinking about HIV—that I sort of resent having to also think about other stuff.

COUNSELOR: So, even though sometimes it might look like you don't care, you really do. In fact, sometimes you kinda get tired of having to care all the time about this stuff.

[Complex reflection directed to Rafael.]

RAFAEL: Right, like, HIV is always there. Every day.

OTTO: I guess I didn't realize that you felt that way. You always seem to handle it so well.

COUNSELOR: In some ways, you guys are both concerned about how Rafael is taking care of himself. You're just focused on different things.

[Dyadic reflection emphasizes common ground.]

OTTO: I just assumed that you were sort of being careless.

RAFAEL: No, trust me, I know what happens then. I've had times, not that long ago, when I was so tired of thinking about this I got bad about taking my meds. My viral load and stuff got really out of whack. It was right as we were getting together actually.

OTTO: Huh. I had the sense there was something going on then. Like, you made some reference to your doctor not being happy with you. But I didn't realize how bad that got.

RAFAEL: Well, it's not something I really love talking about. And the couple of times I've tried to bring it up, I felt like you were not all that interested.

OTTO: Wait, when was that?

COUNSELOR: So, if I could jump in for a second, Rafael, this is something that is tough to talk about—the challenges of living with HIV—and it is also something you would like to be able to be more open about with Otto.

[Dyadic reflection disrupts potential argument conflict and emphasizes the couple's shared desire to discuss the topic.]

RAFAEL: Right. I guess I'm just sort of afraid that getting too far into it will mess things up or something.

OTTO: I feel like it's a little unfair that you've never even given me a chance to understand it all.

COUNSELOR: Otto, you are frustrated because there are things Rafael hasn't told you about fully and you would like to be supportive to him around this.

[Complex reflection explicitly labels Otto's emotion and intention.]

OTTO: Right. He'd have to decide he wants to open up about it.

COUNSELOR: Rafael, I wonder if you could help us understand where—from your perspective—communication around this broke down.

[Question invites Rafael to share his perspective.]

RAFAEL: So, it's not like it's all the time. But sometimes I have tried to tell you about how annoying it is to have to take meds forever and ever. And you jump in with a whole bunch of instructions for how I could make it easier. Or I have talked about the fact that hookups are complicated for me, and you act like it would all be supereasy if I just used condoms. Like that would make it all go away. I think part of why you think I handle being HIV positive well is that you kinda don't want to hear that I don't. You always just want to fix everything.

OTTO: Yikes. I thought I was being helpful.

COUNSELOR: Otto, help us understand what your intention was in those moments. What did you want to have happen?

[Question elicits Otto's intention.]

OTTO: I think I am someone who, when I see a problem, I want to fix it. I can think of examples he's talking about, and I really thought he was looking for was help fixing the problem.

COUNSELOR: You are willing to help. You want to be supportive.

[Reflection emphasizes Otto's intention.]

OTTO: Right. I actually feel really bad that apparently that was just shutting you down.

COUNSELOR: Rafael, what would have been helpful in those moments? What could Otto have done differently when you brought up HIV meds or STI prevention stuff?

[Question elicits Rafael's perspective on how Otto could better achieve his intention to provide support.]

RAFAEL: I just needed him to understand that this isn't always as simple for me as it seems to be for him. In a lot of ways, looking at a condom for me is a big reminder of all the mistakes I made and the problems sex has created in my life. It's not sexy.

COUNSELOR: So when you brought up challenges around medication adherence or condom use, you were not actually asking for help "solving a problem." It might have sounded that way, but the truth is, you don't really need someone to tell you what you "should" be doing—you kinda know that already. What would be helpful is having someone understand that doing "what you should" is hard.

[Summary clarifies Rafael's communication goals and needs.]

RAFAEL: Right. Like, the advice doesn't help. It just makes me feel like a whiner or a failure.

COUNSELOR: Otto, my hunch is that's not the effect you're hoping to have.

[Reflection directs attention to Otto's intentions.]

OTTO: Not at all. That's genuinely never what I meant to do.

RAFAEL: I mean, it doesn't happen all that often. Generally, you're really helpful. It's just around this issue. And I think this issue has been a really big deal for the past month.

COUNSELOR: So, part of what we are learning here is— [Dyadic reflection
whatever decisions you guys make about condom use with summarizes
other partners—sexual health is really important to you common ground.]
both. Rafael's health, how he is managing HIV and taking
care of himself, matters to you both.

OTTO: Yeah, I think that there was a lot that I didn't
necessarily realize was going on.

COUNSELOR: So, I find myself wondering, Rafael, what [Evocative
impact—if any—does all of this have on your thoughts question directed
about condom use and STI prevention? to Rafael.]

RAFAEL: I mean . . . ugh. As much as it's kind of a drag,
I suppose I should give some thought to condoms.

COUNSELOR: It's not your favorite idea. And some things [Complex
about it might be worthwhile. (double-sided)
reflection to
Rafael.]

* * *

Otto and Rafael mutually agreed on the need to discuss sexual health and risk
reduction in the Chapter 6 narrative that illustrated the focusing process. Despite
that agreement on focus, tension, anxiety, and disagreement emerge as the evoking
process moves into the foreground. They agreed sexual risk reduction should be
a topic of focus in session; they did not immediately agree on what they should
go about doing.

The example here included three common communication habits that create
or sustain conflict and serve as barriers to constructive accommodation. These
are exchanges that if left unchecked in session could potentially eclipse any
opportunity for partners to come together around a goal. Recognizing these
exchanges—and understanding why they tend to sustain conflict—provides context for the strategies the counselor used to mitigate conflict and catalyze successful negotiation.

Conflation of (My) Thoughts and (Your)
Feelings—The "I Statement" Gone Wrong

Perhaps the most glaring and overt communication habit that promotes or sustains
relationship discord happens when one partner presents their hunch about what
the other partner is thinking as though it was their own emotion. For example,
Otto says to Rafael: "I feel like *that's an excuse. It's not like nothing else matters.*" The
problem is that: "That's an excuse. It's not like nothing else matters" is not a feeling.

It is Otto's thought, his hunch or hypothesis, about what Rafael is thinking. "Anger," "frustration," "worry," or "concern," are all feelings or emotions Otto might experience in conjunction with this thought; however, instead of accurately naming his own emotion, Otto is narrating what he thinks Rafael is thinking.

These utterances can sound on the surface like the kind of "I statements" that are characteristic of assertive communication (Gordon, 1970); however, their impact is fundamentally different. Correctly executed, "I statements" disclose the speaker's thoughts and feelings accurately, and they "locate the problem inside the speaker" (Burr, 1990, p. 266). They are therefore less likely to be perceived as accusatory or elicit defensiveness (Gordon, 1970). An effective I statement in Otto's situation might be something like: "I'm concerned that you are gonna get another STI, and I'm scared of what that will mean for you and for us." In contrast, the utterances that conflate thoughts and feelings implicitly shift the focus away from the speaker and onto the other person. In this way, they function more like "you statements" that just happen to begin with "I" (Burr, 1990). A statement such as, "I feel like you think I'm unattractive" sounds like an I statement, but it is more likely to be experienced as, "You think I'm unattractive" than "I feel unattractive." As a result, statements that conflate thoughts and feelings are particularly likely to elicit defensiveness from the other partner in a manner similar to the blaming and defensiveness pattern of coercive exchange noted by Christensen et al. (1995).

Responding to the conflation of thoughts and feelings. The narrative provides several examples of the counselor responding strategically to the emergence of conflict arising from the conflation of thoughts and feelings. Timing is a critical component of success here. When one partner makes an utterance that conflates thoughts and feelings, it is likely that the other will respond defensively. One essential aspect of the counselor's strategy then is to interject as quickly as possible after the conflation of thoughts and feelings before a coercive exchange gains momentum.

The counselor accurately labels emotions. The counselor not only interrupts the couple's exchange, but also utilizes individual-level reflections to accurately label the speaker's emotions.

> OTTO: OK, I am sorry to say this, but I feel like that's an excuse. It's not like nothing else matters.
> COUNSELOR: So, Otto—there are ways in which *you still feel concerned* for Rafael. Even though he has HIV, *you still worry* about what would happen if he encountered other STIs.

In effect, the counselor's utterance models an effective I statement or achieves the function an I statement would achieve. It refocuses the conversation on the emotional disclosure implied in Otto's utterance and reduces the likelihood that Rafael will hear Otto's statement as an accusation and respond defensively.

This same objective could be achieved through the use of an open question. In this case, the exchange might look like the following.

OTTO: OK, I am sorry to say this, but I feel like that's an excuse. It's not like nothing else matters.

COUNSELOR: Otto, when you have that thought—that Rafael may be making an excuse for acting like his health is not important—what emotion does that bring up for you? How do you feel when you think that?

Here, the counselor is accurately relabeling Otto's utterance as a disclosure of his thoughts about Rafael. The counselor then asks Otto to label for himself the feeling that he experiences "when he has that thought." The essential element is that the counselor steps into the dialogue to clarify thoughts and feelings accurately before stepping back and inviting Rafael to respond.

Vague or Indirect Communication

Starks, Robles, et al. (2020) observed that misunderstandings or misinterpretation of indirect forms of communication were another common source of relationship discord in session. Implicit or indirect signals are perfectly legitimate forms of communication; however, they rely on the assumption that partners in the exchange understand—or can infer—what the signal means in compatible ways (Yus, 1999). As a result, they are relatively more prone to misunderstandings, especially in instances when partners do not have access to—or do not apply— the same contextual knowledge to the interpretation of what has been conveyed (Yus, 1999).

In the narrative here, one of the reasons why Otto struggled to successfully identify when Rafael was interested in talking about his experiences of living with HIV was because Rafael indicated his desire using vague and indirect cues. He talked about specific challenges with medication adherence or condom use rather than more directly expressing the feelings he was having. Otto's intention was to provide support and assistance; however, Rafael interpreted Otto's suggestions as indicating a lack of interest in his emotional experience. Starks, Robles, et al. (2020) suggested this kind of communication habit may be particularly likely to lead to neglect accommodation response. Both partners feel that they have tried to discuss the issue; both have the sense that the other partner did not respond well; and both let it go because they decide they want to avoid the fight. The phenomenon is similar to the mutual avoidance pattern of communication (Christensen, 1987, 1988; Christensen & Shenk, 1991) discussed in Chapter 9.

Unfortunately, avoidance prevents the development of more effective communication habits. Because Otto and Rafael do not explicitly discuss their misunderstanding, they are not able to align their implicit vocabulary. In this way, the misunderstanding is perpetuated by neglect and becomes a recurring source of frustration. The pattern repeats over and over for the partners because they continue to utilize signals that mean different things to each of them.

Responding to conflict arising from vague or indirect communication. The antidote to this is to facilitate a discussion about these signals. By asking Rafael to identify "what Otto missed," the counselor makes Rafael's implicit and vague re-quest for emotional support explicit. The counselor's move to clarify the meaning of various behavioral signals used by the partners creates the possibility for them to align their implicit vocabularies and communicate more effectively.

Crucial to the execution of this response is the counselor's nonjudgmental stance. The exploration of implicit communication is not undertaken with the intent of finding out "who is at fault" or "which partner got it wrong." Rather, the counselor frames the misunderstanding as arising from an unintentional circumstance in which two people simply had different ways of conveying an idea. It is not so much that one person was communicating correctly and the other was in error, but rather that the couple needs to clarify what particular signals mean for each partner.

Inaccurate Assumptions of Intention

Perceived intention matters. Social information-processing models of aggres-sion in children (e.g., Crick & Dodge, 1994; Dodge & Crick, 1990) and adults (e.g., Linder et al., 2010) have for decades suggested that the way we interpret social cues—the meanings we assign to someone else's behavior—is a determi-nant of how we respond to them. These kinds of assumptions about intention also contributed to the emergence of discord between Otto and Rafael in ses-sion. Even though Otto's intention was to be helpful by providing advice to Rafael about how he could handle HIV medication adherence or condom use, Rafael assumed that Otto's advice signaled a lack of desire to engage meaningfully with his feelings about these struggles. The impetus for conflict was generated not so much by what Otto did, but by Rafael's inferences about the reasons, motivations, or intentions behind Otto's advice giving. As long as Rafael assumes that Otto's advice and suggestions are motivated by a desire to avoid the topic of what it feels like to live with HIV, Otto's attempts at helping are aversive.

Responding to inaccurate assumptions of intention. One way in which inac-curate assumptions of intention sustain conflict is by triggering a cycle of blaming and defensiveness (Christensen et al., 1995). This coercive exchange does little to clarify partners' understandings of one another's motivation. The counselor can diffuse this exchange by interjecting to first draw out and then align assumed and actual intention. In the example, we see this done initially with a question.

OTTO: Yikes. I thought I was being helpful.

COUNSELOR: Otto, help us understand what your intention was in those moments. What did you want to have happen?

Later in the exchange, the counselor uses a reflection to achieve a similar goal:

RAFAEL: Right. Like, the advice doesn't help. It just makes me feel like a whiner or a failure.

COUNSELOR: Otto, my hunch is that's not the effect you're hoping to have.

In these moments, the counselor takes on the role of moderator in the dialogue for a time (O'Leary, 2015). They step in to create space for Otto to explain what his intentions were—and his caring concern for Rafael. The counselor also invites Rafael to explain the response he hoped for from Otto and how this contrasts with the actual effect Otto's advice had on him. Critical to the execution of this strategy is that the counselor's questions are directed to each partner and invite the partner to explain his own experience. In other words, the counselor's questions prime the partners to respond with I statements that contain productive self-disclosure as opposed to you statements that might be more likely to promote and sustain conflict (Gordon, 1970).

ADDITIONAL STRATEGIES FOR RESPONDING TO DYADIC AMBIVALENCE

While some counselor strategies were seen as particularly relevant to specific kinds of conflict, Starks, Robles, et al. (2020) identified a number of additional strategies that counselors used flexibly through the session to facilitate adaptive accommodation and decrease dyadic ambivalence. These can be thought of as more general evoking skills relevant to work with couples. They provide the counselor with a lexicon of strategies that can be used to sustain productive discussions about disagreements and probe the potential for consensus.

Shifting focus. Counselors may already be familiar with the strategy of shifting focus—or "responding to discord [between counselor and client] by redirecting attention and discussion to a less contentions topic or perspective"—as it is used in individual Motivational Interviewing (W. R. Miller & Rollnick, 2013, p. 430). In couples Motivational Interviewing, shifting focus takes on an additional dimension. It can be used to respond to discord between partners by redirecting attention and discussion toward the identification of outcomes more desirable to the couple and away from the apportionment of blame or responsibility.

In the example narrative, Otto and Rafael discussed previous attempts to talk about Rafael's experience of living with HIV. Recounting this kind of event has the potential to activate a blaming and defensiveness exchange as the partners try to determine who bears "fault" or "responsibility" for the conversation not going well. If the counselor allocated attention to arbitrating or litigating this dispute about the burden of blame, it would imperil their maintenance of the nonjudgmental stance that is consistent with the Spirit of Motivational Interviewing. Instead, the counselor shifts focus away from "who is to blame" by refocusing on what Rafael wishes Otto had done.

COUNSELOR: Rafael, what would have been helpful in those moments? What could Otto have done differently when you brought up HIV meds or STI prevention stuff.

This shift—to identify a preferred past—elicits an adaptive behavioral alternative. Rafael tells Otto directly what he could have done—and what he might do in the future—when the topic comes up. An alternative but equivalent shift in focus might explore a more ideal future exchange. This is embodied in the question: "If you found yourself in that situation again, what do you hope you might do?" This ideal future question achieves a similar end. It elicits a discussion of more adaptive and desirable behaviors that can be utilized in the future.

Relationship repair. The strategy of shifting focus, retains an emphasis on the source of conflict. What happens when considering "what couples wish had happened" or "what they hope happens next time" is not enough to alleviate hurt feelings and frustrations? Not every conflict can be solved with instrumental action (Carver et al., 1989). Some decisions cannot be undone; some mistakes cannot be unmade. In these instances, the couple is faced with the task of coping with negative emotions that cannot be addressed by "doing something" about the source of the stressor.

In these instances, counselors may find it useful to focus on the couple's capacity for relationship repair (Starks, Robles, et al., 2020). This redirects attention and discussion toward identifying ways in which partners can help each other feel better. This might involve an exploration of how the couple has gotten through, gotten past, or gotten over prior challenges. Alternatively, the counselor might invite the couple to think about the times and ways that partners have provided care and comfort or effectively expressed concern for one another. The overall goal is to examine the potential for couples to provide emotional support to one another and affirm their relationship even as they tolerate challenges and recover from missteps.

"Common ground" reflections are a particular use of dyadic reflections first introduced in Chapter 4. The initial example narrative in this chapter contains multiple instances in which the counselor points out the Otto and Rafael's shared goals and values, for example: "In some ways, you guys are both concerned about how Rafael is taking care of himself. You're just focused on different things." This kind of reflection serves to highlight areas where the partners agree. It reminds them that they are working together toward some larger shared goal, and that common ground may exist even in the face of disagreement.

In individual Motivational Interviewing, a counselor might utilize a complex reflection to highlight a discrepancy between individual goals and values and a particular behavior. "You have had some struggles in keeping your drinking within the limits you would like to set for yourself, and yet you are generally someone who is really responsible about how you take care of yourself." This kind of reflection amplifies cognitive dissonance in a manner that may motivate the client to bring their behavior in line with their values.

Common ground reflections work in a similar way. The counselor highlights the discrepancy between the couple's agreement around some shared goal or value and their discrepant behavior in a particular moment. The effect is to elicit a conversation about what they could do differently going forward so that their behavior aligns with their values about the relationship. It simultaneously highlights an established success. The couple has reached agreement about some things—their relationship is characterized by some shared values and perspectives—which may facilitate achieving agreement in the present moment.

Dyadic affirmations were discussed in Chapter 4 as an extension of OARS (open questions, affirmations, reflections, and summary statements) and in Chapter 5 as a mechanism to facilitate dyadic functioning. In the evoking process, they become a potential mechanism by which counselors can activate a conversation about how a client might capitalize on prior success or existing resources to create change. Similarly, the counselor's use of dyadic affirmations highlights the couple's potential for change and then creates space to discuss how they might go about doing that.

BEYOND CONFLICT MITIGATION—EVOKING DYADIC MOTIVATION FOR CHANGE

Mitigating relationship discord in session is important; however, it is not the end goal of the evoking phase unto itself. Ideally, the counselor needs to capitalize on adaptive accommodation responses to achieve consensus and then subsequently draw out change talk related to the identified target behavior. The first narrative example in this chapter served primarily to illustrate the use of conflict mitigation strategies. In this second narrative, the counselor intersperses these strategies with more conventional evoking techniques as they continue the discussion about sexual health and risk reduction with Otto and Rafael.

* * *

COUNSELOR: So, we have a lot more context now for understanding why you two might see condoms differently. Rafael, for you condoms represent some things you feel bad about; Otto, for you they are a way of taking care of yourself—something that actually reduces worries. [Dyadic reflection summarizing previous discussion.]

OTTO: Right. Like, now I kinda feel stuck. Because I don't want to make him feel bad about things, but I do genuinely think it would be better if he used condoms.

COUNSELOR: And Rafael, you don't like thinking about condoms, and also some part of you has considered that they might have some benefits. [Double-sided reflection directed to Rafael ending with change talk.]

RAFAEL: Yeah, I mean, I know that.

COUNSELOR: What, from your perspective, are the reasons why anyone might bother to use condoms?

[Evocative question eliciting Rafael's reasons for change.]

RAFAEL: It's not like we haven't just seen the consequences of playing around without them this past month.

COUNSELOR: The last month has not been fun, and you two don't want to be in this place again. Neither of you is crazy about the idea of getting another STI.

[Dyadic reflection of shared reasons for change.]

RAFAEL: I mean, look, using condoms has to have some limits though. Like it's actually easier to consider using them as a top than when I bottom.

OTTO: Surprising. I'd have thought the opposite. It feels more important for the bottom.

RAFAEL: Right, but who wants to ask the guy you are hooking up with to use a condom? That's awkward.

OTTO: I feel like you just say exactly that. You just tell them that.

COUNSELOR: So, for you Otto, that conversation is not hard. It is one you feel confident having regardless of sexual position. But Rafael, you actually are more open to condoms when you're a top because you feel like the decision is easier to make.

[Dyadic reflection accurately labels each partner's view of condom use with an emphasis on change talk.]

OTTO: Why is that? If I can ask. I'm honestly curious.

RAFAEL: I just worry about what they'll think. Or how awkward it is to stop everything and ask a guy to put one on.

OTTO: Honestly, someone who isn't willing to do that doesn't deserve to be hooking up with you.

RAFAEL: Maybe, but it's still hard to be the one who enforces that.

COUNSELOR: Rafael, for you there is something emotionally different about bottoming versus topping.

[Reflection refocuses discussion on Rafael's emotions.]

OTTO: And I guess, I'm sorry to interrupt, but I do actually get that. Like, I say that it's easy to talk about condoms, and I guess for me it is because I'm just pushy like that. But being a bottom can be a lot more vulnerable or whatever.

RAFAEL: That, exactly. In some ways, I think the right thing to do is for me to just not bottom with other people. Like, hooking up with other guys is fine, for like oral sex and maybe topping. But when I think of sex that I regret, it's almost always when I was bottoming and just went along with something I later wish I hadn't.

COUNSELOR: So the idea of using condoms with other partners is something that gets easier to consider if you actually put some limits on what kinds of sex you have there.

[Reflection of Rafael's change talk.]

RAFAEL: Yeah.

COUNSELOR: And that is, in a lot of ways, consistent with you guys' larger goal of keeping some sense of "specialness" about your relationship and your time together. There are maybe some sexual positions that feel more comfortable together than they would with other people.

[Dyadic reflection linking potential change to larger goals and values.]

RAFAEL: Right. I feel really comfortable with Otto, and there's stuff that I just don't have to worry about there.

* * *

In the first narrative of this chapter, Rafael and Otto arrived at a point where they were able to understand and empathize with one another's perspectives about condom use. The counselor successfully catalyzed voice-type accommodation responses to dyadic ambivalence. Rather than arguing about condoms, Rafael and Otto were able to share their thoughts and feelings about the behavior; however, that alone did not help them sort out what they wanted to do. It brought them together, but did not necessarily amplify motivation for change.

In this second narrative, the counselor goes on to flexibly implement traditional evoking skills while attending to dyadic ambivalence in an ongoing way. Both are essential. Imagine how different the conversation might have gone if the counselor had allowed the dialogue to devolve into an argument about whether it should be easy to talk with a sexual partner about using condoms. By rapidly interjecting with a reflection that refocused the discussion on Rafael's feelings, the counselor mitigated the potential discord between partners. At the same time, it is the counselor's utterances that draw out change talk, reflect back and amplify reasons for change, and link potential change to broader goals and values that ultimately generate motivation for change.

CONCLUSIONS AND KEY POINTS

Dyadic ambivalence occurs when partners have divergent perspectives on change. Because partners' influence one another's behavior, this lack of consensus can be a barrier to goal attainment. Exploring areas of disagreement can sometimes elicit relationship discord, or conflict between partners in session. Successful evoking therefore requires a repertoire of skills for mitigating conflict to supplement more traditional skills for drawing out and amplifying change talk. This in turn creates the opportunity for partners to consider one another's perspectives and resolve dyadic ambivalence through consensus. Only after such consensus has been achieved can counselors employ skills to cultivate change talk.

Three common manifestations of dyadic discord—conflict or destructive accommodation—are described. The conflation of thoughts and feelings involves the misuse of I statements. One partner expresses their belief about what the other partner is thinking in terms of their own feelings, for example: "I feel like you think I'm unattractive." Vague and indirect forms of communication lead to conflict when partners fail to recognize one another's signals accurately and interpret their meaning correctly. Inaccurate assumptions of intention involve incorrect inferences about a partner's motivation. Conflict in this instance is less about what a partner did and more about the inferred reason for doing it.

Counselor strategies for responding to relationship discord or conflict in session involve the accurate reflection of emotion, the explication of communication norms, and the clarification of partners' intention. In addition, a number of more general skills are relevant to the mitigation of conflict, including shifting focus away from blame (and toward the exploration of a preferred past or ideal future exchange), consideration of relationship repair, as well as dyadic reflections and relationship affirmations.

8

Planning—Taking Action Together

In the narrative example from Chapter 2, the counselor helped Jarred and Alex identify common ground—to see their two strategies (pre-exposure prophylaxis [PrEP] and condom use) as different routes to achieve a larger goal they both shared (i.e., HIV prevention). In that scenario, the partners shifted toward support for one another's strategy. If the example had gone on, the counselor and couple may have progressed from the exploration of potential change to planning for actual change. The planning process—characterized by the articulation of a clear and actionable goal and the identification of steps that could be taken to achieve it—might have become salient.

Many elements of the planning process with couples are similar to change planning with individual clients. Experienced counselors will likely recognize these components as familiar. This chapter focuses primarily on aspects of change planning that are unique to couples Motivational Interviewing. It utilizes principles from goal-setting (Locke & Latham, 2006) and interdependence theory to conceptualize the role partners play in goal setting and attainment. It concludes with the presentation of three case examples: prototypical planning scenarios commonly encountered in couples Motivational Interviewing. The first two involve instances where partners are able to arrive at a shared goal for change. In the first of these scenarios, change is mutual. Both partners set a goal to change their behavior, and they discuss ways to support one another in a change process that is highly reciprocal. In the second scenario, change is applicable only to one partner in the couple. This scenario demonstrates how one partner can support the other's change process even when they are not changing themselves. The third scenario involves a circumstance where partners are unable to agree on a change goal.

THE ROLE OF PARTNERS IN GOAL FORMATION AND ATTAINMENT

Much about the change planning process in Motivational Interviewing is aligned with goal-setting theory. Decades of research in this area has examined the impact of goals on behavior (Latham, 2001; Locke & Latham, 2006). Interest in the relationship between goal formation and performance spans contexts as diverse as the productivity of logging crews (Latham, 2001) and patient compliance with psychotherapy for psychogenic nonepileptic seizures (Tolchin et al., 2020). Across this large body of work, researchers have identified characteristics of effective goals, mechanisms by which they influence behavior, and factors that moderate their effects.

Characteristics of Effective Goals

Specificity counts. Not all goals are equal in their ability to influence behavior. Setting out to "do your best" to "try hard" or to "make it work this time" may be a subjectively meaningful aspiration; however, these kinds of vague goals are not very good predictors of behavior. The goals that have the most impact on what individuals do are specific (Latham, 2001; Locke & Latham, 2006). They articulate a concrete behavioral objective rather than a vague aspiration. It is the difference between "This is the week I am going to drink less" and "I am only going to drink on 2 days this week, and no more than 3 drinks each time." The first statement expresses an intention to change; however, the second statement provides a description of the actual behavior that is planned.

The impact of goals on behavior increases with their ambition (Latham, 2001; Locke & Latham, 2006). Setting goals high leads individuals to put more effort into accomplishing them. The theoretical mechanism is that goal attainment is reinforcing. Goals become the metric by which we determine how satisfied we are with our own performance (Locke & Latham, 2006). We feel good when we hit the marks we set and finish a job. The harder the job, the greater that sense of accomplishment. Goal setting therefore impacts performance by providing a clear direction for behavior as well as enhancing motivation to work hard and persist.

While ambitious goals may inspire hard work, impossible goals demoralize. There is one important caveat to the notion that ambitious goals enhance achievement. When the ambition of a goal exceeds our capacity to accomplish it, the impact of the goal is diminished (Latham, 2001; Locke & Latham, 2006). The appropriateness of a goal—whether or not it is reasonable or realistically attainable—is therefore dependent on an individual client's circumstances. The degree of ambitiousness—whether a goal is "easy" or "hard" to achieve—must be evaluated in the context of the client's ability, available resources, interpersonal support, and competing priorities.

The characteristics of effective goals outlined in goal-setting theory are commonly captured in the acronym SMART (Clutterbuck & Spence, 2017; Muller & Kotte, 2020; R. S. Rubin, 2002). This framework is broadly popular across a range of disciplines. While there is considerable variability in the exact terms implied by the acronym (R. S. Rubin, 2002), SMART goals are commonly described in some way as being specific, measurable, actionable, realistic, and time bound (Clutterbuck & Spence, 2017). These characteristics remain applicable in the context of goal setting in couples Motivational Interviewing; however, several unique elements emerge when a partner is present in the change process.

Dependence and goal attainment: Implications for Motivational Interviewing with couples. The narrative examples that follow illustrate situations in which counselors work with a couple to not only clarify a goal with SMART features, but also ensure that both partners are invested in goal development. Plans will incorporate ways partners can support one another's efforts and provide feedback to one another while enacting their plans. It is reasonable to wonder why a counselor might place so much emphasis on the development of shared or couple-level goals and change plans. It is possible to imagine a situation in which they instead prioritize developing individualized goals specific to each partner. In this individualized paradigm, counselors might focus on having each partner in the couple identify specific steps they would take toward their own goal without worrying about the roles they might play in supporting one another's efforts.

The rationale for conceptualizing goal formation and change planning as a couple-level activity—something partners do together—was alluded to in the overview of interdependent decision-making. (See Chapter 2.) Sometimes a goal cannot be accomplished without a partner's support. Even when a goal could be accomplished by one partner alone, goal attainment is more likely when a supportive partner promotes success (Righetti et al., 2016; Rusbult & Van Lange, 2008).

Partners' behavior toward one another during the planning process can be understood—at least in part—in terms of the level and mutuality of dependence required to realize their desired outcome (e.g., Rusbult & Van Lange, 2003). When one partner has the ability to realize their goals, meet their needs, or gratify their desires on their own, the situation is defined by a high degree of independence (i.e., low dependence). In contrast, when the ability to realize a goal, meet a need, or achieve a desire relies—all or in part—on the actions of one's partner, the situation is defined by a high degree of dependence.

Consider the situation of Jarred and Alex (from narrative examples in Chapters 1 and 2). Jarred was interested in using PrEP to prevent HIV infection. Imagine a hypothetical situation in which Jarred does not need Alex's logistical support to access PrEP. In this situation, Jarred has his own insurance and ability to pay for any expenses associated with PrEP. He also has access without Alex's assistance or support to medical care and a provider knowledgeable about PrEP. In such a case, whether Jarred makes and keeps an appointment with a physician to discuss PrEP is a decision that he ultimately has the power to make relatively independently of Alex. If he were to get a PrEP prescription, whether or not he takes his daily pill as prescribed, is primarily a behavior under his individual control. Under these circumstances, interdependence theory would label PrEP uptake as an *actor-controlled* behavior (e.g., Rusbult & Van Lange, 2003). This is because Jarred largely has the power to realize his goal on his own if he decided to do so.

Alex's ability to inhibit Jarred's uptake of PrEP in this hypothetical situation arises through social control or influence rather than instrumental power. For example, Alex could encourage and remind Jarred to take his PrEP; alternatively, he could ridicule him for doing so. While neither response directly determines whether Jarred takes his PrEP, Alex's support might help Jarred be more successful; meanwhile, Alex's criticism might diminish Jarred's motivation for PrEP and harm their relationship generally over time.

Now, imagine a contrasting set of hypothetical circumstances in which Jarred has decided to start PrEP, but he is reliant on Alex for medical insurance and financial support. In this case, Alex may be able to exert substantial instrumental power over Jarred's ability to access PrEP. Even though Jarred may have concluded that PrEP is right for him, he will need Alex's support and approval to process the medical insurance claim and pay for the medication. This kind of situation is characterized by a degree of *partner control* (e.g., Rusbult & Van Lange, 2003).

In contrast to goals that fall under actor or partner control, goals that involve *joint control* require both partners to contribute to attainment (Rusbult & Van Lange, 2003). One example of joint control is a couple's decision to be monogamous. If either partner in the relationship decides to deviate from the goal of monogamy, the couple as a whole is nonmonogamous. The couple can only achieve monogamy if both partners work together to maintain behavior consistent with their agreement.

As summarized by Rusbult and Van Lange (2003), the degree of dependence required for goal attainment shapes how partners relate to one another. The more dependent someone is on their partner to achieve a goal—in other words, in a situation characterized by a high degree of partner or joint control—the more attuned they tend to be to their partner. Individuals pay more attention to the nuances of a situation—they dedicate more effort to understanding their partner's perspective and anticipating their partners' actions—in situations where they are dependent on their partner to achieve a desired outcome (Rusbult & Van Lange, 2003).

Once a goal is articulated, Motivational Interviewing counselors can use partners' level and mutuality of dependence to inform the planning process with couples. The way partners negotiate a goal, and the contributions they can make to goal attainment, can be anticipated in part from the level and mutuality of their dependence on one another. This also provides a framework for considering how the counselor might tailor their role in supporting the planning process.

The more dependent partners are—the more they need one another to accomplish a goal because it is under partner or joint control—the more likely they are to spontaneously share information that clarifies their preferences and priorities in goal setting (Rusbult & Van Lange, 2003). In such instances, the counselor may be able to largely assume the role of reflective observer in the planning process. The couple may primarily need the counselor to step s into the dialogue to support adaptive accommodation if dyadic ambivalence emerges or to confirm (through empathic reflections and summaries) that both partners are hearing and understanding one another accurately.

Not all goals characterized by a high degree of dependence will necessarily result in spontaneous and productive negotiation. For a variety of reasons, it is plausible that some couples might struggle to discuss a change plan together even in situations where the partners need one another to achieve a goal. In some instances, partners may lack the communication skills necessary to convey their perspective. In other instances, partners may simply have limited experience working together, and they may be unsure of how to support one another. It is also possible that couples have struggled to work together successfully in the past. In this case, talking about how they can work together toward a change goal now might activate resentments about past actions that derail the planning process.

When goals are dependent and partners struggle to engage with one another in the planning process, counselors may need to assume a more active role to evoke a productive discussion. Part of this involves drawing out each partner's perspectives on goals and related plans. To do so successfully, counselors may need to be prepared to support couples in a variety of ways. This might include the incorporation of communication or problem-solving skills training if challenges emerge around partners' ability to express themselves. See Chapters 9 and 11 for discussions of such practice integration. It might also include ongoing attention to facilitating dyadic functioning when discussions of planning evoke relationship discord.

When goals are under partner control, counselors may need to address power disparities that could emerge during change planning. While situations involving joint control tend to elicit coordination and collaborative problem-solving, situations involving mutual partner control often elicit quid pro quo resolutions involving the exchange of actions (e.g., "If you do this for me, I'll do that for you") (Rusbult & Van Lange, 2003). These exchange-type approaches to planning or problem-solving implicitly assume that there is something each partner can do for the other. Their mutual reliance on one another creates a situation where they can each achieve a desired outcome through a "trade-off" of some kind.

There is no inherent guarantee that partner control is equitably distributed within a couple. When only one partner in the relationship is highly reliant on the other—when dependence is not mutual—they are placed in a position of relative vulnerability. They have less leverage in a negotiation involving a trade-off. A partner with more power may have less motivation to understand or consider their partner's perspective when planning for change. At the same time, a partner with less power may feel pressured to make substantial sacrifices when planning for change because they need their partner in ways that are not particularly mutual. While counselors cannot proscribe equitable change plans without violating the Spirit of Motivational Interviewing, they can help both partners consider the impact of a change plan on their personal well-being and their relationship overall. This might include inviting a partner with relatively more power and control to consider the perspective of the partner with less power. It might also include inviting a partner with less power to evaluate the sacrifices they are willing to make and what they believe they deserve in return from their relationship. The issue of power receives considerable attention in Chapter 9. Strategies for recognizing power disparities in couples communication and responding in ways that enhance equity are discussed there along with relevant procedures for screening and responding to intimate partner violence.

Finally, in situations characterized by low dependence, counselors may need to be more active in drawing out partners' views about change. When partners need one another to accomplish a goal, they may be generally more aware of the potential for their actions to impact one another's outcomes. In contrast, when a goal is largely under actor control, a partner may be less aware of the social and emotional influence of their actions on goal attainment. Counselors may need to actively invite partners to consider how they can support—or avoid inhibiting—change.

PLANNING FOR MUTUAL CHANGE

In this example, we revisit the case of Darin and Simon from Chapter 3. There they discussed an incident in which Darin broke their sexual agreement. While they had agreed to be open, their understanding was that condoms would be used consistently with outside partners. While using cocaine, Darin had sex without a condom and kept that potential risk secret from Simon for a time. In that example, we learned that the couple had presently limited their substance use to only alcohol and cannabis as a result. The conversation in this transcript picks up later in their session. As the transcript begins, it has become evident that the couple also has some concerns about their use of alcohol. Unlike cocaine, which was something only Darin used, both Simon and Darin drink alcohol, and each has recognized that there may be some benefits to decreasing their use at this time.

One interesting element in this example is that Darin and Simon have different views on the details of their goal. They both want to reduce their drinking, but when they begin to elaborate on specifics in the planning process, dyadic ambivalence emerges, and the counselor utilizes skills discussed in Chapter 7 to respond strategically. Another aspect of this narrative is that Darin and Simon have different impressions of how dependent they are on one another to achieve reductions in drinking. While Simone sees drinking as a largely independent behavior, Darin identifies a number of ways in which Simon's drinking might influence his own. The counselor responds by helping partners understand one another's perspective, which allows them to identify ways they can support one another in making change.

* * *

COUNSELOR: Darin has already started making some changes around cocaine use. It sounds like the two of you are coming to the consensus that you would like to reduce your drinking, too. [Dyadic reflection summarizing previous content.]

DARIN: Yeah, I think for me at least, it's really time. And like, knowing you have been thinking that too just makes me thing we really do need to slow down.

SIMON: Yeah, I think that's fair.

COUNSELOR: So, if you two were to think about slowing down, what would that look like? What do you imagine your limits would be ideally?

[Question directed to the couple initiates goal setting.]

DARIN: I want to say, "Oh I'll just drink on the weekends," or something like that. But the truth is, once I start, it's like running downhill for me. I just want to drink until I fall asleep. So I think I need like a full-on break for a while.

SIMON: I get that for you. That's a little frustrating for me because I feel like I probably don't need to be that extreme. I think I could just step back and set a limit of like no more than a couple drinks a couple times a week and be fine with that.

DARIN: You probably could, and I'd like to be able to say I could, too, but the truth is I probably can't. I feel like we learned that with me and coke.

COUNSELOR: So you two have some different limits. Your ideal levels of drinking right now might not be the same. But you both envision drinking quite a lot less than you are now.

[Dyadic reflection emphasizes common ground.]

DARIN: Yes.

COUNSELOR: So, how important is it that the two of you arrive at the exact same limit? Or another way to think about it is, how big a problem would it be if you guys had somewhat different limits around drinking. So you [DARIN] would basically take a full-on break and not drink entirely, while you [Simon] just drank a couple times a week.

[Counselor question probes the impact of dyadic ambivalence about specific change goals.]

DARIN: I think that'd be hard if you drank at home.

SIMON: Really?

DARIN: Honestly yeah. I hate saying this, but I'm impulsive. I feel like if you open a bottle of wine or something, I'll be like "Oh . . . well . . . why not?" And then it'll sort of spiral.

COUNSELOR: Got it, so it's tough for you not to drink when you are around someone who is.

[Reflection captures Darin's perception of goal dependence.]

DARIN: It is honestly.

SIMON: You have done it before though. Like you've been at parties and stuff and not drunk very much because you had a work thing the next day.

DARIN: Yeah.

SIMON: I've seen you do it.

DARIN: Right, but I feel like it's been a long time since I've really made that work.

COUNSELOR: Simon, it sounds like for you not drinking at home, or knowing that you couldn't for a while, would be frustrating. And also Darin, I get the sense that right now, you are not super confident you would be able to stick to your limits if Simon was drinking around you— even if you have been able to do it before.

[Reflection summarizes perceived goal dependence. For Darin, drinking is under some amount of partner control. For Simon, it is largely under actor control.]

SIMON: I mean, it's not like I want to sabotage you. I guess I just don't like the idea that I can't.

COUNSELOR: One thing that I have come to respect about you guys is that you work together. The moves, the job stress, being unemployed—generally, you guys are pretty good at sorting out how to support one another.

[Relationship affirmation.]

DARIN: That's true.

COUNSELOR: And yet this issue feels sticky. Trying to figure out how to tackle drinking together feels different somehow. What makes it harder?

[Question directed to the couple explores dyadic ambivalence.]

SIMON: I think I just resent the idea that I have to give something up entirely just because he wants to. It isn't really that big a deal. Honestly, how much am I really gonna drink on an evening at home when it's just the two of us and you're not drinking? I just don't like the idea that I can't.

COUNSELOR: So the idea of having to give it up doesn't feel great. And also, it's possible that it might not be that big a sacrifice.

[Double-sided reflection to Simon.]

DARIN: And you probably could have a drink if you wanted to. I think the key would be that you don't offer me one, too. And like, don't leave two thirds of a bottle of wine sitting around, because that would be really tempting for me. But I'm not a total child. I wouldn't go nuts if you had a drink at home.

SIMON: I could get like a can of wine or something that I know I would finish and then it wouldn't just be hanging around.

DARIN: Right, I feel like that would probably be OK. And also, if you are thinking about only drinking so much, that might actually be good for you, too.

SIMON: True.

COUNSELOR: So there might actually be a way for you guys to figure out how to navigate this even if you don't have completely identical limits.   [Dyadic reflection.]

SIMON: Knowing that I have a little wiggle room makes it seem like less of a big deal.

COUNSELOR: So Darin, it sounds like, for you, taking a break from drinking means not being around someone who is drinking so much. One way to do that is to limit alcohol in the house, and Simon can help support that by limiting what he drinks at home.

[Summary clarifies goals and Simon's role in Darin's change process.]

I'm wondering, Simon, your goal is to cut back to just a couple drinks on a couple nights. What, if anything, could Darin do that would be helpful to you in doing that?

[Question directs attention to Darin's role in Simon's change process.]

SIMON: Well, if he isn't drinking at all, I'll probably drink less. So there isn't a lot more that he could do. The issue for me will be drinking after work. I do that probably four nights a week. And even though I'm not hammered every night, it's a lot.

COUNSELOR: Got it. So that is the tough spot for you.   [Reflection to Simon.]

SIMON: Right. I'm just gonna have to be a little less social for a while. Or else there's no way around drinking most nights of the week.

COUNSELOR: You may need to change how much you socialize in order to change how much you drink.

[Reflection to Simon.]

SIMON: Hanging out with my coworkers just inevitably ends up at a bar. It's nice to unwind after work for sure, and that's the thing to do.

DARIN: I feel like Stacy and you would probably be able to just go for a walk or something. Sometimes it's just the two of you and I feel like she's not really all that into a bar.

SIMON: Well, that's true.

COUNSELOR: [To SIMON] So there might be some other things that you could do, at least with some of those folks.

[Reflection emphasizes Darin's contribution to Simon's change planning discussion.]

SIMON: That's true.

COUNSELOR: I'm wondering Simon, imagine you found yourself in a tricky spot. Maybe you were tempted to go out after work on a night you felt like you shouldn't. Or you were out and thought you might end up drinking too much. What, if anything, could Darin do to be helpful in those sort of sticky moments?

[Question to Simon probes potential for Darin to support change.]

SIMON: Huh, I had not thought about that. I guess it might actually be nice if I could text you. It would give me an excuse to step away and take stock.

COUNSELOR: Darin, how would that be for you?

[Question elicits Darin's perspective on the proposed role in Simon's change plan.]

DARIN: I'm fine with it as long as I know it's something he wants and not like he would think I was nagging.

* * *

Many counselors will likely recognize a number of elements in the above narrative that look and feel similar to change planning with an individual client. Goals are clarified, action steps are identified, and contingency plans are created for anticipated challenges. The narrative also illustrates two characteristics of planning with couples: ongoing attention to dyadic ambivalence and the specification of partners' roles in one another's change.

Ongoing Attention to Dyadic Ambivalence and Relationship Discord

Chapter 7 made the point that dyadic ambivalence can emerge at any point throughout a session. It is not something that once resolved is gone forever. Coming into this discussion, Darin and Simon had achieved consensus around the broad goal that they should reduce their drinking. The challenge for them was finding a shared perspective on specific goals. Each of them individually had a goal that could be viewed as meeting the SMART criteria; however, these limits were not the same, and Simon initially began to argue against Darin's proposed change goal. One could imagine a scenario in which Darin and Simon progressed into an argument over whether they should stop drinking entirely or just cut back. Similarly, they could have been entangled in a fight about why Darin would ask Simon not to drink at home around him. Instead, the counselor was able to help the couple resolve dyadic ambivalence and find ways to work together toward change. The counselor achieved this by incorporating strategies for responding to relationship discord (see Chapter 7) into the planning process.

The counselor maintained an emphasis on common ground and reframed the partners' specific goals as complementary strategies to achieve an end they both desired. By reminding the couple of their common purpose, the counselor helped to mitigate tension, and the couple was able to tolerate a conversation about change long enough to find a compromise on the points they disagreed.

> COUNSELOR: So you two have some different limits. Your ideal levels of drinking right now might not be the same. But you both envision drinking quite a lot less than you are now.

Chapter 2 noted that successful accommodation may beget successful accommodation. Couples who figure out how to solve one problem together are more likely to solve another. Using dyadic reflections, the counselor reminded Darin and Simon of their shared goals and values—common ground that served to offset and contextualize points of disagreement.

The counselor utilized dyadic affirmations to facilitate dyadic functioning and diffuse relationship discord. Not only did the counselor remind Darin and Simon of points they agreed on, but also they reminded the couple of what works in their relationship.

> COUNSELOR: One thing that I have come to respect about you guys is that you work together. The moves, the job stress, being unemployed— generally, you guys are pretty good at sorting out how to support one another.

By affirming their relationship and emphasizing their caring concern for one another, the counselor increased the likelihood that Darin and Simon would share information about their respective perspectives in productive and constructive ways rather than responding with criticism, judgment, or defensiveness that would sustain conflict and derail working together.

The counselor explored dyadic ambivalence in a way that helped partners understand one another's perspectives. While the counselor consistently moved to mitigate relationship discord, they did not shy away from exploring dyadic ambivalence. In their overview of interdependence theory, Rusbult and Van Lange (2003) noted that when partners have highly similar goals they do not necessarily need to examine or discuss their individual perspectives. They are able to simply move forward with coordinating an agreed-on action. In contrast, when goals diverge, partners may benefit from having more information about one another's perspectives, priorities, and abilities. Consistent with this, the counselor in this example capitalizes on adaptive accommodation by inviting each partner to elaborate on their individual stance in a nonjudgmental context. Understanding one another's concerns helped the partners empathize with one another. This enhanced their willingness to consider ways they could support each other and thereby achieve their shared goal of reduced alcohol use.

The Role of Partners in One Another's Change Plans Are Explored

A common theme in discussions of interdependence theory throughout this text is that partners in high-quality relationships can support one another's efforts toward change—and that their success in doing so is associated with relationship quality. By exploring ways in which each partner can support the other in their change process, the counselor explicitly built these relationship resources into the change plan. Doing so involved specifying both the nature and timing of partner support. Partners identified what would be helpful and also when that help would be most effective. Simply because a partner is willing to help or support change does not necessarily mean that they know which actions will be effective in doing that. By clarifying the nature and timing of support, the counselor maximizes the likelihood that partners will be successful in working together toward change.

PLANNING TOGETHER TO SUPPORT INDIVIDUAL CHANGE

Sometimes a particular goal is much more central or relevant to just one of the partners. It is still possible to think about this goal as one both partners could be invested in. As reviewed in Chapter 7, a wealth of research on dyadic coping has illustrated that the support and coordinated effort of a relationship partner can improve health outcomes (e.g., Badr, 2004; Bodenmann et al., 2011; Kraemer et al., 2011; Revenson, 1994). Notably, this is not a return to an "identified-patient" model. Similar to instances involving mutual change, the planning process here is seen as something the couple is doing together. It is still an act that "they"—the partners—are doing "as a couple." That said, change planning in this case has a slightly different quality compared to planning in instances involving mutual change. One partner is the person primarily responsible for enacting change, while the other is primarily in the role of supporting change. As illustrated in the narrative below, balancing individual autonomy with facilitating dyadic functioning becomes particularly salient.

This example returns to the case of Otto and Rafael from Chapters 4 through 8. In those earlier transcripts, we learned that Rafael is HIV positive and Otto is HIV negative. This transcript comes from a subsequent session. Rafael has received news in the past week that his viral load became detectable. For readers less familiar with HIV care, poor adherence to HIV medication increases the likelihood of drug resistance, adverse health effects of HIV infection, and mortality (e.g., Altice et al., 2019; Luz et al., 2016; Marcus et al., 2016). A detectible level of HIV in his body also increases the chance that he could transmit HIV to a sexual partner (Rodger et al., 2016). In the session just before the transcript begins, Rafael acknowledged some recent challenges with HIV medication adherence. The example begins as the counselor moves to clarify a change goal for HIV medication adherence and develop an associated plan.

One feature worth noting is how Otto's attempts to support Rafael are experienced early on in the session. Whether or not Rafael takes his HIV medication is a goal that is largely under his control. His dependence on Otto with regard to this outcome is very modest. Relationship discord emerges when Rafael responds with frustration to Otto's advice about what he should do. The counselor's responses mitigate this discord and then seek to clarify action steps that are acceptable to Rafael. Doing so allows the couple to identify a supportive role that Otto can play—one that Rafael appreciates rather than being annoyed by.

* * *

COUNSELOR: So, this has been a tough week. Hearing that your viral load was detectible was a gut punch for you, Rafael, and for both of you. Where do we go from here?	[Summary reflection ending with a question that initiates goal setting.]
OTTO: I mean, you have to take your meds. You just do.	
COUNSELOR: Rafael, what do you want to see happen?	[Question elicits Rafael's perspective on change.]
RAFAEL: Yeah. I guess I just didn't realize that I wasn't on top of it. I mean, I knew that I missed some pills here and there, but just how many got away from me.	

COUNSELOR: And that isn't how you want to be managing your HIV.

[Reflection to Rafael.]

RAFAEL: No. I'd been undetectable for so long, I guess I kind of just got lazy.

COUNSELOR: You have been managing HIV for a long time. That gets tiring even though you have been pretty successful at it. And now you have kind of fallen short of where you would like to maintain yourself.

[Reflection to Rafael.]

RAFAEL: Right.

OTTO: So then just take your meds.

RAFAEL: Sure.

COUNSELOR: I get the sense that Rafael getting back to being undetectable after this blip is something that you guys both agree is important.

[Dyadic reflection emphasizes common ground.]

RAFAEL: That's true.

COUNSELOR: Question is, how do we get there? In some ways, "Take your meds" sounds very easy, but what would have to happen to get there?

[Question directed to the couple.]

RAFAEL: That's the thing. This kind of crept up on me. I mostly just didn't do a good job of remembering to take them. It was just sort of easy to get caught up in other stuff and forget. And I didn't realize that started happening more than a couple days a week.

COUNSELOR: So a lot of those missed doses just sort of slipped by.

[Reflection to Rafael.]

OTTO: This is why I think you should do it in the morning. Like we'll just do a little pill box situation and you can take them every morning.

RAFAEL: [to OTTO] Oh my god, I love you, but the morning routine thing makes me crazy. [to COUNSELOR] Sorry, we go around and around about this. We are very different morning people. He like plans his whole day the night before and is great about having every little thing in place each morning. That's just not me. In the evening, I don't want to think about the next workday. When I wake up, I'm focused on what I need to get done and want to get to. It is a tough time of day for me to stop and think about things like packing lunches and taking meds.

COUNSELOR: As similar as you guys are in many ways, you have some pretty different morning habits. They work for both of you, but they are not the same.

[Dyadic reflection emphasizes common ground and acknowledges dyadic ambivalence.]

OTTO: Yeah, I love to be like organized and stuff about the morning. I'm telling you though, I could help you do this.

RAFAEL: Oh my god.

COUNSELOR: So, I just want to pause for a second and say that, I'm not here to tell either of you what to do. Ultimately, everybody gets to make their own choices. There may be a lot that Otto can help with, Rafael, but whether and how you take your meds is still something that no one can ever make you do or make you go about in a way you don't want to.

[Affirmation of Rafael's individual autonomy and acknowledgment of the potential for Otto to provide support.]

RAFAEL: Right. Like the person who has to fix this is me.

OTTO: OK, well, how are ya gonna do that buddy?

COUNSELOR: So, how would you like for you two to go about this, Rafael?

[Question directed to Rafael but worded in the plural to encompass a focus on the couple.]

RAFAEL: So, I think for me, I have to do this in the evening. Like at the end of the day when I'm brushing my teeth or whatever. For some reason I had this sort of belief that vitamins and meds are a morning thing. Even though I'm awful at a morning routine, I sort of felt like I should be doing it then. Which just leads to me failing half the time. I'm better with an evening routine.

COUNSELOR: So switching to taking your medications at night might actually help with this.

[Reflection to Rafael.]

RAFAEL: Yeah. Plus then, if I do get an upset stomach or whatever, I'll be heading to bed anyway and I won't have to like try to get through a morning of work feeling sick.

COUNSELOR: So, it's really clear that Otto wants to help and support you in this. What could he do, if anything, that would be helpful.

[Reflection emphasizes Otto's intention followed by a question inviting Rafael to consider a role for Otto in the change plan.]

RAFAEL: I think part of it honestly is to step back. I know this sucks and I know I need to fix it, but you are so stressed out it's honestly making me feel way worse about all this.

COUNSELOR: [To OTTO] And my hunch is that is not what you intended to do at all.

[Reflection clarifying Otto's intention.]

OTTO: Genuinely no. I don't want to make you feel bad. But I do really want to make sure that you are OK.

COUNSELOR: So, Otto, how does this plan of Rafael's sit with you? This idea of taking his meds at night?

[Question elicits Otto's perspective on Rafael's proposed plan.]

OTTO: I honestly don't care as long as he takes them.

COUNSELOR: So, Rafael, what specifically do you imagine doing. Like what needs to happen for this to work at night?

[Question elaborates action steps.]

RAFAEL: I think if I just have them in the bathroom, like with my toothbrush, it'll be fine. Right now they are in the kitchen, like I'd take them when I get coffee, but they're easy to pass by.

COUNSELOR: So changing location is a part of this.

RAFAEL: Yes.

COUNSELOR: I could imagine a situation where Otto finds himself wondering whether you remembered to take his meds. He is worried about you and really wants to see things turn around. If there was a night where he was wondering whether you took your meds, or if he wanted to remind you to take them, how would that land with you? How, if at all, could he ask about your meds or express that in a way that would feel OK?

[Reflection of Otto's concern ending with a question about the role he might play in supporting Rafael's behavior change.]

OTTO: Oh, yeah, because that will totally happen.

RAFAEL: I think the main thing is to watch your tone. Sometimes when it comes to organizational stuff, you get a little snooty about things. Like asking if I took my meds is fine. But stop there. I don't need you to remind me why I have to do it or make me feel like a child.

OTTO: That's fair.

COUNSELOR: So, it would be OK for Otto to ask if you took your meds. But for that to go over well, the tone needs to be neutral, and you don't want a lecture.

[Reflection clarifying Otto's potential role in the change plan.]

RAFAEL: Yeah, and like it probably will help me remember.

COUNSELOR: So, imagine he went a little too far. Sometimes even with really good intentions we overstep and say a little too much. How might you let Otto know?

[Question troubleshoots a potential problem.]

RAFAEL: [to OTTO] You know how I am. If you see me roll my eyes and wander off you know I'm annoyed and I don't want to fight about something.

OTTO: It's actually not subtle.

COUNSELOR: So, Otto, you can recognize when to step back.

[Reflection to Otto.]

* * *

Respecting Individual Autonomy in Dyadic Change Planning

Respect for autonomy is a central tenant of the Spirit of Motivational Interviewing (W. R. Miller & Rollnick, 2013). This session with Otto and Rafael illustrates that this emphasis on autonomy remains essential even as a counselor seeks to evoke a partner's support for change. Notably, the need to respect individual autonomy while change planning with a couple is applicable regardless of whether change is mutual or individual; however, it is particularly easy to see the concern illustrated in this latter instance.

When partners proscribe change plans or take the expert role, it can elicit relationship discord. Early work on Motivational Interviewing with couples was primarily concerned with the potential for partners to inhibit the change process by arguing against change. Here we see the opposite concern. Dyadic ambivalence has emerged around the change plan even though Otto is making a pro-change argument to Rafael. Otto proposes a solution—he advises Rafael to take his medication regularly in the morning. The problem is, because this plan is not a good fit for Rafael, he is motivated to argue against Otto's suggested plan. In short, Otto's advice-giving elicits sustain talk in a way that is similar to what might happen if the counselor deviated from Motivational Interviewing practice and gave unsolicited advice.

If the counselor "took a side" in the argument about how change should happen, it could potentially exacerbate dyadic ambivalence. Supporting Otto in advocating for his plan would likely intensify Rafael's sustain talk. Meanwhile, defending Rafael's plan could amply Otto's attempts to change Rafael's mind. Instead, consistent with the idea that when goals diverge it is helpful for partners to seek more information about one another's perspectives (Rusbult & Van Lange, 2003), the counselor emphasizes Rafael's autonomy (e.g., W. R. Miller & Rollnick, 2013; Moyers et al., 2014) and creates space for him to share his preferences for enacting change. The key is that, in doing so, the counselor's utterance also emphasizes the possibility that Otto could contribute to change.

> COUNSELOR: So, I just want to pause for a second and say that, I'm not here to tell either of you what to do. Ultimately, everybody gets to make their own choices. *There may be a lot that Otto can help with*, Rafael, but whether and how you take your meds is still something that no one can ever make you do or make you go about in a way you don't want to.

The counselor's following question then makes use of a plural pronoun ("you two") when inviting Rafael to share his perspective on how to go about change.

> COUNSELOR: So, how would you like for *you two* to go about this, Rafael?

This sequence of utterances balances attention to individual autonomy and facilitating dyadic functioning in a way that directs the conversation away from Otto's prescribed plan and toward creation of a plan both partners are invested in.

Partners can negotiate the roles they play in one another's change process. Part of why Otto wants to tell Rafael what to do is that he cares about him. While the impact of his advice is not particularly helpful, his intention is good. Chapter 7 discusses the strategy of clarifying intention as a way to mitigate relationship discord. The counselor uses that strategy here as well.

> RAFAEL: I think part of it honestly is to step back. I know this sucks and I know I need to fix it, but you are so stressed out it's honestly making me feel way worse about all this.
>
> COUNSELOR: [To OTTO] *And my hunch is that is not what you intended to do at all.*
>
> OTTO: Genuinely no. I don't want to make you feel bad. But I do really want to make sure that you are OK.

The narrative between Otto and Rafael then goes on to illustrate the utility of having partners discuss what they can do to be helpful. The counselor specifically elicits Rafael's preferences about how Otto can support him. This gives Otto information about which kinds of social control strategies will be most effective in influencing Rafael's behavior.

In addition to giving Otto a behavioral alternative, specifically negotiating the role partners will play in supporting change also helps to shape how Rafael will interpret Otto's behavior during the week. Rafael is worried about Otto judging him for not taking his medications or treating him in a way that might be somehow condescending. In the course of clarifying their roles in the change plan, the counselor highlights Otto's motivation to support Rafael. This may reduce the potential for relationship discord to arise due to incorrect assumptions of intention (see Chapter 7) in the week ahead.

Consensus Is Meaningful, Even If Only One Partner Is Changing

This narrative illustrates the power of a couple-level goal, even when change is not mutual. Locke and Latham (2006) noted that feedback (on performance) and social support are both predictors of goal attainment. Relationship partners can provide a source of both. Otto is willing and able to provide support to Rafael in the form of encouragement and logistical help if necessary. Rafael cares about Otto's emotional well-being, and knowing that Otto is concerned for him enhances his motivation to take his medications. Unfortunately, in the absence of consensus around how change will happen—it is entirely possible that Otto might unintentionally engage in behaviors that Rafael experiences as coercive or aversive. His attempts to help and support change might actually serve to make change harder by decreasing Rafael's ability to enact a plan that would work better for him. By helping the couple achieve consensus about change, the counselor helps them to capitalize on the support they can provide one another. It brings actions in line with intentions in ways that promote change.

PLANNING WHEN A SHARED GOAL CANNOT BE ACHIEVED

It would be naïve to suggest that a counselor can always help couples agree around a goal and plan for change. It is entirely possible that a counselor could conduct a Motivational Interview with a couple with integrity and fidelity and the partners may still not agree on how to move forward together. The failure to achieve consensus does not mean the counselor necessarily did a "bad job." It may simply mean that the partners have recognized that their individual preferences are incompatible and also that neither of them is prepared to make the sacrifices necessary to achieve consensus.

When this happens, the counselor is faced with the particular challenge of helping a couple to plan for a situation where they cannot work together. In the previous examples, partners sometimes disagreed on how change should happen, but they shared a commitment to a larger goal. Even if they decided to "do different things," those different approaches to change served a common goal that both partners were invested in. This situation is different. Here partners are doing different things because they do not share a common goal.

For this example, we return to Jarred and Alex from Chapters 1 and 2. In those chapters, they discussed HIV prevention options. The example here comes from a session later in their course of treatment. In this narrative, Jarred and Alex discuss methamphetamine use. Both use methamphetamine; however, over the course of several counseling sessions, their use emerged as a point of dyadic ambivalence. Jarred saw reasons to be concerned about their use, and in the narrative he expressed his desire to stop; meanwhile, Alex was less concerned with the status quo and saw no reason to change at this time.

Faced with the reality that the two want different things, the counselor is tasked not only with mitigating relationship discord in session but also with helping the partners consider how they might minimize unnecessary emotional pain and conflict while each works toward their individual goals. This is complicated by the fact that Jarred is concerned that Alex's continued use will prevent him from achieving his goals. He perceives a degree of partner or joint control around this goal. As a result, the couple is faced with the need to consider the possibility of an exit accommodation response (i.e., deferring the decision to move in together) in order to reduce dependence and permit them to progress toward their individual goals.

* * *

COUNSELOR: I get the sense that you guys have a different vision for what the limits on drug use should be. Alex, you don't see a lot of reason to change right now, though you understand why Jarred has concerns. Jarred, you really want to slow down—basically stop using methamphetamine entirely.

[Dyadic reflection summarizes dyadic ambivalence.]

JARRED: Right. I think we've kind of been ignoring that problem for a while and making it work. But, I just don't want to party anymore.

ALEX: I'm not saying you have to.

JARRED: Right, but I also can't be around you when you are using and not do it.

ALEX: So I have to choose you or partying then. That's the deal?

COUNSELOR: First, I know it can be hard to reckon with a situation where you guys want different things. I've been impressed with your willingness to hear and respect one another's viewpoints. I'm not here to tell either one of you what to do. You guys both get to make the decisions that feel right for you. The challenge is, in this case, you two want to head in different directions. Those choices don't feel compatible to you.

[Relationship affirmation; affirmation of individual autonomy; and reflection of dyadic ambivalence.]

ALEX: Right. And it sucks that I'm the one who has to choose whether this is gonna work because his mind is apparently made up.

COUNSELOR: Alex, you are worried that what you decide about meth could make or break this relationship.

[Reflection clarifying Alex's emotion.]

ALEX: Right. I feel like now it's all on me and if we don't work out, it is because I'm the bad guy.

COUNSELOR: Jarred, if I'm understanding Alex correctly, he's concerned that if he doesn't agree to give up using meth, it will ultimately break you guys up. How accurate is that you're your perspective?

[Question elicits Jarred's perspective on assumptions Alex has made.]

JARRED: I guess I don't see it that way right now. At least it is not that cut and dry to me. I'm not saying you have to quit, and I'm not saying I don't want to be with you. But I need to slow down, and I can't do that if you are high around me.

COUNSELOR: So, Jarred, you are OK with Alex's personal decision about using meth. The piece that is important to you right now is that you don't want him to use around you because that will make it hard for you to do what you are trying to do.

[Reflection clarifies Jarred's priorities and what Alex could do to avoid inhibiting Jarred's change plan.]

JARRED: Right. That's all I'm saying.

ALEX: That gets a lot harder if we are gonna do this moving in together.

COUNSELOR: Right now you guys have some ability to do your own thing in your own space. It gets harder to make that work if you live together.

[Dyadic reflection highlights implications of the commitment milestone for partners' level of dependence.]

ALEX: Right. Until now, I could party when I wanted and not have to think about how that involved you.

JARRED: Living together means I'd be around it a lot more.

COUNSELOR: So, where does that leave you in terms of thinking about the move?

[Question exploring implications of dyadic ambivalence for commitment milestone.]

JARRED: I hate to say it, but I honestly think we should wait. I mean, I don't want to move in together and be constantly fighting about this.

ALEX: Right, that would just end with us hating each other.

COUNSELOR: So it might actually be better to sort of hit pause on the move given that you guys are not in the same place around partying.

[Dyadic reflection captures implications of dyadic ambivalence on commitment milestone.]

ALEX: I think we have to. Because I don't want to be sneaking around, and I also don't want to constantly pull you into something that you don't really want to be a part of. I mean, I love it, and I love doing it with you. But I don't want to feel like I'm forcing that on you or like you are forcing me to give it up.

COUNSELOR: One of the things I respect about you two is that you genuinely care about each other. You guys were friends before you were boyfriends, and that concern for one another really comes through.

[Relationship affirmation.]

ALEX: Right, like I respect that he doesn't want to do this. I don't share his concerns, but that doesn't make him a bad person.

JARRED: And I think the same, like I don't think he's awful because he wants to party. I do worry about him, and I hope that someday you also slow down, but I want you to be happy and enjoy yourself.

COUNSELOR: So, one reason to step back from moving in together is that you can then each sort of do your own thing when it comes to partying. If it's OK with you, we could talk about what that looks like for each of you individually.

[Dyadic reflection sets up collaborative proposal to set individual goals.]

JARRED: OK

ALEX: Sure.

COUNSELOR: So, Jarred, your goal for the week is not to use. How do you imagine making that happen? What do you need to do?

[Question initiates planning for Jarred's personal goal.]

JARRED: I think I need to go through my house and clean out all the stuff. Like, there is a pipe that we have at my place and some other stuff we use. For a while anyway, I just want all the kink gear out. I don't want to like see the "stuff" that goes along with that scene.

ALEX: Makes sense. Are we even gonna have sex anymore?

COUNSELOR: Some of the changes Jarred is planning around drug use may change sex for you guys.

[Dyadic reflection clarifies the impact of individual change on the couple.]

JARRED: Honestly, since we've been together, more and more of the sex we have is partying. I have to really think about what it would be like outside of that. Like, we used to have sex without partying. I don't know how into that you really are anymore.

COUNSELOR: What are your thoughts on that Alex?

[Question elicits Alex's perspective.]

ALEX: I mean, sure. I am still into you, and it's not like I have to be high to have sex. Sex is just so much . . . more . . . when you are high.

COUNSELOR: So it's possible you guys will still continue to have sex with each other. And it sounds like, if you do, Alex wouldn't use, because Jarred—you wouldn't be using.

[Reflection clarifies an action step that will reduce the likelihood that Alex inhibits Jarred's change.]

ALEX: It sounds like that would be the deal.

JARRED: I actually want to see what it's like to not always be high when I have sex again.

ALEX; I get that, and if we are gonna go out or something, I would understand that's not what we are gonna do.

COUNSELOR: Alex, I want to also give some thought to your goals this week, too, if that's OK. Partying is something you want to continue to do. I am wondering, what do you see as the limit for you? I hear loud and clear that you don't want to quit totally, but where do you see the limit for yourself? What would feel like "too much?"

[Reflection and question clarifying Alex's personal goal.]

ALEX: Well, I would have to think about how to balance that scene with this relationship if he is not gonna go there with me. I feel like, I probably want to take at least one weekend a month to "indulge" on my own. But that's easy to say, and it might be pretty tempting to do it more than that.

JARRED: And this is what I worry about. Because we started off like that, just now and then, and then it crept up.

COUNSELOR: Alex, what would have to happen in order for you to stick to a limit of only partying once a month?

[Question elaborating Alex's change plan.]

ALEX: Well, I'd have to let some people know. Otherwise, people sort of expect certain things from me. Also, I think it would be helpful if we like set some plans in advance for a while. A lot of weekends we sort of wait and see what's going on, but now I feel like I kinda want to know ahead of time when I'm gonna be able to party.

COUNSELOR: So setting some expectations in advance would be useful for you. That way you can keep partying separate from your time with Jarred. A lot of the time you guys spent together recently involved partying. What do you imagine you might do together if you are not using meth?

[Reflection captures the idea that individual change plans can be compatible. Question troubleshoots a potential challenge in spending time together.]

ALEX: I think if you [Jarred] had suggestions for stuff to do it would help. Otherwise, I feel like I'm giving up a weekend to party and I also have to be the event planner.

JARRED: That's fair. I'm happy to set up some things. It'll probably help me stay busy as well. I'll know when I have to entertain myself.

COUNSELOR: So, you guys can begin to see how you might go your separate ways on this issue. Jarred, you can stop partying. Alex you can continue within the limits you are comfortable with. I am wondering, as you look at the week ahead, where do you think you might run into trouble? Where might this get hard?

[Reflection summarizes individual goals and elicits potential challenges.]

ALEX: I think here you've been really good about making it clear that I can do what I want. I could see us getting into it though if you start like bugging me about what I'm up to or checking in to see if I'm partying all the time.

JARRED: I do want to know if you are being safe though.

COUNSELOR: So, Alex, if Jarred had some questions, how would you want him to go about bringing that up?

[Question troubleshoots potential challenge.]

ALEX: I think as long as he keeps it about what's happening between us, and whether there's anything to worry about passing between us, then it's ok. [To JARRED] If you wanted details of who I did what with that I would get more annoyed. If you don't want to party, then the party isn't your business.

COUNSELOR: Jarred, what challenges do you imagine going forward?

[Question elicits Jarred's perspective on potential challenges.]

JARRED: I think it's gonna be tough knowing that he's out there potentially partying with other people. I think I could wind up getting really jealous.

COUNSELOR: How do you think that might impact the way you guys relate to one another?

[Question troubleshoots potential challenge.]

JARRED: I know when I get like that I have to be really careful about being sarcastic. And I would appreciate it if you didn't like make jokes about who you want to play around with.

ALEX: That is fair.

* * *

Parallel Individual Planning: Minimizing Conflict, Evaluating Dependence, and Reducing Barriers to Change

In many ways, this narrative can be understood as parallel individual change planning. Jarred and Alex have ultimately arrived at the decision that this is not a change that they want to make together. Instead, each of them has resolved to "do his own thing," and they are grappling with the implications of that realization for themselves and their relationship.

Throughout the dialogue, the counselor does three things. First, they actively seek to reduce the intensity of relationship discord even as the couple evaluates the implications of individual change for their relationship. Second, the counselor establishes an individual goal and associated plan with each partner. Third, the counselor examines how partners can avoid getting in the way of one another's plans.

The counselor examines the implications of increasing relationship dependence for dyadic ambivalence. In its overview of interdependence theory, Chapter 2 noted that dyadic ambivalence becomes harder to ignore as dependence increases. This was evident for Jarred and Alex. Their disagreement about drug use is easier to manage while they live separately. They are relatively free to make independent decisions about drug use without relying on one another to maintain harmony in a shared living space.

The decision to halt their plans to move in together represents an exit accommodation response (Rusbult et al., 1982, 1986; Yovetich & Rusbult, 1994). It decreases (or at least it forestalls any increase) in the degree to which Jarred and Alex are dependent on one another. (See Chapter 2 for a review of accommodation.) This kind of destructive accommodation response has substantial potential to evoke conflict between the partners. The counselor uses relationship affirmations and clarifies partners' intentions to mitigate this conflict. This gives Jarred and Alex the opportunity to productively share their concerns about moving in together and consider the implications of the move for their personal goals.

The counselor explores how partners can minimize presenting barriers to one another's goal attainment. In the previous examples, change planning encompassed examining how partners could support one another's change efforts. This frame for change planning would be challenging for Jarred and Alex since they do not particularly support one another's goals. Instead, the counselor invites them to consider how they can avoid creating barriers for one another. Relationship affirmations are used to evoke partners' motivation to "live and let live" rather than to actively support or promote one another's change goals per se.

The counselor also incorporated attention to troubleshooting possible conflict. They actively examined places where partners' behavior would be aversive or disruptive to one another's change plans. Similar to planning with a shared goal, this included attention to the timing and the content of communication. There was greater emphasis here on establishing boundaries and expectations. Since Jarred and Alex are "going their own way" when it comes to drug use, the boundary between shared and personal activities is being reevaluated.

Relationship Termination: Considering a Plan to Break Up

Jarred and Alex stop short of deciding to end their relationship; however, concerns about potential separation emerge in this discussion. Both men express some worries that ultimately, the fact that they cannot agree on drug use will diminish their relationship quality. Their inability to arrive at a shared goal forces Jarred and Alex to reconsider the decision to move in together. This potentially decreases time together, emotional connection, and resource sharing or investment. That may in turn diminish commitment and their intention to persist in the relationship. Still, for the moment they have concluded only that they should suspend plans to move in together. The larger conversation about whether their relationship will endure is left open.

As described in the discussion in Chapter 3 of the Spirit of Motivational Interviewing with couples, it is not the counselor's job to keep partners together. Doing so could potentially be coercive and undermine respect for individual autonomy. By continuing to support dyadic functioning, and by approaching the planning process in a way that minimizes conflict, the counselor provides a format for the couple to consider the possibility of breaking up in a way that minimizes unnecessary pain and suffering. Chapter 11 includes a more extended discussion of special considerations in planning for termination.

CONCLUSIONS AND KEY POINTS

Similar to change planning with individual clients, the planning process with couples involves the articulation of goals that meet the criteria for specificity and ambition implied by goal-setting theory. In other words, goals that are SMART. From the perspective of goal-setting theory, partners can serve as a source of resources for goal attainment and may also provide feedback on progress toward goals. The ability of partners to do so effectively is determined in large part by whether they are mutually invested in the goal.

This chapter considers change planning in three prototypical scenarios—two of which involve situations where partners have a shared goal. Planning for mutual change is relevant in situations where both partners arrive at the decision to modify their behavior. Planning so that the couple can support change relevant for just one partner is relevant in situations where the target behavior is ultimately salient for only one person in the relationship. In both of these scenarios, partners share an investment in the outcome. In both instances, change is something that the partners are working toward together—a couple-level goal. Change plans in these scenarios involve attention to the roles partners play in supporting one another's change.

In contrast, change planning when partners cannot arrive at a shared goal places the emphasis on minimizing the extent to which partners present barriers to one another's desired goals and mitigating conflict between partners outside of session. In this scenario, partners do not share goals and they do not necessarily support one another's goals. As such, their roles in promoting one another's desired change are inherently limited. While not all failures to achieve consensus around a goal necessarily result in relationship termination, this paradigm for change planning is relevant and can be extended to address such circumstances.

9

Communication, Trust, and Power

TYREL J. STARKS AND KENDELL M. DOYLE ■

Previous chapters have given substantial attention to domains of relationship functioning that are salient and explicitly featured in interdependence theory—most notably satisfaction, commitment, and emotional investment. The purpose of this chapter is to provide complementary information on domains of relationship functioning whose position in interdependence theory is relatively subtler or implicit—communication, trust, and power. While they may receive less time in the theoretical spotlight, there is considerable evidence to suggest that these elements of relationship functioning have substantial potential to influence the way couples make decisions together. After reviewing this literature, we examine how intervention research focused on communication, trust, and power might augment and enhance Motivational Interviewing practice with couples.

DYADIC COMMUNICATION: CONFLICT AND NEGOTIATION

The role of communication in interdependence theory is perhaps most obvious in discussions of accommodation—or how partners respond when their interests conflict. For example, as described in Chapter 2, voice (active and constructive) accommodation responses are characterized by instances when partners discuss a problem, share information about their goals and priorities, propose solutions, or attempt to negotiate compromise. In contrast, neglect (passive and destructive) accommodation responses include behaviors like ignoring a partner and refusing to discuss a problem (Rusbult et al., 1982, 1986; Yovetich & Rusbult, 1994). Partners' ability to engage in productive dialogue—whether or not they can reasonably discuss an issue on which they disagree—is clearly inherent in these definitions. It is therefore reasonable that research on couples communication might inform the practice of Motivational Interviewing with couples as counselors seek to mitigate relationship discord and help couples resolve dyadic ambivalence through discussion.

Communication within romantic relationships has been extensively studied for more than four decades. We focus here on two models that have emerged as prominent in the field (Christensen, 1987, 1988; J. M. Gottman, 1982; J. M. Gottman et al., 1976; Sullaway & Christensen, 1983) and describe skills-training options that are aligned with these paradigms (e.g., D. H. Baucom et al., 2008; Christensen & Jacobson, 1998; Dimidjian et al., 2008; Epstein & Baucom, 2002; J. M. Gottman & Gottman, 2008; Gurman, 2008; Jacobson & Margolin, 1979). Together, these models provide counselors with an advanced way of understanding verbal exchanges between partners in session particularly relevant to discussions of dyadic ambivalence. Meanwhile, the associated skills-training strategies may provide additional options for counselors to respond to relationship discord and facilitate dyadic functioning.

Christensen and the Study of Couples Communication Patterns

In their foundational work on couples communication styles during moments of conflict, Christensen and colleagues (Christensen, 1987, 1988; Christensen & Sullaway, 1984; Sullaway & Christensen, 1983) conceptualized maladaptive communication as a pattern of partner interaction rather than focusing on individual communication skills. While individual partners may respond in ways that initiate, sustain, or exacerbate conflict, the quality of interactions is determined by the behavior of both partners—not just one.

Christensen broadly distinguished between two kinds of couple-level communication patterns based on whether partners adopt similar or different stances in an exchange. In symmetrical patterns, partners behave similarly: They mirror one another's behavior or communication strategies. This contrasts with asymmetrical or complementary patterns of communication in which individual partners adopt different roles or strategies (Christensen, 1987, 1988; Christensen & Shenk, 1991).

Importantly, whether a communication pattern is adaptive or maladaptive is only partly separate from the question of symmetry. Christensen and colleagues identified three patterns of maladaptive communication. Two of these—mutual avoidance and mutual blame—are symmetrical. The other one, demand/withdraw, represents an asymmetrical pattern of communication. In contrast, Christensen and colleagues suggested that constructive communication patterns were uniformly symmetrical, involving mutual discussion, negotiation, or exchange. So, while symmetry does not guarantee constructive communication, asymmetry is uniquely maladaptive in this paradigm.

Mutual avoidance—Both partners actively eschew discussions of topics that would produce conflict. This might be achieved by both partners avoiding the topic entirely: No one brings it up. It might also be achieved by one partner ignoring the other partner's mention of the topic or withholding information that could inform or sustain such a discussion. This pattern of communication aligns with neglect (passive and destructive) accommodation responses (Rusbult et al., 1996; Rusbult & Zembrodt, 1983) discussed in Chapter 2. The difference is that mutual avoidance arises from an exchange in which both partners participate. It occurs when both partners adopt a stance of neglect toward an issue that produces conflict.

Mutual blame, "pointing fingers" at one another during discussions of conflict (Christensen, 1987, 1988; Christensen & Shenk, 1991; Futris et al., 2010; Sullaway & Christensen, 1983). In contrast to mutual avoidance—when partners evade or distract from conflict—couples who adopt a mutual blame pattern actively accuse, blame, or criticize one another for the role they played in the problem. This pattern is often characterized as overt arguments or fighting— verbal exchanges in which partners "attack" each other. These behaviors also partially align with situations where both partners opt for neglect accommodation responses. Rusbult et al. (1982) specified that some neglect responses—including insults or criticism—may appear "active" on the surface, but they are "passive" with respect to problem resolution.

Demand/withdraw—When attempts at problem-solving are met with avoidance (Christensen, 1987, 1988; Christensen & Shenk, 1991; Sullaway & Christensen, 1983). This asymmetrical pattern of maladaptive communication has garnered the most attention in research. It has a strong and reliable association with relationship problems and poor relationship functioning (B. R. Baucom et al., 2010; Caughlin & Huston, 2002; J. M. Gottman & Levenson, 2000; Heavey et al., 1995; Schrodt et al., 2014; Sullaway & Christensen, 1983). This substantial body of work suggests that there are two ways couples might fall into a demand/withdraw pattern. *Discuss/avoid* exchanges (Christensen, 1987, 1988; Christensen & Shenk, 1991; Futris et al., 2010; Sullaway & Christensen, 1983) might be thought of as those in which one partner makes an attempt at a voice response (Rusbult et al., 1996; Rusbult & Zembrodt, 1983). They set out with the goal of productively discussing the topic; however, their attempt elicits an exit or neglect response from their partner, whose goal is to escape from the conversation. Alternatively, in a *criticize/defend* exchange (Christensen, 1987, 1988; Christensen & Shenk, 1991; Futris et al., 2010; Sullaway & Christensen, 1983) the partner initiating the discussion may do so using a neglect response characterized by nagging, criticism, or demands (S. Cohen & Lichtenstein, 1990; Lewis & Rook, 1999), which motivates the other partner to respond by refuting the criticism.

Constructive communication—Mutual discussion, mutual negotiation, and mutual expression (Christensen, 1987, 1988; Christensen & Heavey, 1990; Christensen & Shenk, 1991; Heavey et al., 1996). Similar to maladaptive communication that sustains conflict, adaptive communication is understood in terms of patterns of interaction between partners. It is characterized by the presence of three components: mutual discussion, mutual negotiation, and mutual expression (Christensen, 1988; Futris et al., 2010). In *mutual discussion*, both partners explain their perspective on a problem. They do not necessarily examine ways to resolve the disagreement. Instead, they share information with one another, which increases each partner's understanding of the other's stance. In contrast, *mutual negotiation* involves joint engagement in problem-solving. Both partners outline possible solutions or offer areas of potential compromise. *Mutual expression* occurs when partners disclose their thoughts and feelings to one another in a mutual, assertive, and respectful manner.

Mutual discussion, negotiation, and expression are all consistent with the broad concept of a voice accommodation response. The difference is that the couple-level pattern of constructive communication arises only when both partners assume a voice response. One could imagine a situation in which either of the partners responds to an attempt at discussion by withdrawing or ignoring the issue. In this case, a demand/withdraw pattern would emerge despite the fact that one partner in the couple gave a voice response to conflict.

Gottman and Communication Sequences

J. M. Gottman and colleagues' (J. M. Gottman et al., 1977 J. M. Gottman, 1982, 1999; J. M. Gottman & Gottman, 2008; J. M. Gottman et al., 1976;) proposed an alternative conceptualization of couples communication derived by contrasting conflict exchanges between satisfied couples with those who were less satisfied. J. M. Gottman's sequences comprise a series of partners' utterances whose overall organization results in either adaptive or maladaptive interactions. For example, if one partner responds to the other's complaint with a complaint of their own, conflict amplifies. Alternatively, if one partner's complaint is followed by the other validating their viewpoint and offering an alternative solution for the problem, conflict may be mitigated. For J. M. Gottman, it was not inevitable that conflict follows from the initial criticism. It is determined by the nature and the sequencing of utterances in an exchange between partners.

In Christensen's paradigm, adaptive patterns of communication were uniformly symmetrical. J. M. Gottman's work introduced the possibility that sequences comprising some asymmetrical responses may be adaptive. Utterances that validate the speaker's input or paraphrase shifts in attitudes during a negotiation may diffuse conflict. They serve to break up a sequence of utterances that might otherwise comprise solely parallel self-disclosure and permit partners to demonstrate that they are listening effectively to one another.

Cross-complaining sequences—Complaint and countercomplaint (J. M. Gottman et al., 1977; J. M. Gottman, 1982). In Chapter 1, Jarred and Alex discussed HIV prevention and their preferences for pre-exposure prophylaxis (PrEP) versus condom use diverged. One could imagine a cross-complaining exchange emerging if their conversation there had continued unchecked.

JARRED: Well, I'm sorry, but I just don't like the idea of PrEP.
ALEX: I'm sorry, too, because condoms are just not something we can be successful at.
JARRED: But PrEP is an everyday thing. Are we gonna have sex with someone every day?

ALEX: The point is that condoms have to happen every time you have sex, and that is a spoiler.

This cross-complaining sequence could readily extend or exacerbate conflict. It prevents both men from actively listening to one another's perspective and inhibits their ability to engage in a constructive discussion about problems.

Validation responses disrupt cross-complaining. Validation responses are brief verbal (e.g., reflections, summary statements, or intercalary vocalizations expressing assent, including "mmm-hmm," "yeah," "oh," etc.) and nonverbal cues (e.g., head nods, eye contact) that the individual is actively listening to their partner. Their effect in a communication sequence is to contextualize utterances that follow, placing them in a more neutral or nonconfrontational frame (J. M. Gottman et al., 1977; J. M. Gottman, 1982). Gottman argued that this type of validation sequence aims to substantiate the partner's complaint (J. M. Gottman et al., 1977), and lowers the odds of a negative response when a countercomplaint is then offered.

Imagine what might have happened in the previous brief exchange if Jarred and Alex had validated or acknowledged one another's point of view before offering their own perspective. Note that validating utterances are italicized for clarity.

JARRED: Well, I'm sorry, but I just don't like the idea of PrEP.
ALEX: *I understand that you have concerns about PrEP.* My concern is that condoms are just not something we can be successful at.
JARRED: *So, you are OK with condoms if we could be reliable, and you think PrEP is actually easier than trying to do that.*
ALEX: Exactly.
JARRED: I don't necessarily agree.

The use of validation by Alex and Jarred does not automatically produce agreement. It does prevent the escalation of conflict. Validation allows Alex and Jarred to confirm that they are understanding one another and expresses an openness to one another's perspectives even if they have not reached agreement.

Counterproposal sequences—The endless exchange of suggestions (J. M. Gottman, 1982). Similar to cross-complaining, sequences in which partners focus on making the argument for their own solution to a problem can exacerbate conflict. Partners focusing on making the argument for their preferred plan prevents them from hearing and understanding one another's perspectives. Again, one might imagine such an exchange between Alex and Jarred:

ALEX: Ultimately, I think PrEP is the right plan for us. At least I know it is for me.
JARRED: I don't think you've really considered condom use. What are you gonna do about gonorrhea and chlamydia and stuff? That doesn't matter?
ALEX: Say what you want, PrEP offers the best protection with the least amount of fuss.

JARRED: Condoms actually offer *more* projection if you think about it.

The utterances in this sequence are not complaints per se. Rather than bemoaning the problems with one another's ideas, Jarred and Alex are focused on presenting the merits of their own solution. The overall effect, though, is sustained conflict. Compromise is difficult to achieve when neither partner demonstrates that they are actively listening to the argument presented.

Contracting sequences acknowledge, accept, or agree with a suggestion before providing additional problem-solving suggestions. Similar to validating utterances, contracting utterances acknowledge the initial proposal, relay understanding of this proposal, and express an openness to joint problem-solving. Contracting sequences may depict mutual negotiation between partners or a partner's modified viewpoint over the course of the conversation (J. M. Gottman et al., 1977; J. M. Gottman, 1982). This alternative example discussion between Alex and Jarred incorporates the use of contracting statements, which have been italicized for clarity.

> ALEX: Ultimately, I think PrEP is the right plan for us. At least I know it is for me.
>
> JARRED: *So, you are settled on PrEP. I respect that and I could see that for you.* I am also worried about gonorrhea and chlamydia and stuff. Condoms provide more of that protection.
>
> ALEX: *You are right. HIV isn't the only concern.* I guess it is the thing I am most worried about, so PrEP offers the best protection in my mind with the least amount of fuss.
>
> JARRED: *For HIV, if you don't believe condoms are gonna happen, I guess you are right.* But I think we have to decide what we are gonna do about stuff other than HIV then.

Again, the use of contracting utterances does not immediately lead to agreement; however, conflict is diminished by the partners' acknowledgment of the merits of one another's ideas.

Nonverbal Communication

Much of the research on couples communication focuses on verbal behavior—what partners say to one another. It is worth acknowledging that nonverbal cues may be important elements in these exchanges as well. In particular, avoidance of conflict or withdrawal is often conveyed nonverbally. Even when partners respond with silence, they may roll their eyes, avoid eye contact, or present closed-off body language (e.g., crossed arms, stiff postures, facing away) (Kelly et al., 2003; Weiss & Heyman, 1990). Nonverbal maladaptive communication can also be depicted through facial expressions (e.g., frowning, sneering, or looks of disgust, despair, frustration, or anger) as well as tone of voice (e.g., sarcastic, tense, impatient, cold, or sad tones) (J. M. Gottman et al., 1977; J. M. Gottman, 1980).

Similarly, constructive communication patterns or sequences can manifest in the form of nonverbal behavior ques. More specifically, active engagement in discussions may be observed through eye contact, head nodding, facing one's partner, and positive facial expressions (e.g., smiling). Couples may also minimize distance between them, lean toward each other, or engage in physical touch, such as holding hands. Couples may also appear generally more relaxed in their body posture, and messages are communicated with more empathetic, warm, affectionate, or neutral vocal tones (J. M. Gottman et al., 1977; J. M. Gottman, 1980).

IMPLICATIONS FOR MOTIVATIONAL INTERVIEWING PRACTICE

There is a robust compliment of interventions designed to foster the development of constructive communication in session (see Gurman, 2008, for a review). These aim to then generalize skills introduced in session to interactions outside the counseling setting. Chapter 7 introduced a number of counselor strategies for mitigating relationship discord. Those strategies were introduced in the context of responding to dyadic ambivalence about change. The communication strategies introduced here are intended to mitigate conflict more broadly. Their integration provides Motivational Interviewing counselors with a wider range of options for responding to conflict that may disrupt a session but be unrelated to the target behavior.

Integrative behavioral couples therapy (IBCT). Although Christensen and colleagues work on communication patterns influenced a number of couples interventions (see Gurman, 2008, for a review), it directly informed the communication skill-building and problem-solving strategies that comprise integrative behavioral couples therapy (IBCT) (Christensen & Jacobson, 2000; Christensen et al., 1995; Dimidjian et al., 2008). Motivational Interviewing counselors working with couples who wish to focus on improving communication or joint problem-solving skills may draw on IBCT as one model for achieving these goals.

In IBCT, communication skill building involves three processes: leveling (e.g., expressing oneself), validating (e.g., active listening and helping partners feel heard and understood), and editing (e.g., correcting maladaptive communicative responses). *Leveling* occurs when counselors encourage couples to openly express their thoughts, feelings, opinions, and perspectives by facilitating equal engagement as both the speaker and listener. When communication goes awry, counselors should disrupt the couple's exchange and invite partners to revise— or *edit*—their maladaptive utterances to exclude blaming, shaming, or contempt. Couples are instructed in the effective use of "I statements" and summary statements (or paraphrasing) to *validate* or demonstrate that they are actively attending to one another (Christensen & Jacobson, 2000; Christensen et al., 1995; Dimidjian et al., 2008).

Consistent with the Spirit of Motivational Interviewing with couples, IBCT counselors aim to foster a collaborative environment during the problem-solving portion of sessions. Counselors facilitate an open discussion of the problem by encouraging couples to accurately define the source of conflict and honestly acknowledge the ways in which they contributed to the problem at hand (e.g., take ownership of their role or accept responsibility). Partners are coached to collaboratively identify solutions or compromises to address their mutually agreed-on problem. Couples are instructed to use their new communication techniques to effectively problem-solve and negotiate an effective solution. Counselors guide couples through the discussion and negotiation phase of the session by identifying moments where communication goes awry and encouraging the use of constructive communication skills (Christensen et al., 1995; Dimidjian et al., 2008).

Combatting the Four Horsemen—Gottman and colleagues' "recipe" for successful relationships. J. M. Gottman's work yielded an influential taxonomy of maladaptive communicative responses that may serve as a particularly useful framework to help counselors recognize problematic exchanges in session and encourage the use of more adaptive communication skills (J. M. Gottman, 1999; J. M. Gottman & Gottman, 2008). Gottman's four maladaptive communicative behaviors, referred to as the Four Horsemen of the Apocalypse (J. M. Gottman, 1994, 1999; J. M. Gottman & Gottman, 2008; J. M. Gottman & Silver, 2015), include

1. **Criticism** (e.g., attacking a partner's character or personality, attributing blame to partner through attacks on their character)
2. **Defensiveness** (e.g., denying or avoiding one's role in producing the conflict)
3. **Contempt** (e.g., displaying superiority over a partner through insulting, mocking, or name-calling)
4. **Stonewalling** (e.g., emotionally disengaging or withdrawing from the conflict interaction as a result of being emotionally overwhelmed)

The utility of J. M. Gottman's approach is enhanced by the fact that it specifies "antidotes" or alternative constructive responses for each of the Four Horsemen (J. M. Gottman, 1999; J. M. Gottman & Gottman, 2008).

When **criticism** emerges in session, J. M. Gottman and colleagues suggested counselors should encourage couples to express feelings using I statements instead of "you" statements. (See Chapters 4 and 7 for additional information on pronoun use and I statements in session.) Additionally, counselors may instruct couples to reframe complaints into requests they make to one another.

In response to **defensiveness**, counselors can encourage partners to accept responsibility for their contribution to the problem. This exploration of how the problem arose needs to enhance partners' awareness of one another's perspective. Part of accepting one's own responsibility in creating or sustaining a problematic situation is understanding how the other person views one's actions and the situation overall.

J. M. Gottman and colleagues recommended that counselors immediately disrupt **contempt** statements. They suggested that counselors provide couples with information that allows them to recognize and avoid the use of contempt. Counselors should cultivate an environment of respect—one in which the use of contempt would be antithetical—by having partners verbalize what they appreciate and admire about one another.

Stonewalling presents a unique challenge. It is characterized by disengagement from conflict. This escape precludes the couple having any opportunity to engage in productive discussion. As a result, the first step in responding to stonewalling is to help partners learn and practice emotion regulation skills—self-soothing techniques (e.g., mindfulness, breathing exercises, progressive muscle relaxation)—that reduce physiological arousal. Effective use of emotion regulation allows partners to tolerate prolonged engagement in the discussion of a problem or disagreement without becoming overwhelmed. This creates an opportunity for partners to engage in a more adaptive communication exchange.

TRUST: DOUBT VERSUS BELIEF IN THE RELIABILITY OF OTHERS

The potential relevance of trust to Motivational Interviewing with couples was foreshadowed in Chapter 6. That chapter examined ways in which a lack of trust might undermine the focusing process. There we offered a behavioral conceptualization of trust that has proven useful in our clinical work.

> **Trust might be thought of as the expectancy that a partner's verbal behavior (i.e., "what they say") is a reasonably accurate predictor of what they have done or what they will do.**

When true deficits in trust are present, any negotiation becomes perfunctory because partners ultimately do not believe one another's statements. Communication is also undermined when a partner does not believe that they are being believed. Why should someone make an effort to explain themselves if there is no chance a partner will accept their statement as genuine?

Chapter 6 suggested that when deficits in trust are present, rebuilding trust may need to be a preparatory step in the change process. In this section, we review research on trust and provide an overview of counseling strategies relevant to addressing mistrust. The goal is to provide a framework for counselors to recognize the emergence of mistrust and options for responding strategically to it.

Research on trust in romantic relationships has been largely organized around two different theoretical perspectives. Both can be viewed as examining how an individual answers questions like: "Will my partner be there for me?" or "Can I rely or depend on my partner?" **Dispositional perspectives on trust provide an intra-individual answer to such questions.** They suggest that past experiences predispose individuals to a certain degree of trust in others generally (Bowlby, 1969, 1973; Deutsch, 1973; Hazan & Shaver, 1994; J. A. Simpson, 1990) or define trust as a facet of individual personality (Rotter, 1971, 1980). These global or general expectations about the degree to which others are trustworthy then color an individual's perception of their specific relationship. **In contrast, interpersonal conceptualizations of trust view it through a relationship-specific lens rather than as a global expectancy that generalizes across people.** Trust represents an individual's belief or expectancy about how their partner will behave. These expectancies are generated and informed by observing the extent to which a partner displays prosocial behaviors toward one another, responds benevolently to one's needs, or prioritizes couple-level goals (Holmes & Rempel, 1989; Kelley et al., 2003; Rempel et al., 1985; Wieselquist et al., 1999).

Dispositional Theories of Trust

Dispositional conceptualizations of trust suggested that individuals enter relationships with previously formed beliefs and attitudes regarding how trustworthy others are, irrespective of context or relationship type (Deutsch, 1973; Rotter, 1980). One of the most well-known examples of a dispositional model of trust stems from attachment theory (Ainsworth, 1985; Ainsworth et al., 1978; Bowlby, 1969, 1973). It suggests that childhood experiences with caregiving relationships shape perceptions—or internal working models—of what romantic relationships "should" look like.

Attachment is conceptualized as a developmental process that begins in early childhood through the formation of affectional bonds with primary caregivers. These bonds serve as a mechanism to regulate emotion and manage distress. Children develop systematic patterns of behaviors, emotional expression, and interpersonal expectations based on their interactions with caregivers. These systematic patterns of behavior, affect, and expectancies are referred to as an attachment style or orientation (Ainsworth et al., 1978; Fraley & Shaver, 2000; Shaver & Mikulincer, 2002). Consistently responsive, caring, and loving caregiving interactions facilitate the development of secure attachment. Securely attached infants anticipate a caregiver will be responsive, and they are distressed when a caregiver is absent; however, they are readily soothed and happy on reunion with the caregiver. In contrast, unresponsive, insensitive, cold, and inconsistent caregiving interactions result in the development of insecure attachment styles (Ainsworth et al., 1978).

Attachment orientation, initially formed in childhood, then continues to inform and guide social behavior and relationship attitudes into adulthood (N. L. Collins & Read, 1990; Feeney & Noller, 1990; Fraley & Shaver, 2000). During adulthood, secure attachment is characterized as being comfortable with close relationships and interpersonal dependence. Adults with greater attachment security report greater levels of trust in their romantic partners, compared to their anxiously or avoidantly attached counterparts (Fitzpatrick & Lafontaine, 2017; Hazan & Shaver, 1987; Mikulincer, 1998; J. A. Simpson, 1990). In contrast, avoidantly attached individuals eschew close relationships, interpersonal dependence, and intimacy, while anxious attachment is expressed as fear of rejection and abandon-ment, leading to interpersonal dependence (Mikulincer et al., 2003).

Although attachment orientations are found to be relatively stable over time (Fraley et al., 2011), attachment styles are not fixed or wholly immutable (Arriaga & Kumashiro, 2019). While early interactions with caregivers exert a powerful influence, insecure attachment is also developed, reinforced, and maintained through maladaptive interactions with romantic partners in adulthood (S. M. Johnson, 2004, 2008; S. M. Johnson & Greenberg, 1985, 1988). S. M. Johnson (2008) suggested that trust is eroded in relationships with maladaptive communi-cative responses, as these patterns maintain and reinforce attachment insecurity.

Interpersonal Conceptualizations of Trust

Directly informed by or aligned with interdependence theory (and our own proposed definition of trust used in this text), interpersonal conceptualizations of trust posit that it is accrued or reinforced in moments when partners engage in prosocial behaviors toward one another (Holmes & Rempel, 1989; Kelley et al., 2003; Rusbult & Van Lange, 2008; J. A. Simpson, 2007a, 2007b; Wieselquist et al., 1999; Yovetich & Rusbult, 1994). When one partner reliably responds in prosocial ways during moments of potential conflict, the other partner comes to anticipate this behavior. This anticipation that a partner will behave well in turn increases the likelihood that prosocial actions will be reciprocated in return (Kelley et al., 2003; Wieselquist et al., 1999).

Implications for Motivational Interviewing Practice With Couples

Mistrust may be evident in the way couples communicate with one another. There is evidence to suggest that couples' communication patterns are predicted by partners' attachment style (Ebrahimi & Ali Kimiaei, 2014). Attachment se-curity has been associated with more constructive communication. In contrast, anxious attachment has been associated with diminished constructive commu-nication. Avoidant attachment is uniquely associated with the occurrence of de-mand/withdraw exchanges (Ebrahimi & Ali Kimiaei, 2014). Aligned with this, Starks, Castro, et al. (2016) examined associations between attachment and com-munication skills in a sample of unpartnered sexual minority men. They found that both attachment anxiety and avoidance were associated with diminished as-sertive communication skills. In addition, avoidance was associated with dimin-ished emotional communication skills (i.e., the ability to accurately convey one's feelings and emotions to a conversational partner).

Mistrust has the potential to be a self-fulfilling prophesy (in communication at least). Because anxious and avoidant attachment styles predict maladaptive communication, they potentially inhibit the kind of constructive communication exchange that would ultimately enhance trust. A partner who fears rejection may be hesitant to share their perspective in conversation. This robs the other partner of the opportunity to demonstrate understanding and respect. A partner who avoids dependence—one who does not allow themselves to develop reliance on a relationship—may see little reason to respond adaptively to dyadic ambivalence. Their partner may in turn come to expect this lack of consideration and also respond destructively.

Counselors therefore need to address mistrust in part by disrupting couples' typical conversational exchanges. Research on attachment-related interventions suggest that trust is amenable to clinical interventions focused on disrupting maladaptive interactions between partners (e.g., emotionally focused couples therapy; S. M. Johnson, 2004). These interventions help partners communicate more effectively and work to restructure emotional expression in order to alter maladaptive interactions patterns. The result is that the intervention may build trust by facilitating attachment security between partners. When partners are worried about rejection, counselors may need to do more to elicit their perspective and convey acceptance. When partners are hesitant to become invested in a relationship, counselors may need to do more to facilitate dyadic functioning and invite the partners to consider what they value about their relationship and one another.

Successful focusing during a couples Motivational Interview may build trust in and of itself. Interpersonal formulations of trust emphasize that it is formed by partners' observation of one another's behavior during interactions involving accommodation. In this way, the focusing and engaging processes of a couples Motivational Interview provide opportunities for counselors to catalyze trust by creating the space for partners to express their goals, priorities, and motivations to one another in a nonjudgmental atmosphere. The counselor's expression of empathic interest and unconditional positive regard for both partners—the balanced expression of the Spirit of Motivational Interviewing—provides a model for how partners might take a similar stance toward one another during the discussion of difficult topics.

Strategies that mitigate relationship discord—and promote the use of constructive communication skills—may build trust. Holmes and Rempel (1989) suggested that trust could be improved through behaviors consistent with constructive communication, such as recognizing partner needs, negotiation, compromise, affirmations of partner worth, and engaging in prosocial behavior that prioritizes partner- or relationship-level goals over self-interest (see also Simpson, 2007a). Unfortunately, low-trust individuals have been found to disengage and withdraw from situations in which trust can be forged through such constructive interactions (Rempel et al., 2001). Intervention by the counselor that disrupts conflict between partners and cues the use of more prosocial or adaptive communication may function to catalyze trust. Strategies for doing so are discussed in Chapter 7 and the previous section on couples communication. In addition, Chapter 11 discusses the potential for integrating problem-solving and social skills training into Motivational Interviewing practice with couples. These strategies may also be useful for disrupting conflict and redirecting the couple toward a more adaptive conversational exchange.

Counselor strategies that afford partners the opportunity to clarify their intentions to one another may indirectly serve to enhance trust. Chapter 7 introduced the notion that conflict can be sustained by one partner's inaccurate assumptions about the other's intention. Research on trust is syntonic with this assertion that assumption of intention matters. Simply engaging in prosocial behaviors may not be enough to increase trust in a relationship. Holmes and Rempel (1989) found that individuals who report low levels of trust are less likely to interpret a partner's behavior as prosocial and often discount the possibility that their partner would prioritize their needs or relationship-level goals over their own immediate self-interests. So even if one partner engages in a prosocial action, there is the danger that deficits in trust may diminish the other partner's ability to recognize the action as prosocial. Counselors can counteract this tendency by creating opportunities for partners to share their assumptions of one another's intentions and provide feedback to one another on the accuracy of these assumptions.

POWER: IMPLICATIONS FOR NEGOTIATION AND DECISION-MAKING

A substantial portion of this text has attended to how partners influence one another's behavior. Previous chapters have alluded to the idea that dependence— the extent to which partners rely on one another to achieve a desired goal—is not inherently equitable (Rusbult & Van Lange, 2003, 2008). Sometimes one partner is substantially more reliant on the relationship than the other. In these instances, the less reliant partner is situated in a position of relative power. They need their partner and the relationship less in order to accomplish their goals.

In this section, we consider the implications of relationship power for Motivational Interviewing practice with couples. Counselors need to be able to recognize indicators of power disparities, anticipate the ways power may impact interactions between partners, and adopt strategies that address challenges introduced by power disparities. Counselors must also be able to recognize instances when disparities in power may be accompanied by severe manifestations of conflict that warrant services beyond what a typical Motivational Interview may provide.

The Basis of Relationship Power

Interdependence theory has generally considered power from a situational perspective—the degree of control a partner has over a particular outcome. This conceptualization gives relatively limited attention to dispositional- or structural-level factors that determine the degree of power individuals have across a wide range of social situations (e.g., Bowleg, 2012; Crenshaw, 1989; Goffman, 1963; Link & Phelan, 2001; Solar & Irwin, 2010). Due to their position in society (the basis of their power) and access to resources, some individuals simply have a more pervasive capacity to enact their goals and desires than others (Dahl, 1957).

Partners who possess stigmatized or marginalized identities experience diminished relationship power. Across a wide range of studies conducted in the United States, data indicate that participants who identify as a racial or ethnic minority (e.g., Capaldi et al., 2012; C. C. Huang et al., 2010) or women (in heterosexual couples) (e.g., Bay-Cheng et al., 2018; Connell, 1987; McCarthy et al., 2018) have less power than participants who identify as majority White or men. Notably, this association between stigmatized identities and relationship power is not limited to race, ethnicity, or gender. Of particular relevance to sexual and gender minority people in relationships, "outness" (disclosure of one's sexual or gender minority identity to others) and gender conformity (behaving in ways that correspond to prescribed gender norms) predict greater relationship power (Goldenberg et al., 2016).

Access to or control over resources enhances power. Studies consistently suggest that older partners (e.g., Kim et al., 2008), those who earn more money (e.g., Capaldi et al., 2012; Goldenberg et al., 2016; Perry et al., 2016) or have more education (e.g., Goldenberg et al., 2016; Pulerwitz et al., 2000) also have more power in a relationship. Age, wealth, and education tend to increase together, and collectively they signal a situation where someone is increasingly likely to have the experience and resources necessary to independently achieve their goals.

Healthier partners tend to have more power. Partners who experience chronic health conditions that impair functioning may be more reliant on their partners to provide emotional support, assistance with healthcare needs, and other resources (e.g., Frambes et al., 2018; Franks et al., 2006). Of particular relevance, stigmatized health conditions—notably HIV infection (Berenson et al., 2015; Perry et al., 2016) and substance use (Caetano et al., 2017; Capaldi et al., 2012; Duncan et al., 2018)—have specifically been associated with diminished relationship power.

Power Disparities and Communication Between Relationship Partners

A substantial amount of research on power has indicated that equity between partners is an indicator of better dyadic functioning. Having power in the relationship is not inherently bad, but power disparities between partners can become problematic (D. H. Baucom et al., 2008; Finneran & Stephenson, 2014; Giordano et al., 2016; Gray-Little, 1982; S. M. Johnson, 2004, 2008; Whisman & Jacobson, 1990). Many of these studies conceptualize power in some way as implying influence over decision-making (D. H. Baucom et al., 2008; Broderick, 1993; Gray-Little & Burks, 1983; Szinovacz, 1981). For example, the Sexual Relationship Power scale asks a respondent to indicate agreement with items, such as "My partner has more say than I do about important decisions that affect us" or "When my partner and

I disagree, he gets his way most of the time" (Pulerwitz et al., 2000). When power is operationalized this way, power disparities imply that one partner has substantially more control over decisions that impact both people in the relationship. It is therefore reasonable to expect that disparities in power might be manifest in the way partners communicate with one another, particularly in discussions characterized by dyadic ambivalence.

Power as conversational dominance. Some argue that the partner who talks more or dominates conversation holds greater power in the relationship (e.g., Gray-Little, 1982; Kollock et al., 1985; Whisman & Jacobson, 1990). One partner can also assert conversational dominance by interrupting the other. Talking more, talking over, and interrupting a partner all convey the message that the conversationally dominant partner's perspectives, emotions, and priorities are more important than those of the partner who is left in the position of listening to them (Kollock et al., 1985).

The power of withholding information. Power imbalances can also manifest in the withholding of information (i.e., withdrawing) and being unreceptive—or not actually listening—to the speaker (Jacobson & Holtzworth-Munroe, 1986). Refusing to discuss problems or respond to a partner's demands asserts an individual's power to maintain the status quo even if a partner objects (Christensen & Heavey, 1990; Holmes & Murray, 1996). Similar to conversational dominance, withdrawal sends the message that the more powerful partner does not need to bother to acknowledge, respond to, or understand the perspective, emotions, or priorities of the partner with less power.

Contempt and coercing partner compliance. While conversational dominance and withdrawal may be implicit assertions of relationship power, partners may overtly express power through communication tactics such as threats, blame, criticism, guilt, and nagging. These coercive tactics enforce a partner's compliance through the use of what might be considered verbal or social punishment (Sullaway & Christensen, 1983). They expressly, directly, and aggressively convey the more powerful partner's disregard for or devaluation of the less powerful partner.

Psychological attachment—Power over a partner's emotions. The concept of psychological attachment was introduced in Chapter 5 (Agnew et al., 1998; Rusbult, Marvetz, et al., 1998). As psychological attachment increases, partners exert greater influence over one another's emotions. One partner's happiness tends to make the other happy; one partner's distress tends to distress the other (Agnew et al., 1998). Similar to dependence, there is nothing that inherently guarantees that psychological attachment develops in simultaneous and equitable ways for both partners. Power disparities can emerge because of a lack of reciprocity in partners' ability to influence one another's emotions (Cook et al., 1995; J. M. Gottman et al., 1999; J. M. Gottman & Notarius, 2000). In other words, the partner who is most sensitive to the other's emotions has less power. Alternatively, the partner who cares the least about the other's feelings has relatively more power.

Implications for Motivational Interviewing With Couples

Power is potentially expressed in the way partners communicate with one another. This implies that Motivational Interviewing counselors can use their observation of the couple's interaction to draw some inferences about partners' respective power and influence on decision-making. It provides a source of information that goes beyond recognition of demographic characteristics, exposure to stigma, and access to resources that may also impact the distribution of power in a relationship.

Perhaps even more importantly, at least some couples' interventions posit that counselors can indirectly address power imbalances by restructuring the way partners communicate (S. M. Johnson, 2004, 2008). Given what is known about power and communication, there are a number of ways in which counselors might adapt their approach to a couples Motivational Interview in response to observed power disparities. Doing so requires the counselor to actively assume the roles of host and moderator (O'Leary, 2015)—establishing communication norms and disrupting or redirecting the couple's typical way of communicating. Their broad goal is to enhance the mutuality of the partners' awareness of one another's perspectives, consideration of one another's needs, and empathy for one another's experience.

Disrupting conversational dominance—Creating opportunities for the expression of goals, needs, and priorities serves as a mechanism to empower partners (S. M. Johnson, 2004). When one partner is accustomed to speaking and the other is equally accustomed to being spoken to—or being in the listener role—the counselor will likely need to do more to draw out the partner who ordinarily speaks less often. In doing so, their goal is to convey respect for both partners. This requires a two-fold strategy. First, counselors may need to disrupt the flow of the partner who is typically conversationally dominant. Second, they need to empower the less conversational partner to speak.

For someone accustomed to speaking uninterrupted, the experience of an intrusion on their flow of ideas may be jarring. The use of accurate reflections to demonstrate empathy and understanding toward the conversationally dominant partner may help to mitigate the emergence of discord between them and the counselor. These strategies convey that the counselor cares about the conversationally dominant partner's perspective even as they create space and direct attention to the other partner.

In a symmetrical way, for a partner who is rarely given the opportunity to express themselves, the sudden realization that it is "their turn to talk" may be disconcerting. Finding the right words to convey a thought can be challenging. If someone does not often speak, they may need time to decide what they want to say and how to say it. Counselors can support partners who are typically not conversationally dominant in several ways. First, they can simply hold the space in conversation for them to speak. In their role as moderator (O'Leary, 2015), the counselor can pause—and ask the partner who typically dominates conversation to pause as well—and give time to formulate a reply. Second, the counselor can use reflections and affirmations of any content offered by the customarily quiet partner to clarify and affirm their contribution to the conversation. Finally, they can emphasize the typically quiet partner's autonomy and convey that it is OK not to speak. The counselor's goal is not to compel speech, but to offer an opportunity.

Engaging as an antidote to withdrawal. When thinking about responding to a partner who withdraws, many counselors may be tempted to think of an instance when withdrawal is motivated by anxiety, insecurity, or fear of judgment. They may think of withdrawal as signaling a lack of power in line with the behavior of a partner who is less conversationally dominant. In those instances, creating opportunities to speak, establishing an atmosphere of safety and respect, and demonstrating empathy and acceptance may reduce anxiety and facilitate engagement in session.

When a partner chooses to assert power by not speaking, the counselor is presented with a different challenge. When formulating a response, it is important to note that withdrawal in this case is an expression of power—not the lack thereof. The message conveyed by a partner's silence is that they do not need to explain themselves or respond to what the other partner has said. Directing a partner to speak not only violates the Spirit of Motivational Interviewing but also may potentially invoke discord between the counselor and the partner who is withdrawn. Instead, the counselor must adopt strategies that acknowledge autonomy and evoke motivation for session engagement.

An initial response may be to affirm autonomy and acknowledge that everyone in the room has the ability to decide what they want to share. This acknowledges the reality that the counselor cannot compel either partner to speak. Much like acknowledging that clients do not have to change can sometimes make it easier for them to discuss the possibility of change (W. R. Miller & Rollnick, 2013), acknowledging that someone does not have to talk in session may make it easier for them to consider a response. One extreme manifestation of this strategy might even be to acknowledge that the couple does not have to continue in counseling together. By acknowledging that both partners have the power to withdraw consent and end their sessions together, the counselor may make it easier for a partner who is withdrawn to talk about what they hope could be accomplished in session.

Counselors can invite a partner who withdraws to talk about their motivation for not speaking. In some instances, withdrawal may serve as an expression of negative affect (e.g., anger, frustration, or resentment toward a partner). In other instances, withdrawal may be motivated by the desire to protect priorities from a partner. Perhaps the partner who has withdrawn believes they would ultimately have to forfeit their own priorities in any discussion. Drawing out and acknowledging these concerns may help the couple to engage in relationship repair, convey respect for one another's priorities, and work together more effectively.

Finally, while counselors cannot compel someone to speak, they can examine the consequences of not speaking. A partner who withdraws has still elected to attend the session. Counselors might juxtapose a partner's decision to withdraw with their broader goals for counseling. They might invite partners to consider the impact of withholding information or not discussing an issue on each other and their relationship. Doing so may afford opportunities for counselors to develop discrepancy (W. R. Miller & Rollnick, 2013)—or to position withdrawal as incongruent with a partner's broader goals and values—and thereby motivate engagement.

Combatting contempt and coercion—Establishing an atmosphere of acceptance and respect. Expressions of contempt—coercive statements that focus on a partner's behavior (e.g., shaming, blaming, criticizing)—are featured among J. M. Gottman's Four Horsemen (J. M. Gottman, 1999; J. M. Gottman & Gottman, 2008). As described previously in this chapter, J. M. Gottman and colleagues advised that counselors interrupt such statements immediately, help the couple to recognize the use of such statements, and implement more adaptive alternative forms of communication that accurately express personal thoughts and feelings without criticism or judgment of the other partner.

While this strategy involves elements of educating and redirecting client communication, it is nevertheless broadly consistent with the Spirit of Motivational Interviewing with couples. In articulating the counselor's role as host, O'Leary (2015) suggested that part of their role is to establish norms for behavior in session. Creating an atmosphere of acceptance and respect—one consistent with the Spirit of Motivational Interviewing—means establishing the expectation that partners will speak and listen to one another. Allowing one partner to belittle or demean the other in session implicitly conveys that such behavior is acceptable to the counselor—or at least not sufficiently concerning to warrant disruption. In contrast, J. M. Gottman's strategy of disrupting and replacing contempt communication in session reorients power and shifts the focus to an examination of each partner's own emotional experience, perspective, and sense of responsibility (J. M. Gottman, 1999; J. M. Gottman & Gottman, 2008).

Catalyzing collaborative decision-making. Couples interventions that incorporate decision-making, negotiation, and problem-solving skills training also give counselors a mechanism to address power disparities in negotiations (D. H. Baucom et al., 2008; Dimidjian et al., 2008). Counselors can facilitate the distribution of relationship power by encouraging both partners to offer their perspectives on a goal, generate possible solutions, and evaluate the merits of those potential solutions (Coleman, 2014). In doing so, the partners exchange information about their relevant thoughts and feelings. Ideally, this process enhances partners' ability to empathize with one another, facilitates joint control in decision-making, and yields a change plan that both partners are more invested in. The use of such strategies is discussed further in Chapter 11 in the context of practice integration.

Special Considerations for Couples Experiencing Intimate Partner Violence

Power disparities predict more than just how a couple communicates and makes decisions. They may also manifest in the occurrence of physical, sexual, or emotional violence between partners in heterosexual (Capaldi et al., 2012; Giordano et al., 2016; Robertson & Murachver, 2011) and same-sex couples (e.g., Bosco et al., 2022; Finneran & Stephenson, 2014; McKenry et al., 2006). While Motivational Interviewing has been utilized as a component of intimate partner violence interventions (e.g., Kistenmacher & Weiss, 2008; Musser et al., 2008; Stith et al., 2012; Taft et al., 2001), these interventions also incorporate specialty services that are potentially beyond the scope of what many Motivational Interviewing counselors can provide in their practice. While there is evidence that it enhances motivation to engage in violence prevention services, Stith et al. (2012) specifically cautioned that Motivational Interviewing should not be used in place of such specialty services.

Motivational Interviewing with couples was not developed as a specialty service to address the occurrence of intimate partner violence. In fact, due to the potential need for specialty services, couples were excluded from our intervention development studies if either partner reported the occurrence of physical or sexual intimate partner violence and stated that they did not feel safe in their current relationship (Starks, Adebayo, et al., 2022; Starks, Dellucci, et al., 2019; Starks, Feldstein Ewing, et al., 2019; Starks, Kyre, et al., 2021; Starks, Millar, et al., 2018; Starks, Robles, et al., 2020). While it is certainly possible that future research may identify ways that couples Motivational Interviewing could be integrated into interventions that address intimate partner violence, this has not been a component of our work to date.

We strongly recommend that any couples' counselor who does not specialize in the treatment of intimate partner violence develop a set of appropriate referral procedures and resources to help couples who are experiencing violence access specialty services. We also recommend developing initial screening procedures that can identify the need for such specialty services at the outset of the counseling relationship. In addition, counselors should also monitor for signs of intimate partner violence over the course of treatment.

Routine Screening to identify the need for specialty services. For more than two decades, scholars have urged counselors to screen all couples seeking services for intimate partner violence (e.g., Aldarondo & Straus, 1994; Bograd & Mederos, 1999; Todahl & Walters, 2011). The practice of universal screening is recommended by a wide range of organizations, among them the American Medical Association, the National Association of Social Workers, and the American Psychological Association (Todahl & Walters, 2011). The rationale is that intimate partner violence occurs with sufficient frequency to warrant routine evaluation; it is unlikely to be disclosed spontaneously; it is associated with poor health outcomes; and its identification is essential to insuring safe and adequate care. While screening questionnaires may be completed on intake, they might also be used periodically over the course of counseling. Some counselors may readminister progress evaluations at regular intervals. Others may utilize such measures on an as-needed basis.

Before administering universal screening, it is recommended that counselors refer to resources outlining best practices for intimate partner

violence screening (e.g., Paterno & Draughon, 2016) **and violence prevention** (e.g., Niolon et al., 2017) **to ensure client safety, familiarize themselves with mandated reporting laws in their area, and develop an intimate partner violence screening and response protocol** (Paterno & Draughon, 2008). Once they have familiarized themselves with this guidance, a range of screening instruments is available. Examples include the Partner Violence Screen (PVS) and Humiliation, Afraid, Rape, Kick (HARK) (for full review, see Curry et al., 2018; Paterno & Draughon, 2016). Counselors interested in a measure tailored for male couples might also consider the Intimate Partner Violence for Gay and Bisexual Men (IPV-GMB) scale (Stephenson & Finneran, 2013).

Couples communication may signal concerns about intimate partner violence. The way a couple communicates is potentially indicative of how power is distributed in their relationship. Counselors can therefore use their observation of a couple's interaction as another source of ongoing information about the risk or potential presence of intimate partner violence. Violence in relationships is associated with engagement in maladaptive communication patterns, such as demand/withdraw communication (Babcock et al., 1993; Feldman & Ridley, 2000); hostile communication (Robertson & Murachver, 2007); threats, blame, and criticism (Feldman & Ridley, 2000); contempt, defensiveness, stonewalling, demanding, and withdrawing communication (T. L. Cornelius et al., 2010).

Counselors may notice the signs or consequences of conflict. Additional risk factors and correlates of intimate partner violence include relationship conflict, displays of hostility, and physical aggression (Niolon et al., 2017; World Health Organization, 2012b). Counselors may therefore look for the physical and psychological signs of conflict and hostility. Physical signs might include bruising, black eyes, and other unexplained injuries sustained in an altercation. Psychological signs may include symptoms of anxiety, depression (including suicide attempt and self-injury), post-traumatic stress disorder, low self-esteem, and increased substance use.

Indications of control or monitoring. Violence may also take the form of isolating, monitoring, or controlling a partner (e.g., World Health Organization, 2012b). Counselors should be concerned if they notice indications that one partner is systematically isolating the other from their social network of family and friends, monitoring their communication (perhaps by going through their cell phone or regulating when they are allowed to see certain people), or restricting access to money, transportation, or other resources.

Responding to indications of violence. Paterno and Draughon (2016) provided guidance for counselors responding to indications of intimate partner violence detected through routine screening. Immediate responses include acknowledgment of the experience, exploring the client's desire for help, and providing referrals and support. They also suggested additional procedures for assessing the level of immediate danger and engaging in related safety planning.

In addition to procedures for responding to violence reported at screening, counselors should develop protocols for responding to instances where indications of violence emerge at other points in the course of treatment. Beyond providing the couple with referrals for specialty services, counselors may need to engage in more immediate safety planning. This might include identifying triggers or factors associated with the occurrence of violence in the relationship (e.g., substance use); constructing de-escalation procedures with the couple (e.g., timeouts); and establishing safety plans (e.g., removing weapons from the home). When the risk of violence is particularly acute, partners may need to be separated to complete the safety planning process, and the plan may include maintenance of that separation when the risk for violence is particularly high (for a full review, see Karakurt et al., 2014).

A range of additional resources is available to counselors who are developing procedures around screening and referrals for intimate partner violence. While most of these resources were developed for heterosexual couples, they provide some starting point for counselors working with diverse couples. Extensive information is available through the National Domestic Violence Hotline's (https://www.thehotline.org) website. This includes a detailed overview of warning signs of abuse and safety planning procedures. The website also facilitates telephone- and chat-based support for survivors. The National Center on Domestic and Sexual Violence (http://www.ncdsv.org) provides counselor training and resources. Its website includes templates for safety plans and related protocols.

CONCLUSIONS AND KEY POINTS

While they arguably receive less explicit attention in the literature on interdependence theory, communication, trust, and power are essential components of relationship functioning. All three concepts are in some way related to how couples manage conflict, solve problems, and make decisions together. All three have the potential to inform a counselor's understanding of interactions between partners in session. Likewise, all of them have the potential to guide how counselors participate in conversations with couples. Collectively, they provide guidance and strategies for reducing conflict and enhancing adaptive interactions between partners during a Motivational Interview.

Much of the research on couples communication has focused on the way partners interact during times of conflict. This body of research is particularly relevant to discussions characterized by dyadic ambivalence. Unlike accommodation responses—which have largely been conceptualized in terms of the behavior of individual partners—the interaction patterns studied by Christensen and colleagues and the communication sequences identified by J. M. Gottman and colleagues are conceptualized as exchanges involving both partners. As such, they provide a framework for conceptualizing how the behavior of both partners during moments of disagreement may sustain or mitigate conflict. Research in this area has also produced guidance for counselors on how to recognize and disrupt maladaptive communication between partners and redirect the exchange toward the use of more adaptive forms of communication characterized by the productive and respectful exchange of information.

Research on trust in romantic relationships has been largely organized around two different theoretical perspectives: dispositional and interpersonal. The former focus on intra-individual factors. They suggest that past experiences, particularly interactions with caregivers in childhood, predispose individuals to a certain degree of trust in others generally. These expectations then shape expectations and perceptions across relationships broadly. In contrast, interpersonal conceptualizations of trust view it through a relationship-specific lens rather than as a generalized expectancy. Trust represents an individual's belief about how their partner will behave. This expectancy is arrived at through observing the extent to a partner displays prosocial behavior, responds benevolently to one's needs, and prioritizes couple-level goals.

Similar to research on communication, both dispositional and interpersonal conceptualizations of trust provide counselors with a framework for understanding interactions between partners in session. Intervention research suggests that facilitating prosocial interactions between partners, fostering the use of adaptive communication in session, may cultivate trust. This means that research on couples' communication and conflict may do more than expand counselor strategies for responding to relationship discord; it may provide a mechanism to address challenges related to mistrust in session.

Finally, as mentioned in previous chapters, there is no guarantee that dependence is distributed equally between partners in a couple. Sometimes one partner is substantially more reliant on the relationship than the other. In these instances, the less reliant partner is situated in a position of relative power. They need their partner and the relationship less in order to accomplish their goals. Partners who have a stigmatized or marginalized identity, those who have less experience or access to resources, and those who experience health challenges are all likely to experience diminished power in their relationships.

Power manifests in the way partners communicate with one another. Motivational Interviewing counselors can look for conversational dominance (one partner speaking more or interrupting the other); withdrawal (withholding information or refusing to acknowledge what a partner has said); or expressions of contempt or coercion as indicators of relationship power. They can also increase egalitarianism in session by ensuring that partners who typically talk less are given the opportunity to speak, engaging partners who express power through withdrawal, and establishing norms for session communication that preclude the use of contempt or coercion.

At its extreme, relationship power and power disparities may manifest in violence between relationship partners. While Motivational Interviewing has been incorporated into a number of violence interventions for people in relationships, the treatment of violence requires specialty services, and Motivational Interviewing should not be used to address violence in the absence of such services. More specifically, Motivational Interviewing with couples was not created to address the occurrence of violence.

Consistent with guidance on best practices, we recommend that counselors adopt initial screening procedures that can identify the need for specialty services to address intimate partner violence at the outset of treatment as well as monitor for signs of intimate partner violence over the course of their work with a couple. Counselors should also develop referral procedures and identify local resources to help couples who are experiencing violence access these specialty services if the need is identified. In addition to procedures for responding to violence reported at initial screening, counselors should develop protocols for responding to instances when indications of violence emerge at other points in the course of treatment. This should include the development of procedures for the ongoing evaluation of risk and the creation of safety plans with couples in addition to providing referrals to specialty services.

10

Discussing Sex as Both a Goal and Context

TREY V. DELLUCCI AND TYREL J. STARKS ■

The framework for couples Motivational Interviewing articulated in the previous chapters was derived from work at the intersection of drug use and sexual behavior among sexual minority men. In this way, this text is consistent with the World Health Organization's (WHO's) stance that sexuality is a "central aspect of being human throughout life" (WHO, 2021). It also fits with recent calls to integrate attention to sexual behavior, sexual health, and HIV-related outcomes in psychotherapy generally (Pantalone & Budge, 2020). This kind of integration challenges counselors to interact with the schemas and scripts—the habits, norms, or conventions—couples develop around sex. To do this, counselors must understand a number of issues related to normative sexual development, the intersection of sexual relationship quality, and relationship functioning, as well as the link between drug use and sex. The purpose of this chapter is to provide an introduction to these issues and examples of strategies and techniques relevant to engaging couples in discussions around sex that can be integrated into Motivational Interviewing practice.

NORMATIVE SEXUALITY DEVELOPMENT

While it is normative for young children and even infants to engage in self-stimulating behavior involving manipulation of their genitals (Bolin et al., 2021), for most the emergence of adult sexual interests focused on achieving orgasm and involving intercourse coincides with the onset of puberty in adolescence (Herman-Giddens et al., 2012; S. Jackson & Goossens, 2020; Susman et al., 2010). Although sex and sexuality are integral to adolescent identity formation, sex during adolescence has historically been viewed as a deviant behavior, and some public health policies have prescribed abstinence as the only presumed healthy behavior during adolescence (Santelli et al., 2017). At the same time, there has been a growing movement in the field to conceptualize sexuality development as a normative process that emphasizes the developmental nature of sexuality from adolescence to adulthood (e.g., Diamond & Savin-Williams, 2009; Harden, 2014; Schalet, 2011; Tolman & McClelland, 2011).

For most people, sexual behavior emerges in adolescence, with the average age of sexual debut around 15 years old (Cavazos-Rehg et al., 2009; Sandfort et al., 2008). Contemporaneously, this is also when most youth report initial dating and relationship experiences. This is important to highlight because sexual arousal is not considered the primary motive for engaging in sex during adolescence (Araji, 2004). For most adolescents, engaging in sex is typically a way of increasing intimacy and desire within a relationship (Dawson et al., 2008). For others, sex may provide a behavioral strategy for managing one's affect by increasing pleasure and distraction or by enhancing self-esteem (Dawson et al., 2008; Robinson et al., 2007).

For sexual minority individuals, adolescence is a critical period for sexual identity development as well (Savin-Williams & Cohen, 2015). While the average age of first awareness of same-sex attraction has been estimated at 9.3 years, self-identification as gay or lesbian tends to occur in adolescence, around age 13–14. This is commonly followed by identity disclosure to friends and parents a year later on average (D'Augelli, 2006).

Older theories of sexual identity development suggested that the process of articulating a sexual minority identity begins with an awareness of being different from one's peers (e.g., Cass, 1979; Rosario et al., 1996; Troiden, 1988). This difference may be first noticed in gender expression (K. M. Cohen, 2002). Another source of feeling different emerges when adolescents begin to have fantasies and feelings for other same-sex individuals (Savin-Williams, 2009). While there is some variability in details, older theories of sexual identity development typically suggested that the initial felt sense of differentness was reliably followed by exploration of same-sex sexual behavior and ultimately by the assumption of a sexual minority identity that was integrated into one's overall personality (e.g, Cass, 1979; Troiden, 1988). More recent research on sexual identity development has suggested this sequence is more variable than originally thought. Some evidence indicates that recent cohorts of youth are more likely to assume a sexual minority identity prior to engaging in sexual behavior with same-sex youth (Rosario et al., 2006). Furthermore, work with sexual minority women has illustrated the potential for fluidity in attraction, behavior, and identity over time from adolescence into emerging adulthood (Diamond, 2008).

Same-sex romantic relationships are common during adolescence and provide a unique context for exploration and experimentation regarding sexuality and the synthesis of one's sexual identity (Connolly & McIsaac, 2009). In their study of sexual minority youth aged 16 to 20 in the Chicago area, Starks, Newcomb, et al. (2015), 35.7% indicated they started dating before the age of 15. Approximately half of these youth (48.8%) reporting having at least six different dating partners, and about half (54.2%) reported having at least two dating partners they considered to be a "serious" relationship.

Relationships remain common into emerging adulthood and beyond. While data on sexual minority women and transgender people in relationships are extremely sparse, large cross-sectional survey studies of sexual minority men indicated that approximately 50% to 82% were in relationships (Parsons et al., 2013; Starks, Robles, Bosco, Dellucci, et al., 2019). These relationships were stable, with the majority of relationships lasting at least 2 years. Similarly, the recognition of same-sex marriage in the United States created the opportunity for sexual minority couples to access this relationship milestone. In 2019, of those in same-sex households, 58% were married (Walker & Taylor, 2021).

SEXUALITY, HEALTH, AND RELATIONSHIP QUALITY

While many of the narrative examples in this text reflect an integrated focus on drug use and sexual health, Motivational Interviewing can address sexual health broadly, even in the absence of drug use (see a review by Bahner & Stenqvist, 2020). Before discussing how Motivational Interviewing can be applied to improve sexual health, it is potentially useful to consider the definition of sexual health and the history of addressing sex in counseling and psychotherapy. The way in which we understand "sexual health" has evolved across the decades and is shaped, at least partly, by political, social, and historical events (Edwards & Coleman, 2004). To date, the WHO defines sexual health as

> a state of physical, emotional, mental and social well-being in relation to sexuality; it is not merely the absences of disease, dysfunction or infirmity. Sexual health requires a positive and respectful approach to sexuality and sexual relationships, as well as the possibility of having pleasurable and safe sexual experiences, free of coercion, discrimination and violence. For sexual health to be attained and maintained, the sexual rights of a persons must be respected, protected, and fulfilled. (WHO, 2006)

Despite the very definition arguing that sexual health goes beyond "disease, dysfunction or infirmity," the majority of the work in psychological and clinical research on sexual health has historically focused on the treatment of sexual dysfunctions and disease.

Sexual dysfunctions (e.g., sexual desire disorders, sexual arousal disorders, orgasm disorders, and sexual pain disorders) made their first appearance in the third version of the *Diagnostic and Statistical Manual of Mental Disorders* (*DSM-III*) in 1980 (American Psychiatric Association, 1980). Until the publication of its fifth edition (*DSM-5*) in 2013 (American Psychiatric Association, 2013), there had been little guidance on differentiating between sexual difficulties and dysfunctions (Sungur & Gündüz, 2014), potentially creating a bias for sexual dysfunction diagnoses. The *DSM-5* has since introduced criteria to improve differentiating diagnoses of sexual dysfunctions, including duration and frequency, the need for marked distress or impairment within the individual, and important differences associated with sex assigned at birth. While *DSM-5* has made these improvements, these diagnoses often do not capture the experiences of sexual and gender minorities in the manual's current version.

Sexuality as a Specialization Versus Integration in Health Services

In many respects, sex has been treated as a specialty topic within the psychotherapy and counseling disciplines (Binik & Meana, 2009). The reputation of "sex therapy" as a specialization can be dated to Masters and Johnson's publication of *Human Sexual Inadequacy* in 1970. Following the sexual revolution, this work was influential in continuing a trend that reduced the stigma around sex and creating a "safe space" for addressing sexual dysfunction in psychotherapy. More recent scholars—arguing for greater integration of sex into psychotherapy generally—have pointed out that the principles that underlie most sex therapy interventions are shared by other orientations (Binik & Meana, 2009). Consistent with this, others have characterized sex therapy as a specific application of cognitive behavioral therapy since its inception (Meana & Jones, 2011). This conceptual and theoretical overlap has substantive consequences for psychotherapy practice. Many counselors may view issues related to sex and sexuality as outside their typical range of competence and requiring referral to such a specialist; however, relegating sex to specialty services potentially creates an arbitrary professional distinction that does not map to how clients experience their lives.

In 2001, Surgeon General David Satcher emphasized the centrality of sexuality to the human experience (Satcher, 2001). Despite this, researchers examining general health and well-being over the lifespan have typically not included a focus on healthy expressions of sexuality (Diamond & Huebner, 2012). Instead, attention to sex has commonly been restricted to a relatively narrow focus on sexually transmitted infections (STIs), unintended pregnancy, sexual dysfunction, or sexual violence and coercion (Dixon-Mueller, 1993; Higgins et al., 2010).

In the past two decades, subdisciplines of psychology have called for a paradigm shift, emphasizing the need to study the positive, normative, and pleasurable dimensions of sex, rather than focusing solely on sexual risks and problems (R. M. Anderson, 2013; Harden, 2014; Impett et al., 2014; Philpott et al., 2006; Pick et al., 2005; Russell, 2005). This is particularly salient in the field of HIV, where Pantalone and Budge (2020) have asked the field to move away from the typical public health model. The shift from risks and dangers of sex to a "sex-positive approach" to conceptualizing sexual health is important because positive aspects of sex contribute to an individual's overall well-being (Satcher, 2001). Similarly, cross-sectional and longitudinal studies have consistently found that positive aspects of sex are associated with health in both middle and late adulthood and life expectancy (Diamond & Huebner, 2012; Lindau & Gavrilova, 2010; Onder et al., 2003; Palmore, 1982; Smith et al., 1997).

Sexual Relationship Quality: Associations With General Relationship Functioning and Health

Chapter 5 opened with a review of the robust literature establishing the association between general relationship quality and health. There is also a well-developed—if admittedly smaller—literature linking the narrower domain of sexual relationship quality to health outcomes. This literature underscores the legitimacy of calls to integrate attention to healthy sexuality and sexual relationship quality into more general mental and physical healthcare.

Much like the larger literature on relationship functioning (see Chapter 5), there is variability in how the quality of sexual interactions has been conceptualized and measured in research. Some studies have focused on sexual frequency as a proxy for sexual quality (e.g., Schoenfeld et al., 2017). The assumption here is that couples that have sex more are having higher quality sex. In contrast, others have focused on partners' subjective sense of satisfaction with sex rather than absolute sexual frequency (e.g., Yeh et al., 2006). Still others have used relevant aspects of relationship functioning as indicators of sexual relationship quality. Such examples include sexual intimacy, or the degree to which partners reciprocate love and respect during sex (Lafontaine et al., 2018), and sexual communication, or the degree to which partners share their preferences and seek change within their sexual relationships (Simon & Gagnon, 1986). Similarly, studies of sexual minority men have conceptualized the quality of sexual interactions across broad domains, including (but not limited to) sexual satisfaction, sexual communication, and frequency of sex (e.g., Parsons et al., 2012).

Therapists, researchers, and the general public view the quality of a couple's relationship and their sex life as intrinsically connected (Sprecher, 1998; Wincze & Weisberg, 2001). Decades of research have demonstrated a strong, positive association between relationship functioning and sexual satisfaction among both heterosexual and same-sex couples (e.g., Byers, 2005; Fallis et al., 2016; Peplau & Fingerhut, 2007). Similarly, dissatisfaction with sex and the perception that sex does not occur with sufficient frequency in a relationship are common reasons for couples to seek therapy (Doss et al., 2004; Geiss & O'Leary, 1981 Veroff, Kulka, & Douvan, 1981) and are often associated with negative relationship outcomes, such as mistrust and jealousy (Fortenberry, 2019).

Some theorists have suggested that the quality of sex impacts the overall quality of a relationship in a unidirectional fashion (Hassebrauck & Fehr, 2002; Sprecher & Cate, 2004). Evidence for this proposition comes from a limited, but compelling, group of longitudinal studies examining causal pathways between relationship satisfaction and sexual satisfaction (Byers, 2005; Fallis et al., 2016; Sprecher, 2002; Yeh et al., 2006). The most recent involved 113 heterosexual couples assessed at baseline and a follow-up 2 years later (Fallis et al., 2016). Results suggested that one's own sexual satisfaction at baseline predicted his or her own—but not their partner's—relationship satisfaction at follow-up. In contrast, relationship satisfaction at baseline was not predictive of sexual satisfaction over time. These results were consistent with three previous longitudinal studies, which also found that sexual satisfaction was predictive of relationship satisfaction over time (Byers, 2005; Sprecher, 2002; Yeh et al., 2006).

Others have challenged the assumption of a unidirectional association between sexual and overall relationship quality—suggesting that the association is instead reciprocal in nature. Lawrance and Byers (1995) proposed the interpersonal exchange model of sexual satisfaction. Based on social exchange theory (Homans, 1974), and highly consistent with principles of interdependence theory—the model posits that sexual satisfaction is based on four factors over time: (1) the individual's perceptions of the rewards associated with the sexual relationship; (2) the costs associated with the sexual relationship; (3) perceived comparison with one's expectations; and (4) perceived level of equity of the couple's rewards and costs. Longitudinal data gathered by Lawrance and Byers (1995) provided evidence supporting a reciprocal hypothesis. Pathways from sexual satisfaction to relationship satisfaction and from relationship satisfaction to sexual satisfaction were significant.

Ultimately, whether sexual relationship quality has a unidirectional or a recursive association with overall relationship quality is less important for counselors than the larger observation that healthy, satisfying sexual interactions between partners are predictive of relationship functioning. Despite their points of divergence, these studies all suggested that counselors who wish to help couples improve their relationship functioning overall may overlook an important determinant of relationship quality if they are unable or unwilling to incorporate attention to a couple's sexual functioning. They also suggested that components that aim to reduce sexual dissatisfaction and improve the quality of a couple's sexual interactions may be meaningful additions to psychological interventions that address the general mental and physical health of couples.

Attachment: Interpersonal Expectancies About Relationships—Sex and Sexual Satisfaction in Relationships

The concept of attachment was introduced in Chapter 9. The discussion there focused primarily on the implications of attachment orientation on perceptions of trust and relationship power. Attachment has also been linked to sexual relationship functioning more specifically. Research conducted primarily among heterosexual people in relationships suggested that attachment style predicts how people approach sex.

Anxiously attached individuals employ hyperactivation strategies, whose function is to achieve or maintain closeness within the relationship (Ainsworth, 1989; Bowlby, 1969, 1977; Fraley & Shaver, 2000). For these individuals, sex serves as a maintenance behavior to reduce feelings of insecurity and establish closeness with partners. At the same time, these individuals often have lower self-efficacy for sexual negotiation and lower levels of orgasmic responsivity (Birnbaum, 2007; J. A. Feeney & Noller, 2004; Schachner & Shaver, 2004), which leads to lower sexual satisfaction overall. Among sexual minority men specifically, having an anxiously attached partner is associated with less frequent sex between main partners (Starks & Parsons, 2014). Attachment anxiety has also been linked to concerns that condom use will convey mistrust or a lack of emotional closeness between partners (Starks et al., 2016). These concerns about intimacy interference have in turn been linked to sexual risk-taking or attitudes towards HIV prevention strategies among sexual minority men in a number of studies (e.g., Gamarel & Golub, 2015, 2019; Golub et al., 2012; Starks et al., 2016; Starks, Payton, et al., 2014).

In contrast, avoidantly attached individuals engage in deactivating strategies in hopes of maintaining independence and self-reliance, while also denying emotional needs from the relationship (Ainsworth, 1989; Bowlby, 1969, 1977; Fraley & Shaver, 2000). Avoidantly attached individuals often have less restrictive attitudes toward sex, avoid intimacy in the context of sex, and have higher numbers of casual partners (Gentzler & Kerns, 2004; Schachner & Shaver, 2004). For these individuals, lower sexual satisfaction is thought to be driven by the discomfort of integrating intimacy and sex with their main partners (Butzer & Campbell, 2008). Among sexual minority men specifically, having an avoidantly attached partner is associated with decreased frequency of sex between main partners—similar to anxious attachment. In addition, men who were avoidantly attached reported more frequent condomless sex with casual partners than both secure and anxiously attached men (Starks & Parsons, 2014). Avoidant attachment has also been linked to concerns that condoms interfere with sexual pleasure (Starks et al., 2016).

DRUG USE AND SEXUAL BEHAVIOR

As outlined in Chapter 1, there is a well-established link between drug use and sexual behavior generally—as well as sexual risk-taking specifically (e.g., Daskalopoulou et al., 2014; Ottaway et al., 2017; Rendina et al., 2015; Starks, Sauermilch, et al., 2021). For example, 27.2% of sexual minority men reported using cannabis; 5.6% reported using stimulants (e.g., cocaine, crack, amphetamines); and 4.1% reported the use of other illicit drugs concurrently with sex (Feinstein, Moody, et al., 2018). Concurrent drug use and sex were also common among sexual minority men in relationships. Previous studies have estimated that 12.5% (illicit drugs) to 33% (cannabis) of partnered sexual minority men used drugs during sex with their main partner, while 10.6% to 31% used illicit drugs or cannabis during sex with their casual partners (e.g., Mitchell, 2016; Mitchell et al., 2016; Parsons & Starks, 2014). To begin to integrate attention to sex into drug use interventions, it is potentially useful to have some awareness of factors that might explain this association.

For some people, there is a belief that drug use will help facilitate sex by influencing their sexual intimacy, pleasure, and risk-taking. These beliefs are often conceptualized under expectancy theory (Dermen & Cooper, 1994; G. T. Wilson & Lawson, 1976), which emphasizes the importance of internalized expectations about the effects of substance use on sexual behaviors. Individuals expect that substance use will increase their ability to express their desires for others (Mullens et al., 2010) and their own ability to be social and accepted by others (Dermen & Cooper, 1994) and to enhance sexual performance (Mullens et al., 2011). Studies have consistently found that these expectances are associated with the use of substances generally (Flory et al., 2004; Starks, Millar, Tuck, et al., 2015), drinking and drug use before sex, and condomless sex after drinking (Patrick & Maggs, 2009; White et al., 2009).

For others, sexual interactions provide a context in which drug use is reinforced or normative. These interactions are sometimes referred to as *party and play* (PnP) or *chemsex*—colloquial terms popular in the United States and the United Kingdom—indicating sex that occurs under the influence of drugs, particularly among sexual minority men (Bourne et al., 2015; Souleymanov et al., 2021). PnP offers sexual minority men an escape from oppression and stigma (Pollard et al., 2018), opportunities for self-expression and pleasure (Race, 2017), and a context for producing social connectedness (Race, 2015).

Many describe using drugs initially as a means of decreasing sexual inhibitions so that they can introduce more variety into their sexual experiences—engaging in behaviors they otherwise would not try (Kurtz, 2005). Specific substances, namely methylmethcathione ("mephedrone"), gamma-hydroxybutyric acid ("GHB"), and crystal methamphetamine, are common drugs used in conjunction with sex in the PnP scene because they induce euphoria, increase energy, and enhance sexual arousal and stamina (Bourne et al., 2015). A recent qualitative study found that many sexual minority men described experiencing multiple domains of pleasure when combining drug use and sex (Milhet et al., 2019). For example, some described experiences of becoming someone's "special person" in the moments of using drugs during sex. Others also described PnP as a unique context for making social connections that allowed for the formation of transient but intense bonds with other individuals. Finally, some described PnP as giving them a space to completely let go and experience feeling physical sensations that they had not experienced before. Combined, these physiological, social, and affective pleasures reinforce a belief that drug use is somehow essential to experience sexual pleasure and satisfaction.

Implications for Motivational Interviewing Practice

Failure to attend to sex and sexual satisfaction may diminish the relevance of drug use interventions. Whether through sexual expectancies or PnP, sex can be a primary motivator for drug use for some people. Exploring this possibility requires that counselors feel confident in their ability to facilitate conversations at the intersection of drug use and sex. At the same time, many training programs forgo topics addressing healthy sexual functioning and only teach counselors about sexual dysfunctions broadly (Hanzlik & Gaubatz, 2012). Often this leads counselors to ignore or not address sex in session unless it is specifically brought up by the client or in the context of medical illness (S. A. Miller & Byers, 2008); however, by ignoring sex a counselor may miss a major function of drug use.

The intersection of sex and drugs may shape clients' perceptions of behavior change goals. Clients vary in the extent to which drug use and sex are interrelated behaviors. For some clients, the link between them is very tenuous. For these individuals, drug use and sex might sometimes happen together, but they may also happen separately. At the other end of the spectrum, drug use and sex may be deeply connected—nearly synonymous—behaviors for some clients. Engaging in one behavior may essentially imply engaging in the other. These clients may routinely use drugs with their sexual partners, and the overwhelming majority of their sex may happen while intoxicated.

The extent to which drug use and sex are interrelated has the potential to shape client perceptions of behavior change. Where drug use and sex are largely unrelated behaviors, clients may readily be able to imagine changes in one behavior that are more or less independent of changes made in the other. In contrast, clients for whom sex and drugs are highly related may perceive any change in one of these behaviors as directly implying change in the other. For a client who cannot imagine having sex sober, reducing or abstaining from drug use means also forfeiting sexual activity. In these cases, exploring the possibility of sober sex—developing social skills necessary to meet sexual partners, negotiate a sexual encounter, and fully engage in pleasurable sex—may be a prerequisite or contemporaneous goal to enable the client to consider changes in drug use.

DISCUSSING SEX WITH OUTSIDE PARTNERS IN MOTIVATIONAL INTERVIEWING PRACTICE

While existing empirically supported couples interventions, such as (J. M. Gottman & Gottman, 2008) and S. Johnson's "Emotionally Focused Couple Therapy" (S. M. Johnson & Bradley, 2009), do not shy away from exploring sex and intimacy within the relationship, these interventions historically have assumed a secure bond cannot be established within the context of a consensual nonmonogamous relationship. This assumption runs counter to research on nonmonogamy among sexual minority male couples presented in Chapters 1 and 5 and similar research on heterosexual couples (see review by Moors et al., 2017). Additionally, it contrasts with clinical guidance for counselors to be flexible in their own ideas about sexual relationships and their views on commitment in order to best help the couple (LaSala, 2004, 2005).

Since many existing approaches to couples therapy view nonmonogamy as inherently problematic, Motivational Interviewing counselors seeking a model for how they might engage couples around the issue of sexual agreements and the occurrence of sex with outside partners must look elsewhere for one that is consistent with the Spirit of Motivational Interviewing. One such model is offered in couples' HIV testing and counseling (CHTC). CHTC was discussed previously in Chapter 4, where it provided a model for conceptualizing pathways of communication between the counselor, partners, and couple in a Motivational Interviewing session. In addition to this, the coverage and sequencing of content in CHTC substantively influenced and informed how Motivational Interviewing counselors introduced and navigated the discussion of sexual agreements and sex with outside partners in the *Couples Health Project* intervention (Starks, Adebayo, et al., 2021; Starks, Millar, et al., 2018).

A Model for Discussing Sex and Sexual Agreements in Counseling

As a single-session intervention, CHTC emphasizes the importance of couples testing and receiving their results together (Painter, 2001; WHO, 2012a). While a detailed presentation of CHTC is beyond the scope of this chapter, it is important to highlight that CHTC is inclusive of seven core elements: (1) introduction and consent for treatment; (2) preparation for the HIV test; (3) exploration of the couple's relationship; (4) discussion of HIV risk concerns; (5) sexual agreements; (6) delivering test results; and (7) developing a treatment and/ or prevention plan based on testing results. This allows for mutual disclosure of HIV status within the couple, facilitation of support, and connection to a healthcare provider.

Although CHTC was not originally developed specifically as a Motivational Interviewing intervention per se, its general principles and approach to helping couples negotiate sexual safety are highly consistent with the spirit and practice of Motivational Interviewing. Of particular relevance are Steps 4, 5, and 7, which focus largely on clarifying the couple's approach to HIV and STI risk management; the explication of the couple's sexual agreement; and the development of an HIV prevention or care plan that both partners are invested in. This sequencing mirrors the focusing, evoking, and planning processes that characterize couples Motivational Interviewing.

Unlike interventions that presume nonmonogamy is inherently problematic, the counselor in CHTC does not have an agenda about what a couple's agreement "should be." Clarification of the agreement provides a foundation for exploring the sufficiency of the couple's sexual health or prevention planning. It serves as a jumping off point for evoking motivation to reduce sexual risk-taking in the context of the couple's overall goal for their sexual agreement. An example of this work is provided in the Chapter 6 narrative involving Rafael and Otto. In this example, Otto brought up concerns around sex organically. The counselor learned quickly that the couple had defined their sexual agreement as being open and allowing for sexual partners outside the relationship with limited rules or boundaries.

Introducing the Topic of Sex in Counseling

Unlike with the case of Rafael and Otto in Chapter 6, not all clients introduce the topic of sex organically. In these instances, it may be incumbent on the counselor to broach the topic when they suspect it could be relevant. Notably, some have suggested that assessing sex and sexual functioning should routinely be included as a component of general couples counseling (e.g., J. S. Gottman & Gottman, 2015). Here we offer a few recommendations for engaging couples around the topic of sex in a couples Motivational Interview; these recommendations were drawn from a combination of Motivational Interviewing practice guidance and CHTC.

Consider the timing of sexual content relative to the establishment of rapport. CHTC deliberately explores the couple's relationship generally (in Step 3) before progressing to a more focused discussion of sexual health practices and clarification of the sexual agreement (Painter, 2001; WHO, 2012a). Step 3 provides an opportunity for rapport building and identification of the couple's strengths, which then can be used to address challenges or disagreements should they be encountered later in session. This sequencing—which positions rapport building and an exploration of relationship functioning ahead of focusing specifically on a behavioral target—mirrors our presentation of Motivational Interviewing processes. Counselors who rush to introduce the topic of sex or sexual safety before establishing sufficient rapport and understanding of the strengths and challenges a couple might be facing generally may find the topic more difficult to examine.

In our practice, we have generally found that when counselors move to discuss sexual behavior or sexual risk-taking before talking about the relationship more generally, the transitions are more difficult, and some disruption in rapport is more likely (Starks, Adebayo, et al., 2021; Starks, Dellucci, et al., 2019; Starks, Feldstein Ewing, et al., 2019; Starks, Kyre, et al., 2021; Starks, Robles, Pawson. et al., 2019). In contrast, there is something of a natural progression in content that can occur across the engaging, facilitating, and focusing processes when counselors approach sex by discussing the relationship generally first. These are described informally to trainees as "Tell me about yourselves"; "Tell me about your relationship"; and then "Tell me what is happening for you guys around sex"; and finally (if relevant), "How do manage HIV risk in your relationship?" That flow, from general to specific, mirrors the sequencing of content in CHTC and the salience of Motivational Interviewing processes over time.

Acceptance matters—Particularly when talking about sex. Consistent with the Spirit of Motivational Interviewing with couples, when broaching the topic of sex, the counselor must seek to actively convey a nonjudgmental stance toward the couple's handling of sex and a genuine curiosity about the couple's sexual goals and priorities. This recommendation is in line with the idea that counselors should seek to actively express acceptance throughout a Motivational Interview. It is particularly important when bringing up the topic of sex because clients may be particularly likely to anticipate judgment if their agreement or behavior violates what they believe the counselor's values and norms to be.

One way to actively convey a nonjudgmental stance is to consider language use. As mentioned in Chapter 5, some people have an implicit tendency to use the term "commitment" as synonymous with monogamy. Such use has the potential to unintentionally convey to nonmonogamous couples that their relationships are inherently less than fully committed. Terms like "cheating" or "infidelity" tend to connote that someone has done something wrong. While there may be instances in which these terms are meaningful to clients in ways that warrant their use, counselors should be cautious about introducing such language because it may unintentionally convey a specific viewpoint on sex with partners outside the primary relationship.

Counselors may utilize strategies such as normalizing and affirmations of sexual autonomy to explicitly assume a nonjudgmental stance toward sex during a couples Motivational Interview. Emphasizing autonomy is a central component of Motivational Interviewing Spirit (W. R. Miller & Rollnick, 2013), and statements supportive of autonomy or self-efficacy are specifically valued as a counseling technique (e.g., S.-F. Wang et al., 2007). These kinds of statements can be applied specifically to introduce sex in a Motivational Interviewing consistent way. Consider the following example, which contains prototype language drawn from the CHTC protocol in italics (Painter, 2001; WHO, 2012a):

COUNSELOR: If it is OK with you guys, I was wondering if we could talk a bit about the rules or understandings you guys have about sex with partners outside your relationship. *Many couples have agreements or understandings about how they have sex together and with partners outside their relationships. Some couples may be monogamous or exclusive. Some couples may be open, which means one or both partners may have sex with other people. Other couples go for something in the middle.* I am not here to tell you what your agreement should be, but I am curious what rules or understandings you guys have.

EXPLORING SEXUAL SATISFACTION: UNPACKING AND MODIFYING SEXUAL SCRIPTS

While CHTC provides a model for how counselors might navigate a conversation about sex with partners outside the primary relationship, it is less well suited to guide a discussion of the sex main partners have together. Enhancing sexual functioning and sexual satisfaction in couples was a primary focus of Masters and Johnson's work (Masters & Johnson, 1966, 1970). They conceptualized sex as a natural function and proposed a set of specific and structured suggestions (including defined practice exercises or homework) for physical–sexual touch and discovery intended to address sexual dysfunction in couples (Weiner & Avery-Clark, 2014) by redirecting focus away from expectations of an emotional or physical response (Linschoten et al., 2016).

Masters and Johnson (1970) suggested that natural functions were (1) innate, (2) not teachable, and (3) outside voluntary control. Building on the idea that sex is a natural function, they proposed that deficits in sexual pleasure and performance arose in part because people try to control aspects of the sexual encounter that they cannot—resulting in anxiety and ineffective communication between partners. Their exercises were intended to refocus people on those aspects of the sexual encounter that they could control: their engagement in the physical act of touching and the mindful experience of the sensations experienced in their own body. Since one cannot "make" or "force" a natural sexual response, pressure to do so produces anxiety and paradoxically diminishes enjoyment. Engaging in sexual touch for the sake of one's self and focusing on tactile sensation rather than arousal per se free the individual from anxiety as they allow themselves to experience a natural sexual response rather than manufacture a particular sexual goal like arousal or orgasm.

Practice integration is discussed in greater detail in Chapter 11. For at least some couples who experience deficits in sexual satisfaction together, the integration of sensate focus activities into a Motivational Interview may provide a powerful vehicle for counselors to support clients in the development of change plans that enhance a couple's sex together. It enhances the universe of activities that counselors might draw on when clients identify challenges related to pleasure, arousal, or orgasm during sex together.

While potentially useful, sensate focus activities primarily center on behavior immediately preceding and during the act of sex itself. Some couples may experience barriers to having sex together that occur outside this relatively immediate context of sex. Challenges may emerge in the interactions that lead up to sex as partners signal their desire for sex and assess one another's interest and intention. In this case, sexual satisfaction is diminished not by sexual performance per se, but by the misalignment of partners' expectations about when sex should happen and how it might come about.

In Chapter 5, the narrative between Otto and Rafael ended with the realization that both men had some desire to have sex together more frequently. This came as something of a surprise, particularly to Rafael. Here, the counselor continues this discussion. As the conversation progresses, the counselor achieves two primary goals. First, they elaborate on each partner's perception of how interest in sex is conveyed. Second, they highlight points where partners' perceptions of one another's intentions are misaligned. Doing so clarifies partners' sexual needs and goals. It also enhances the accuracy of sexual communication.

* * *

| COUNSELOR: OK, so where's the best place for us to start in on this? We could begin by focusing on what's going on with other people or on sex between you two. What makes sense? | [Collaborative question directed to the couple.] |

RAFAEL: So, I don't know about you, but I am really curious about this idea that you actually want to have sex more. Because that is news to me.

OTTO: Oh god, I'm in trouble. [laughs]

COUNSELOR: Ha! Well, Otto, how would you feel if we jump into things there?

[Collaborative question.]

OTTO: Sure. Why not. I put it out there. Though honestly, I'm surprised that's news to you. I think it's pretty obvious that I've been frustrated.

RAFAEL: Ummm . . . has it? I feel like you have not said this before.

OTTO: I have; I just think you haven't noticed.

COUNSELOR: So, Rafael, help us understand why you were thinking that Otto didn't want to have sex very much. What signaled to you that he wasn't interested.

[Question elicits Rafael's perception of the couple's interaction.]

RAFAEL: Well, sometimes I feel like I try to start something and you sort of shut it down.

OTTO: When does that happen?

RAFAEL: Just this past weekend. We were out at the bar. He met me after my shift, and we just stayed out together. It was nice; we had fun. Then we got home, and I like tried to start stuff and you just wanted to go to bed.

OTTO: I was very drunk, and honestly, sex did not seem like a great idea just then. So that's fair, but that's like one time.

COUNSELOR: Got it. So I really want to come back to that question of how substance use impacts sex for you two. But, if it's OK, I'm curious to go back to this idea of why Rafael might have gotten the impression you were not into the idea of having sex so much. Rafael, sounds like part of it is sometimes you try to initiate and the overture is not always well received. But what else, if anything, do you notice? What else gave you that idea?

[Summary followed by a question that maintains a focus on understanding Rafael's perception of the couple's interaction.]

RAFAEL: Well, I guess also you—and I'm sorry to say this, we don't have to talk about it if you don't want to—but you seem really like frustrated with your body and stressed out about being in shape. I don't necessarily know how to respond to that. I think you look fine, but I feel like any time sex or being attractive comes up you get really frustrated.

OTTO: Ugh . . . well, that's true. I do not feel good about how I look. I guess I kind of assume that when we don't have sex it's because I'm not attractive.

RAFAEL: I have definitely never said that.

COUNSELOR: Got it. So when you guys don't have sex, Otto, you often end up worrying that it is because of how you look.

[Reflection clarifies Otto's feeling and disrupts what could be a defensive exchange.]

OTTO: Yeah. I mean, that sounds stupid, but he's around really hot guys at the bar the entire day. I feel like there's no way I can compete.

COUNSELOR: Part of you is worried that Rafael is comparing you to other people.

[Reflection clarifies Otto's assumptions about how Rafael evaluates him sexually.]

OTTO: I am certainly comparing myself. I feel like it's just what you do as a gay man. There's a lot of pressure to look a certain way. [to RAFAEL] Don't you think? And like, especially with some of the guys at the bar.

RAFAEL: That is true. There is definitely a look. Everyone wants a great profile picture for the apps or whatever. But honestly, I never go around thinking like, "Otto is ugly, and I wish I had someone hotter." Like, that's not what's happening for me.

COUNSELOR: Otto, I'm curious, what, if anything, is Rafael doing or saying—what are you picking up on—that would indicate to you he is comparing you to other guys?

[Question elicits Otto's perspective on the couple's interaction.]

OTTO: Honestly, for the most part he's really good. He's always very nice about how I look. So, it isn't like he's insulting me. If anything, he's probably nicer about my body than I am. I guess I think about it a lot when I think he's hooking up with someone else. Like, clearly he wants to have sex, but not with me.

COUNSELOR: Rafael, what are your thoughts on that?

[Question to Rafael.]

RAFAEL: So, that's definitely not the case. I mean, sometimes hooking up is fun because it's just sex. There's so many other things that connect us other than just sex. Sometimes sex with a hookup is just easy. But like, it's never a situation where I'm thinking, "Oh I'm horny and you are gross" which is what I feel like you are assuming.

OTTO: Not quite that childish.

RAFAEL: Right, but you know what I mean.

COUNSELOR: Right now, it sounds like Otto assumes that when you, Rafael, hook up with someone else, it's because you're not attracted to him. And it sounds like that's not what is really going on for you.

[Dyadic reflection clarifies discrepancy between Otto's perception and Rafael's intention.]

RAFAEL: Right. I actually feel really bad that's what you have been thinking. I feel like we do a really good job of being kind to one another, and it bothers me you'd make that assumption.

OTTO: I know. I really do know that's not you. It's just hard not to feel that way.

COUNSELOR: It's really clear that you guys genuinely don't want to hurt one another.

[Relationship affirmation.]

RAFAEL: Right. I've seen couples that are shady to each other. And we've never been into that kind of petty argument stuff.

OTTO: We have never been into that kind of drama.

COUNSELOR: I am wondering if we could go back to this moment this past weekend when Rafael tried to initiate sex. Given the conversation we just had, Rafael, what is your hunch about how Otto was feeling that evening.

[Question revisits Rafael's perception of couple's interaction.]

RAFAEL: Huh . . . well, that's a good question.
I mean, we had a really good evening. I thought we
were having a good time anyway.

COUNSELOR: And what is your hunch about how   [Question to Rafael.]
he may have been feeling, or what may have been
going through his head about you guys having sex?

RAFAEL: I guess in all honesty, I kind of don't know
now.

COUNSELOR: Totally OK. No judgments. Otto,   [Question invites
what was that moment like for you?   disclosure from Otto.]

OTTO: Honestly, it was frustrating. Because the
truth is, I was tired and very drunk. So I didn't really
want to have sex because I wanted to go to bed. But
I also felt really bad for not being into it because
I spend so much time wishing we had sex more
often. So oddly, I was kind of angry about it because
I felt like you picked a time when you knew I was
kinda out of it.

RAFAEL: I definitely did not know that. How would
I possibly know that?

COUNSELOR: Right, so you guys were in two really   [Dyadic reflection
different places just then. If you could go back in captures misaligned
time, what do you wish had happened?   expectations. Question
                                                     shifts focus to a
                                                     preferred past.]

RAFAEL: I guess I could have just not done
anything. But then you're mad because we never
have sex.

COUNSELOR: Right, so doing nothing doesn't feel   [Dyadic reflection of
like the best approach. But what could have made   common ground and
that evening go better. It sounds like neither of you question.]
quite wanted it to end the way it did.

OTTO: I think I could have done a better job of just
saying, "Not now, but later." Things got shut down
in a way that was kind of cold and maybe sort of
resentful, when, like, I really did want to have sex,
just not right then.

COUNSELOR: What would that have looked like?   [Question to Otto
                                                     clarifies communication
                                                     strategy.]

OTTO: I mean, I could have just said: "This is hot, but we gotta wait until the morning."

COUNSELOR: [to RAFAEL] How would that go?   [Question to Rafael elicits his perspective on the strategy.]

RAFAEL: I think it'd be fine. Then I'd know. At the time, I just felt like I was annoying you.

OTTO: No, that was definitely not it.

* * *

Some of the challenges Rafael and Otto experience can be understood in terms of sensate focus principles. Both men are in some ways concerned about the other's level of attraction or interest in sex. A sensate focus would suggest that neither of them can control the other's interest in or arousal during sex, and therefore this preoccupation with one another's responses increases their own anxiety and diminishes the enjoyment of sex.

On another level, though, Rafael and Otto are struggling to accurately convey and recognize one another's interest in sex. Otto has incorrectly assumed that he is generally not attractive to Rafael and Rafael is uninterested in sex with him. Rafael incorrectly assumed that Otto is uninterested in sex and that approaching sex will activate Otto's discomfort with his own appearance. This is not necessarily a problem of sexual interest, arousal, or orgasm per se. The problem is that Otto and Rafael have made incorrect assumptions about one another's intentions, goals, and desires. Their implicit or nonverbal communication about sex is misaligned. Their struggle illustrates the lived experience that a couple's ability to have open and honest communication about sex is central to sexual satisfaction (MacNeil & Byers, 2005).

The challenge faced by Otto and Rafael can be understood in part by thinking in terms of the alignment of their sexual scripts. A sexual script is a cognitive narrative that organizes people's beliefs about how to act, what to feel, and how to understand partners' behaviors during sexual interactions (Simon & Gagnon, 1986). They define the time, behaviors, persons, and purpose of engaging in sex . These cognitions often guide behaviors in a manner similar to self-fulfilling prophecies. They dictate the enactment of behaviors that tend to elicit anticipated interactions, reinforcing beliefs in the script itself and making it difficult to behave in a way that is outside the sexual script. Unlike the sensate focus paradigm, in which sex is conceptualizalized as a natural response, sexual script theory proposes that sexuality is not only a biological response independent of culture and historical context but also a set of learned behaviors reflecting cultural norms. Simon and Gagnon (1986) argued that there are three components to sexual scripts that interact to create specific sexual encounters.

At the cultural level, scripts provide guidelines for which sexual behaviors are considered appropriate for a specific group. At the interpersonal level, individuals are then motivated to ensure their own behavior during sexual encounters reflects the culturally proscribed script. At this interpersonal level, the construction of sexual scripts is made more complex by the interaction between sexual partners. A sexual script may be modified if an individual feels that their sexual behavior is dissimilar to the expectations of their sexual partner. At the final, intrapsychic level, an individual begins to integrate their own personal beliefs and values into their sexual script.

Misaligned scripts—Missed opportunities and misconstrued signals. In truth, both Rafael and Otto desire to have sex more often. Both find each other attractive. Both are capable of a normative sexual response. Much of what prevents them from having sex together can be understood in terms of a misalignment in their sexual scripts. Otto does not believe that he looks the way he "should." His body does not conform to a culturally proscribed model of attractiveness. Otto therefore discounts Rafael's degree of attraction to him in ways that are not accurate from Rafael's perspective. Both men have misunderstood one another's intentions and misconstrued one another's nonverbal behavior as a result.

The counselor in this narrative utilizes a number of techniques, previously introduced in Chapter 7 to respond to dyadic discord, in order to unpack the couple's sexual script and begin to cultivate alignment. When Otto expresses his concerns about his own attractiveness in terms of his belief about what Rafael is thinking, the counselor accurately reflects back Otto's emotion. When both men describe their assumptions about one another's intention, the counselor intervenes and creates opportunities to verify and correct these impressions. As these misalignments are identified, the couple has an opportunity to then develop a mutual or shared script that reflects more accurate understandings of one another's goals and intentions.

This emphasis on deconstructing and reimagining a couple's sexual script does not negate the value of sensate focus. The two strategies can serve complementary purposes. A sexual script provides context for the complex set of interactions that lead up to the opportunity for sex and also encourages examination of culturally proscribed concepts of what constitutes a "normative" or acceptable sexual response. Within this larger cultural and interpersonal context, sensate focus activities are potentially powerful tools to help couples enhance enjoyment and pleasure during the immediate act of sex.

CONCLUSIONS AND KEY POINTS

Sex and sexuality emerge as natural components of human development. There is a substantial body of literature demonstrating that a satisfying sex life is related to overall health, and sexual relationship quality is associated with general relationship quality. Despite this evidence and recent calls to view sexuality as a normative component of well-being, dominant conceptualizations in psychology and healthcare have typically focused on sexual dysfunction and the prevention of STIs or pregnancy. Sex has been further divorced from overall mental health care and well-being by the bifurcation of services that render sex therapy a specialty field.

The merit of integrating sex into general mental and physical health services is particularly obvious in the area of substance use. For many clients, drug use may occur in conjunction with sex, and sex may serve as a motivation for use. Counselors who are unwilling or believe they are unable to address issues of sex may therefore overlook or ignore critical aspects of substance use.

Beyond implications for substance use intervention, Motivational Interviewing offers a framework for working with couples to achieve a healthy and fulfilling sexual relationship. In this context, sex takes on the quality of a target behavior unto itself, and counselors may draw on techniques and processes that they would use to explore any other target behavior. This point is particularly important because it emphasizes that counselors trained in Motivational Interviewing are already equipped with the skills needed to work with a couple on topics of sex. When additional intervention strategies are needed, interventions such as CHTC and sensate focus as well as research on sexual script theory provide models for how Motivational Interviewing counselors might integrate attention to sex as both a context for drug use and a goal unto itself in counseling.

11

Integration, Future Directions, and Limitations

DANIEL SAUERMILCH AND TYREL J. STARKS ■

This text represents just one strain in the longer story of the development and expansion of Motivational Interviewing. Arguably, one of the most remarkable qualities of Motivational Interviewing is its potential for innovation. Initially developed to address substance use, it has proven applicable, with varying degrees of success, to dozens of health behaviors. Counselors, nutritionists, pharmacists, parole officers, and many others now regularly use techniques, strategies, and interventions guided by the Motivational Interviewing paradigm (e.g., Abughosh et al., 2017; Iarussi & Powers, 2018; W. R. Miller & Rollnick, 2002; Ogu et al., 2013).

Motivational Interviewing has proven highly amenable to practice integration, particularly in conjunction with cognitive behavioral therapy. While not all have received empirical support in clinical trials (e.g., Parsons et al., 2018; H. B. Simpson et al., 2010; Starks, Skeen, Jones, Gurung, et al., 2021; Westra et al., 2016), at least some interventions that blend Motivational Interviewing and cognitive behavioral therapy components have demonstrated considerable potential (e.g., Hsieh et al., 2012; C. L. Randall & McNeil, 2017; Riper et al., 2014). Naar and Safren (2017) discuss and synthesize the research in support of this particular configuration of treatment approaches. In many instances, Motivational Interviewing has been integrated with cognitive behavioral or dialectical behavioral therapy as a means of developing motivation for change (Dietz & Dunn, 2014; Naar & Safren, 2017; Riper et al., 2014). It serves as a precursor intervention for cognitive behavioral components that focus on skill acquisition and implementation (Naar & Safren, 2017). It may also attenuate variability in motivation experienced by clients over the course of treatment (Naar & Safren, 2017; Tolchin et al., 2020).

The success of at least some of these integrated interventions that fuse Motivational Interviewing with cognitive behavioral therapies points to the potential to integrate couples Motivational Interviewing with elements of other existing couples interventions. In this kind of synergy, the intervention being blended with Motivational Interviewing may expand the universe of "what happens in session." It may also provide the counselor with tools to generalize or extend the work in session into a couple's life through homework assignments and activities. Meanwhile, Motivational Interviewing might provide the framework for guiding "how the counselor enacts the intervention." It contributes a nuanced linguistic and interpersonal understanding of the processes relevant to introducing, examining, and enacting potential change. It may enhance initial motivation to engage in skill-building components or sustain motivation over the course of a longer integrated treatment.

In the spirit of promoting such development, this chapter offers examples of potential areas for future growth and innovation in couples Motivational Interviewing. We begin by considering the potential for practice integration, drawing inspiration from existing interventions that blend Motivational Interviewing and other counseling disciplines, notably cognitive behavioral therapy. Next we discuss some special challenges in the consent and termination processes with couples that warrant ongoing attention as the paradigm evolves. Finally, we discuss the limitations of research on couples Motivational Interviewing to date and the potential for future work to expand and inform the paradigm.

PRACTICE INTEGRATION: EXPANDING THE UNIVERSE OF "WHAT HAPPENS" IN SESSION

One way to understand why practice integration may be so vital is to consider a session in which the counselor and couple get a bit stuck. Here we return to Darin and Simon. We met them first in Chapter 3, and in Chapter 8 they developed a plan to reduce drinking. This excerpt is from a later session. They are talking with the counselor about how general stressors impact their interactions with each other as well as the decisions they make about cannabis use and sexual behavior. The example begins with an emphasis on evocation. Notice the challenge encountered as the planning phase becomes salient.

* * *

COUNSELOR: The more we talk about marijuana, the more I get the sense that you two are under a lot of pressure right now. [Dyadic reflection.]

SIMON: Yes. We've been struggling.

DARIN: The past few months have been crazy. Your mom got sick. You are helping her. I hate this new job, but I'm stuck in it.

SIMON: It's been rough for sure.

COUNSELOR: So, how do you guys take care of each other through all this?

[Question directed to the couple.]

DARIN: Simon was so supportive when I lost my job. He pushed me to apply for a new one for sure, but I never doubted he was gonna take care of us while I worked it out. I would have been so terrified otherwise.

SIMON: And I think that goes both ways. There've been a lot of times when I've had to prioritize going home to take care of Mom and Darin has gotten that. He has even come and helped out where he could. [to DARIN] You even cleaned her entire house that one time.

COUNSELOR: So in a lot of ways, you look out for one another.

[Relationship affirmation.]

DARIN: Absolutely. But I also think it's frustrating because sometimes we just don't know what to do. Like sometimes I can tell Simon is upset or something, and I feel like whatever I do to help will be wrong.

SIMON: Really?

DARIN: Yeah. Like, if I ask too many questions, I'll just be pestering you. And if I leave it alone, then I'm ignoring you.

SIMON: I get that. I didn't realize. That is basically what happens for me with you. You are so upset about work so much of the time that I kinda just don't know what to say anymore. I want to be helpful, but whenever we talk it just seems to make you more upset.

COUNSELOR: So there are some times when you guys really want to be present for each other—you want to help and be supportive—but you don't quite know how to do that.

[Dyadic reflection.]

DARIN: Yeah, exactly. And honestly, a lot of those times, we just end up smoking together and watching TV.

SIMON: And oddly, like, that's not the worst thing. It's kind of comforting to just be quiet and together and know he is there.

COUNSELOR: And also, part of you both wishes that there was something else you could do for one another in those moments other than just get high together.	[Dyadic reflection.]
DARIN: Otherwise it ends up feeling like there are fewer and fewer things that are safe to talk about or do together. I don't love that.	
SIMON: It's kinda sad to hear you say that, but you are not wrong.	
COUNSELOR: So, one thing that both of you would be interested in is thinking about ways to connect generally. And also you want to find more satisfying ways to help one another in these moments where right now you just don't know what to say or do.	[Dyadic reflection establishes potential change goal.]
DARIN: Yes.	
SIMON: Definitely.	
COUNSELOR: What has worked for you guys in the past when one of you is upset?	[Question to the couple that elicits their perspective on how they could go about change.]
DARIN: Honestly, not really sure. Basically getting stoned and chilling out together. Drinking maybe? But we've cut that back now.	
COUNSELOR: These moments where one of you is stressed and the other wants to help have always kinda been a stumper.	[Dyadic reflection.]
SIMON: Yeah. Honestly, I think we have always just sort of avoided them. The first few times we tried it went badly, and I think we learned we do better if we just leave each other be.	
COUNSELOR: Which also robs you of the chance to be present for each other in ways that you'd like to be.	[Complex reflection extends Simon's thought.]
SIMON: Right.	
COUNSELOR: When you think about those moments—Simon, when you are stressed about family, or Darin, when you are stressed about work—what would be helpful? What do you want the other person to do?	[Question to the couple attempts to elicit possible steps in a change plan.]

DARIN: God, I honestly don't even know. Because it isn't him I'm mad at.

SIMON: Same. Like, it's not on him.

COUNSELOR: And yet those moments impact you both. They take a toll on your relationship.

[Dyadic reflection.]

DARIN: I worry a lot that my stupid work stuff will sort of spoil things for us.

SIMON: Again, same. I worry that at some point, I'm gonna be so consumed with family stuff that I'm no fun to be around.

COUNSELOR: Over the past few weeks, you guys have been really successful at working together around drinking. What makes this different? What, if anything, did we learn there that could help you here?

DARIN: I don't know honestly. I get what you are saying, and like it feels like this shouldn't be all that different.

SIMON: I think the issue is that there we knew what we needed from each other.

DARIN: Right, and here . . . I dunno.

COUNSELOR: Got it. You're not sure what you need, but you know you don't like where things are headed. That's a hard spot to be in. Where do we go from here?

[Dyadic reflection followed by a question to the couple again attempting to draw out potential steps toward change.]

SIMON: I honestly don't know. I think we have been asking ourselves that for a long time.

DARIN: Fortunately, we have been stoned most of that time, so it hasn't hurt so much.

SIMON: And . . . he thinks he's funny.

DARIN: I am funny. You know it. [to COUNSELOR] But seriously, I was hoping you might be able to tell us. Like, what can we do?

* * *

Consider for a moment what the counselor in this session might do next. There is reasonably clear consensus on the desire for change. We would have hoped that as the planning process became salient, the couple would consider steps to achieve their goal of providing more effective support in moments of stress. This might thereby reduce their use of cannabis as a coping strategy in such moments. Unfortunately, that road forward is blocked by a lack of behavioral knowledge and skill. Darin and Simon do not know what to do. Consistent with a strengths-based focus (Rapp, 1998), the counselor has used core Motivational Interviewing skills to explore past successes and elicit the couple's view on how they would like to go about changing; however, the couple is stumped each time. They have the will, but cannot identify the behavioral means.

These kinds of moments—in which a lack of knowledge impedes planning—are particularly illustrative of the power of practice integration. As W. R. Miller and Rollnick (2013) acknowledged, there are a host of existing behavior change technologies that have demonstrated empirical support. Why not reach for those tools and techniques in this moment? The utility of this was evident in the discussion in Chapter 9 of communication skills training. Here we provide examples of other manifestations of practice integration relevant to the challenge encountered in the session with Darin and Simon. These are not intended to be an exhaustive list, but rather exemplars of the kind of innovative practice adaptations we hope to inspire in future work.

Social and Problem-Solving Skills Training

One way to understand the problem faced by Darin and Simon is that, in specific social situations, they struggle to identify an effective behavior that they could enact. The challenges of identifying, executing, and evaluating the effectiveness of behavior in social situations have been articulated and addressed in the context of social skills (Liberman et al., 1989) and problem-solving skills training (Crick & Dodge, 1994; D'Zurilla & Goldfried, 1971). One way the counselor might help support Darin and Simon is to draw on strategies from these paradigms.

Social skills training traditionally hinges on a counselor's ability to model interpersonal skills via role-play, deliver constructive feedback in response to clients' behavioral enactments, and provide assignments for clients to practice these skills in their day-to-day lives (Liberman et al., 1989; Mueser et al., 2013). Problem-solving training is an approach to resolving interpersonal problems via a series of programmatic techniques: defining the problem, considering solutions, and identifying the solution of best fit (Crick & Dodge, 1994; D'Zurilla & Goldfried, 1971). These two approaches are often implemented together to optimize their effectiveness (Mueser et al., 2013).

A number of relationship skill-building interventions have been developed (e.g., Davila et al., 2021; Pentel, 2020; Whitton et al., 2016). Furthermore, several existing interventions addressing sexual risk among sexual minority couples integrate relationship skill building (e.g., Gamarel et al., 2019;

Newcomb et al., 2017; Wu et al., 2010). At least some of these intervention models are informed by Motivational Interviewing—or are readily amenable to Motivational Interviewing (Gamarel et al., 2019; Newcomb et al., 2017). While relationship skill building is incorporated in all of these interventions, only one includes relationship skill building beyond communication skills training (Newcomb et al., 2017).

There are a number of ways in which Motivational Interviewing may be synergistically integrated with social and problem-solving skill paradigms. Worksheets that structure problem-solving and related communication have been developed for couples (e.g., Ludgate & Grubr, 2018). Options are available online and free of charge in some cases (e.g., Human Performance Resources by CHAMP, 2018). Counselors might invite the couple to complete these kinds of worksheets together as an activity in session. Used this way, the worksheet provides a structure that guides partners through the steps of problem-solving. The counselor is present to provide guidance and support. The worksheet, once completed in session, becomes a product that the couple can leave with—a physical representation of both the problem-solving process and any plan on which they decided. Alternatively, these kinds of materials might be offered to the couple to complete outside of session. In this way, they serve as a guide for the couple to practice skills independently of the counselor.

Counselors might also coach couples in the use of problem-solving skills through role-play practice in session. Darin and Simon have specifically struggled to successfully discuss their respective life stressors. After multiple failed attempts at providing support, they have resorted to forgoing the conversation and smoking together has been a preferred alternative. If the couple were to enact that conversation with the counselor present, the counselor might be able to help the partners identify where things go awry, brainstorm more effective responses, and coach partners on the use of adaptive communication skills (Crick & Dodge, 1994). Done this way, the role-play conversation in session may serve as a blueprint for future conversations. Role-play problem-solving has been integrated, to some extent, in existing interventions for male couples (e.g., Newcomb et al., 2017). Also aligned with this, couples HIV testing and counseling incorporates a role-play in which the couple practices how they might go about discussing a breach in their sexual agreement if one were to occur (Grabbe et al., 2014).

Behavioral Activation

Another challenge Darin and Simon face is that the universe of enjoyable activities they engage in together has shrunk. As the demands of life and external stressors have increased, the time they spend simply enjoying one another's company has diminished. In terms of interdependence theory (Rusbult & Van Lange, 2003), the rewards of their relationship have diminished, and they are somewhat less satisfied with the relationship than they used to be. Behavioral activation strategies are potentially relevant to addressing this kind of challenge.

As a treatment approach unto itself, behavioral activation has a rich history in the treatment of depression (e.g., Beck, 1979; Lewinsohn, 1974, 1975) and has since found utility in the treatment of psychosis (Gaudiano et al., 2015; Mairs et al., 2011); substance use (Banducci et al., 2013; Daughters et al., 2018; Pott et al., 2021); and anxiety (Stein et al., 2020), among other behavioral health concerns. Broadly, the approach is premised on the notion that maladaptive cognitions or behaviors (e.g., depression) emerge when an individual does not experience requisite positive reinforcement from the environment. As such, behavioral activation has traditionally been used to enable clients to overcome deficiencies in environmental reinforcement through the active pursuit of behaviors that may generate such contingencies (Lewinsohn, 1974).

The techniques that comprise behavioral activation have typically fallen into three primary domains: (1) evaluative techniques (i.e., activity monitoring and assessing values or valued activity domains); (2) activation strategies (i.e., activity scheduling and forming avoidance targeting procedures); and (3) maintenance techniques (i.e., forging contingency management procedures to sustain behavior via reward) (e.g., Fuchs & Rehm, 1977; Kanter et al., 2010; Lewinsohn, 1974; Martell et al., 2001, 2010). These techniques follow a sequence whereby counselors help their clients chart their current activity, facilitate a discussion of their client's goals and values, and schedule activities with these values in mind to build positive reinforcement with extant environmental stimuli. To maintain this behavioral change, counselors then work with clients to address points when maladaptive behaviors may be reinforced or when positive behavior change is not reinforced by the client's environment (Kanter et al., 2010; Lewinsohn, 1974; Lewinsohn et al., 1970).

For a number of theoretical reasons, Motivational Interviewing and behavioral activation techniques are a natural pairing. Both approaches are client centered and share in the perspective that collaboration between counselor and client is key to successful treatment (Balán et al., 2016; W. R. Miller & Rollnick, 2013; Naar & Safren, 2017). Both assume that a client's values and goals should influence the direction of counseling itself (Balán et al., 2016). Perhaps as a result, interventions that have integrated techniques from both approaches have been implemented successfully (e.g., Choi et al., 2016; Chu et al., 2009; J. R. Cornelius et al., 2011; Kertes et al., 2011; Meinzer et al., 2021; Ponsford et al., 2016; Terry et al., 2020).

Scheduling pleasant (shared) activities. There is a history of couples interventions that integrate behavioral activation—in the form of pleasant event scheduling—for a range of behavioral outcomes (e.g., Emanuels-Zuurveen & Emmelkamp, 1996; Manos et al., 2009; Sautter et al., 2011; Zrenchik, 2015). In addition, there are at least two examples of couples interventions that incorporate a behavioral activation component in addressing sexual risk-taking and/or drug use among sexual minority men (Newcomb et al., 2017; Starks, Adebayo, et al., 2022). These interventions generally assume that the behavioral activation activity serves to enhance relationship satisfaction and lay a foundation of successful engagement in shared or joint activities, which may then support future engagement in collaborative efforts for change in the target behavior. Beyond these specific applications, it is plausible to see how pleasant event scheduling might be readily integrated into couples Motivational Interviewing practice more generally. Couples Motivational Interviewing techniques might be used to explore the jointly held values or goals that would inform the subsequent selection of shared activities. The Motivational Interviewing counselor might then elicit motivation to complete the activity outside of session and plan the specifics of such activity completion.

Contingency management—Partners as a source of reinforcement. As mentioned in the overview of goal-setting theory (see Chapter 9), partners may serve as a source of support and feedback to one another during the process of goal attainment (Locke & Lantham, 2006). Contingency management strategies represent one way to formalize the role partners play in providing feedback and reinforcement for goal attainment. Consistent with this, behavioral couples therapy (Fals-Stewart et al., 2004) incorporates the development of contingency management plans with couples. The couple identifies specific reinforcers that are delivered by partners to one another after completion of steps that are consistent with progression toward intervention goals. In applications specific to substance use, contingency management plans involve partners providing reinforcement for reductions in use or abstinence. The counselor helps to develop the contingency management plan (which involves identifying potential reinforcers and clarifying the schedule of reinforcement delivery) and assess its ongoing success (Falconier & Epstein, 2019).

Contingency management components represent one way Motivational Interviewing counselors may clarify the role partners play in change plans. They specifically call attention to how partners respond to one another after they have performed a behavior consistent with an established change plan (or failed to do so successfully). In examples of change planning offered thus far, counselors have largely explored the role partners might play before and during the performance of a behavior. For example, in the first narrative of Chapter 8, Darin and Simon discussed ways they could support one another's drinking goals by modifying their behavior around one another during times when drinking might be likely. One could imagine such a conversation going further and identifying ways in which the partners might actively reinforce one another's success in meeting established goals. For example, they might agree to go to a movie together—or engage in some other mutually enjoyable activity—over the weekend if both of them adhere to the limits they set for alcohol consumption. Similarly, Darin and Simon might benefit from a discussion of ways in which they could mutually reinforce one another for successful attempts at communication during times of stress.

Exploring shared values—Enhancing the salience of relationship investment. Another way to understand the challenge encountered by Darin and Simon in session is that they have a diminished sense of relationship investment (Rusbult, 1980). As outside stressors have encroached and their interactions have been less rewarding, they are beginning to feel like they share less and less. Each of them, in their own way, voices some concern that the durability of the relationship—an indicator of commitment—might be compromised. One novel approach to addressing this concern has been the integration of a particular kind of values exploration activity—specifically the values card sort activity—into Motivational Interviewing practice with couples (Starks, Adebayo, et al., 2022).

A range of values clarification activities has been used in established interventions to explore client values and consider their relative significance (e.g., agenda mapping, goal setting, valued living questionnaires) (e.g., Durrant et al., 2007; S. C. Hayes et al., 2006; G. T. Wilson et al., 2010). We based our initial application of values clarification in couples Motivational Interviewing (Starks, Adebayo, et al., 2022) on the format of a personal values card sort, a technique characteristic of individual Motivational Interviewing (W. R. Miller et al., 2001) and one sometimes used to help establish a focus or goal for treatment (Bean et al., 2011; W. R. Miller et al., 2001; W. R. Miller & Rollnick, 2013). Such activities have also been used to engage clients or evoke change talk in interventions tailored for sexual minority men (e.g., Parsons et al., 2014, 2018; Starks, Robles, Pawson, et al., 2019) and people living with HIV (e.g., Naar et al., 2020; Starks, Skeen, Jones, Gurung, et al., 2021). In all of these interventions, clients sort a set of cards, each of which contains a value or priority, into categories indicating its importance. The sorted cards are then used by counselors to engage clients in a discussion of their personal values and consider how these values are reflected in decisions they make about the target behavior.

In our intervention, the card sort activity served a novel purpose: to highlight the couple's shared goals and values. In other words, we use the activity to make aspects of relationship investment explicit and salient, thereby enhancing the couple's capacity to work together toward change. Once shared goals and values are identified, they can be juxtaposed with partners' behavior to evoke change talk later in session.

In completing the couple's value card sort, partners work together to sort cards into four piles as depicted in Figure 11.1. Values that are important to both partners are placed centrally. Each partner keeps a pile of values that matter primarily to them but not to the other. Values that are not important to either partner are placed separately. The counselor then invites each partner to identify and describe their three most important values from the pile that is shared. The effect in session is generally to enhance partners' awareness of common ground—and potentially examine the importance of their investment in one another. This provides a foundation for considering consensus in the face of dyadic ambivalence and tends to enhance motivation to respond to dyadic discord in session with adaptive accommodation .

Homework Activities

Use of many of the strategies described above might potentially invoke a plan to then implement skills discussed in session during interactions outside the counseling. Such homework assignments are a common feature of cognitive behavioral approaches (Beck, 1979). Counselors assign varied tasks (e.g., practicing

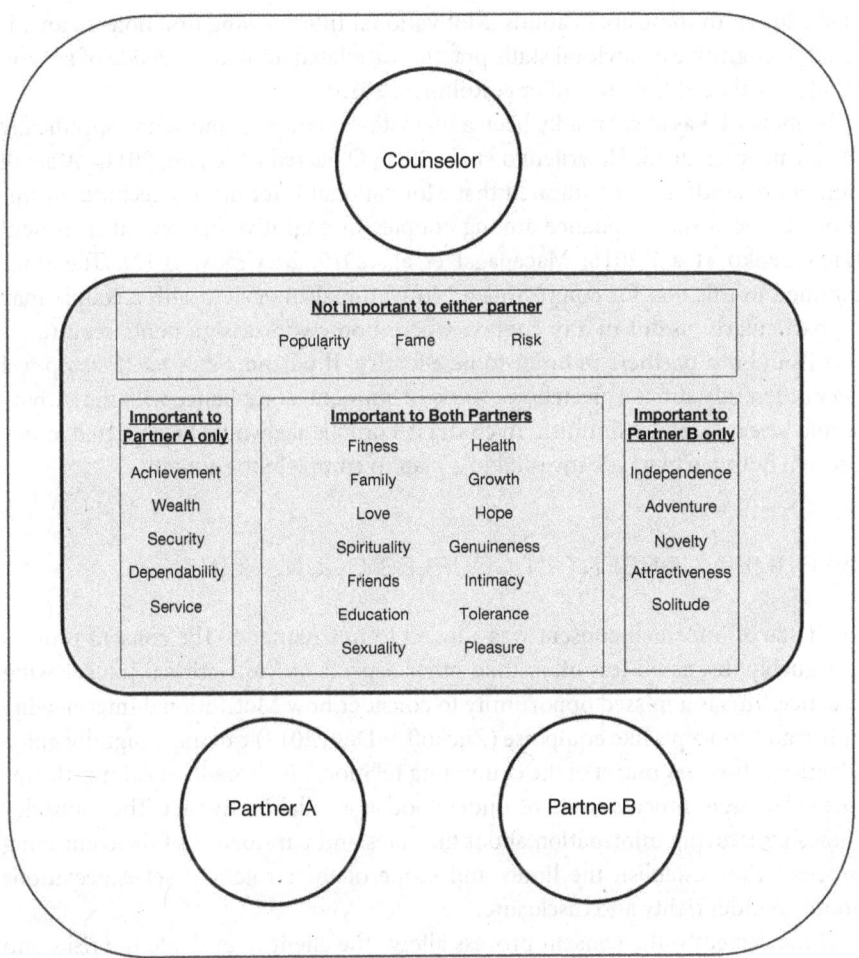

Figure 11.1 Diagram of couples values card sort.

coping strategies, rehearsing social skills, monitoring destructive beliefs, re-
flexive writing activities) as a means of deepening clients' psychoeducation and
to create opportunities for clients to develop skills in their daily lives (Beck,
1979). In its broadest sense, homework has been found to be beneficial for
clients in cognitive behavioral interventions (e.g., Kazantzis et al., 2010, 2016).
For example, in the treatment of adults with depression, the completion of
homework between sessions was correlated with an improvement in symptoms
(Conklin & Strunk, 2015).

Research has indicated that Motivational Interviewing techniques improve com-
pliance with cognitive behavioral skills practice outside of session (e.g., Aviram &
Westra, 2011; Soleymani et al., 2018). There is precedent for the integration of
Motivational Interviewing skills to enhance homework activities—particularly
self-monitoring diary cards—with sexual minority men (Parsons et al., 2018) and
HIV-positive clients specifically (Parsons et al., 2007; Starks, Skeen, Jones, Gurung,

et al., 2021). In these applications, Motivational Interviewing functions as an adjunct to cognitive behavioral skills practice or related activities outside of session (Callan et al., 2012; W. R. Miller & Rollnick, 2013).

Homework has also broadly been a mainstay in couples counseling specifically (e.g., Falconier, 2015; Hawrilenko et al., 2016; O'Farrell & Schein, 2011). A small number of studies have indicated that Motivational Interviewing techniques improve homework compliance among couples in cognitive behavioral treatment (Hawrilenko et al., 2016; Macapagal et al., 2019; McCrady, 2012). The skills outlined in this text for completing a Motivational Interview with a couple may be particularly useful in any context where homework assignments require effort from both partners in order to be effective. If partners in a relationship feel very differently about a given homework assignment, compliance with the activity would be expected to diminish. In contrast, compliance would be expected to improve if both partners are invested in a plan to complete the activity.

INFORMED CONSENT IN COUPLES COUNSELING

The issue of informed consent was alluded to in Chapter 6. The consent process is arguably discussed less often than other aspects of Motivational Interviewing practice. This is a missed opportunity to consider how Motivational Interviewing Spirit, and concepts like equipoise (Zuckoff & Dew, 2012) can meaningfully guide practice at the very outset of the counseling relationship. Broadly speaking, the informed consent process could be understood as a collaborative act. The counselor shares structuring information about the rules and parameters of the counseling process. They establish the limits and scope of their role and set expectations about confidentiality and disclosure.

Done correctly, the consent process allows the client to evaluate the risks and benefits of counseling and make an informed decision about whether or not to proceed. When clients are unsure of whether engaging in counseling is right for them, counselors may take a stance of equipoise. They can demonstrate respect for the client's autonomy by affirming their capacity to choose and helping them evaluate the potential consequences of counseling in the context of the client's broader goals and values from a place of neutrality.

A small but meaningful body of scholarship discusses ethical issues unique to informed consent and confidentiality with couples. For a review of these issues, see the work of Bass and Quimby (2006). Here we consider two particularly salient decisions a counselor must make at the outset of the process. First, counselors must decide whether they are open to conducting private sessions with individual partners during the course of the couple's treatment. If these sessions are to occur, expectations around confidentiality must be further explicated. Second, regardless of whether individual sessions will occur or not, counselors must decide whether they will conduct initial consent procedures with the couple together or whether partners will be consented individually.

Individual Sessions

Will individual sessions be part of the course of treatment? There is variability in whether counselors who work with couples treat partners as a couple as well as individually. There are, in fact, no clinical mandates that forbid couples counselors from seeing either or both partners independently and conjointly (American Psychological Association, 2017). Counselors decide for themselves how to navigate such treatment options, and the benefits and challenges of treating relationship partners separately as well as together has long been a focus of discussion (Knauss & Knauss, 2012). Counselors who allow for individual sessions may utilize them when session content emerges that is particularly fraught or challenging or when partners may benefit from space to process independently (e.g., Tie & Poulsen 2013). Other counselors (e.g., Ignacio & Taylor, 2017) may eschew individual sessions as a means to minimize opportunity for a breach of confidentiality between partners. Simply, there are opportunities and challenges that come with either approach.

Obtaining Initial Consent

Will partners be consented individually or together? Regardless of whether they conduct sessions with individual partners or not, obtaining consent from both partners together has largely been the historical norm for couples counselors (Knauss & Knauss, 2012; Margolin, 1982). The purpose of completing consent together is to minimize potential miscommunication or misunderstandings about confidentiality over the course of treatment. Presumably, if everyone is present together when confidentiality expectations are established, everyone should have a common understanding of what they have agreed to.

While there are benefits to obtaining consent from partners jointly, there is also a clear pitfall to this option. Relationship partners may not feel equally ready or willing to pursue couples counseling. One relationship partner may feel much more committed to the notion of treatment than their partner, or one may be open to counseling but would prefer individual treatment for a variety of reasons. In such cases, consent given in the presence of one's relationship partner may arise from coercion as opposed to genuine desire for counseling.

Counselors who intend to utilize a combination of individual and couples sessions may address this option during the informed consent process. This may include establishing the purpose and timing of individual sessions. This is also an opportunity to establish the limits of confidentiality partners can expect with regard to "secrets" (e.g., infidelity, health concerns, etc.) disclosed in individual sessions (Bass & Quimby, 2006; Gottlieb et al., 2008; Gurman & Burton, 2014). Some counselors may offer substantial guarantees of confidentiality for individual sessions. In such cases, information from individual sessions would be expected to be kept confidential between an individual partner and counselor unless or until the partner chooses to disclose it in a joint session. Other counselors may establish an expectation that they will retain some discretion around disclosure. In these cases, if a counselor determined that it was in the couple or partner's best interest to share content disclosed in an individual session, they might do so without needing explicit permission following initial consent.

Because of concerns about potential coercion, our own research studies have utilized an alternative approach in which partners are consented individually prior to any engagement in joint activities. This is true whether study participation involves a qualitative interview with the couple (e.g., Bosco et al., 2019; Starks, Pawson, et al., 2018) or receipt of an intervention (e.g., Starks, Adebayo, et al., 2022; Starks, Dellucci, et al., 2019; Starks, Feldstein Ewing, et al., 2019; Starks, Kyre et al., 2021). Even though our approach to Motivational Interviewing works exclusively with the partners together—rather than incorporating individual as well as dyadic sessions—we conduct informed consent individually. This provides an opportunity to make sure that both partners have adequate time to personally understand the potential risks and benefits of participation. It allows us to assess for the potential that one partner has been threatened or coerced to participate in ways that might indicate safety concerns.

SPECIAL CONSIDERATIONS WHEN RELATIONSHIPS TERMINATE

Supporting the separation process. The consideration of relationship dissolution has been discussed at several points in this text, most notably in Chapters 3 and 8. Consistent with the stance in previous chapters, the literature widely indicates that couples counselors ought not view separation as a failure of the counseling process (Lebow, 2015; Margolin, 1982). Rather, separation is understood as a resolution that may have only been reached through the opportunity to explore relationship processes and partner perspectives provided by the counseling process. In the absence of this time and exploration, couples may languish for far longer before reaching the conclusion to separate.

Motivational Interviewing counselors who wish for a model of how to approach the separation process might look to discernment counseling, a brief intervention for couples designed to support the thoughtful consideration of separation (Doherty et al., 2011, 2016; Emerson et al., 2021). Notably, discernment counseling is an approach that relies heavily on individual sessions with each partner conducted by the same counselor (Doherty et al., 2016). Partners separate and engage with their counselor in a discussion of their own contributions to the extant challenges in their relationship. Over the course of counseling, counselors may disclose their impressions of one partner's sessions to their counterpart individually before bringing both partners together for joint sessions (Doherty et al., 2016). Research on discernment counseling has found that while this counseling approach may reduce ambivalence around divorce, joint sessions provide space and time for partners to acknowledge and share concerns with one another not previously disclosed or understood before counseling began (Emerson et al., 2021).

Although most sessions in discernment counseling are conducted with individual partners, the relationship itself is still the primary focus. As such, Motivational Interviewing techniques may be used for both partners individually to explore communication deficits in their relationship—as well as apparent strengths—and ultimately build momentum toward a relationship outcome that is mutually agreed on by both partners (i.e., remain together, formally separate, or pursue couples therapy to remediate the concerns discussed) (Doherty et al., 2016). Considering that this form of counseling blends individual and couples sessions, the potential for integrated interventions that fuse individual and couples Motivational Interviewing strategies with discernment counseling may be a fruitful area of future inquiry.

Individual therapy if the couple's work ends. How is a couples Motivational Interviewing counselor accountable—and to which partner—postseparation should partners decide to end their relationship? There is no field-wide consensus about the correct answer to this ethical question. Motivational Interviewing counselors working with couples will need to develop their own practice conventions that reflect their areas of expertise, personal skill set, and theoretical orientation as well as relevant idiosyncratic client concerns. Our own work thus far has tested brief, time-limited interventions ranging from one (Starks, Dellucci, et al., 2019) to three sessions (Starks, Adebayo, et al., 2022). Break-ups during the course of treatment have been rare. Since session attendance was incentivized in our multisession intervention, we planned from the outset to offer clients the opportunity to attend sessions individually if the relationship ended before all three sessions were complete. This was done to avoid the potential for coercion. We did not want to force ex-partners to attend a session together merely to obtain compensation. While our decision reflects the ethics of decision-making in the context of research, it represents one possible real-world solution to the question of whether a counselor remains engaged with partners following the dissolution of their relationship.

Guidance for how a counselor ought to negotiate or clarify their role in the case of relationship dissolution is, like many couples counseling didactics, quite subjective to the counselor (Lebow, 2015). Practitioners may refer both partners to separate counselors in some cases. In the event that the dissolution of the relationship may not be entirely mutual, a counselor may choose to continue treatment with the partner who did not advocate for separation to mitigate the sense of loss that may be exacerbated by the simultaneous termination of the relationship with their partner and the counselor (Lebow, 2015).

Individual counseling that continues after a couple separates might involve relction on the relationship that has just ended. Counselors may facilitate a discussion regarding the challenges faced in the former relationship and—similarly to discernment counseling—explore the client's own contributions to the dissolution of their relationship. Such a discussion might help to elucidate features of the relationship that were desirable—and might be sought in future relationships—and those that were undesirable. Using affirming and reflective techniques, counselors may then shape client language in the direction of changing the behaviors discussed in anticipation of future relationships.

When counselors agree to see one of the former partners (or both) as an individual client for some limited duration after a couple separates in order to facilitate a transition, they might consider employing Motivational Interviewing techniques to build client change talk in the direction of finding an alternative counselor to continue their individual treatment and then provide referrals for care. In this way, the target behavior becomes the referral, and individual Motivational Interviewing becomes an intercalary intervention designed to bridge the former partner or partners to another counselor with whom they can begin a new working relationship.

EXTENSIONS AND FUTURE APPLICATIONS OF COUPLES MOTIVATIONAL INTERVIEWING

Beyond Emerging Adult Sexual Minority Men in the United States

Admittedly, the framework described in this text has been derived primarily from work that has focused all or in large part on English-speaking, cisgender sexual minority men. An emphasis on HIV prevention has narrowed the scope of this work further to emerging adults (aged 18–29) and those sexual minority men who use drugs. While undoubtedly there are factors unique to sexual minority men in relationships—and the prevalence of HIV infection in this population provides a strong rationale for developing tailored interventions with this group (see Chapter 1)—the reach of couples Motivational Interviewing would be considerably limited if it remained so restricted. Fortunately, there is a legacy of Motivational Interviewing research that suggests the potential for the framework laid out in this text to generalize to other populations.

The practice has expanded across linguistic and cultural contexts (F. F. Huang et al., 2015; Oh & Lee, 2016; Saito et al., 2012). Motivational Interviewing interventions have been applied internationally (e.g., Bahafzallah et al., 2020; F. F. Huang et al., 2015; Saito et al., 2012) as well as in work with specific ethnic groups within the United States (e.g., American Indian/Alaskan Native Americans and Latinx Americans) (Calhoun et al., 2010; C. S. Lee et al., 2013; Venner et al., 2016). While more ethnically expansive work on such adaptations is needed, the efficacy of Motivational Interviewing when tailored for treatment seekers' cultural contexts (i.e., immigration circumstances, familial relationships, acculturative stress, and discrimination) shows significant potential for future practice with diverse mental health consumers (Lee et al., 2013). As such, there are apparent inroads for couples Motivational Interviewing for couples of many cultural and linguistic backgrounds beyond the focus on English speaking, cis men in relationships.

Motivational Interviewing has also proven effective across the lifespan, with practice applications emerging for a range of behavioral outcomes with adolescents (e.g., Cushing et al., 2014; D'Amico et al., 2015; Naar-King & Suarez, 2011) as well as older adults (e.g., Chang et al., 2015; Purath et al., 2014). As with adults, Motivational Interviewing with adolescents has been shown effective for a variety of health behaviors and conditions, from asthma to metabolic functioning, besides that of substance use (Cushing et al., 2014). Research has therefore proffered comprehensive instruction on special considerations for Motivational Interviewing with adolescents in particular (Naar-King & Suarez, 2011). More recently, Brummel-Smith (2015) has articulated formal guidance for Motivational Interviewing with older adults. Similar to adolescents, Motivational Interviewing with older adults has demonstrated efficacy for myriad health conditions and behaviors beyond substance use, including diabetes maintenance and heart health (Purath et al., 2014).

The demonstrated efficacy of Motivational Interviewing across the lifespan has implications for couples Motivational Interviewing. This evidence base positions Motivational Interviewing with couples as a plausible approach for the treatment of relationship partners well beyond those aged 18–29. Early work suggested that relationship functioning among sexual minority male adolescents predicts attitudes toward couples HIV testing (Starks, Lovejoy, et al., 2021) as well as sexual risk-taking with male partners. This work has indicated that such couples may find couples HIV testing a signal of low as well as high relationship commitment—and that either may serve as a barrier to engagement (Starks, Lovejoy, et al., 2021). Most notably, perceptions of relationship seriousness—which is synonymous with commitment in this age group (Starks, Dellucci, et al., 2021)—have been linked to condomless sex with main partners (Newcomb et al., 2014). Meanwhile, adolescent sexual minority males with higher relationship satisfaction report fewer instances of condomless anal sex with male partners generally (Starks, Dellucci, et al., 2021). These formative indications of the relevance of relationships to sexual risk in adolescents have provided the foundation for initial intervention development efforts that draw on (Starks, Dellucci, et al., 2021) or are aligned with (Gamarel et al., 2019) the couples Motivational Interviewing principles outlined in this text.

Heterosexual and gender minority couples have benefited from individual Motivational Interviewing interventions or practice informed by Motivational Interviewing. The work that has informed the development of the couples Motivational Interviewing paradigm described in this text has been focused on sexual minority male couples. This focus stands in contrast to most other couples therapy paradigms, which have largely been developed from work with heterosexual couples (e.g., Reiter & Chenail, 2017; Wiebe & Johnson, 2016).

There is no a priori reason why the principles, processes, and practices outlined in this text would be inherently limited to application with male couples. Individual Motivational Interviewing interventions have demonstrated efficacy across populations that are diverse with respect to gender (e.g., Arayasirikul et al., 2020; Vogel et al., 2019). It is entirely plausible that Motivational Interviewing practice would demonstrate similar generalizability. Early work applying Motivational Interviewing to marital satisfaction in heterosexual couples showed initial promise (Cordova et al., 2001). Burgeoning research on the treatment of lesbian couples (Pentel, 2020) as well as couples that include at least one transgender or gender nonconforming partner using therapy based on Motivational Interviewing has been found to be effective in increasing relationship satisfaction for such couples (Minten & Dykeman, 2021). Such examples signal potentially broad applications of Motivational Interviewing with couples across a range of sexual and gender identities. Future work may seek to explore principles that generalize across practice with these various groups as well as elements that are unique to engaging couples with specific sexual and gender identities.

Finally, Motivational Interviewing with couples may attend to concerns beyond that of substance use and sexual risk. Both this chapter and Chapter 1 have emphasized the broad success of Motivational Interviewing in applications across a wide range of health behaviors. There is reason to hope that Motivational Interviewing practice with couples would demonstrate a similar propensity for applications across outcomes. While the content of counseling sessions may vary dramatically with target behavior—sessions focused on smoking cessation (e.g., Lindson-Hawley et al., 2015; Manuel et al., 2013) cover very different content from sessions focused on the prevention of re-incarceration (e.g., Polcin et al., 2018; Stinson & Clark, 2017)—the core processes, principles, and techniques of Motivational Interviewing are common across these apparently disparate interventions. It is our hope that innovative researchers and clinicians will find similar promise in drawing on the contents of this text to address targets that go well beyond our formative emphasis on drug use and sexual health.

Beyond Main or Primary Relationship Partner Dyads

While this text has a particular focus on main or primary relationship partner dyads, these are not the only interdependent relationships. There is at least some theoretical reason to believe that the principles, processes, and practices outlined in this text might find application with other kinds of client relationships. While interdependence theory has been applied extensively to understand functioning in main or primary relationships, Kelley and Thibaut's original formulation of the theory was not specifically restricted to these relationships (Kelley & Thibaut, 1978; Thibaut & Kelley, 1959). Research in industrial organization psychology has used interdependence theory to understand functioning between government and business (Tjosvold et al., 2008); within the hospitality, service, and tourism industries (J. J. Lee et al., 2014; Özel & Kozak, 2017; Solomon et al., 1985); and in team sports (B. Jackson et al., 2010), among other industries and settings. Given this, we provide some initial suggestions for applications of couples Motivational Interviewing practice outside of primary partnerships.

The parent/guardian–adolescent dyad. A multitude of dyadic interventions have been developed for parent/guardian–adolescent participation—from the treatment of attention deficit hyperactivity disorder (ADHD) and substance use among adolescents to the improvement of communication within the parent/guardian–adolescent relationship (e.g., Colegrove et al., 2018; J. M. Gottman et al., 1997; Sibley et al., 2020; Tolou-Shams et al., 2017). A number of such studies have specifically implemented Motivational Interviewing techniques with parents or guardians and their children broadly (e.g., Bianchi-Hayes et al., 2018; Sibley et al., 2016, 2020; Spirito et al., 2011; Thomas et al., 2017; Winters & Leitten, 2007). Interventions based on Motivational Interviewing to treat substance use among adolescents have shown greater reductions in use when parents or guardians are included in session (Spirito et al., 2011; Winters & Leitten, 2007). While the integration of Motivational Interviewing practice has been largely successful in the treatment of parent/guardian–adolescent dyads regarding adolescent ADHD and parental stress, the effects of treatment on adolescents have been shown to attenuate over time (Sibley et al., 2016).

These findings may allude to a challenge similar to that found in early work on Motivational Interviewing with couples: what to do when a partner argues against change? Analogously, counselors might struggle when adolescents and parents or guardians disagree about counseling goals. In these instances, principles described in this text might provide guidance on how to mitigate conflict, develop consensus, and work toward joint planning. The process of facilitating dyadic functioning—and counselor techniques such as dyadic reflections and relationship affirmations particularly relevant to this process—might be readily generalized to consider the quality of the parent/guardian–child relationship.

Individuals with acute or chronic health conditions and their caregivers. A number of studies have focused on the development of interventions designed for individuals with health conditions (e.g., cognitive decline, cancer, injury, etc.) and their caregivers (e.g., Badr et al., 2015, 2019; Hanser et al., 2011; Kreitzer et al., 2018; Moon & Adams, 2012; Northouse et al., 2010). Though many of these interventions are successful in mitigating caregiver burden and increasing quality of life for both caregivers and patients, the frame of treatment (i.e., patient focused, caregiver focused, or dyad focused) seems to moderate treatment outcomes (Badr et al., 2019; Kreitzer et al., 2018). Namely, while interventions that focus primarily on caregivers only may be more effective in alleviating mental and somatic health outcomes for both parties, those interventions that focus on the dyad itself are likewise efficacious. In fact, a dyadic intervention for cancer patients and their caregivers has shown that such interventions are feasible and acceptable for dyadic counterparts (Ketcher, Thompson, et al., 2020). While dyadic interventions of this kind show promise, further research is needed to compare efficacy of dyadic to individual interventions with respect to symptom alleviation for patients and psychological outcomes for both members of the dyad (Badr et al., 2019).

Motivational Interviewing with couples, as articulated here, provides a framework for conceptualizing the couple as client. It might therefore serve as a useful starting point for enhancing the dyadic focus of patient and caregiver interventions. The potential for such integration is hinted at by the recent success of an 8-minute intervention focused on improving dyadic communication and clarifying shared goals for caregiver–patient dyads (Ketcher, Ellington, et al., 2020). Qualitative findings from the study indicated that this brief intervention had potential to mitigate distress and promote dyadic coping It emphasized the importance of interventions that cast attention on communication as a foundation for positive health outcomes for such dyads (Ketcher, Ellington, et al., 2020).

Notably, early work has integrated Motivational Interviewing into patient–caregiver interventions for the treatment of comorbid schizophrenia and substance use (Barrowclough et al., 2001). This limited work, much like the dyadic interventions designed for adolescent–caregiver dyads, has also functioned via an identified-client paradigm. The paradigm outlined in this text would suggest that viewing the patient–caregiver dyad in toto as the client might ameliorate barriers to intervention progress encountered when patients and caregivers have divergent views of health behaviors.

Tailoring Individual Motivational Interviewing practice for people in relationships. As mentioned in Chapter 5 and discussions of the informed consent process, couples counseling requires dyadic participation. Engagement in couples counseling inherently involves joint effort in the form of session attendance by both partners. Based on the principles of interdependence theory, one would expect that those couples with the poorest dyadic functioning would face the most challenges in achieving consensus about engaging in couples counseling and working together to coordinate session attendance. Some couples researchers have indicated concerns that dyadic participation may bias samples toward relatively higher functioning couples (Starks, Millar, & Parsons, 2015; Yucel & Gassanov, 2010). Similarly, the idea that counseling services for people in relationships will always involve dyadic intervention might very well exclude partnered people who are very much in need of care that is tailored to address relationship factors relevant to their behavioral decision-making.

This idea—that not all partnered people who may benefit from Motivational Interviewing can be engaged in dyadic sessions with their partner—has led to the development of a novel intervention protocol that circumvents this barrier to care (Starks, Robles, Pawson, et al., 2019). Project PARTNER incorporates the process of facilitating dyadic functioning into an individually delivered intervention. Communication skills and relationship strengths and challenges are discussed in session with the goal of identifying more effective ways the client might interact with their partner outside of session. The intervention also explicitly incorporates attention to partner attitudes toward the target behavior and examines ways that clients might engage relationship partners in their change processes. While these interventions are not couples Motivational Interviewing per se, they attest to the fact that relationship science generally—and Motivational Interviewing practice with couples specifically—may enhance Motivational Interviewing practice with individuals in relationships.

CONCLUSIONS AND KEY POINTS

Motivational Interviewing with couples is a counseling approach in its own right, and also there are clear opportunities for its integration with other approaches and techniques. From the consent process for couples entering and pursuing a course of therapy to more granular aspects of value clarification and social skills training, couples Motivational Interviewing Spirit and techniques may enhance counselor efficacy to engage with a more diverse range of clients in a wide array of dyadic relationships besides relationship partners and for presenting concerns beyond substance use and sexual risk. While there are clear limitations to Motivational Interviewing, these challenges may be surmounted by further study and practice to increase the applicability of these techniques for those who may stand to most benefit from treatment.

ACKNOWLEDGMENT

I can think of a handful of times in my life when a mentor or friend had a better eye for my horizon than I had myself. Diane Ketel believed I could play Schumann's *Introduction and Allegro Appassionato*. Dr. Barbara Yutrenka suggested I should minor in statistics as an undergraduate student. Dr. Ann Fisher put me forward to teach Psychology of Women when I was her dissertation student. Each of those endeavors began primarily because I had more faith in their judgment than I had in my own abilities; and each turned into an experience I still think about today. Thanks to them (and to all of my teachers and mentors) for the role they played in getting me here.

Keeping with that theme, there was no scenario in the fall of 2019 in which I believed I was ready to write a book. I thought writing a book was something you did once you had figured things out. I definitely did not feel like I had things figured out in the fall of 2019. So first and foremost, I have to thank Dr. Karen Ingersoll. Ultimately, I proposed this book because she told me it was a good idea. She insisted—very wisely—that writing it was how I would do the figuring out. Fortunately for me, Sarah Harrington at Oxford University Press also thought it was a good idea. Her enthusiasm set this in motion.

The research most central to the development of the ideas in this book was largely funded through grants from the National Institute on Drug Abuse (particularly R34 DA043422 and R34 DA036419). Many thanks to Drs. Richard Jenkins and Sonia Lee at the National Institutes of Health for their good counsel over the years. I also owe a tremendous debt to the research teams that supported and carried out this work. In particular, Christine Cowles, Mark Pawson, Andrew Cortopassi, Mark Stratton, Kory Kyre, Michael Suarez, Jonathan Ohadi, Nahuel Smith-Becerra, and Ruben Jimenez, as well as Drs. Gabriel Robles and Brett Millar and data managers Juan Castiblanco-Bustos, Kris Ali, Trinae Adebayo, Scott Jones, and Chloe Mirzayi, who were integral to these studies. Thanks also to my current team, who have kept things running through the monumental challenges of the pandemic. This includes Christine, Kory, Juan, and Trinae, as well as Beeta Salsabilian, Christel Adhemar, and Joseph Hillesheim.

Enormous thanks to my graduate students, Stephen Bosco, Trey Dellucci, Kendell Doyle, and Daniel Sauermilch, who have been with me through a whole lot of "figuring things out" over the past years. I am honored by their commitment, grateful for their patience, and inspired by their tenacity. The projects, the papers, the work overall—none would have been the same without them. Three of them have made contributions to this book specifically. What they offer here is just a preview of their potential. I could not have made this book what it is without them. Thanks also to Stephen P. Sullivan, MPH, for his tremendous help with the graphic design of the figures in this text.

Despite the excellent intervention supervision and training I received in Motivational Interviewing and substance use treatment from Drs. Juline Koken and John Pachankis, I am not sure I fully understood what I was trying to do in Motivational Interviewing with couples until I had to explain it to someone else. So much of how I now think about this work was sorted out in supervision sessions. I am therefore forever indebted to my clinical supervisees who worked on *We Test* and *The Couples Health Project*: Dr. Gabriel Robles, Paula Bertone, and Dr. Cynthia Cabral as well as Stephen Bosco, Kendell Doyle, Dr. Raymond Moody, Dr. Thomas Whitfield, Alex Brousset, and Dr. Jonathan Lassiter. Their curiosity and skill were a gift. Seeing what made sense to them helped me make sense of things.

Finally, I owe the biggest thank you of all to my husband, Michael Zimmerman. Practically speaking, we took some long, pandemic road trips in the summer of 2020. On those drives, Michael—who is the real writer in the family—talked me through how to plan and sequence the content in a book. Without his insight into process, this whole enterprise might have gone off the rails. More importantly, he has stood by me and made any number of sacrifices through all the anxiety and madness of my early career. His knack for seeing things that feel impossible as just another practical problem to solve—while sometimes maddening—has given me hope in a great many dark moments. Even when things are not perfect, they are still pretty great. That I think is a certain kind of perfect all its own.

REFERENCES

Abughosh, S., Wang, X., Serna, O., Esse, T., Mann, A., Masilamani, S., Holstad, M. M., Essien, E. J., & Fleming, M. (2017). A Motivational Interviewing intervention by pharmacy students to improve medication adherence. *Journal of Managed Care & Specialty Pharmacy*, *23*(5), 549–560.

Agnew, C. R., Van Lange, P. A. M., Rusbult, C. E., & Langston, C. A. (1998). Cognitive interdependence: Commitment and the mental representation of close relationships. *Journal of Personality and Social Psychology*, *74*(4), 939–954.

Ainsworth, M. D. (1985). Attachments across the life span. *Bulletin of the New York Academy of Medicine*, *61*(9), 792–812.

Ainsworth, M. D. (1989). Attachments beyond infancy. *American Psychologist*, *44*(4), 709–716.

Ainsworth, M. D., Blehar, M. C., Water, E., & Wall, S. (1978). *Patterns of attachment: A psychological study of the strange situation*. Lawrence Erlbaum Associates.

Aldarondo, E., & Straus, M. A. (1994). Screening for physical violence in couple therapy: Methodological, practical, and ethical considerations. *Family Process*, *33*(4), 425–439.

Altice, F., Evuarherhe, O., Shina, S., Carter, G., & Beaubrun, A. C. (2019). Adherence to HIV treatment regimens: Systematic literature review and meta-analysis. *Patient Preference and Adherence*, *13*, 475–490.

American Psychiatric Association. (1980). *Diagnostic and statistical manual of mental disorders* (3rd ed., revised).

American Psychiatric Association. (2013). *Diagnostic and statistical manual of mental disorders* (5th ed.).

American Psychological Association. (2012). Practice guidelines for lesbian, gay, and bisexual clients. *American Psychologist*, *67*(1), 10–42.

American Psychological Association. (2015). Guidelines for psychological practice with transgender and gender nonconforming people. *American Psychologist*, *70*(9), 832–864.

American Psychological Association. (2017). *Ethical principles of psychologists and code of conduct (2002, amended effective June 1, 2010, and January 1, 2017)*. https://www.apa.org/ethics/code/ethics-code-2017.pdf

Anderson, P. L., Glidden, D. V., Liu, A., Buchbinder, S., Lama, J. R., Guanira, J. V., McMahan, V., Bushman, L. R., Casapía, M., Montoya-Herrera, O., Veloso, V. G.,

Mayer, K. H., Chariyalertsak, S., Schechter, M., Bekker, L. G., Kallás, E. G., & Grant, R. M. (2012). Emtricitabine-tenofovir concentrations and pre-exposure prophylaxis efficacy in men who have sex with men. *Science Translational Medicine*, 4(151), 151ra125.

Anderson, R. M. (2013). Positive sexuality and its impact on overall well-being. *Bundesgesundheitsblatt-Gesundheitsforschung-Gesundheitsschutz*, 56(2), 208–214.

Anton, R. F., O'Malley, S. S., Ciraulo, D. A., Cisler, R. A., Couper, D., Donovan, D. M., Gastfriend, D. R., Hosking, J. D., Johnson, B. A., LoCastro, J. S., Longabaugh, R., Mason, B. J., Mattson, M. E., Miller, W. R., Pettinati, H. M., Randall, C. L., Swift, R., Weiss, R. D., Williams, L. D., & Zweben, A. (2006). Combined pharmacotherapies and behavioral interventions for alcohol dependence: The COMBINE study: A randomized controlled trial. *Journal of the American Medical Association*, 295(17), 2003–2017.

Apodaca, T. R., Magill, M., Longabaugh, R., Jackson, K. M., & Monti, P. M. (2013). Effect of a significant other on client change talk in Motivational Interviewing. *Journal of Consulting and Clinical Psychology*, 81(1), 35–46.

Araji, S. K. (2004). Preadolescents and adolescents: Evaluating normative and non-normative sexual behaviours and development. In G. O'Reilly, W. L. Marshall, A. Carr, & R. C. Beckett (Eds.), *The handbook of clinical intervention with young people who sexually abuse* (pp. 19–51). Psychology Press.

Arayasirikul, S., Turner, C., Trujillo, D., Le, V., Beltran, T., & Wilson, E. C. (2020). Does the use of Motivational Interviewing skills promote change talk among young people living with HIV in a digital HIV care navigation text messaging intervention? *Health Promotion Practice*, 21(5), 738–743.

Aron, A., Aron, E. N., & Smollan, D. (1992). Inclusion of Other in the Self scale and the structure of interpersonal closeness. *Journal of Personality and Social Psychology*, 63(4), 596–612.

Arriaga, X. B., & Kumashiro, M. (2019). Walking a security tightrope: Relationship-induced changes in attachment security. *Current Opinion in Psychology*, 25, 121–126.

Asay, T. P., & Lambert, M. J. (1999). In M. A. Hubble, B. L. Duncan, & S. D. Miller (Eds.), *The heart and soul of change; What works in therapy* (pp. 23–55). American Psychological Association.

Austin, E. L., & Bozick, R. (2012). Sexual orientation, partnership formation, and substance use in the transition to adulthood. *Journal of Youth and Adolescence*, 41(2), 167–178.

Aviram, A., & Westra, H. A. (2011). The impact of Motivational Interviewing on resistance in cognitive behavioural therapy for generalized anxiety disorder. *Psychotherapy Research*, 21(6), 698–708.

Babcock, J. C., Waltz, J., Jacobson, N. S., & Gottman, J. M. (1993). Power and violence: The relation between communication patterns, power discrepancies, and domestic violence. *Journal of Consulting and Clinical Psychology*, 61(1), 40.

Babor, T., & Del Boca, F. K. (2003). *Treatment matching in alcoholism*. Cambridge University Press.

Bacon, M. (2019). *Family therapy and the treatment of substance use disorders: The family matters model*. Routledge.

Badr, H. (2004). Coping in marital dyads: A contextual perspective on the role of gender and health. *Personal Relationships, 11*(2), 197–211.

Badr, H., Acitelli, L. K., & Taylor, C. L. C. (2008). Does talking about their relationship affect couples' marital and psychological adjustment to lung cancer? *Journal of Cancer Survivorship, 2*(1), 53–64.

Badr, H., Bakhshaie, J., & Chhabria, K. (2019). Dyadic interventions for cancer survivors and caregivers: State of the science and new directions. *Seminars in Oncology Nursing, 35*(4), 337–341.

Badr, H., Smith, C. B., Goldstein, N. E., Gomez, J. E., & Redd, W. H. (2015). Dyadic psychosocial intervention for advanced lung cancer patients and their family caregivers: Results of a randomized pilot trial. *Cancer, 121*(1), 150–158.

Bahafzallah, L., Hayden, K. A., Raffin Bouchal, S., Singh, P., & King-Shier, K. M. (2020). Motivational Interviewing in ethnic populations. *Journal of Immigrant and Minority Health, 22*(4), 816–851.

Bahner, J., & Stenqvist, K. (2020). Motivational Interviewing as evidence-based practice? An example from sexual risk reduction interventions targeting adolescents and young adults. *Sexuality Research and Social Policy, 17*(2), 301–313.

Balán, I. C., Lejuez, C. W., Hoffer, M., & Blanco, C. (2016). Integrating Motivational Interviewing and brief behavioral activation therapy: Theoretical and practical considerations. *Cognitive and Behavioral Practice, 23*(2), 205–220.

Banducci, A. N., Lejuez, C. W., & MacPherson, L. (2013, Summer). Pilot of a behavioral activation-enhanced smoking cessation program for substance users with elevated depressive symptoms in residential treatment. *Addictions Newsletter (American Psychological Association, Division 50), 2013*, 16–20.

Bariola, E., Lyons, A., & Leonard, W. (2015). The mental health benefits of relationship formalisation among lesbians and gay men in same-sex relationships. *Australian and New Zealand Journal of Public Health, 39*(6), 530–535.

Barrowclough, C., Haddock, G., Tarrier, N., Lewis, S. W., Moring, J., O'Brien, R., Schofield, N., & McGovern, J. (2001). Randomized controlled trial of motivational interviewing, cognitive behavior therapy, and family intervention for patients with comorbid schizophrenia and substance use disorders. *American Journal of Psychiatry, 158*(10), 1706–1713.

Bass, B., & Quimby, J. (2006). Addressing secrets in couples counseling: An alternative approach to informed consent. *Family Journal, 14*(1), 77–80.

Baucom, B. R., McFarland, P. T., & Christensen, A. (2010). Gender, topic, and time in observed demand–withdraw interaction in cross-and same-sex couples. *Journal of Family Psychology, 24*(3), 233–242.

Baucom, B. R., Sheng, E., Christensen, A., Georgiou, P. G., Narayanan, S. S., & Atkins, D. C. (2015). Behaviorally-based couple therapies reduce emotional arousal during couple conflict. *Behavior Research and Therapy, 72*, 49–55.

Baucom, D. H., Epstein, N. B., LaTaillade, J. J., & Kirby, J. S. (2008). Cognitive-behavioral couple therapy. In A. S. Gurman (Ed.), *Clinical handbook of couple therapy* (4th ed., pp. 31–72). Guilford Press.

Bay-Cheng, L. Y., Maguin, E., & Bruns, A. E. (2018). Who wears the pants: The implications of gender and power for youth heterosexual relationships. *Journal of Sex Research, 55*(1), 7–20.

Beach, S. R. H., Sandeen, E. E., & O'Leary, D. K. (1990). *Depression in marriage*. Guilford Press.

Bean, M. K., Mazzeo, S. E., Stern, M., Bowen, D., & Ingersoll, K. (2011). A values-based Motivational Interviewing (MI) intervention for pediatric obesity: Study design and methods for MI values. *Contemporary Clinical Trials, 32*(5), 667–674.

Beck, A. T. (1979). *Cognitive therapy of depression*. Guilford Press.

Berenson, K. R., Paprocki, C., Fishman, M. T., Bhushan, D., El-Bassel, N., & Downey, G. (2015). Rejection sensitivity, perceived power, and HIV risk in the relationships of low-income urban women. *Women & Health, 55*(8), 900–920.

Bianchi-Hayes, J., Schoenfeld, E., Cataldo, R., Hou, W., Messina, C., & Pati, S. (2018). Combining activity trackers with Motivational Interviewing and mutual support to increase physical activity in parent-adolescent dyads: Longitudinal observational feasibility study. *JMIR Pediatrics Parent, 1*(1), e3.

Bierstetel, S. J., & Slatcher, R. B. (2020). Couples' behavior during conflict in the lab and diurnal cortisol patterns in daily life. *Psychoneuroendocrinology, 115*(5), 104633.

Binik, Y. M., & Meana, M. (2009). The future of sex therapy: Specialization or marginalization? *Archives of Sexual Behavior, 38*(6), 1016–1027.

Birnbaum, G. E. (2007). Attachment orientations, sexual functioning, and relationship satisfaction in a community sample of women. *Journal of Social and Personal Relationships, 24*(1), 21–35.

Blashill, A. J., Wilson, J. M., O'Cleirigh, C. M., Mayer, K. H., & Safren, S. A. (2014). Examining the correspondence between relationship identity and actual sexual risk behavior among HIV-positive men who have sex with men. *Archives of Sexual Behavior, 43*(1), 129–137.

Bodenmann, G., Meuwly, N., & Kayser, K. (2011). Two conceptualizations of dyadic coping and their potential for predicting relationship quality and individual well-being: A comparison. *European Psychologist, 16*(4), 255–266.

Bograd, M., & Mederos, F. (1999). Battering and couples therapy: Universal screening and selection of treatment modality. *Journal of Marital and Family Therapy, 25*(3), 291–312.

Bolin, A., Whelehan, P., Vernon, M., & Antoine, K. (2021). *Human sexuality: Biological, psychological, and cultural perspectives*. Routledge.

Bosco, S. C., Pawson, M., Parsons, J. T., & Starks, T. J. (2019). Biomedical HIV prevention among gay male couples: A qualitative study of motivations and concerns. *Journal of Homosexuality, 68*(8), 1353–1370.

Bosco, S. C., Robles, G., Stephenson, R., & Starks, T. J. (2022). Relationship power and intimate partner violence in sexual minority male couples. *Journal of Interpersonal Violence, 37*(1–2), NP671–NP695.

Bourke, E., Magill, M., & Apodaca, T. R. (2016). The in-session and long-term role of a significant other in motivational enhancement therapy for alcohol use disorders. *Journal of Substance Abuse Treatment, 64*, 35–43.

Bourne, A., Reid, D., Hickson, F., Torres-Rueda, S., & Weatherburn, P. (2015). Illicit drug use in sexual settings ("chemsex") and HIV/STI transmission risk behaviour among gay men in south London: Findings from a qualitative study. *Sexually Transmitted Infections, 91*(8), 564–568.

Bowlby, J. (1969). *Attachment and loss: Vol. 1 Attachment*. Basic Books.

Bowlby, J. (1973). *Attachment and loss: Vol. 2. Separation: Anxiety and anger*. Basic Books.

Bowlby, J. (1977). The making and breaking of affectional bonds. *British Journal of Psychiatry, 130*(3), 201–210.

Bowleg, L. (2012). The problem with the phrase women and minorities: Intersectionality— An important theoretical framework for public health. *American Journal of Public Health, 102*(7), 1267–1273.

Braithwaite, S. R., Delevi, R., & Fincham, F. D. (2010). Romantic relationships and the physical and mental health of college students. *Personal Relationships, 17*(1), 1–12.

Braithwaite, S. R., & Holt-Lunstad, J. (2017). Romantic relationships and mental health. *Current Opinion in Psychology, 13*, 120–125.

Branscum, P., & Sharma, M. (2010). A review of Motivational Interviewing-based interventions targeting problematic drinking among college students. *Alcoholism Treatment Quarterly, 28*(1), 63–77.

Broderick, C. B. (1993). *Understanding family process: Basics of family systems theory*. Sage.

Brummel-Smith, K. (2015). Motivational Interviewing for older adults. In G. M. Sullivan & A. K. Pomidor (Eds.), *Exercise for aging adults: A guide for practitioners* (pp. 59–66). Springer International Publishing.

Buehlman, K. T., Gottman, J. M., & Katz, L. F. (1992). How a couple views their past predicts their future: Predicting divorce from an oral history interview. *Journal of Family Psychology, 5*, 295–318.

Bui, K. V. T., Raven, B. H., & Schwarzwald, J. (1994). Influence strategies in dating relationships: The effects of relationship satisfaction, gender, and perspective. *Journal of Social Behavior & Personality, 9*(3), 429–442.

Burr, W. R. (1990). Beyond I-statements in family communication. *Family Relations, 39*(3), 266–273.

Butzer, B., & Campbell, L. (2008). Adult attachment, sexual satisfaction, and relationship satisfaction: A study of married couples. *Personal Relationships, 15*(1), 141–154.

Byers, E. S. (2005). Relationship satisfaction and sexual satisfaction: A longitudinal study of individuals in long-term relationships. *Journal of Sex Research, 42*(2), 113–118.

Byers, E. S., Henderson, J., & Hobson, K. M. (2009). University students' definitions of sexual abstinence and having sex. *Archives of Sexual Behavior, 38*, 665–674.

Caetano, R., Schafer, J., & Cunradi, C. B. (2017). Alcohol-related intimate partner violence among White, Black, and Hispanic couples in the United States. In M. Natarajan (Ed.), *Domestic violence: The five big questions* (pp. 153–160). Routledge.

Cain, D., Samrock, S., Jones, S. S., Jimenez, R. H., Dilones, R., Tanney, M., Outlaw, A., Friedman, L., Naar, S., & Starks, T. J. (2021). Marijuana and illicit drugs: Correlates of condomless anal sex among adolescent and emerging adult sexual minority men. *Addictive Behaviors, 122*, 107018.

Calhoun, D., Brod, R., Kirlin, K., Howard, B. V., Schuldberg, D., & Fiore, C. (2010). Effectiveness of Motivational Interviewing for improving self-care among Northern Plains Indians with type 2 diabetes. *Diabetes Spectrum, 23*(2), 107.

Callan, J. A., Dunbar-Jacob, J., Sereika, S. M., Stone, C., Fasiczka, A., Jarrett, R. B., & Thase, M. E. (2012). "Barriers to Cognitive Behavioral Therapy Homework Completion Scale–Depression Version": Development and psychometric evaluation. *International Journal of Cognitive Therapy, 5*(2), 219–235.

Capaldi, D. M., Knoble, N. B., Shortt, J. W., & Kim, H. K. (2012). A systematic review of risk factors for intimate partner violence. *Partner Abuse, 3*(2), 231–280.

Caponnetto, P., Maglia, M., Floresta, D., Ledda, C., Vitale, E., Polosa, R., & Rapisarda, V. (2020). A randomized controlled trial to compare group Motivational Interviewing to very brief advice for the effectiveness of a workplace smoking cessation counseling intervention. *Journal of Addictive Diseases, 38*(4), 465–474.

Cardo, D. M., Culver, D. H., Ciesielski, C. A., Srivastava, P. U., Marcus, R., Abiteboul, D., Heptonstall, J., Ippolito, G., Lot, F., & McKibben, P. S. (1997). A case–control study of HIV seroconversion in health care workers after percutaneous exposure. *New England Journal of Medicine, 337*(21), 1485–1490.

Cartwright, D. (Ed.). (1952). *Field theory in social science: Selected theoretical papers by Kurt Lewin.* Social Science Paperbacks.

Carver, C. S., Scheier, M. F., & Weintraub, J. K. (1989). Assessing coping strategies—A theoretically based approach. *Journal of Personality and Social Psychology, 56*(2), 267–283.

Cass, V. C. (1979). Homosexual identity formation: A theoretical model. *Journal of Homosexuality, 4*(3), 219–235.

Caughlin, J. P., & Huston, T. L. (2002). A contextual analysis of the association between demand/withdraw and marital satisfaction. *Personal Relationships, 9*(1), 95–119.

Cavazos-Rehg, P. A., Krauss, M. J., Spitznagel, E. L., Schootman, M., Bucholz, K. K., Peipert, J. F., Sanders-Thompson, V., Cottler, L. B., & Bierut, L. J. (2009). Age of sexual debut among U.S. adolescents. *Contraception, 80*(2), 158–162.

Centers for Disease Control and Prevention. (2019). *PrEP basics.* https://www.cdc.gov/hiv/basics/prep.html

Centers for Disease Control and Prevention. (2021a). *Deciding to take PrEP.* https://www.cdc.gov/hiv/basics/prep/prep-decision.html

Centers for Disease Control and Prevention. (2021b). Monitoring selected national HIV prevention and care objectives by using HIV surveillance data—United States and 6 dependent areas, 2019. *HIV Surveillance Supplemental Report, 26*(2). https://www.cdc.gov/hiv/library/reports/hiv-surveillance/vol-26-no-2/index.html

Centers for Disease Control and Prevention: US Public Health Service. (2021c). Preexposure prophylaxis for the prevention of HIV infection in the United States— 2021 Update: a clinical practice guideline. https://www.cdc.gov/hiv/pdf/risk/prep/cdc-hiv-prep-guidelines-2021.pdf. Last accessed March 31, 2022.

Cepeda, J. A., Solomon, S. S., Srikrishnan, A. K., McFall, A. M., Kumar, M. S., Vasudevan, C. K., Anand, S., Celentano, D. D., Lucas, G. M., & Mehta, S. H. (2017). Injection drug network characteristics are important markers of HIV risk behavior and lack of viral suppression. *Journal of Acquired Immune Deficiency Syndromes, 75*(3), 257–264.

Chang, Y. P., Compton, P., Almeter, P., & Fox, C. H. (2015). The effect of Motivational Interviewing on prescription opioid adherence among older adults with chronic pain. *Perspectives in Psychiatric Care, 51*(3), 211–219.

Chen, J., Li, X., Xiong, Y., Fennie, K. P., Wang, H., & Williams, A. B. (2016). Reducing the risk of HIV transmission among men who have sex with men: A feasibility study of the Motivational Interviewing counseling method. *Nursing and Health Sciences, 18*(3), 400–407.

Choi, K.-H., Jaekal, E., & Lee, G.-Y. (2016). Motivational and behavioral activation as an adjunct to psychiatric rehabilitation for mild to moderate negative symptoms in individuals with schizophrenia: A proof-of-concept pilot study. *Frontiers in Psychology, 7,* 1759.

Christensen, A. (1987). Detection of conflict patterns in couples. In K. Hahlweg & M. J. Goldstein (Eds.), *Understanding major mental disorder: The contribution of family interaction research* (pp. 250–265). Family Process Press.

Christensen, A. (1988). Dysfunctional interaction patterns in couples. In P. F. M. A. Noller (Ed.), *Perspectives on marital interaction* (pp. 31–55). Multilingual Matters.

Christensen, A., Dimidjian, S., & Martell, C. R. (1995). Integrative behavioral couples therapy. In A. S. Gurman, J. L. Lebow, & D. K. Snyder (Eds.), *Clinical handbook of couples therapy* (5th ed., pp. 61–94). Guilford Press.

Christensen, A., & Heavey, C. L. (1990). Gender and social structure in the demand/withdraw pattern of marital conflict. *Journal of Personality and Social Psychology, 59*(1), 73–81.

Christensen, A., & Jacobson, N. S. (1998). *Acceptance and change in couples therapy: A therapist's guide to transforming relationships.* Norton.

Christensen, A., & Jacobson, N. S. (2000). *Reconcilable differences.* Guilford Press.

Christensen, A., & Sullaway, M. (1984). *Communication patterns questionnaire.* University of California.

Christensen, A., & Shenk, J. L. (1991). Communication, conflict, and psychological distance in nondistressed, clinic, and divorcing couples. *Journal of Consulting and Clinical Psychology, 59*(3), 458–463.

Chu, B. C., Colognori, D., Weissman, A. S., & Bannon, K. (2009). An initial description and pilot of group behavioral activation therapy for anxious and depressed youth. *Cognitive and Behavioral Practice, 16*(4), 408–419.

Clutterbuck, D., & Spence, G. (2017). Working with goals in coaching. In T. Bachkirova, G. Spense, & D. Drake (Eds.), *The SAGE handbook of coaching* (pp. 218–237). SAGE.

Cohen, K. M. (2002). Relationships among childhood sex-atypical behavior, spatial ability, handedness, and sexual orientation in men. *Archives of Sexual Behavior, 31*(1), 129–143.

Cohen, S., & Lichtenstein, E. (1990). Partner behaviors that support quitting smoking. *Journal of Consulting and Clinical Psychology, 58*(3), 304.

Colegrove, V. M., Havighurst, S. S., Kehoe, C. E., & Jacobsen, S. L. (2018). Pilot randomized controlled trial of tuning relationships with music: Intervention for parents with a trauma history and their adolescent. *Child Abuse & Neglect, 79,* 259–268.

Coleman, P. T. (2014). Power and conflict. In P. T. Coleman, M. Deutsch, & E. C. Marcus (Eds.), *The handbook of conflict resolution: Theory and practice* (pp. 137–167). Jossey-Bass/Wiley.

Collins, N. L., & Read, S. J. (1990). Adult attachment, working models, and relationship quality in dating couples. *Journal of Personality and Social Psychology, 58*(4), 644–663.

Collins, W. A. (2003). More than myth: The developmental significance of romantic relationships during adolescence. *Journal of Research on Adolescence, 13*(1), 1–24.

Conklin, L. R., & Strunk, D. R. (2015). A session-to-session examination of homework engagement in cognitive therapy for depression: Do patients experience immediate benefits? *Behavioral Research & Therapy, 72,* 56–62.

Connell, R. W. (1987). *Gender and power: Society, the person, and sexual politics.* Stanford University Press.

Connolly, J. A., & McIsaac, C. (2009). Romantic relationships in adolescence. In R. M. Lerner & L. Steinberg (Eds.), *Handbook of adolescent psychology: Contextual influences on adolescent development* (pp. 104–151). John Wiley & Sons.

Cook, J., Tyson, R., White, J., Rushe, R., Gottman, J. M., & Murray, J. (1995). Mathematics of marital conflict: Qualitative dynamic mathematical modeling of marital interaction. *Journal of Family Psychology, 9*(2), 110.

Cordova, J. V., Warren, L. Z., & Gee, C. B. (2001). Motivational Interviewing and an intervention for at-risk couples. *Journal of Marital and Family Therapy, 27*(3), 315–326.

Cornelius, J. R., Douaihy, A., Bukstein, O. G., Daley, D. C., Wood, S. D., Kelly, T. M., & Salloum, I. M. (2011). Evaluation of cognitive behavioral therapy/motivational enhancement therapy (CBT/MET) in a treatment trial of comorbid MDD/AUD adolescents. *Addictive Behavaviour, 36*(8), 843–848.

Cornelius, T. L., Shorey, R. C., & Beebe, S. M. (2010). Self-reported communication variables and dating violence: Using Gottman's marital communication conceptualization. *Journal of Family Violence, 25*(4), 439–448.

Cornwell, B. (2012). Spousal network overlap as a basis for spousal support. *Journal of Marriage and Family, 74*, 229–238.

Cortopassi, A. C., Wells, B. E., Parsons, J. T., & Starks, T. J. (2018). Linguistic correlates of the Communication Patterns Questionnaire: The correspondence of language and quantitative measures of perceived communication patterns among emerging adult gay male couples. *Couple and Family Psychology: Research and Practice, 7*(3–4), 158–170.

Crenshaw, K. (1989). Demarginalizing the intersection of race and sex: A black feminist critique of antidiscrimination doctrine, feminist theory and antiracist politics. *University of Chicago Legal Forum, 1989*(1), 139–168.

Crick, N. R., & Dodge, K. A. (1994). A review and reformulation of social-information-processing mechanisms in children's social adjustment. *Psychological Bulletin, 115*(1), 74–101.

Curry, S. J., Krist, A. H., Owens, D. K., Barry, M. J., Caughey, A. B., Davidson, K. W., . . . & US Preventive Services Task Force. (2018). Screening for intimate partner violence, elder abuse, and abuse of vulnerable adults: US Preventive Services Task Force final recommendation statement. *JAMA, 320*(16), 1678–1687.

Cushing, C. C., Jensen, C. D., Miller, M. B., & Leffingwell, T. R. (2014). Meta-analysis of Motivational Interviewing for adolescent health behavior: Efficacy beyond substance use. *Journal of Consulting and Clinical Psychology, 82*(6), 1212–1218.

Dahl, R. A. (1957). The concept of power. *Behavioral Science, 2*(3), 201–215.

D'Amico, E. J., Houck, J. M., Hunter, S. B., Miles, J. N. V., Osilla, K. C., & Ewing, B. A. (2015). Group Motivational Interviewing for adolescents: Change talk and alcohol and marijuana outcomes. *Journal of Consulting and Clinical Psychology, 83*(1), 68–80.

Daskalopoulou, M., Rodger, A., Phillips, A. N., Sherr, L., Speakman, A., Sollins, S., Elford, J., Johnson, M. A., Gilson, R., Fisher, M., Wilkins, E., Anderson, J., McDonnell, J., Edwards, S., Perry, N., O'Connell, R., Lascar, M., Jones, M., Jonhnson, A. M., . . . Lampe, F. C. (2014). Recreational drug use, polydrug use, and sexual beahvior in HIV-diagnosed men who have sex with men in the US: Results from cross-sectional ASTRA study. *Lancet HIV, 1*, e22–e31.

D'Augelli, A. R. (2006). Developmental and contextual factors and mental health among Lesbian, gay, and bisexual youths. In A. M. Omoto & H. S. Kurtzman (Eds.), *Sexual orientation and mental health: Examining identity and development in Lesbian, gay, and bisexual people* (pp. 37–53). American Psychological Association.

Daughters, S. B., Magidson, J. F., Anand, D., Seitz-Brown, C. J., Chen, Y., & Baker, S. (2018). The effect of a behavioral activation treatment for substance use on post-treatment abstinence: A randomized controlled trial. *Addiction, 113*(3), 535–544.

Davidovich, U., de Wit, J. B. F., & Stroebe, W. (2004). Behavioral and cognitive barriers to safer sex between men in steady relationship: Implications for prevention strategies. *AIDS Education & Prevention, 16*(4), 301–314.

Davidovich, U., de Wit, J. B. F., & Stroebe, W. (2006). Relationship characteristics and risk of HIV infection: Rusbult's investment model and sexual risk behavior of gay men in steady relationships. *Journal of Applied Social Psychology, 36*(1), 22–40.

Davila, J., Bradbury, T. N., Cohan, C. L., & Tochluk, S. (1997). Marital functioning and depressive symptoms: Evidence for a stress generation model. *Journal of Personality and Social Psychology, 73*, 849–861.

Davila, J., Stroud, C. B., & Star, L. (2014). Depression in couples and families. In I. Gotlib & C. Hammen (Eds.), *Handbook of depression* (3rd ed., pp. 410–428). Guilford Press.

Davila, J., Zhou, J., Norona, J., Bhatia, V., Mize, L., & Lashman, K. (2021). Teaching romantic competence skills to emerging adults: A relationship education workshop. *Personal Relationships, 28*(2), 251–275.

Dawson, L. H., Shih, M. C., de Moor, C., & Shrier, L. A. (2008). Reasons why adolescents and young adults have sex: Associations with psychological characteristics and sexual behavior. *Journal of Sex Research, 45*(3), 225–232.

DeBord, K. A., Fischer, A. R., Bieschke, K. J., & Perez, R. M. (Eds.). (2017). *Handbook of sexual orientation and gender diversity in counseling and psychotherapy.* American Psychological Association.

Dellucci, T. V., Carmichael, C., & Starks, T. J. (2020). Arrangements versus agreements: Evaluating two approaches to measuring male couples' rules and understandings around sex with outside sex partners. *Archives of Sexual Behavior, 50*(3), 1689–1700.

Dermen, K. H., & Cooper, M. L. (1994). Sex-related alcohol expectancies among adolescents: II. Prediction of drinking in social and sexual situations. *Psychology of Addictive Behaviors, 8*(3), 161–168.

Deutsch, M. (1973). *The resolution of conflict: Constructive and destructive processes.* Yale University Press.

Diamond, L. M. (2008). *Sexual fluidity.* Wiley Online Library.

Diamond, L. M., & Huebner, D. M. (2012). Is good sex good for you? Rethinking sexuality and health. *Social and Personality Psychology Compass, 6*(1), 54–69.

Diamond, L. M., & Savin-Williams, R. C. (2009). Adolescent sexuality. In R. M. Lerner & L. Steinberg (Eds.), *Handbook of adolescent psychology: Individual bases of adolescent development* (pp. 479–523). John Wiley & Sons.

DiClemente, C. C., Corno, C. M., Graydon, M. M., Wiprovnick, A. E., & Knoblach, D. J. (2017). Motivational interviewing, enhancement, and brief interventions over the last decade: A review of reviews of efficacy and effectiveness. *Psychology of Addictive Behavior, 31*(8), 862–887.

Dietz, A. R., & Dunn, M. E. (2014). The use of Motivational Interviewing in conjunction with adapted dialectical behavior therapy to treat synthetic cannabis use disorder. *Clinical Case Studies, 13*(6), 455–471.

Dimidjian, S., Martell, C. R., & Christensen, A. (2008). Integrative behavioral couple therapy. In A. S. Gurman (Ed.), *Clinical handbook of couple therapy* (4th ed., pp. 73–103). Guilford Publications.

Dixon-Mueller, R. (1993). The sexuality connection in reproductive health. *Studies in Family Planning, 24*(5), 269–282.

Dodge, K. A., & Crick, N. R. (1990). Social information-processing bases of aggressive behavior in children. *Personality and Social Psychology Bulletin, 16*(1), 8–22.

Doherty, W. J., Harris, S. M., & Wilde, J. L. (2016). Discernment counseling for "mixed-agenda" couples. *Journal of Marital and Family Therapy, 42*(2), 246–255.

Doherty, W. J., Willoughby, B. J., & Peterson, B. (2011). Interest in reconciliation among divorcing parents. *Family Court Review, 19*, 48–52.

Doss, B. D., Simpson, L. E., & Christensen, A. (2004). Why do couples seek marital therapy. *Professional Psychology: Research and Practice, 35*(6), 608–614.

Drigotas, S. M., Rusbult, C. E., & Verette, J. (1999). Level of commitment, mutuality of commitment, and couple well-being. *Personal Relationships, 6*, 389–409.

Due, P., Holstein, B., Lund, R., Modvig, J., & Avlund, K. (1999). Social relations: Network, support and relational strain. *Social Science & Medicine, 48*, 661–673.

Duncan, D. T., Goedel, W. C., Stults, C. B., Brady, W. J., Brooks, F. A., Blakely, J. S., & Hagen, D. (2018). A study of intimate partner violence, substance abuse, and sexual risk behaviors among gay, bisexual, and other men who have sex with men in a sample of geosocial-networking smartphone application users. *American Journal of Men's Health, 12*(2), 292–301.

Durrant, C., Clarke, I., Tolland, A., & Wilson, H. (2007). Designing a CBT service for an acute inpatient setting: A pilot evaluation study. *Clinical Psychology & Psychotherapy, 14*(2), 117–125.

Dyer, O. (2019). Gilead to give up Truvada exclusivity and donate drug to some in US. *BMJ: British Medical Journal (Online), 365*, I2173. https://doi.org/http://dx.doi.org/10.1136/bmj.l2173

D'Zurilla, T. J., & Goldfried, M. R. (1971). Problem solving and behavior modification. *Journal of Abnormal Psychology, 78*(1), 107–126.

Ebrahimi, E., & Ali Kimiaei, S. (2014). The study of the relationship among marital satisfaction, attachment styles, and communication patterns in divorcing couples. *Journal of Divorce & Remarriage, 55*(6), 451–463.

Edwards, W. M., & Coleman, E. (2004). Defining sexual health: A descriptive overview. *Archives of Sexual Behavior, 33*(3), 189–195.

Eldridge, N. S. (1987). Gender issues in counseling same-sex couples. *Professional Psychology: Research and Practice, 18*(6), 567–572.

Emanuels-Zuurveen, L., & Emmelkamp, P. M. (1996). Individual behavioural-cognitive therapy v. marital therapy for depression in maritally distressed couples. *British Journal of Psychiatry, 169*(2), 181–188.

Emerson, A. J., Harris, S. M., & Ahmed, F. A. (2021). The impact of discernment counseling on individuals who decide to divorce: Experiences of post-divorce communication and coparenting. *Journal of Marital and Family Therapy, 47*(1), 36–51.

Enns, C. Z. (1993). Twenty years of feminist counseling and therapy: From naming biases to implementing multifaceted practice. *Counseling Psychologist, 21*(1), 3–87.

Epstein, N. B., & Baucom, D. H. (2002). *Enhanced cognitive-behavioral therapy for couples: A contextual approach.* American Psychological Association.

Falconier, M. K. (2015). TOGETHER—A couples' program to improve communication, coping, and financial management skills: Development and initial pilot-testing. *Journal of Marital and Family Therapy*, *41*(2), 236–250.

Falconier, M. K., & Epstein, N. B. (2019). Contingency contracting in couple and family therapy. In J. L. Lebow, A. L. Chambers, & D. C. Breunlin (Eds.), *Encyclopedia of couple and family therapy* (pp. 583–585). Springer International Publishing.

Fallis, E. E., Rehman, U. S., Woody, E. Z., & Purdon, C. (2016). The longitudinal association of relationship satisfaction and sexual satisfaction in long-term relationships. *Journal of Family Psychology*, *30*(7), 822.

Fals-Stewart, W., O'Farrell, T. J., & Birchler, G. R. (2004). Behavioral couples therapy for substance abuse: Rationale, methods, and findings. *Science & Practice Perspectives*, *2*(2), 30–41.

Fals-Stewart, W., O'Farrell, T. J., & Lam, W. K. K. (2009). Behavioral couples therapy for gay and lesbian couples with alcohol use disorders. *Journal of Substance Abuse Treatment*, *37*(4), 379–387.

Farmer, C., & Geller, M. (2005). The integration of psychodrama with Bowen's theory of couples therapy. *Journal of Group Psychotherapy Psychodrama and Sociometry*, *58*(2), 70–85.

Feeney, B. C., & Collins, N. L. (2015). New look at social support: A theoretical perspective on thriving through relationships. *Personality and Social Psychology Review*, *19*(2), 113–147.

Feeney, J. A., & Noller, P. (1990). Attachment style as a predictor of adult romantic relationships. *Journal of Personality and Social Psychology*, *58*(2), 281–291.

Feeney, J. A., & Noller, P. (2004). Attachment and sexuality in close relationships. In J. H. Harvey, A. Wenzel, & S. Sprecher (Eds.), *The handbook of sexuality in close relationships* (pp. 193–212). Lawrence Erlbaum Associates Publishers.

Feinstein, B. A., Dellucci, T. V., Sullivan, P. S., & Mustanski, B. (2018). Characterizing sexual agreements with one's most recent sexual partner among young men who have sex with men. *AIDS Education and Prevention*, *30*(4), 335–349.

Feinstein, B. A., Moody, R. L., John, S. A., Parsons, J. T., & Mustanski, B. (2018). A three-city comparison of drug use and drug use before sex among young men who have sex with men in the United States. *Journal of Gay & Lesbian Social Services*, *30*(1), 82–101.

Feldman, C. M., & Ridley, C. A. (2000). The role of conflict-based communication responses and outcomes in male domestic violence toward female partners. *Journal of Social and Personal Relationships*, *17*(4–5), 552–573.

Felmlee, D. (2001). No couple is an island: A social network perspective on dyadic stability. *Social Forces*, *79*(4), 1259–1287.

Finneran, C., & Stephenson, R. (2014). Antecedents of intimate partner violence among gay and bisexual men. *Violence and Victims*, *29*(3), 422–435.

Fitzpatrick, J., & Lafontaine, M. F. (2017). Attachment, trust, and satisfaction in relationships: Investigating actor, partner, and mediating effects. *Personal Relationships*, *24*(3), 640–662.

Fitzsimons, G. M., & Kay, A. C. (2004). Language and interpersonal cognition: Causal effects of variations in pronoun usage on perceptions of closeness. *Personality and Social Psychology Bulletin*, *30*(5), 547–557.

Fleming, M. (2014, February 22). *Why "condomless sex" is the new barebacking. Q Project Q Atlanta.* https://www.projectq.us/why-condomless-sex-is-the-new-barebacking/

Fletcher, G. J. O., Simpson, J. A., & Thomas, G. (2000). The measurement of perceived relationship quality components: A confirmatory factor analytic approach. *Personality and Social Psychology Bulletin, 26*(3), 340–354.

Flory, K., Lynam, D., Milich, R., Leukefeld, C., & Clayton, R. (2004). Early adolescent through young adult alcohol and marijuana use trajectories: Early predictors, young adult outcomes, and predictive utility. *Development and Psychopathology, 16*(1), 193–213.

Fortenberry, J. D. (2019). Trust, sexual trust, and sexual health: An interrogative review. *Journal of Sex Research, 56*(4–5), 425–439.

Fraley, R. C., & Shaver, P. R. (2000). Adult romantic attachment: Theoretical developments, emerging controversies, and unanswered questions. *Review of General Psychology, 4*(2), 132–154.

Fraley, R. C., Vicary, A. M., Brumbaugh, C. C., & Roisman, G. I. (2011). Patterns of stability in adult attachment: An empirical test of two models of continuity and change. *Journal of Personality and Social Psychology, 101*(5), 974–992.

Frambes, D., Given, B., Lehto, R., Sikorskii, A., & Wyatt, G. (2018). Informal caregivers of cancer patients: Review of interventions, care activities, and outcomes. *Western Journal of Nursing Research, 40*(7), 1069–1097.

Franks, M. M., Stephens, M. A., Rook, K. S., Franklin, B. A., Keteyian, S. J., & Artinian, N. T.. (2011). Spouses' provision of health-related support and control to patients participating in cardiac rehabilitation. *Journal of Family Psychology, 20*(2), 311–318.

Freud, S. (1993). Observations on transference-love: Further recommendations on the technique of psycho-analysis III. *Journal of Psychotherapy Practice and Research, 2*(2), 171–180.

Frost, D. M., & Forrester, C. (2013). Closeness discrepancies in romantic relationships: Implications for relational well-being, stability, and mental health. *Personality and Social Psychology Bulletin, 39*(4), 456–469.

Fuchs, C. Z., & Rehm, L. P. (1977). A self-control behavior therapy program for depression. *Journal of Consulting and Clinical Psychology, 45*(2), 206–215.

Funk, J. L., & Rogge, R. D. (2007). Testing the ruler with item response theory: Increasing precision of measurement for relationship satisfaction with the Couples Satisfaction Index. *Journal of Family Psychology, 21*(4), 572–583.

Futris, T. G., Campbell, K., Nielsen, R. B., & Burwell, S. R. (2010). The communication patterns questionnaire-short form: A review and assessment. *Family Journal, 18*(3), 275–287.

Gamarel, K. E., Darbes, L. A., Hightow-Weidman, L., Sullivan, P., & Stephenson, R. (2019). The development and testing of a relationship skills intervention to improve HIV prevention uptake among young gay, bisexual, and other men who have sex with men and their primary partners (We Prevent): Protocol for a randomized controlled trial. *JMIR Research Protocols, 8*(1), e10370.

Gamarel, K. E., & Golub, S. A. (2015). Intimacy motivations and pre-exposure prophylaxis (PrEP) adoption intentions among HIV-negative men who have sex with men (MSM) in romantic relationships. *Annals of Behavioral Medicine, 49*(2), 177–186.

Gamarel, K. E., & Golub, S. A. (2019). Closeness discrepancies and intimacy interference: Motivations for HIV prevention behavior in primary romantic relationships. *Personality and Social Psychology Bulletin, 45*(2), 270–283.

Gamarel, K. E., Neilands, T. B., Golub, S. A., & Johnson, M. O. (2014). An omitted level: An examination of relational orientations and viral suppression among HIV serodiscordant male couples. *Journal of Acquired Immune Deficiency Syndromes*, *66*(2), 193–196.

Gamarel, K. E., Reisner, S. L., Darbes, L. A., Hoff, C. C., Chakraborty, D., Nemoto, T., & Operario, D. (2016). Dyadic dynamics of HIV risk among transgender women and their primary male sexual partners: The role of sexual agreement types and motivations. *AIDS Care*, *28*(1), 104–111.

Gamarel, K. E., Reisner, S. L., Laurenceau, J. P., Nemoto, T., & Operario, D. (2014). Gender minority stress, mental health, and relationship quality: A dyadic investigation of transgender women and their cisgender male partners. *Journal of Family Psychology*, *28*(4), 437–447.

Gamarel, K. E., Starks, T. J., Dilworth, S. E., Neilands, T. B., Taylor, J. M., & Johnson, M. O. (2014). Personal or relational? Examining sexual health in the context of HIV serodiscordant same-sex male couples. *AIDS and Behavior*, *18*(1), 171–179.

Garanzini, S., Yee, A., Gottman, J. M., Gottman, J. S., Cole, C., Preciado, M., & Jasculca, C. (2017). Results of Gottman method couples therapy with gay and lesbian couples. *Journal of Marital and Family Therapy*, *43*(4), 674–684.

Garfield, R. (2010). Male emotional intimacy: How therapeutic men's groups can enhance couples therapy. *Family Process*, *49*, 109–122.

Gaudiano, B. A., Busch, A. M., Wenze, S. J., Nowlan, K., Epstein-Lubow, G., & Miller, I. W. (2015). Acceptance-based behavior therapy for depression with psychosis: Results from a pilot feasibility randomized controlled trial. *Journal of Psychiatric Practice*, *21*(5), 320–333.

Geiss, S. K., & O'Leary, K. D. (1981). Therapist ratings of frequency and severity fo marital problems: implications for research. *Journal of Marital and Family Therapy*, *7*(4), 515–520.

Gentzler, A. L., & Kerns, K. A. (2004). Associations between insecure attachment and sexual experiences. *Personal Relationships*, *11*(2), 249–265.

Giordano, P. C., Copp, J. E., Longmore, M. A., & Manning, W. D. (2016). Anger, control, and intimate partner violence in young adulthood. *Journal of Family Violence*, *31*(1), 1–13.

Goffman, E. (1963). *Stigma: Notes on the management of spoiled identity*. Simon & Schuster.

Goldenberg, T., Clarke, D., & Stephenson, R. (2013). "Working together to reach a goal": MSM's perceptions for dyadic HIV care for same-sex male couples. *Journal of Acquired Immune Deficiency Syndromes*, *64*(0 1), S52–S61.

Goldenberg, T., Finneran, C., Andes, K. L., & Stephenson, R. (2015). "Sometimes people let love conquer them": How love, intimacy, and trust in relationships between men who have sex with men influence perceptions of sexual risk and sexual decision-making. *Culture, Health & Sexuality*, *17*(5), 607–622.

Goldenberg, T., Stephenson, R., & Bauermeister, J. (2019). Cognitive and emotional factors associated with sexual risk-taking behaviors among young men who have sex with men. *Archives of Sexual Behavior*, *48*(4), 1127–1136.

Goldenberg, T., Stephenson, R., Freeland, R., Finneran, C., & Hadley, C. (2016). "Struggling to be the alpha": Sources of tension and intimate partner violence in same-sex relationships between men. *Culture, Health & Sexuality*, *18*(8), 875–889.

Golub, S. A., Starks, T. J., Payton, G., & Parsons, J. T. (2012). The critical role of intimacy in the sexual risk behaviors of gay and bisexual men. *AIDS and Behavior, 16*(3), 626–632.

Gomez, A. M., Beougher, S. C., Chakravarty, D., Neilands, T. B., Mandic, C. G., Darbes, L. A., & Hoff, C. C. (2012). Relationship dynamics as predictors of broken agreements about outside sexual partners: Implications for HIV prevention among gay couples. *AIDS and Behavior, 16*(6), 1584–1588.

González-Álvarez, S., Madoz-Gúrpide, A., Parro-Torres, C., Hernández-Huerta, D., & Ochoa Mangado, E. (2019). Relationship between alcohol consumption, whether linked to other substance use or not, and antiretroviral treatment adherence in HIV+ patients. *Adicciones, 31*(1), 8–17.

Goodreau, S. M., Carnegie, N. B., Vittinghoff, E., Lama, J. R., Sanchez, J., Grinsztejn, B., Koblin, B. A., Mayer, K. H., & Buchbinder, S. P. (2012). What drives the US and Peruvian HIV epidemics in men who have sex with men (MSM)? *PLoS One, 7*(11), e50522.

Goodreau, S. M., Carnegie, N. B., Vittinghoff, E., Lama, J. R., Sanchez, J., Grinsztejn, B., Koblin, B. A., Mayer, K. H., & Buchbinder, S. P. (2013). Correction: What drives the US and Peruvian HIV epidemics in men who have sex with men (MSM)? *PLoS One, 8*(7). https://doi.org/10.1371/annotation/9a6a0c8e-2d01-4f36-9ab8-f9fdfce6497b

Gordon, T. (1970). *Parent effectiveness training.* Wyden.

Gottlieb, M. C., Lasser, J., & Simpson, G. L. (2008). Legal and ethical issues in couple therapy. In: A. S. Gurman (Ed.), *Clinical handbook of couple therapy* (pp. 698–717). Guilford Press.

Gottman, J. M., Markman, H., & Notarius, C. (1977). The topography of marital conflict: A sequential analysis of verbal and nonverbal behavior. *Journal of Marriage and the Family, 39*(3),461–477.

Gottman, J. M., Swanson, C., & Murray, J. (1999). The mathematics of marital conflict: Dynamic mathematical nonlinear modeling of newlywed marital interaction. *Journal of Family Psychology, 13*(1), 3–19.

Gottman, J. M. (1980). Consistency of nonverbal affect and affect reciprocity in marital interaction. *Journal of Consulting and Clinical Psychology, 48*(6), 711–717.

Gottman, J. M. (1982). Emotional responsiveness in marital conversations. *Journal of Communication, 32*(3), 108–120.

Gottman, J. M. (1994). *What predicts divorce? The relationship between marital processes and marital outcomes.* Lawrence Erlbaum Associates.

Gottman, J. M. (1999). *The marriage clinic: A scientifically-based marital therapy.* Norton & Company.

Gottman, J. M., & Gottman, J. S. (2008). Gottman method couple therapy. In A. S. Gurman (Ed.), *Clinical handbook of couple therapy* (4th ed., pp. 138–164). Guilford Press.

Gottman, J. M., Katz, L. F., & Hooven, C. (1997). *Meta-emotion: How families communicate emotionally.* Lawrence Erlbaum Associates.

Gottman, J. M., & Levenson, R. W. (2000). The timing of divorce: Predicting when a couple will divorce over a 14-year period. *Journal of Marriage and the Family, 62*(3), 737–745.

Gottman, J. M., & Notarius, C. I. (2000). Decade review: Observing marital interaction. *Journal of Marriage and Family, 62*(4), 927–947.

Gottman, J. M., Notarius, C., & Markman, H. (1976). *A couple's guide to communication.* Research Press.

Gottman, J. M., & Silver, N. (2015). *The seven principles for making marriage work: A practical guide from the country's foremost relationship expert.* Harmony.

Gottman, J. S., & Gottman, J. M. (2015). *10 principles for doing effective couples therapy.* W. W. Norton & Company.

Grabbe, K., Jones, R., Barnes, J. L., McWilliams, A., Stephenson, R., Sullivan, P., Coury-Doniger, P., & Schwartz, A. (2014). *Couples HIV testing and counseling (CHTC) in the United States.* Centers for Disease Control and Prevention.

Graham, J. M., & Barnow, Z. B. (2013). Stress and social support in gay, lesbian, and heterosexual couples: Direct effects and buffering models. *Journal of Family Psychology, 27*(4), 569–578.

Gray-Little, B. (1982). Marital quality and power processes among Black couples. *Journal of Marriage and the Family, 44*(3), 633–646.

Gray-Little, B., & Burks, N. (1983). Power and satisfaction in marriage: A review and critique. *Psychological Bulletin, 93*(3), 513.

Greenan, D. E., & Tunnell, G. (2003). *Couple therapy with gay men.* Guilford Press.

Grov, C., Starks, T. J., Rendina, H. J., & Parsons, J. T. (2014). Rules about casual sex partners, relationship satisfaction, and HIV risk in partnered gay and bisexual men. *Journal of Sex & Marital Therapy, 40*(2), 105–122.

Guanipa, C., & Woolley, S. R. (2000). Gender biases and therapists' conceptualization of couple difficulties. *American Journal of Family Therapy, 28*(2), 181–191.

Gurman, A. S. (2008). *Clinical handbook of couple therapy* (4th ed.). Guilford Press.

Gurman, A. S., & Burton, M. (2014). Individual therapy for couple problems: Perspectives and pitfalls. *Journal of Marital and Family Therapy, 40*(4), 470–483.

Gute, G., Eshbaugh, E. M., & Wiersma, J. (2008). Sex for you, but not for me: Discontinuity in undergraduate emerging adults' definitions of "having sex." *Journal of Sex Research, 45*(4), 329–337.

Haefner, J. (2014). An application of Bowen family systems theory. *Issues in Mental Health Nursing, 35*(35), 835–841.

Halkitis, P. N., Levy, M. D., & Solomon, T. M. (2016). Temporal relations between methamphetamine use and HIV seroconversion in gay, bisexual, and other men who have sex with men. *Journal of Health Psychology, 21*(1), 93–99.

Hanser, S. B., Butterfield-Whitcomb, J., Kawata, M., & Collins, B. E. (2011). Home-based music strategies with individuals who have dementia and their family caregivers. *Journal of Music Therapy, 48*(1), 2–27.

Hanzlik, M. P., & Gaubatz, M. (2012). Clinical PsyD trainees' comfort discussing sexual issues with clients. *American Journal of Sexuality Education, 7*(3), 219–236.

Harden, K. P. (2014). A sex-positive framework for research on adolescent sexuality. *Perspectives on Psychological Science, 9*(5), 455–469.

Hassebrauck, M., & Fehr, B. (2002). Dimensions of relationship quality. *Personal Relationships, 9*(3), 253–270.

Hawrilenko, M., Eubanks Fleming, C. J., Goldstein, A. S., & Cordova, J. V. (2016). Motivating action and maintaining change: The time-varying role of homework following a brief couples' intervention. *Journal of Marital and Family Therapy, 42*(3), 396–408.

Hayes, J. A., Gelso, C. J., Goldberg, S., & Kivlighan, D. M. (2018). Contertransference management and effective psychotherapy: Meta-analytic findings. *Psychotherapy, 55*(4), 496–507.

Hayes, S. C., Luoma, J. B., Bond, F. W., Masuda, A., & Lillis, J. (2006). Acceptance and commitment therapy: Model, processes and outcomes. *Behaviour Research and Therapy, 44*(1), 1–25.

Hays, P. A., & Iwamasa, G. Y. (2006). *Culturally responsive cognitive-behavioral therapy: Assessment, practice, and supervision.* American Psychological Association.

Hazan, C., & Shaver, P. R. (1987). Romantic love conceptualized as an attachment process. *Journal of Personality and Social Psychology, 52*(3), 511–524.

Hazan, C., & Shaver, P. R. (1994). Attachment as an organizational framework for research on close relationships. *Psychological Inquiry, 5*(1), 1–22.

Heavey, C. L., Christensen, A., & Malamuth, N. M. (1995). The longitudinal impact of demand and withdrawal during marital conflict. *Journal of Consulting and Clinical Psychology, 63*(5), 797–801.

Heavey, C. L., Larson, B. M., Zumtobel, D. C., & Christensen, A. (1996). The Communication Patterns Questionnaire: The reliability and validity of a constructive communication subscale. *Journal of Marriage and the Family,* 796–800.

Hendrick, S. A. (1988). A generic measure of relationship satisfaction. *Journal of Marriage and the Family, 50*(1), 93–98.

Hendrix, H., Hunt, H. L., Luquet, W., & Carlson, J. (2015). Using the Imago dialogue to deepen couples therapy. *Journal of Individual Psychology, 71*(3), 253–272.

Henry, W. P., Schacht, T. E., & Strupp, H. H. (1990). Patient and therapist introject, interpersonal process, and differential psychotherapy outcome. *Journal of Consulting and Clinical Psychology, 58*(6), 768–774.

Herman-Giddens, M. E., Steffes, J., Harris, D., Slora, E., Hussey, M., Dowshen, S. A., Wasserman, R., Serwint, J. R., Smitherman, L., & Reiter, E. O. (2012). Secondary sexual characteristics in boys: Data from the pediatric research in office settings network. *Pediatrics, 130*(5), e1058–e1068.

Higgins, J. A., Trussell, J., Moore, N. B., & Davidson, J. K. (2010). Virginity lost, satisfaction gained? Physiological and psychological sexual satisfaction at heterosexual debut. *Journal of Sex Research, 47*(4), 384–394.

Hirschman, A. O. (1970). *Exit, voice, and loyalty: Responses to decline in firms, organizations, and states.* Harvard University Press.

Hirschman, A. O. (1974). "Exit, voice, and loyalty": Further reflections and a survey of recent contributions. *Social Science Information, 1974,* 13, 7–26.

Hoff, C. C., & Beougher, S. C. (2010). Sexual agreements among gay male couples. *Archives of Sexual Behavior, 39*(3), 774–787.

Hoff, C. C., Chakravarty, D., Beougher, S. C., Neilands, T. B., & Darbes, L. A. (2012). Relationship characteristics associated with sexual risk behavior among MSM in committed relationships. *AIDS Patient Care and STDs, 26*(12), 738–745.

Holmes, J. G., & Murray, S. L. (1996). Conflict in close relationships. In E. T. Higgins & A. Kruglanski (Eds.), *Social psychology: Handbook of basic principles* (pp. 622–654). Guilford Press.

Holmes, J. G., & Rempel, J. K. (1989). Trust in close relationships. In C. Hendrick (Ed.), *Review of personality and social psychology* (Vol. 10, pp. 187–220). SAGE.

Homans, G. C. (1974). *Social behavior: Its elementary forms* (Revised ed.) Harcourt Brace Jovanovich.

Howard, J. A., Blumstein, P., & Schwartz, P. (1986). Sex, power, and influence tactics in intimate relationships. *Journal of Personality and Social Psychology, 52,* 102–109.

Howe, C. J., Cole, S. R., Napravnik, S., Kaufman, J. S., Adimora, A. A., Elston, B., Eron, J. J., Jr., & Mugavero, M. J. (2014). The role of at-risk alcohol/drug use and treatment in appointment attendance and virologic suppression among HIV(+) African Americans. *AIDS Research and Human Retroviruses*, *30*(3), 233–240.

Hsieh, M.-Y., Ponsford, J., Wong, D., Schönberger, M., Taffe, J., & McKay, A. (2012). Motivational Interviewing and cognitive behaviour therapy for anxiety following traumatic brain injury: A pilot randomised controlled trial. *Neuropsychological Rehabilitation*, *22*(4), 585–608.

Huang, C. C., Son, E., & Wang, L. R. (2010). Prevalence and factors of domestic violence among unmarried mothers with a young child. *Families in Society*, *91*(2), 171–177.

Huang, F. F., Jiao, N. N., Zhang, L. Y., Lei, Y., & Zhang, J. P. (2015). Effects of a family-assisted smoking cessation intervention based on motivational interviewing among low-motivated smokers in China. *Patient Education and Counseling*, *98*(8), 984–990.

Human Performance Resources by CHAMP. (2018, October). *Problem solving for couples*. Retrieved January 18, 2022, from https://www.hprc-online.org/social-fitn ess/couples-intimacy/problem-solving-couples-pdf

Hunt, J. (2011). Motivational Interviewing and people with diabetes. *European Diabetes Nursing*, *8*(2), 68b–73b.

Iarussi, M. M., & Powers, D. (2018). Outcomes of Motivational Interviewing training with probation and parole officers: Findings and lessons learned. *Federal Probation*, *82*, 28.

Ignacio, L., & Taylor, G. (2017). Combining couple therapy with individual therapy by the same therapist team using early memories: Exploration of a new model. *Group*, *41*(4), 323–336.

Impett, E. A., Muise, A., & Peragine, D. (2014). Sexuality in the context of relationships. In *APA handbook of sexuality and psychology, Vol. 1: Person-based approaches* (pp. 269–315). American Psychological Association.

Jackson, B., Grove, J. R., & Beauchamp, M. R. (2010). Relational efficacy beliefs and relationship quality within coach-athlete dyads. *Journal of Social and Personal Relationships*, *27*(8), 1035–1050.

Jackson, S., & Goossens, L. (2020). *Handbook of adolescent development*. Routledge.

Jacobson, N. S., Christensen, A., Prince, S. E., Cordova, J., & Eldridge, K. (2000). Integrative behavioral couple therapy: An acceptance-based, promising new treatment for couple discord. *Journal of Consulting and Clinical Psychology*, *68*(2), 351–355.

Jacobson, N. S., & Holtzworth-Munroe, A. (1986). Marital therapy: A social-learning perspective. In N. S. Jacobson & A. S. Gurman (Eds.), *Clinical handbook of marital therapy* (pp. 29–70). Guilford Press.

Jacobson, N. S., & Margolin, G. (1979). *Marital therapy: Strategies based on social learning and behavior exchange principles*. Brunner/Mazel.

Janis, I. L., & Mann, L. (1977). *Decision making: A psychological analysis of conflict, choices and commitment*. Free Press.

John, S. A., Starks, T. J., Rendina, H. J., Grov, C., & Parsons, J. T. (2018). Should I convince my partner to go on pre-exposure prophylaxis (PrEP)? The role of personal and relationship factors on PrEP-related social control among gay and bisexual men. *AIDS and Behavior*, *22*(4), 1239–1252.

Johnson, D. J., & Rusbult, C. E. (1989). Resisting temptation: Devaluation of alternative partners as a means of maintaining commitment in close relationships. *Journal of Personality and Social Psychology, 57*(6), 967–980.

Johnson, S. M., & Bradley, B. (2009). Emotionally focused couple therapy: Creating loving relationships. In J. H. Bray & M. Stanton (Eds.), *The Wiley-Blackwell handbook of family psychology* (pp. 402–415). Wiley Blackwell.

Johnson, S. M. (2004). *The practice of emotionally focused couple therapy: Creating connection* (2nd ed.). Brunner-Routledge.

Johnson, S. M. (2008). Emotionally focused couple therapy. In A. S. Gurman (Ed.), *Clinical handbook of couple therapy* (4th ed., pp. 107–137). Guilford Publications.

Johnson, S. M. (2020). *The practice of emotionally focused couple therapy: Creating connection* (3rd ed.). Routledge, Taylor & Francis Group.

Johnson, S. M., & Greenberg, L. S. (1985). Differential effects of experiential and problem-solving interventions in resolving marital conflict. *Journal of Consulting and Clinical Psychology, 53*(2), 175–184.

Johnson, S. M., & Greenberg, L. S. (1988). Relating process to outcome in marital therapy. *Journal of Marital and Family Therapy, 14*(2), 175–183.

Jones, C. M., Clayton, H. B., Deputy, N. P., Roehler, D. R., Ko, J. Y., Esser, M. B., Brookmeyer, K. A., & Herta, M. F. (2020). Prescription opioid misuse and use of alcohol and other substances among high school students—Youth Risk Behavior Survey, United States, 2019. *MMWR Morbidity and Mortality Weekly Report, 69*(Suppl. 1), 38–46.

Kahle, E. M., Sharma, A., Sullivan, S., & Stephenson, R. (2020). The influence of relationship dynamics and sexual agreements on perceived partner support and benefit of PrEP use among same-sex male couples in the U.S. *AIDS and Behavior, 24*(7), 2169–2177.

Kahler, C. W., Pantalone, D. W., Mastroleo, N. R., Liu, T., Bove, G., Ramratnam, B., Monti, P. M., & Mayer, K. H. (2018). Motivational Interviewing with personalized feedback to reduce alcohol use in HIV-infected men who have sex with men: A randomized controlled trial. *Journal of Consulting and Clinical Psychology, 86*(8), 645–656.

Kalichman, S. C. (1998). Post-exposure prophylaxis for HIV infection in gay and bisexual men: Implications for the future of HIV prevention. *American Journal of Preventive Medicine, 15*(2), 120–127.

Kanter, J. W., Manos, R. C., Bowe, W. M., Baruch, D. E., Busch, A. M., & Rusch, L. C. (2010). What is behavioral activation? A review of the empirical literature. *Clinical Psychology Review, 30*(6), 608–620.

Karakurt, G., Anderson, A., Banford, A., Dial, S., Korkow, H., Rable, F., & Doslovich, S. F. (2014). Strategies for managing difficult clinical situations in between sessions. *American Journal of Family Therapy, 42*(5), 413–425.

Kazantzis, N., Whittington, C., & Dattilio, F. (2010). Meta-analysis of homework effects in cognitive and behavioral therapy: A replication and extension. *Clinical Psychology: Science and Practice, 17*(2), 144–156.

Kazantzis, N., Whittington, C., Zelencich, L., Kyrios, M., Norton, P. J., & Hofmann, S. G. (2016). Quantity and quality of homework compliance: A meta-analysis of relations with outcome in cognitive behavior therapy. *Behavioral Therapy, 47*(5), 755–772.

Kelley, H. H. (1979), *Personal relationships: Their structures and processes*. Lawrence Erlbaum Associates Publishers.

Kelley, H. H., Holmes, J. G., Kerr, N. L., Reis, H. T., Rusbult, C. E., & Van Lange, P. A. (2003). *An atlas of interpersonal situations*. Cambridge University Press.

Kelley, H. H., & Thibaut, J. W. (1978). *Interpersonal relations: A theory of interdependence*. John Wiley & Sons.

Kelly, A. B., Fincham, F. D., & Beach, S. R. H. (2003). Communication skills in couples: A review and discussion of emerging perspectives. In J. O. Greene & B. R. Burleson (Eds.), *Handbook of communication and social interaction skills* (pp. 723–751). Lawrence Erlbaum Associates Publishers.

Kertes, A., Westra, H. A., Angus, L., & Marcus, M. (2011). The impact of Motivational Interviewing on client experiences of cognitive behavioral therapy for generalized anxiety disorder. *Cognitive and Behavioral Practice, 18*(1), 55–69.

Ketcher, D., Ellington, L., Baucom, B. R. W., Clayton, M. F., & Reblin, M. (2020). "In eight minutes we talked more about our goals, relationship, than we have in years": A pilot of patient–caregiver discussions in a neuro-oncology clinic. *Journal of Family Nursing, 26*(2), 126–137.

Ketcher, D., Thompson, C., Otto, A. K., Reblin, M., Cloyes, K. G., Clayton, M. F., Baucom, B. R. W., & Ellington, L. (2020). The me in we dyadic communication intervention is feasible and acceptable among advanced cancer patients and their family caregivers. *Palliative Medicine, 35*(2), 389–396.

Kim, H. K., Laurent, H. K., Capaldi, D. M., & Feingold, A. (2008). Men's aggression toward women: A 10-year panel study. *Journal of Marriage and Family, 70*(5), 1169–1187.

Kistenmacher, B. R., & Weiss, R. L. (2008). Motivational interviewing as a mechanism for change in men who batter: A randomized controlled trial. *Violence and Victims, 23*(5), 558–570.

Knauss, L. K., & Knauss, J. W. (Eds.). (2012). *Ethical issues in multiperson therapy*. American Psychological Association.

Kollock, P., Blumstein, P., & Schwartz, P. (1985). Sex and power in interaction: Conversational privileges and duties. *American Sociological Review, 50*(1), 34–46.

Kraemer, L. M., Stanton, A. L., Meyerowitz, B. E., Rowland, J. H., & Ganz, P. A. (2011). A longitudinal examination of couples' coping strategies as predictors of adjustment to breast cancer. *Journal of Family Psychology, 25*(6), 963–972.

Krakower, D. S., Daskalakis, D. C., Feinberg, J., & Marcus, J. L. (2020). Tenofovir alafenamide for HIV preexposure prophylaxis: What can we DISCOVER about its true value? *Annals of Internal Medicine, 172*(4), 281–282.

Kreitzer, N., Kurowski, B. G., & Bakas, T. (2018). Systematic review of caregiver and dyad interventions after adult traumatic brain injury. *Archives of Physical Medicine and Rehabilitation, 99*(11), 2342–2354.

Krueger, E. A., Fish, J. N., & Upchurch, D. M. (2020). Sexual orientation disparities in substance use: Investigating social stress mechanisms in a national sample. *American Journal of Preventive Medicine, 58*(1), 59–68.

Kurdek, L. A. (1995). Assessing multiple determinants of relationship commitment in cohabitating gay, cohabitating lesbian, dating heterosexual, and married heterosexual couples. *Family Relations, 44*(3), 261–266.

Kurtz, S. P. (2005). Post-circuit blues: Motivations and consequences of crystal meth use among gay men in Miami. *AIDS and Behavior*, *9*(1), 63–72.

Lafontaine, M. F., Hum, L., Gabbay, N., & Dandurand, C. (2018). Examination of the psychometric properties of the Personal Assessment of Intimacy in Relationships with Individuals in Same-Sex Couple Relationships. *Journal of GLBT Family Studies*, *14*(4), 263–294.

LaSala, M. C. (2000). Lesbians, gay men, and their parents: Family therapy for the coming-out crisis. *Family Process*, *39*(1), 67–81.

LaSala, M. C. (2001). Monogamous or not: Understanding and counseling gay male couples. *Families in Society*, *82*(6), 605–611.

LaSala, M. C. (2004). Extradyadic sex and gay male couples: Comparing monogamous and nonmonogamous relationships. *Families in Society*, *85*(3), 405–412.

LaSala, M. C. (2005). Monogamy of the heart: Extradyadic sex and gay male couples. *Journal of Gay & Lesbian Social Services*, *17*(3), 1–24.

Latham, G. P. (2001). The reciprocal effects of science on practice: Insights from the practice and science of goal setting. *Canadian Psychology*, *42*(1), 1–11.

Lawrance, K. A., & Byers, E. S. (1995). Sexual satisfaction in long-term heterosexual relationships: The interpersonal exchange model of sexual satisfaction. *Personal Relationships*, *2*(4), 267–285.

Lebow, J. L. (2015). Separation and divorce issues in couple therapy. In A. S. Gurman, J. L. Lebow, & D. K. Snyder (Eds.), *Clinical handbook of couple therapy* (5th ed., pp. 445–463). Guilford Press.

Lee, C. S., López, S. R., Colby, S. M., Rohsenow, D., Hernández, L., Borrelli, B., & Caetano, R. (2013). Culturally adapted motivational interviewing for Latino heavy drinkers: Results from a randomized clinical trial. *Journal of Ethnicity in Substance Abuse*, *12*(4), 356–373.

Lee, J. J., Capella, M. L., Taylor, C. R., Luo, M., & Gabler, C. B. (2014). The financial impact of loyalty programs in the hotel industry: A social exchange theory perspective. *Journal of Business Research*, *67*(10), 2139–2146.

Lehmiller, J. J. (2012). Perceived marginalization and its association with physical and psychological health. *Journal of Social and Personal Relationships*, *29*(4), 451–469.

Lehmiller, J. J., & Agnew, C. R. (2006). Marginalized relationships: The impact of social disapproval on romantic relationship commitment. *Personality and Social Psychology Bulletin*, *32*(1), 40–51.

Lehmiller, J. J., & Agnew, C. R. (2007). Perceived marginalization and the prediction of romantic relationship stability. *Journal of Marriage and the Family*, *69*(4), 1036–1049.

Leibert, T. W., Smith, J. B., & Agaskar, V. R. (2011). Relationship between the working alliance and social support on counseling outcome. *Journal of Clinical Psychology*, *67*(7), 709–719.

Lewinsohn, P. M. (1974). A behavioral approach to depression. In R. J. Friedman & M. M. Katz (Eds.), *The psychology of depression: Contemporary theory and research* (pp. 157–174). John Wiley & Sons.

Lewinsohn, P. M. (1975). The behavioral study and treatment of depression. In M. Hersen, R. M. Eisler, & P. M. Miller (Eds.), *Progress in behavior modification* (Vol. 1, pp. 19–64). Elsevier.

Lewinsohn, P. M., Weinstein, M. S., & Alper, T. (1970). A behavioral approach to the group treatment of depressed persons: A methodological contribution. *Journal of Clinical Psychology*, *26*(4), 525–532.

Lewis, M. A., Gladstone, E., Schmal, S., & Darbes, L. A. (2006). Health-related social control and relationship interdependence among gay couples. *Health Education Research, 21*(4), 488–500.

Lewis, M. A., McBride, C. M., Pollak, K. I., Puleo, E., Butterfield, R. M., & Emmons, K. M. (2006). Understanding health behavior change among couples: An interdependence and communal coping approach. *Social Science & Medicine, 62*(6), 1369–1380.

Lewis, M. A., & Rook, K. S. (1999). Social control in personal relationships: Impact on health behaviors and psychological distress. *Health Psychology, 18*(1), 63.

Liberman, R. P., DeRisi, W. J., & Mueser, K. T. (1989). *Social skills training for psychiatric patients*. Pergamon Press.

Lick, D. J., Durso, L. E., & Johnson, K. L. (2013). Minority stress and physical health among sexual minorities. *Perspectives on Psychological Science, 8*(5), 521–548.

Lindau, S. T., & Gavrilova, N. (2010). Sex, health, and years of sexually active life gained due to good health: Evidence from two US population based cross sectional surveys of ageing. *BMJ, 340*, c810.

Linder, J. R., Werner, N. E., & Lyle, K. A. (2010). Automatic and controlled social information processing and relational aggression in young adults. *Personality and Individual Differences, 49*(7), 778–783.

Lindson-Hawley, N., Thompson, T. P., & Begh, R. (2015). Motivational interviewing for smoking cessation. *Cochrane Database of Systematic Reviews, 7*(7), CD006936.

Linehan, M. M. (2015). *DBT skills training manual (2nd ed.)*. Guilford Press.

Link, B. G., & Phelan, J. C. (2001). Conceptualizing stigma. *Annual Review of Sociology, 27*(1), 363–385.

Linschoten, M., Weiner, L., & Avery-Clark, C. (2016). Sensate focus: A critical literature review. *Sexual and Relationship Therapy, 31*(2), 230–247.

Locke, E. A., & Lantham, G. P. (2006). New directions in goal-setting theory. *Current Directions in Psychological Science, 15*(5), 265–268.

Loving, T. J., & Slatcher, R. B. (2013). *Romantic relationships and health*. In J. A. Simpson & L. Campbell (Eds.), *The Oxford handbook of close relationships* (pp. 617–637). Oxford University Press.

Loza, O., Curiel, Z. V., Beltran, O., & Ramos, R. (2020). Methamphetamine use and sexual risk behaviors among men who have sex with men in a Mexico-US border city. *American Journal on Addictions, 29*(2), 111–119.

Ludgate, J. W., & Grubr, T. N. (2018). *The CBT couples toolbox*. PESI Publishing and Media.

Luz, P. M., Girouard, M. P., Grinsztejn, B., Freedberg, K. A., Veloso, V. G., Losina, E., Struchiner, C. J., MacLean, R. L., Parker, R. A., Paltiel, A. D., & Walensky, R. P. (2016). Survival benefits of antiretroviral therapy in Brazil: A model-based analysis. *Journal of the International AIDS Society, 19*(1), 20623.

Macapagal, K., Feinstein, B. A., Puckett, J. A., & Newcomb, M. E. (2019). Improving young male couples' sexual and relationship health in the 2GETHER program: Intervention techniques, environments of care, and societal considerations. *Cognitive and Behavioral Practice, 26*(2), 254–269.

MacNeil, S., & Byers, E. S. (2005). Dyadic assessment of sexual self-disclosure and sexual satisfaction in heterosexual dating couples. *Journal of Social and Personal Relationships, 22*(2), 169–181.

Madson, M. B., Loignon, A. C., & Lane, C. (2009). Training in Motivational Interviewing: A systematic review. *Journal of Substance Abuse Treatment*, 36(1), 101–109.

Magill, M., Mastroleo, N. R., Apodaca, T. R., Barnett, N. P., Colby, S. M., & Monti, P. M. (2010). Motivational Interviewing with significant other participation: Assessing therapeutic alliance and patient satisfaction and engagement. *Journal of Substance Abuse Treatment*, 39(4), 391–398.

Mairs, H., Lovell, K., Campbell, M., & Keeley, P. (2011). Development and pilot investigation of behavioral activation for negative symptoms. *Behavior Modification*, 35(5), 486–506.

Malone, J., Syvertsen, J. L., Johnson, B. E., Mimiaga, M. J., Mayer, K. H., & Bazzi, A. R. (2018). Negotiating sexual safety in the era of biomedical HIV prevention: Relationship dynamics among male couples using pre-exposure prophylaxis. *Culture, Health & Sexuality*, 20(6), 658–672.

Manos, R. C., Kanter, J. W., Rusch, L. C., Turner, L. B., Roberts, N. A., & Busch, A. M. (2009). Integrating functional analytic psychotherapy and behavioral activation for the treatment of relationship distress. *Clinical Case Studies*, 8(2), 122–138.

Manuel, J. K., Houck, J. M., & Moyers, T. B. (2012). The impact of significant others in motivational enhancement therapy: Findings from Project MATCH. *Behavioural and Cognitive Psychotherapy*, 40, 297–312.

Manuel, J. K., Lum, P. J., Hengl, N. S., & Sorensen, J. L. (2013). Smoking cessation interventions with female smokers living with HIV/AIDS: A randomized pilot study of motivational interviewing. *AIDS Care*, 25(7), 820–827.

Marcus, J. L., Chao, C. R., Leyden, W. A., Xu, L., Quesenberry, C. P., Jr., Klein, D. B., Towner, W. J., Horberg, M. A., & Silverberg, M. J. (2016). Narrowing the gap in life expectancy between HIV-infected and HIV-uninfected individuals with access to care. *Journal of Acquired Immune Deficiency Syndromes*, 73(1), 39–46.

Margolin, G. (1982). Ethical and legal considerations in marital and family therapy. *American Psychologist*, 37(7), 788–801.

Martell, C. R., Addis, M. E., & Jacobson, N. S. (2001). *Depression in context: Strategies for guided action*. W. W. Norton & Co.

Martell, C. R., Dimidjian, S., Herman-Dunn, R., & Lewinsohn, P. M. (2010). *Behavioral activation for depression: A clinician's guide*. Guilford Publications.

Martinez, O., Munoz-Laboy, M., Levine, E. C., Starks, T., Dolezal, C., Dodge, B., Icard, L., Moya, E., Chavez-Baray, S., Rhodes, S. D., & Fernandez, M. I. (2017). Relationship factors associated with sexual risk behavior and high-risk alcohol consumption among Latino men who have sex with men: Challenges and opportunities to intervene on HIV risk. *Archives of Sexual Behavior*, 46(4), 987–999.

Martín-Pérez, C., Navas, J. F., Perales, J. C., López-Martín, Á., Cordovilla-Guardia, S., Portillo, M., Maldonado, A., & Vilar-López, R. (2019). Brief group-delivered motivational interviewing is equally effective as brief group-delivered cognitive-behavioral therapy at reducing alcohol use in risky college drinkers. *PLoS One*, 14(12), e0226271.

Masters, W., & Johnson, V. E. (1966). *Human sexual response*. Little, Brown and Company.

Masters, W., & Johnson, V. E. (1970). *Human sexual inadequacy*. Little, Brown and Company.

McCarthy, K. J., Mehta, R., & Haberland, N. A. (2018). Gender, power, and violence: A systematic review of measures and their association with male perpetration of IPV. *PLoS One*, 13(11), e0207091.

McCarty-Caplan, D., Jantz, I., & Swartz, J. (2014). MSM and drug use: A latent class analysis of drug use and related sexual risk behaviors. *AIDS and Behavior, 18*(7), 1339–1351.

McCrady, B. S. (2012). Treating alcohol problems with couple therapy. *Journal of Clinical Psychology, 68*(5), 514–525.

McCrady, B. S., Stout, R., Noel, N., Abrams, D., & Nelson, F. (1991). Effectiveness of three types of spouse-involved behavioral alcoholism treatment. *British Journal of Addiction, 86*, 1415–1424.

McGeough, B. (2021). A systematic review of substance use treatments for sexual minority women. *Journal of Gay & Lesbian Social Services, 33*(2), 180–210.

McKenry, P. C., Serovich, J. M., Mason, T. L., & Mosack, K. (2006). Perpetration of gay and lesbian partner violence: A disempowerment perspective. *Journal of Family Violence, 21*(4), 233–243.

McNaughton, N., DeYoung, C. G., & Corr, P. J. (2016). Approach/avoidance. In J. R. Absher & J. Cloutier (Eds.), *Neuroimaging personality, social cognition, and character* (pp. 25–49). Academic Press.

Meana, M., & Jones, S. (2011). Developments and trends in sex therapy. *Advancements in Psychosomatic Medicine, 31*, 57–71.

Medley, G., Lipari, R. N., Bose, J., Cribb, D. S., Kroutil, L. A., & McHenry, G. (2016). *Sexual orientation and estimates of adult substance use and mental health: Results from the 2015 National Survey on Drug Use and Health.* https://www.samhsa.gov/data/sites/default/files/NSDUH-SexualOrientation-2015/NSDUH-SexualOrientation-2015/NSDUH-SexualOrientation-2015.htm

Meinzer, M. C., Oddo, L. E., Vasko, J. M., Murphy, J. G., Iwamoto, D., Lejuez, C. W., & Chronis-Tuscano, A. (2021, February). Motivational Interviewing plus behavioral activation for alcohol misuse in college students with ADHD. *Psychology of Addictive Behavior, 35*(7), 803–816. https://doi.org/10.1037/adb0000663

Meltzer, D., Chung, J., Khalili, P., Marlow, E., Arora, V., Schumock, G., & Burt, R. (2010). Exploring the use of social network methods in designing healthcare quality improvement teams. *Social Science & Medicine, 71*(6), 1119–1130.

Mikulincer, M. (1998). Attachment working models and the sense of trust: An exploration of interaction goals and affect regulation. *Journal of Personality and Social Psychology, 74*(5), 1209.

Mikulincer, M., Shaver, P. R., & Pereg, D. (2003). Attachment theory and affect regulation: The dynamics, development, and cognitive consequences of attachment-related strategies. *Motivation and Emotion, 27*(2), 77–102.

Milhet, M., Shah, J., Madesclaire, T., & Gaissad, L. (2019). Chemsex experiences: Narratives of pleasure. *Drugs and Alcohol Today, 19*(1), 11–22.

Miller, S. A., & Byers, E. S. (2008). An exploratory examination of the sexual intervention self-efficacy of clinical psychology graduate students. *Training and Education in Professional Psychology, 2*(3), 137–144.

Miller, W. R., Benefield, R. G., & Tonigan, J. S. (1993). Enhancing motvation for change in problem drinking: A controlled comparison of two therapists styles. *Journal of Consulting and Clinical Psychology, 61*(455–461).

Miller, W. R., C'de Baca, J., & Matthews, D. B. (2001). *Personal values card sort.* University of New Mexico.

Miller, W. R., & Rollnick, S. (2002). *Motivational Interviewing* (2nd ed.). Guilford Publications.

Miller, W. R., & Rollnick, S. (2013). *Motivational Interviewing: Helping people change* (3rd ed.). Guilford Press.

Miller, W. R., & Rose, G. S. (2009). Toward a theory of Motivational Interviewing. *American Psychologist, 64*(6), 527–537.

Miller, W. R., & Rose, G. S. (2010). Motivational Interviewing in a relational context. *American Psychologist, 65*(4), 298–299.

Miller, W. R., & Rose, G. S. (2015). Motivational Interviewing and decision balance: Contrasting responses to client ambivalence. *Behavioral and Cognitive Psychotherapy, 43*, 129–141.

Miller-Matero, L. R., & Cano, A. (2015). Encouraging couples to change: A motivational assessment to promote well-being in people with chronic pain and their partners. *Pain Medicine, 16*(2), 348–355.

Mimiaga, M. J., Closson, E. F., Kothary, V., & Mitty, J. A. (2014). Sexual partnerships and considerations for HIV antiretroviral pre-exposure prophylaxis utilization among high-risk substance using men who have sex with men. *Archives of Sexual Behavior, 43*(1), 99–106.

Mimiaga, M. J., Reisner, S. L., Grasso, C., Crane, H. M., Safren, S. A., Kitahata, M. M., Schumacher, J. E., Mathews, W. C., & Mayer, K. H. (2013). Substance use among HIV-infected patients engaged in primary care in the United States: Findings from the centers for AIDS research network of integrated clinical systems cohort. *American Journal of Public Health, 103*(8), 1457–1467.

Minten, M. J., & Dykeman, C. (2021). The impact of a marriage checkup with transgender couples. *Sexologies, 30*(2), e93–e99.

Mirkarimi, K., Kabir, M. J., Honarvar, M. R., Ozouni-Davaji, R. B., & Eri, M. (2017). Effect of Motivational Interviewing on weight efficacy lifestyle among women with overweight and obesity: A randomized controlled trial. *Iranian Journal of Medical Sciences, 42*(2), 187–193.

Mitchell, J. W. (2014). Characteristics and allowed behaviors of gay male couples' sexual agreements. *Journal of Sex Research, 51*(3), 316–328.

Mitchell, J. W. (2016). Differences in gay male couples' use of drugs and alcohol with sex by relationship HIV status. *American Journal of Men's Health, 10*(4), 262–269.

Mitchell, J. W., Boyd, C., McCabe, S., & Stephenson, R. (2014). A cause for concern: Male couples' sexual agreements and their use of substances with sex. *AIDS and Behavior, 18*(7), 1401–1411.

Mitchell, J. W., Harvey, S. M., Champeau, D., Moskowitz, D. A., & Seal, D. W. (2012). Relationship factors associated with gay male couples' concordance on aspects of their sexual agreements: Establishment, type, and adherence. *AIDS and Behavior, 16*(6), 1560–1569.

Mitchell, J. W., Pan, Y., & Feaster, D. (2016). Actor-partner effects of male couples substance use with sex and engagement in condomless anal sex. *AIDS and Behavior, 20*(12), 2904–2913.

Mitchell, J. W., & Petroll, A. E. (2013). Factors associated with men in HIV-negative gay couples who practiced UAI within and outside of their relationship. *AIDS and Behavior, 17*(4), 1329–1337.

Monti, P. M., Colby, S. M., Mastroleo, N. R., Barnett, N. P., Gwaltney, C. J., Apodaca, T. R., Rohsenow, D. J., Magill, M., Gogineni, A., Mello, M. J., Biffle, W. L., & Cioffi, W. G. (2014). Individual versus significant-other-enhanced brief motivational intervention for alcohol in emergency care. *Journal of Consulting and Clinical Psychology, 82*(6), 936–948.

Moon, H., & Adams, K. B. (2012). The effectiveness of dyadic interventions for people with dementia and their caregivers. *Dementia, 12*(6), 821–839.

Moors, A. C., Matsick, J. L., & Schechinger, H. A. (2017). Unique and shared relationship benefits of consensually non-monogamous and monogamous relationships. *European Psychologist, 22*(1), 55–71.

Moyers, T. B., Manuel, J. K., & Ernst, D. (2014). *Motivational Interviewing treatment integrity coding manual 4.0.* https://casaa.unm.edu/download/miti4_2.pdf. Last accessed 4/23/2022.

Mueser, K. T., Gottlieb, J. D., & Gingerich, S. (2013). Social skills and problem-solving training. In S. G. Hofmann (Ed.), *The Wiley handbook of cognitive behavioral therapy* (pp. 243–272). Wiley-Blackwell.

Mullens, A. B., Young, R. M., Dunne, M., & Norton, G. (2010). The Cannabis Expectancy Questionnaire for Men Who Have Sex With Men (CEQ-MSM): A measure of substance-related beliefs. *Addictive Behaviors, 35*(6), 616–619.

Mullens, A. B., Young, R. M., Dunne, M. P., & Norton, G. (2011). The Drinking Expectancy Questionnaire for Men Who Have Sex With Men (DEQ-MSM): A measure of substance-related beliefs [Article]. *Drug & Alcohol Review, 30*(4), 372–380.

Muller, A. A., & Kotte, S. (2020). Of SMART, GROW and goals gone wild—A systematic literature review on the relevance of goal activities in workplace coaching. *International Coaching Psychology Review, 15*(2), 69–97.

Musser, P. H., Semiatin, J. N., Taft, C. T., & Murphy, C. M. (2008). Motivational interviewing as a pregroup intervention for partner-violent men. *Violence and Victims, 23*(5), 539–557.

Naar, S., Robles, G., Macdonell, K. E., Dinaj-Koci, V., Simpson, K. N., Lam, P., Parsons, J. T., Sizemore, K. M., & Starks, T. J. (2020). Intervention to improve health behaviors among youth living with HIV: A randomized clinical trial. *Journal of the American Medical Association Open Network, 3*(8), e2014650.

Naar, S., & Safren, S. A. (2017). *Motivational interviewing and CBT: Combining strategies for maximum effectiveness.* Guilford Press.

Naar-King, S., Outlaw, A., Green-Jones, M., Wright, K., & Parsons, J. T. (2009). Motivational Interviewing by peer outreach workers: A pilot randomized clinical trial to retain adolescents and young adults in HIV care. *AIDS Care, 21*(7), 868–873.

Naar-King, S., & Suarez, M. (2011). *Motivational interviewing with adolescents and young adults.* Guilford Press.

National Center on Domestic and Sexual Violence. (n.d.) Home page. Retrieved January 18, 2022, from http://www.ncdsv.org/

National Domestic Violence Hotline. (2020, December). Home page. Retrieved January 18, 2022, from https://www.thehotline.org

National Domestic Violence Hotline. (2020, December). Safety planning. https://www.thehotline.org/search-our-resources/?search=safety+planning

National Domestic Violence Hotline. (2021, November 29). *Warning signs of abuse.* Retrieved January 18, 2022, from https://www.thehotline.org/identify-abuse/domestic-abuse-warning-signs/

National Institute of Allergy and Infectious Disease. (2020a, July 7). Long-acting injectible form of HIV prevention outperforms daily pill in NIH study. https://www.

niaid.nih.gov/news-events/long-acting-injectable-form-hiv-prevention-outperfo rms-daily-pill-nih-study

National Institute of Allergy and Infectious Disease. (2020b, November 9). *NIH study finds long-acting injectable drug prevents HIV acquisition in cisgender women.* https://www.niaid.nih.gov/news-events/statement-nih-study-finds-long-acting-inj ectable-drug-prevents-hiv-acquisition

Navidian, A., Kermansaravi, F., Tabas, E. E., & Saeedinezhad, F. (2016). Efficacy of group Motivational Interviewing in the degree of drug craving in the addicts under the methadone maintenance treatment (MMT) in South East of Iran. *Archives of Psychiatric Nursing, 30*(2), 144–149.

Neilands, T. B., Chakravarty, D., Darbes, L. A., Beougher, S. C., & Hoff, C. C. (2009). Development and validation of the Sexual Agreement Investment Scale. *Journal of Sex Research, 47*(1), 24–37.

Neilands, T. B., LeBlanc, A. J., Frost, D. M., Bowen, K. S., Sullivan, P. S., Hoff, C. C., & Chang, J. (2020). Measuring a new stress domain: Validation of the Couple-Level Minority Stress Scale. *Archives of Sexual Behavior, 49*(1), 249–265.

Newcomb, M. E., Macapagal, K. R., Feinstein, B. A., Bettin, E., Swann, G., & Whitton, S. W. (2017). Integrating HIV prevention and relationship education for young same-sex male couples: A pilot trial for the 2GETHER intervention. *AIDS and Behavior, 21*(8), 2464–2478.

Newcomb, M. E., Ryan, D. T., Garofalo, R., & Mustanski, B. S. (2014). The effects of sexual partnership and relationship characteristics on three sexual risk variables in young men who have sex with men. *Archives of Sexual Behavior, 43*(1), 61–72.

Niolon, P. H., Kearns, M., Dills, J., Rambo, K., Irving, S., Armstead, T., & Gilbert, L. (2017). *Preventing intimate partner violence across the lifespan: A technical package of programs, policies, and practices.* National Center for Injury Prevention and Control, Centers for Disease Control and Prevention.

Nolan, S., Walley, A. Y., Heeren, T. C., Patts, G. J., Ventura, A. S., Sullivan, M. M., Samet, J. H., & Saitz, R. (2017). HIV-infected individuals who use alcohol and other drugs, and virologic suppression. *AIDS Care, 29*(9), 1129–1136.

Northouse, L. L., Katapodi, M. C., Song, L., Zhang, L., & Mood, D. W. (2010). Interventions with family caregivers of cancer patients: Meta-analysis of randomized trials. *CA: A Cancer Journal for Clinicians, 60*(5), 317–339. https://doi.org/10.3322/caac.20081

Norton, R. (1983). Measuring marital quality: A critical look at the dependent variable. *Journal of Marriage and Family, 1*, 141–151.

Noyes, E. T., & Schlauch, R. C. (2018). Examination of approach and avoidance inclinations on the reinforcing value of alcohol. *Addictive Behaviors, 79*, 61–67.

O'Farrell, T. J., & Schein, A. Z. (2000). Behavioral couples therapy for alcoholism and drug abuse. *Journal of Substance Abuse Treatment, 18*(1), 51–54.

O'Farrell, T. J., & Schein, A. Z. (2011). Behavioral couples therapy for alcoholism and drug abuse. *Journal of Family Psychotherapy, 22*(3), 193–215.

Ogu, L. C., Janakiram, J., Hoffman, H. J., McDonough, L., Valencia, A. P., Mackey, E. R., & Klein, C. J. (2013). Hispanic overweight and obese children: Thirty cases managed with standard WIC counseling or Motivational Interviewing. *ICAN: Infant, Child, & Adolescent Nutrition, 6*(1), 35–43.

Oh, H., & Lee, C. (2016). Culture and motivational interviewing. *Patient Education and Counseling, 99*(11), 1914–1919.

O'Leary, C. J. (2008). Response to couples and families in distress: Rogers' six conditions lived with respect for the unique medium of relationship therapy. *Person-Centered & Experiential Psychotherapies, 7*, 294–307.

O'Leary, C. J. (2012). A couple and family therapist's view of nondirectivity. *Person-Centered & Experiential Psychotherapies, 11*, 215–224.

O'Leary, C. J. (2015). Person-centered couple and family therapy: The effects of an extra beat of time. *Person-Centered & Experiential Psychotherapies, 14*(3), 236–247.

Onder, G., Penninx, B. W. J. H., Guralnik, J. M., Jones, H., Fried, L. P., Pahor, M., & Williamson, J. D. (2003). Sexual satisfaction and risk of disability in older women. *Journal of Clinical Psychiatry, 64*(10), 1177–1182.

Ottaway, Z., Finnerty, F., Amlani, A., Pinto-Sander, N., Szanyi, J., & Richardson, D. (2017). Men who have sex with men diagnosed with a sexually transmitted infection are significantly more likely to engage in sexualised drug use. *International Journal of STD & AIDS, 28*(1), 91–93.

Özel, Ç. H., & Kozak, N. (2017). An exploratory study of resident perceptions toward the tourism industry in Cappadocia:A social exchange theory approach. *Asia Pacific Journal of Tourism Research, 22*(3), 284–300.

Pachankis, J. E. (2007). The psychological implications of concealing a stigma: A cognitive-affective-behavioral model. *Psychological Bulletin, 133*(2), 328–345.

Pachankis, J. E., Goldfried, M. R., & Ramrattan, M. E. (2008). Extension of the rejection sensitivity construct to the interpersonal functioning of gay men. *Journal of Consulting and Clinical Psychology, 76*(2), 306–317.

Pachankis, J. E., Hatzenbuehler, M. L., & Starks, T. J. (2014). The influence of structural stigma and rejection sensitivity on young sexual minority men's daily tobacco and alcohol use. *Social Science & Medicine, 103*, 67–75.

Painter, T. M. (2001). Voluntary counseling and testing for couples: A high-leverage intervention for HIV/AIDS prevention in sub-Saharan Africa. *Social Science & Medicine, 53*, 1397–1411.

Palmore, E. B. (1982). Predictors of the longevity difference: A 25-year follow-up. *Gerontologist, 22*(6), 513–518.

Pantalone, D. W., & Budge, S. L. (2020). Psychotherapy research is needed to improve clinical practice for clients with HIV. *Psychotherapy, 57*(1), 1–6.

Pantalone, D. W., Nelson, K. M., Batchelder, A. W., Chiu, C., Gunn, H. A., & Horvath, K. J. (2020). A systematic review and meta-analysis of combination behavioral interventions co-targeting psychosocial syndemics and HIV-related health behaviors for sexual minority men. *Journal of Sex Research, 57*(6), 681–708.

Parsons, J. T., Golub, S. A., Rosof, E., & Holder, C. (2007). Motivational Interviewing and cognitive-behavioral intervention to improve HIV medication adherence mong hazardous drinkers: A randomized controlled trial. *Journal of Acquired Immune Deficiency Syndromes, 46*(4), 443–450.

Parsons, J. T., John, S. A., Millar, B. M., & Starks, T. J. (2018). Testing the efficacy of combined Motivational Interviewing and cognitive behavioral skills training to reduce methamphetamine use and improve HIV medication adherence among HIV-positive gay and bisexual men. *AIDS and Behavior, 22*(8), 2674–2686.

Parsons, J. T., Kutnick, A. H., Halkitis, P. N., Punzalan, J. C., & Carbonari, J. P. (2005). Sexual risk behaviors and substance use among alcohol abusing HIV-positive men who have sex with men. *Journal of Psychoactive Drugs, 37*(1), 27–36.

Parsons, J. T., Lelutiu-Weinberger, C., Botsko, M., & Golub, S. A. (2014). A randomized controlled trial utilizing motivational interviewing to reduce HIV risk and drug use in young gay and bisexual men. *Journal of Consulting and Clinical Psychology*, *82*(1), 9–18.

Parsons, J. T., & Starks, T. J. (2014). Drug use and sexual arrangements among gay couples: Frequency, interdependence and associations with sexual risk. *Archives of Sexual Behavior*, *43*(1), 89–98.

Parsons, J. T., Starks, T. J., Dubois, S., Grov, C., & Golub, S. A. (2013). Alternatives to monogamy among gay male couples in a community survey: Implications for mental health and sexual risk. *Archives of Sexual Behavior*, *42*(2), 303–312.

Parsons, J. T., Starks, T. J., Gamarel, K. E., & Grov, C. (2012). (Non)monogamy and sexual relationship quality among same-sex male couples. *Journal of Family Psychology*, *26*(5), 669–677.

Paterno, M. T., & Draughon, J. E. (2016). Screening for intimate partner violence. *Journal of Midwifery & Women's Health*, *61*(3), 370–375.

Patrick, M. E., & Maggs, J. L. (2009). Does drinking lead to sex? Daily alcohol–sex behaviors and expectancies among college students. *Psychology of Addictive Behaviors*, *23*(3), 472–481.

Patterson, G. R., & Chamberlain, P. (1994). A functional analysis of resistance during patient training therapy. *Clinical Psychology: Science and Practice*, *1*(1), 53–70.

Pearson, R. E. (1990). *Counseling and social support: Perspectives and practice*. SAGE Publications.

Pentel, K. Z. (2020). *Cognitive-behavioral couple therapy for same-sex female couples: A pilot study* (Publication Number 28023889) [Doctoral dissertation, University of North Carolina at Chapel Hill]. ProQuest Dissertations and Theses Global.

Peplau, L. A., & Fingerhut, A. W. (2007). The close relationships of lesbians and gay men. *Annual Review of Psychology*, *58*, 405–424.

Perry, N. S., Huebner, D. M., Baucom, B. R., & Hoff, C. C. (2016). Relationship power, sociodemographics, and their relative influence on sexual agreements among gay male couples. *AIDS and Behavior*, *20*(6), 1302–1314.

Pett, W. (2019, February). *Post-exposure prophylaxes (PEP)*. AIDSmap.com. https://www.aidsmap.com/about-hiv/post-exposure-prophylaxis-pep

Philpott, A., Knerr, W., & Boydell, V. (2006). Pleasure and prevention: When good sex is safer sex. *Reproductive Health Matters*, *14*(28), 23–31.

Pick, S., Givaudan, M., & Kline, K. F. (2005). Sexual pleasure as a key component of integral sexual health. *Feminism & Psychology*, *15*(1), 44–49.

Pitasi, M. A., Beer, L., Cha, S., Lyons, S. J., Hernandez, A. L., Prejean, J., Valleroy, L. A., Crim, S. M., Trujillo, L., Hardman, D., Painter, E. M., Petty, J., Mermin, J. H., Daskalakis, D. C., & Hall, H. I. (2021). Vital signs: HIV Infection, diagnosis, treatment, and prevention among gay, bisexual, and other men who have sex with men—United States, 2010–2019. *MMWR Morbidity & Mortality Weekly Report*, *70*, 1669–1675.

Polcin, D. L., Bond, J., Korcha, R., Nayak, M. B., Galloway, G. P., & Evans, K. (2014). Randomized trial of intensive motivational interviewing for methamphetamine dependence. *Journal of Addictive Diseases*, *33*(3), 253–265.

Polcin, D. L., Korcha, R., Witbrodt, J., Mericle, A. A., & Mahoney, E. (2018). Motivational Interviewing case management (MICM) for persons on probation or parole entering sober living houses. *Criminal Justice and Behavior*, *45*(11), 1634–1659.

Pollard, A., Nadarzynski, T., & Llewellyn, C. (2018). Syndemics of stigma, minority-stress, maladaptive coping, risk environments and littoral spaces among men who have sex with men using chemsex. *Culture, Health & Sexuality, 20*(4), 411–427.

Ponsford, J., Lee, N. K., Wong, D., McKay, A., Haines, K., Alway, Y., Downing, M., Furtado, C., & O'Donnell, M. L. (2016). Efficacy of motivational interviewing and cognitive behavioral therapy for anxiety and depression symptoms following traumatic brain injury. *Psychological Medicine, 46*(5), 1079–1090.

Poortman, A. R., & Mills, M. (2012). Investments in marriage and cohabitation: The role of legal and interpersonal commitment. *Journal of Marriage and Family, 74*(2), 357–376.

Pott, S. L., Delgadillo, J., & Kellett, S. (2021). Is behavioral activation an effective and acceptable treatment for co-occurring depression and substance use disorders? A meta-analysis of randomized controlled trials. *Journal of Substance Abuse Treatment, 132,* 108478.

Powers, M. B., Vedel, E., & Emmelkamp, P. M. G. (2008). Behavioral couples therapy for alcohol and drug use disorders: A meta-analysis. *Clinical Psychology Review, 28*(6), 952–962.

Prochaska, J. O., Redding, C. A., & Evers, K. E. (2008). The transtheoretical model and stages of change. In K. Glanz, B. K. Rimer, & K. Viswanath (Eds.), *Health behavior and health education: Theory, research and practice* (4th ed., pp. 97–121). John Wiley and Sons.

Pulerwitz, J., Gortmaker, S. L., & DeJong, W. (2000). Measuring sexual relationship power in HIV/STD research. *Sex Roles, 42*(7–8), 637–660.

Purath, J., Keck, A., & Fitzgerald, C. E. (2014). Motivational interviewing for older adults in primary care: A systematic review. *Geriatric Nursing, 35*(3), 219–224.

Race, K. (2015). "Party and Play": Online hook-up devices and the emergence of PNP practices among gay men. *Sexualities, 18*(3), 253–275.

Race, K. (2017). Thinking with pleasure: Experimenting with drugs and drug research. *International Journal of Drug Policy, 49,* 144–149.

Randall, C. L., & McNeil, D. W. (2017). Motivational interviewing as an adjunct to cognitive behavior therapy for anxiety disorders: A critical review of the literature. *Cognitive and Behavioral Practice, 24*(3), 296–311.

Randall, H. E., & Byers, E. S. (2003). What is sex? Students definitions of having sex, sexual partner, and unfaithful sexual behavior. *Canadian Journal of Human Sexuality, 12*(2), 87–96.

Rapp, C. A. (1998). *The strengths model: Case management with people suffering from severe and persistent mental illness* (C. A. Rapp, Trans.). Oxford University Press.

Rauer, A. J., Karney, B. R., Garvan, C. W., & Hou, W. (2008). Relationship risks in context: A cumulative risk approach to understanding relationship satisfaction. *Journal of Marriage and the Family, 70*(5), 1122–1135.

Reiter, M. D., & Chenail, R. J. (2017). *Behavioral, humanistic-existential, and psychodynamic approaches to couples counseling.* Routledge.

Rempel, J. K., Holmes, J. G., & Zanna, M. P. (1985). Trust in close relationships. *Journal of Personality and Social Psychology, 49*(1), 95.

Rempel, J. K., Ross, M., & Holmes, J. G. (2001). Trust and communicated attributions in close relationships. *Journal of Personality and Social Psychology, 81*(1), 57–64.

Rendina, H. J., Moody, R. L., Ventuneac, A., Grov, C., & Parsons, J. T. (2015). Aggregate and event-level associations between substance use and sexual behavior among gay and bisexual men: Comparing retrospective and prospective data. *Drug and Alcohol Dependence, 154,* 199–207.

Rentscher, K. E., Soriano, E. C., Rohrbaugh, M. J., Shoham, V., & Mehl, M. R. (2017). Partner pronoun use, communal coping, and abstinence during couple-focused intervention for problematic alcohol use. *Family Process, 56,* 348–363.

Rescorla, R. A. (1988). Pavlovian condition: It's not what you think it is. *American Psychologist, 43*(3), 151–160.

Revenson, T. A. (1994). Social support and marital coping with chronic illness. *Annals of Behavioral Medicine, 16*(2), 122–130.

Righetti, F., Rusbult, C. E., & Finkenauer, C. (2016). Regulatory fit and the Michelangelo phenomenon: How close partners promote one another's ideal selves. *Journal of Experimental Social Psychology, 46*(6), 972–985.

Rios-Spicer, R., Darbes, L., Hoff, C., Sullivan, P. S., & Stephenson, R. (2019). Sexual agreements: A scoping review of measurement, prevalence and links to health outcomes. *AIDS and Behavior, 23*(1), 259–271.

Riper, H., Andersson, G., Hunter, S. B., de Wit, J., Berking, M., & Cuijpers, P. (2014). Treatment of comorbid alcohol use disorders and depression with cognitive-behavioural therapy and motivational interviewing: A meta-analysis. *Addiction, 109*(3), 394–406.

Robertson, K., & Murachver, T. (2007). It takes two to tangle: Gender symmetry in intimate partner violence. *Basic and Applied Social Psychology, 29*(2), 109–118.

Robertson, K., & Murachver, T. (2011). Women and men's use of coercive control in intimate partner violence. *Violence and Victims, 26*(2), 208–217.

Robinson, M. L., Holmbeck, G. N., & Paikoff, R. (2007). Self-esteem enhancing reasons for having sex and the sexual behaviors of African American adolescents. *Journal of Youth and Adolescence, 36*(4), 453–464.

Robles, G., Dellucci, T. V., Gupta, S. K., Rosenthal, L., & Starks, T. J. (2022). Identity and relationship-based discrimination, and mental health in a sample of sexual minority male couples. *Journal of Gay & Lesbian Mental Health, 26*(1), 76–97. https://doi.org/10.1080/19359705.2021.1926389

Robles, T. F., Slatcher, R. B., Trombello, J. M., & McGinn, M. M. (2014). Marital quality and health: A meta-analytic review. *Psychological Bulletin, 140*(1), 140–187.

Rodger, A. J., Cambiano, V., Bruun, T., Vernazza, P., Collins, S., van Lunzen, J., Corbelli, G. M., Estrada, V., Geretti, A. M., Beloukas, A., Asboe, D., Viciana, P., Gutierrez, F., Clotet, B., Pradier, C., Gerstoft, J., Weber, R., Westling, K., Wandeler, G., ... PARTNER Study Group. (2016). Sexual activity without condoms and risk of HIV transmission in serodifferent couples when the HIV-positive partner is using suppressive antiretroviral therapy. *Journal of the American Medical Association, 316*(2), 171–181.

Rogers, C. R. (1946). Significant aspects of client-centered therapy. *American Psychologist, 1*(10), 415–422.

Rogers, C. R. (1949). The attitude and orientation of the counselor in client-centered therapy. *Journal of Consulting and Clinical Psychology, 13*(2), 82–94.

Rogers, C. R. (1979). The foundations of the person-centered approach. *Education, 100*(2), 98–107.

Rohrbaugh, M. J., Mehl, M. R., Shoham, V., Reilly, E. S., & Ewy, G. A. (2008). Prognostic significance of spouse we talk in couples coping with heart failure. *Journal of Consulting and Clinical Psychology, 76*(5), 781–789.

Roland, M. E., Neilands, T. B., Krone, M. R., Katz, M. H., Franses, K., Grant, R. M., Busch, M. P., Hecht, F. M., Shacklett, B. L., & Kahn, J. O. (2005). Seroconversion following nonoccupational postexposure prophylaxis against HIV. *Clinical Infectious Diseases, 41*(10), 1507–1513.

Rosario, M., Meyer-Bahlburg, H. F. L., Hunter, J., Exner, T. M., Gwadz, M., & Keller, A. M. (1996). The psychosexual development of urban lesbian, gay, and bisexual youths. *Journal of Sex Research, 33*(2), 113–126.

Rosario, M., Schrimshaw, E. W., Hunter, J., & Braun, L. (2006). Sexual identity development among lesbian, gay, and bisexual youths: Consistency and change over time. *Journal of Sex Research, 43*(1), 46–58.

Rosenthal, L., Deosaran, A., Young, D. L., & Starks, T. J. (2019). Relationship stigma and well-being among adults in interracial and same-sex relationships. *Journal of Social and Personal Relationships, 36*(11–12), 3408–3428.

Rosenthal, L., & Starks, T. J. (2015). Relationship stigma and relationship outcomes in interracial and same-sex relationships: Examination of sources and buffers. *Journal of Family Psychology, 29*(6), 818–830.

Rothblum, E. D. (Ed.). (2020). *The Oxford handbook of sexual and gender minority mental health.* Oxford University Press.

Rotter, J. B. (1971). Generalized expectancies for interpersonal trust. *American Psychologist, 26*(5), 443–452.

Rotter, J. B. (1980). Interpersonal trust, trustworthiness, and gullibility. *American Psychologist, 35*(1), 1–7.

Rubin, R. S. (2002). Will the real SMART goals please stand up? *Industrial-Organizational Psychologist, 39*(4), 26–27.

Rubin, Z. (1970). Measurement of romantic love. *Journal of Personality and Social Psychology, 16*(2), 265–273.

Rusbult, C. E. (1980). Commitment and satisfaction in romantic associations: A test of the investment model. *Journal of Experimental Social Psychology, 16*(2), 172–186.

Rusbult, C. E. (1983). A longitudinal test of the investment model: The development (and deterioration) of satisfaction and commitment in heterosexual involvements. *Journal of Personality and Social Psychology, 45*(1), 101–117.

Rusbult, C. E., Bissonnette, V. L., Arriaga, X. B., Cox, C. L., & Bradbury, T. N. (1998). Accommodation processes during the early years of marriage. In T. N. Bradbury (Ed.), *The developmental course of marital dysfunction* (pp. 74–113). Cambridge University Press.

Rusbult, C. E., & Buunk, B. P. (1993). Commitment processes in close relationships: An interdependence analysis. *Journal of Social and Personal Relationships, 10*(2), 175–204.

Rusbult, C. E., Johnson, D. J., & Morrow, G. D. (1986). Impact of couple patterns of problem solving on distress and nondistress in dating relationships. *Journal of Personality and Social Psychology, 50*(4), 744–753.

Rusbult, C. E., Martz, J. M., & Agnew, C. R. (1998). The investment model scale: Measuring commitment level, satisfaction level, quality of alternatives, and investment size. *Personal Relationships, 5*(4), 357–391.

Rusbult, C. E., & Van Lange, P. A. M. (1996). Interdependence processes. In E. T. Higgins & A. W. Kruglanski (Eds.), *Social psychology: Handbook of basic principles* (pp. 564–596). Guilford Press.

Rusbult, C. E., & Van Lange, P. A. (2003). Interdependence, interaction, and relationships. *Annual Review of Psychology*, *54*(1), 351–375.

Rusbult, C. E., & Van Lange, P. A. M. (2008). Why we need interdependence theory. *Social and Personality Psychology Compass*, *2*(5), 2049–2070.

Rusbult, C. E., Verette, J., Whitney, G. A., Slovik, L. F., & Lipkus, I. (1991). Accommodation processes in close relationships: Theory and preliminary empirical evidence. *Journal of Personality and Social Psychology*, *60*(1), 53–78.

Rusbult, C. E., Yovetich, N. A., & Verette, J. (1996). An interdependence analysis of accommodation processes. In G. J. O. Fletcher & J. Fitness (Eds.), *Knowledge structures in close relationships: A social psychological approach* (pp. 63–90). Lawrence Erlbaum Associates.

Rusbult, C. E., & Zembrodt, I. M. (1983). Responses to dissatisfaction in romantic invomvents: A multidimensional scaling analysis. *Journal of Experimental Social Psychology*, *19*(3), 274–293.

Rusbult, C. E., Zembrodt, I. M., & Gunn, L. K. (1982). Exit, voice, loyalty, and neglect: Responses to dissatisfaction in romantic involvements. *Journal of Personality and Social Psychology*, *43*(6), 1230–1242.

Russell, S. T. (2005). Conceptualizing positive adolescent sexuality development. *Sexuality Research and Social Policy*, *2*(3), 4–12.

Rutter, P. (2012). Sex therapy with gay male couples using affirmative therapy. *Sexual and Relationship Therapy*, *27*, 35–45.

Saito, M., Nodate, Y., Maruyama, K., Tsuchiya, M., Watanabe, M., & Niwa, S.-i. (2012). Establishment of a practical training program in smoking cessation for use by pharmacists using cognitive-behavioral therapy and the motivational interview method. *Yakugaku zasshi*, *132*(3), 369–379.

Salazar, L. F., Stephenson, R., Sullivan, P. S., & Tarver, R. (2013). Development and validation of HIV-related dyadic measures for men who have sex with men. *Journal of Sex Research*, *50*(2), 164–177.

Sandfort, T. G. M., Orr, M., Hirsch, J. S., & Santelli, J. (2008). Long-term health correlates of timing of sexual debut: Results from a national US study. *American Journal of Public Health*, *98*(1), 155–161.

Santa Ana, E. J., LaRowe, S. D., Armeson, K., Lamb, K. E., & Hartwell, K. (2016). Impact of group motivational interviewing on enhancing treatment engagement for homeless veterans with nicotine dependence and other substance use disorders: A pilot investigation. *American Journal on Addictions*, *25*(7), 533–541.

Santelli, J. S., Kantor, L. M., Grilo, S. A., Speizer, I. S., Lindberg, L. D., Heitel, J., Schalet, A. T., Lyon, M. E., Mason-Jones, A. J., & McGovern, T. (2017). Abstinence-only-until-marriage: An updated review of US policies and programs and their impact. *Journal of Adolescent Health*, *61*(3), 273–280.

Satcher, D. (2001). The surgeon general's call to action to promote sexual health and responsible sexual behavior. *American Journal of Health Education*, *32*(6), 356–368.

Sautter, F. J., Armelie, A. P., Glynn, S. M., & Wielt, D. B. (2011). The development of a couple-based treatment for PTSD in returning veterans. *Professional Psychology: Research and Practice*, *42*(1), 63–69.

Savin-Williams, R. C. (2009). *The new gay teenager*. Harvard University Press.

Savin-Williams, R. C., & Cohen, K. M. (2015). Developmental trajectories and milestones of lesbian, gay, and bisexual young people. *International Review of Psychiatry*, *27*(5), 357–366.

Schachner, D. A., & Shaver, P. R. (2004). Attachment dimensions and sexual motives. *Personal Relationships, 11*(2), 179–195.

Schalet, A. T. (2011). Beyond abstinence and risk: A new paradigm for adolescent sexual health. *Women's Health Issues, 21*(3), S5–S7.

Scharff, J. S., & Scharff, D. E. (1997). Object relations couple therapy. *Amican Journal of Psychotherapy, 51*(2), 141–173.

Scheffel, K., Amidei, C., & Fitzgerald, K. A. (2019). Motivational Interviewing: Improving confidence with self-care management in postoperative thoracolumbar spine patients. *Journal of Neuroscience Nursing, 51*(3), 113–118.

Schoenfeld, E. A., Loving, T. J., Pope, M. T., Huston, T. L., & Štulhofer, A. (2017). Does sex really matter? Examining the connections between spouses' nonsexual behaviors, sexual frequency, sexual satisfaction, and marital satisfaction. *Archives of Sexual Behavior, 46*(2), 489–501.

Schrodt, P., Witt, P. L., & Shimkowski, J. R. (2014). A meta-analytical review of the demand/withdraw pattern of interaction and its associations with individual, relational, and communicative outcomes. *Communication Monographs, 81*(1), 28–58.

Schulenberg, J. E., Marline, A. C., Johnston, L. D., O'Malley, P. M., & Laetz, V. B. (2005). Trajectories of marijuana use during the transition to adulthood: The big picture based on national panel data. *Journal of Drug Issues, 35*(2), 255–279.

Schumm, W. R., Scanlon, E. D., Crow, C. L., Green, D. M., & Buckler, D. L. (1983). Characteristics of the Kansas marital satisfaction scale in a sample of 79 married couples. *Psychological Reports, 53*(2), 583–588.

Scott, S., Whitton, S., & Buzzella, B. (2018). Providing relationship interventions to same-sex couples: Clinical considerations, program adaptations, and continuing education. *Cognitive and Behavioral Practice, 26*(2), 270–284.

Sewell, K. K., McGarrity, L. A., & Strassberg, D. S. (2017). Sexual behavior, definitions of sex, and the role of self-partner context among lesbian, gay, and bisexual adults. *Journal of Sex Research, 54*(7), 825–831.

Sewell, K. K., & Strassberg, D. S. (2015). How do heterosexual undergraduate students define having sex? A new approach to an old question. *Journal of Sex Research, 52*(5), 507–516.

Sharma, A., Garofalo, R., Hidalgo, M. A., Hoehnle, S., Mimiaga, M. J., Brown, E., Thai, J., Bratcher, A., Wimbly, T., Sullivan, P. S., & Stephenson, R. (2019). Do male couples agree on their sexual agreements? An analysis of dyadic data. *Archives of Sexual Behavior, 48*(4), 1203–1216.

Sharma, A., Kahle, E., Sullivan, S., & Stephenson, R. (2021). Sexual agreements and intimate partner violence among male couples in the U.S.: An analysis of dyadic data. *Archives of Sexual Behavior, 50*(3), 1087–1105.

Shaver, P. R., & Mikulincer, M. (2002). Attachment-related psychodynamics. *Attachment and Human Development, 4*(2), 133–161.

Shick, V. R., Rosenberger, J. G., Herbenick, D., Collazo, E., Sanders, S. A., & Reece, M. (2016). The behavioral definitions of "having sex with a man" and "having sex with a woman" identified by women who have engaged in sexual activity with both men and women. *Journal of Sex Research, 53*(4–5), 578–587.

Sibley, M. H., Graziano, P. A., Kuriyan, A. B., Coxe, S., Pelham, W. E., Rodriguez, L., Sanchez, F., Derefinko, K., Helseth, S., & Ward, A. (2016). Parent-teen behavior therapy + Motivational Interviewing for adolescents with ADHD. *Journal of Consulting Clinical Psychology, 84*(8), 699–712.

Sibley, M. H., Rodriguez, L., Coxe, S., Page, T., & Espinal, K. (2020). Parent–teen group versus dyadic treatment for adolescent ADHD: What works for whom? *Journal of Clinical Child & Adolescent Psychology*, *49*(4), 476–492.

Simmons, R. A., Gordon, P. C., & Chambless, D. L. (2005). Pronouns in marital interaction: What do "you" and "I" say about marital health? *Psychological Science*, *16*(12), 932–936.

Simon, W., & Gagnon, J. H. (1986). Sexual scripts: Permanence and change. *Archives of Sexual Behavior*, *15*(2), 97–120.

Simpson, H. B., Zuckoff, A. M., Maher, M. J., Page, J. R., Franklin, M. E., Foa, E. B., Schmidt, A. B., & Wang, Y. (2010). Challenges using motivational interviewing as an adjunct to exposure therapy for obsessive-compulsive disorder. *Behaviour Research and Therapy*, *48*(10), 941–948.

Simpson, J. A. (1990). Influence of attachment styles on romantic relationships. *Journal of Personality and Social Psychology*, *59*(5), 971–980.

Simpson, J. A. (2007a). *Foundations of interpersonal trust*. Guilford Press.

Simpson, J. A. (2007b). Psychological foundations of trust. *Current Directions in Psychological Science*, *16*(5), 264–268.

Skeen, S. J., Starks, T. J., Jimenez, R. H., Rendina, H. J., & Cain, D. (2021, May). Heterosexual cisgender men partnered with transgender women exhibit higher HIV/STI sexual risk than their gay, bisexual and queer counterparts: Findings from a U.S.-based convenience sample recruited online. *AIDS and Behavior*, *25*(10), 3279–3291. https://doi.org/10.1007/s10461-021-03314-9

Skinner, B. F. (1953). *The science of human behavior*. Macmillan.

Smith, G. D., Frankel, S., & Yarnell, J. (1997). Sex and death: Are they related? Findings from the Caerphilly cohort study. *BMJ*, *315*(7123), 1641–1644.

Solar, O., & Irwin, A. (2010). *A conceptual framework for action on the social determinants of health*. WHO Document Production Services.

Soleymani, S., Britt, E., & Wallace-Bell, M. (2018). Motivational interviewing for enhancing engagement in intimate partner violence (IPV) treatment: A review of the literature. *Aggression and Violent Behavior*, *40*, 119–127.

Soller, B. (2014). Caught in a bad romance: Adolescent romantic relationships and mental health. *Journal of Health and Social Behavior*, *55*(1), 56–72.

Solomon, M. R., Surprenant, C., Czepiel, J. A., & Gutman, E. G. (1985). A role theory perspective on dyadic interactions: The service encounter. *Journal of Marketing*, *49*(1), 99–111.

Souleymanov, R., Brennan, D. J., Logie, C. H., Allman, D., Craig, S. L., & Halkitis, P. N. (2021). Party-n-play and online information and communication technologies: A socio-linguistic perspective. *Sexualities*, *24*(3), 388–408.

Spanier, G. B. (1976). Measuring dyadic adjustment: New scales for assessing the quality of marriage and similar dyads. *Journal of Marriage and the Family*, *38*(1), 15–28.

Spirito, A., Sindelar-Manning, H., Colby, S. M., Barnett, N. P., Lewander, W., Rohsenow, D. J., & Monti, P. M. (2011). Individual and family motivational interventions for alcohol-positive adolescents treated in an emergency department: Results of a randomized clinical trial. *Archives of Pediatrics & Adolescent Medicine*, *165*(3), 269–274.

Spitalnick, J. S., & McNair, L. D. (2005). Couples therapy with gay and lesbian clients: An analysis of important clinical issues. *Journal of Sex & Marital Therapy*, *31*(1), 43–56.

Sprecher, S. (1998). Social exchange theories and sexuality. *Journal of Sex Research*, *35*(1), 32–43.

Sprecher, S. (2002). Sexual satisfaction in premarital relationships: Associations with satisfaction, love, commitment, and stability. *Journal of Sex Research*, *39*(3), 190–196.

Sprecher, S., & Cate, R. M. (2004). Sexual satisfaction and sexual expression as predictors of relationship satisfaction and stability. In J. H. Harvey, A. Wenzel, & S. Sprecher (Eds.), *The handbook of sexuality in close relationships* (pp. 245–266). Lawrence Erlbaum Associates Publishers.

Sprecher, S., & Felmlee, D. (2000). Romantic partners' perception s of social network attributes with the passage of time and relationship transitions. *Personal Relationships*, *7*(4), 325–340.

Stabb, S. D., Cox, D. L., & Harber, J. L. (1997). Gender-related therapist attributions in couples therapy: A preliminary multiple case study investigation. *Journal of Marital and Family Therapy*, *23*(3), 335–346.

Stanton, S. C. E., & Campbell, L. (2014). Psychological and physiological predictors of health in romantic relationships: An attachment perspective. *Journal of Personality*, *82*(6), 528–538.

Starks, T. J., Adebayo, T., Kyre, K. D., Millar, B. M., Stratton, M. J., Gandhi, M., & Ingersoll, K. S. (2022). Pilot randomized controlled trial of motivational interviewing with sexual minority male couples to reduce drug use and sexual risk: The Couples Health Project. *AIDS and Behavior*, *26*(2), 310–327.

Starks, T. J., Cabral, C., & Talan, A. (2020). Drug use among sexual and gender minority populations. In E. D. Rothblum (Ed.), *The Oxford handbook of sexual and gender minority mental health* (pp. 101–112). Oxford University Press.

Starks, T. J., Castro, M. A., Castiblanco, J. P., & Millar, B. M. (2016). Modeling interpersonal correlates of condomless anal sex among gay and bisexual men: An application of attachment theory. *Archives of Sexual Behavior*, *46*(4), 1089–1099.

Starks, T. J., Dellucci, T. V., Gupta, S., Robles, G., Stephenson, R., Sullivan, P., & Parsons, J. T. (2019). A pilot randomized trial of intervention components addressing drug use in couples HIV testing and counseling (CHTC) with male couples. *AIDS and Behavior*, *23*, 2407–2420.

Starks, T. J., Dellucci, T. V., Lovejoy, T. I., Robles, G., Jimenez, R., Cain, D., Naar, S., & Ewing, S. W. F. (2021). Adolescent sexual minority males, relationship functioning, and condomless sex. *Journal of Adolescent Health*, *68*(2), 419–421.

Starks, T. J., Doyle, K. M., Bosco, S. C., & Revenson, T. A. (2022). Partners' consensus about joint effort predicts COVID-19 prevention among sexual minority men. *Archives of Sexual Behavior*, *51*(1), 217–230.

Starks, T. J., Doyle, K. M., Millar, B. M., & Parsons, J. T. (2017). Eriksonian intimacy development, relationship satisfaction, and depression in gay male couples. *Psychology of Sexual Orientation and Gender Diversity*, *4*(2), 241–250.

Starks, T. J., Doyle, K. M., Shalhav, O., John, S. A., & Parsons, J. T. (2019). An examination of gay couples' motivations to use (or forego) pre-exposure prophylaxis expressed during couples HIV testing and counseling (CHTC) sessions. *Prevention Science*, *20*(1), 157–167.

Starks, T. J., Doyle, K. M., Stewart, J. L., Bosco, S. C., & Ingersoll, K. S. (2022). Development of Motivational Interviewing Treatment Integrity (MITI) fidelity codes assessing Motivational Interviewing with couples. *AIDS and Behavior*, *26*(1), 13–20.

Starks, T. J., Feldstein Ewing, S. W., Lovejoy, T., Gurung, S., Cain, D., Fan, C. A., Naar, S., & Parsons, J. T. (2019). Adolescent male couples-based HIV testing intervention

(We Test): Protocol for a Type 1, hybrid implementation-effectiveness trial. *JMIR Research Protocols, 8*(6), e11186.

Starks, T. J., Gamarel, K. E., & Johnson, M. O. (2014). Relationship characteristics and HIV transmission risk in same-sex male couples in HIV serodiscordant relationships. *Archives of Sexual Behavior, 43*(1), 139–147.

Starks, T. J., Jones, S., Kyre, K., Robles, G., Cain, D., Jimenez, R., Stephenson, R., & Sullivan, P. (2020). Testing the drug use and condomless anal sex link among sexual minority men: The predictive utility of marijuana and interactions with relationship status. *Drug and Alcohol Dependence, 216,* 108318.

Starks, T. J., Kyre, K., Cowles, C., Castiblanco, J., Washington, C., Parker, J., Kahle, E., & Stephenson, R. (2021). A full-factorial randomized controlled trial of adjunct couples HIV testing and counseling components addressing drug use and communication skills among sexual minority male couples. *BMC Public Health, 21,* 2158.

Starks, T. J., Lovejoy, T., Sauermilch, D., Robles, G., Stratton, M. J., Jr., Cain, D., Naar, S., & Ewing, S. W. F. (2021). Developmental barriers to couples' HIV testing and counseling among adolescent sexual minority males: A dyadic socio-ecological perspective. *AIDS and Behavior, 25*(3), 787–797.

Starks, T. J., Millar, B. M., Doyle, K. M., Bertone, P. B., Ohadi, J., & Parsons, J. T. (2018). Motivational Interviewing with couples: A theoretical framework for clinical practice illustrated in substance use and HIV prevention intervention with gay couples. *Psychology of Sexual Orientation and Gender Diversity, 5*(4), 490–502.

Starks, T. J., Millar, B. M., & Parsons, J. T. (2015). Correlates of individual versus joint participation in online survey research with same-sex male couples. *AIDS and Behavior, 19*(6), 963–969.

Starks, T. J., Millar, B. M., Tuck, A. N., & Wells, B. E. (2015). The role of sexual expectancies of substance use as a mediator between adult attachment and drug use among gay and bisexual men. *Drug and Alcohol Dependence, 153,* 187–193.

Starks, T. J., Newcomb, M. E., & Mustanski, B. (2015). A longitudinal study of interpersonal relationships among lesbian, gay, and bisexual adolescents and young adults: Mediational pathways from attachment to romantic relationship quality. *Archives of Sexual Behavior, 44*(7), 1821–1831.

Starks, T. J., & Parsons, J. T. (2014). Adult attachment among partnered gay men: Patterns and associations with sexual relationship quality. *Archives of Sexual Behavior, 43*(1), 107–117.

Starks, T. J., & Parsons, J. T. (2018). Drug use and HIV prevention with young gay and bisexual men: Partnered status predicts intervention response. *AIDS and Behavior, 22*(9), 2788–2796.

Starks, T. J., Pawson, M., Stephenson, R., Sullivan, P., & Parsons, J. T. (2018). Dyadic qualitative analysis of condom use scripts among emerging adult gay male couples. *Journal of Sex & Marital Therapy, 44*(3), 269–280.

Starks, T. J., Payton, G., Golub, S. A., Weinberger, C., & Parsons, J. T. (2014). Contextualizing condom use: Intimacy interference, stigma, and unprotected sex. *Journal of Health Psychology, 19*(6), 711–720.

Starks, T. J., Robles, G., Bosco, S. C., Dellucci, T. V., Grov, C., & Parsons, J. T. (2019). The prevalence and correlates of sexual arrangements in a national cohort of HIV-negative gay and bisexual men in the United States. *Archives of Sexual Behavior, 48*(1), 369–382.

Starks, T. J., Robles, G., Bosco, S. C., Doyle, K. M., & Dellucci, T. V. (2019). Relationship functioning and substance use in same-sex male couples. *Drug and Alcohol Dependence, 201*, 101–108.

Starks, T. J., Robles, G., Doyle, K. M., Pawson, M., Bertone, P. B., Millar, B. M., & Ingersoll, K. S. (2020). Motivational Interviewing with male couples to reduce substance use and HIV risk: Manifestations of partner discord and strategies for facilitating dyadic functioning. *Psychotherapy, 57*(1), 58–67.

Starks, T. J., Robles, G., Pawson, M., Jimenez, R. H., Gandhi, M., Parsons, J. T., & Millar, B. M. (2019). Motivational Interviewing to reduce drug use and HIV incidence among young men who have sex with men in relationships and are high priority for pre-exposure prophylaxis (Project PARTNER): Randomized controlled trial protocol. *JMIR Research Protocols, 8*(7), e13015.

Starks, T. J., Sauermilch, D., Adebayo, T., Kyre, K. D., Stratton, M., & Darbes, L. A. (2021). Day-level associations between drug use and sexual behavior in male couples: Actor partner interdependence modeling of timeline follow-back data. *Drug and Alcohol Dependence, 225*, 108758.

Starks, T. J., Skeen, S. J., Jones, S. S., Gurung, S., Millar, B. M., Ferraris, C., Ventuneac, A., Parsons, J. T., & Sparks, M. A. (2022). Effectiveness of a combined motivational interviewing and cognitive behavioral intervention to reduce substance use and improve HIV-related immune functioning. *AIDS and Behavior, 26*(4), 1138–1152.

Starks, T. J., Skeen, S. J., Jones, S. S., Millar, B. M., Gurung, S., Ferraris, C., Ventuneac, A., Parsons, J. T., & Sparks, M. A. (2021 May). The importance of domain-specific self-efficacy assessment for substance use and HIV care continuum outcomes among adults in an urban HIV clinic network. *AIDS Care.* https://doi.org/10.1080/09540 121.2021.1904501

Stein, A. T., Carl, E., Cuijpers, P., Karyotaki, E., & Smits, J. A. J. (2020). Looking beyond depression: A meta-analysis of the effect of behavioral activation on depression, anxiety, and activation. *Psychological Medicine, 51*(9), 1491–1504.

Stephenson, R., & Finneran, C. (2013). The IPV-GBM scale: A new scale to measure intimate partner violence among gay and bisexual men. *PLoS ONE, 8*(6), e62592. https://doi.org/10.1371/journal.pone.0062592

Stephenson, R., Freeland, R., Sullivan, S. P., Riley, E., Johnson, B. A., Mitchell, J., McFarland, D., & Sullivan, P. S. (2017). Home-based HIV testing and counseling for male couples (Project Nexus): A protocol for a randomized controlled trial. *JMIR Research Protocols, 6*(5), e101.

Stephenson, R., Grabbe, K. L., Sidibe, T., McWilliams, A., & Sullivan, P. S. (2016). Technical assistance needs for successful implementation of couples HIV testing and counseling (CHTC) intervention for male couples at US HIV testing sites. *AIDS and Behavior, 20*, 841–847.

Stephenson, R., Suarez, N. A., Garofalo, R., Hidalgo, M. A., Hoehnle, S., Thai, J., Mimiaga, M. J., Brown, E., Bratcher, A., Wimbly, T., & Sullivan, P. (2017). Project stronger together: Protocol to test a dyadic intervention to improve engagement in HIV care among sero-discordant male couples in three US cities. *JMIR Research Protocols, 6*(8), e170--170.

Sternberg, R. J. (1997). Construct validation of a triangular love scale. *European Journal of Social Psychology, 27*(3), 313–335.

Stinson, J. D., & Clark, M. D. (2017). *Motivational Interviewing with offenders: Engagement, rehabilitation, and reentry*. Guilford Press.

Stith, S. M., McCollum, E. E., Amanor-Boadu, Y., & Smith, D. (2012). Systemic perspectives on intimate partner violence treatment. *Journal of Marital and Family Therapy, 38*(1), 220–240.

Stotts, A. L., Schmitz, J. M., Rhoades, H. M., & Grabowski, J. (2001). Motivational interviewing with cocaine-dependent patients: A pilot study. *Journal of Consulting and Clinical Psychology, 69*(5), 858–862.

Strupp, H. H., & Binder, J. L. (1984). *Psychotherapy in a new key*. Basic Books.

Sullaway, M., & Christensen, A. (1983). Assessment of dysfunctional interaction patterns in couples. *Journal of Marriage and the Family*, 653–660.

Sullivan, P. S., Salazar, L., Buchbinder, S., & Sanchez, T. H. (2009). Estimating the proportion of HIV transmissions from main sex partners among men who have sex with men in five US cities. *AIDS, 23*(9), 1153–1162.

Sullivan, P. S., Stephenson, R., Grazter, B., Wingood, G., DiClemente, R. J., Allen, S., Hoff, C. C., Salazar, L., Scales, L., Montgomery, J., Schwartz, A., Barnes, J., & Grabbe, K. (2014). Adaptation of the African couples HIV testing and counseling model for men who have sex with men in the United States: An application of the ADAPT-ITT framework. *SpringerPlus, 3*(1), 249–280.

Sultan, B., Benn, P., & Waters, L. (2014). Current perspectives in HIV post-exposure prophylaxis. *HIV/AIDS (Auckland, NZ), 6*, 147–158.

Sungur, M. Z., & Gündüz, A. (2014). A comparison of *DSM-IV-TR* and *DSM-5* definitions for sexual dysfunctions: Critiques and challenges. *Journal of Sexual Medicine, 11*(2), 364–373.

Susman, E. J., Houts, R. M., Steinberg, L., Belsky, J., Cauffman, E., DeHart, G., Friedman, S. L., Roisman, G. I., & Halpern-Felsher, B. L. (2010). Longitudinal development of secondary sexual characteristics in girls and boys between ages 9½ and 15½ years. *Archives of Pediatrics & Adolescent Medicine, 164*(2), 166–173.

Szinovacz, M. E. (1981). Relationship among marital power measures: A critical review and an empirical test. *Journal of Comparative Family Studies, 12*(2), 151–169.

Taft, C. T., Murphy, C. M., Elliott, J. D., & Morrel, T. M. (2001). Attendance-enhancing procedures in group counseling for domestic abusers. *Journal of Counseling Psychology, 48*(1), 51.

Terry, J. D., Weist, M. D., Strait, G. G., & Miller, M. (2020). Motivational Interviewing to promote the effectiveness of selective prevention: An integrated school-based approach. *Prevention Science, 22*(6), 799–810.

Thibaut, J. W., & Kelley, H. H. (1959). *The social psychology of groups*. Wiley.

Thomas, R., Abell, B., Webb, H. J., Avdagic, E., & Zimmer-Gembeck, M. J. (2017). Parent-child interaction therapy: A meta-analysis. *Pediatrics, 140*(3), e20170352.

Thorndike, E. (1920). A constant error in psychological ratings. *Journal of Applied Psychology, 4*, 24–29.

Thorley, L., Lut, I., Crenna-Jennings, W., Benton, L., Jeffries, J., Kirwan, P., Hibbert, M., Okala, S., Asboe, D., Kunda, C., Mbewe, R., Morris, S., Morton, J., Nelson, M., Paterson, H., Reeves, I., Ross, M., Sharp, L., Seruma, W., . . . Hudson, A. (2016 July). *Stigma in the age of undetectability*. International AIDS Conference [Conference Session]. Durban, South Africa.

Tie, S., & Poulsen, S. (2013). Emotionally focused couple therapy with couples facing terminal illness. *Contemporary Family Therapy, 35*, 557–567.

Tjosvold, D., Peng, A. C., Chen, Y. F., & Su, F. (2008). Business and government interdependence in China: Cooperative goals to develop industries and the marketplace. *Asia Pacific Journal of Management, 25*(2), 225–249.

Todahl, J., & Walkders, E. (2011). Universal screening for intimate partner violence: A systematic review. *Journal of Marital and Family Therapy, 37*(3), 355–369.

Tolchin, B., Baslet, G., Martino, S., Suzuki, J., Blumenfeld, H., Hirsch, L. J., Altalib, H., & Dworetzky, B. A. (2020). Motivational interviewing techniques to improve psychotherapy adherence and outcomes for patients with psychogenic nonepileptic seizures. *Journal of Neuropsychiatry and Clinical Neuroscience, 32*(2), 125–131.

Tolman, D. L., & McClelland, S. I. (2011). Normative sexuality development in adolescence: A decade in review, 2000–2009. *Journal of Research on Adolescence, 21*(1), 242–255.

Tolou-Shams, M., Dauria, E., Conrad, S. M., Kemp, K., Johnson, S., & Brown, L. K. (2017). Outcomes of a family-based HIV prevention intervention for substance using juvenile offenders. *Journal of Substance Abuse Treatment, 77*, 115–125.

Totenhagen, C. J., Randall, A. K., & Lloyd, K. (2018). Stress and relationship functioning in same-sex couples: The vulnerabilities of internalized homophobia and outness. *Family Relations, 67*(3), 399–413.

Tran, B. X., Nguyen, L. T., Do, C. D., Nguyen, Q. L., & Maher, R. M. (2014). Associations between alcohol use disorders and adherence to antiretroviral treatment and quality of life amongst people living with HIV/AIDS. *BMC Public Health, 14*(1), 27.

Triandis, H. C. (2018). *Individualism and collectivism*. Routledge.

Troiden, R. R. (1988). Homosexual identity development. *Journal of Adolescent Health Care, 9*(2), 105–113.

Tunnell, G. (2012). Gay male couple therapy: An attachment-based model. In J. J. Bigner & J. L. Wetchler (Eds.), *Handbook of LGBT-affirmative couple and family therapy* (pp. 25–42). Routledge.

Ukatt Research Team. (2005). Effectiveness of treatment for alcohol problems: Findings of the randomised UK Alcohol Treatment Trial (UKATT). *BMJ, 331*(7516), 541–544.

U.S. Department of Health and Human Services. (2005). Antiretroviral postexposure prophylaxis after sexual, injection-drug use, or other nonoccupational exposure to HIV in the United States: Recommendations from the U.S. Department of Health and Human Services. *MMWR Morbidity & Mortality Weekly Reports Recommendations and Reports, 54*(RR-2), 1–20. https://www.cdc.gov/mmwr/prev iew/mmwrhtml/rr5402a1.htm

U.S. Department of Health and Human Services. (2021). About PEP. https://www.cdc. gov/hiv/basics/pep/about-pep.html. Last accessed March 31, 2022.

U.S. Department of Health and Human Services. (2021a, April 21) What is PEP? https:// www.hiv.gov/hiv-basics/hiv-prevention/using-hiv-medication-to-reduce-risk/ post-exposure-prophylaxis

U.S. Department of Health and Human Services. (2021b, December 21). NIH Celebrates of long-acting injectable PrEP. https://www.nih.gov/news-events/ news-releases/nih-celebrates-fda-approval-long-acting-injectable-drug-hiv-pre vention

Venner, K. L., Greenfield, B. L., Hagler, K. J., Simmons, J., Lupee, D., Homer, E., Yamutewa, Y., & Smith, J. E. (2016). Pilot outcome results of culturally adapted evidence-based substance use disorder treatment with a Southwest Tribe. *Addictive Behaviors Reports, 3*, 21–27.

Verma, T. (2019). Managing online video gaming-related addictive behaviors through motivational interviewing. *Indian Journal of Social Psychiatry, 35*(3), 217–219.

Veroff, J., Kulka, R. A., & Douvan, E. (1981). *Mental health in America.* New York: Basic Books.

Vogel, E. A., Belohlavek, A., Prochaska, J. J., & Ramo, D. E. (2019). Development and acceptability testing of a Facebook smoking cessation intervention for sexual and gender minority young adults. *Internet Interventions, 15*, 87–92.

Vosburgh, H. W., Mansergh, G., Sullivan, P. S., & Purcell, D. W. (2012). A review of the literature on event-level substance use and sexual risk behavior among men who have sex with men. *AIDS and Behavior, 16*(6), 1394–1410.

Wagner, C. C., & Ingersoll, K. S. (2012). *Motivational Interviewing in groups.* Guilford Press.

Walker, L., & Taylor, D. (2021). *Same-sex couple households: 2019.* American Community Survey Briefs (Report number ACSBR-005). U.S. Census Bureau.

Wang, K., & Pachankis, J. E. (2016). Gay-related rejection sensitivity as a risk factor for condomless sex. *AIDS and Behavior, 20*(4), 763–767.

Wang, S.-F., Li, Y.-C., Chang, J.-R., Courtney, M., & Chang, Y.-L. (2007). The application of self-efficacy counseling skills to health education in patients with diabetes. *Journal of Nursing, 54*(1), 70–77.

Wang, Z., Lau, J. T. F., Ip, M., Ho, S. P. Y., Mo, P. K. H., Latikin, C., Ma, Y. L., & Kim, Y. (2018). A randomized controlled trial evaluating efficacy of promoting a home-based HIV self-testing with online counseling on increasing HIV testing among men who have sex with men. *AIDS and Behavior, 22*(1), 190–201.

Watkins, C. L., Wathan, J. V., Leathley, M. J., Auton, M. F., Deans, C. F., Dickinson, H. A., Jack, C. I. A., Sutton, C. J., Broek, M. D. v. d., & Lightbody, C. E. (2011). The 12-month effects of early Motivational Interviewing after acute stroke. *Stroke, 42*(7), 1956–1961.

Weiner, L., & Avery-Clark, C. (2014). Sensate focus: Clarifying the Masters and Johnson's model. *Sexual and Relationship Therapy, 29*(3), 307–319.

Weiss, R. L., & Heyman, R. E. (1990). Observation of marital interaction. In F. D. Fincham & T. N. Bradbury (Eds.), *The psychology of marriage: Basic issues and applications* (pp. 87–117). Guilford Press.

Wells, B. E., Golub, S. A., & Parsons, J. T. (2011). An integrated theoretical approach to substance use and risky sexual behavior among men who have sex with men. *AIDS and Behavior, 15*(3), 509–520.

Westra, H. A., Constantino, M. J., & Antony, M. M. (2016). Integrating motivational interviewing with cognitive-behavioral therapy for severe generalized anxiety disorder: An allegiance-controlled randomized clinical trial. *Journal of Consulting and Clinical Psychology, 84*(9), 768–782.

Whisman, M. A., & Jacobson, N. S. (1990). Power, marital satisfaction, and response to marital therapy. *Journal of Family Psychology, 4*(2), 202.

White, H. R., Fleming, C. B., Catalano, R. F., & Bailey, J. A. (2009). Prospective associations among alcohol use-related sexual enhancement expectancies, sex after alcohol use, and casual sex. *Psychology of Addictive Behaviors, 23*(4), 702–707.

Whitton, S. W., Dyar, C., Newcomb, M. E., & Mustanski, B. (2018a). Effects of romantic involvement on substance use among young sexual and gender minorities. *Drug and Alcohol Dependence, 191*, 215–222.

Whitton, S. W., Dyar, C., Newcomb, M. E., & Mustanski, B. (2018b). Romatic involvement: A protective factor for psychological health in racially-diverse young sexual minorities. *Journal of Abnormal Psychology, 127*(3), 265–275.

Whitton, S. W., & Kuryluk, A. D. (2012). Relationship satisfaction and depressive symptoms in emerging adults: Cross-sectional associations and moderating effects of relationship characteristics. *Journal of Family Psychology, 26*(2), 226–235.

Whitton, S. W., & Kuryluk, A. D. (2014). Associations between relationship quality and depressive symptoms in same-sex couples. *Journal of Family Psychology, 28*(4), 571–576.

Whitton, S. W., Weitbrecht, E. M., Kuryluk, A. D., & Hutsell, D. W. (2016). A randomized waitlist-controlled trial of culturally sensitive relationship education for male same-sex couples. *Journal of Family Psychology, 30*(6), 763–768.

Wiebe, S. A., & Johnson, S. M. (2016). A review of the research in emotionally focused therapy for couples. *Family Process, 55*(3), 390–407.

Wieselquist, J., Rusbult, C. E., Foster, C. A., & Agnew, C. R. (1999). Commitment, pro-relationship behavior, and trust in close relationships. *Journal of Personality and Social Psychology, 77*(5), 942.

Wilson, G. T., & Lawson, D. M. (1976). Expectancies, alcohol, and sexual arousal in male social drinkers. *Journal of Abnormal Psychology, 87*(3), 587–594.

Wilson, K. G., Sandoz, E. K., Kitchens, J., & Roberts, M. (2010). The Valued Living Questionnaire: Defining and measuring valued action within a behavioral framework. *Psychological Record, 60*(2), 249–272.

Wincze, J. P., & Weisberg, R. B. (2001). *Sexual dysfunction: A guide for assessment and treatment* (3rd ed.). Guilford Press.

Winters, K. C., & Leitten, W. (2007). Brief intervention for drug-abusing adolescents in a school setting. *Psychology of Addictive Behavior, 21*(2), 249–254.

WHO.int [Internet]. Geneva. World Health Organization: c1948–2018. Defining sexual health; c2006 [updated 2010, cited 2018 Mar 24]; [about 3 screens]. Available from: http://www.who.int/reproductivehealth/topics/sexual_health/sh_definitions/en/

World Health Organization. (2012a). *Guidance on couples HIV testing and counseling including antiretroviral therapy for treatment and prevention in serodiscordant couples: Recommendations for a public health approach.* https://apps.who.int/iris/bitstream/handle/10665/44646/9789241501972_eng.pdf

World Health Organization. (2012b). *Understanding and addressing violence against women: Intimate partner violence* (No. WHO/RHR/12.36). https://apps.who.int/iris/bitstream/handle/10665/77432/?sequence=1

World Health Organization. (2019). *What's the 2+1+1? Event-driven oral pre-exposure prophylaxis to prevent HIV for men who have sex with men.* https://www.who.int/publications-detail-redirect/what-s-the-2-1-1-event-driven-oral-pre-exposure-prophylaxis-to-prevent-hiv-for-men-who-have-sex-with-men

World Health Organization. (2021). Sexual and reproductive health. https://www.who.int/reproductivehealth/topics/en/

Wright, B. L., & Loving, T. J. (2011). Health implications of conflict in close relationships. *Social and Personality Psychology Compass, 5/8*, 552–562.

Wrzus, C., Hanel, M., Wagner, J., & Neyer, F. J. (2013). Social network changes and life events across the life span: A meta-analysis. *Psychological Bulletin, 139*(1), 53–80.

Wu, E., El-Bassel, N., McVinney, L. D., Fontaine, Y. M., & Hess, L. (2010). Adaptation of a couple-based HIV intervention for methamphetamine-involved African American men who have sex with men. *Open AIDS Journal, 4,* 123–131.

Wu, E., El-Bassel, N., McVinney, L. D., Hess, L., Remien, R. H., Charania, M., & Mansergh, G. (2011). Feasibility and promise of a couple-based HIV/STI preventive intervention for methamphetamine-using, black men who have sex with men. *AIDS and Behavior, 15*(8), 1745–1754.

Yakovenko, I., Quigley, L., Hemmelgarn, B. R., Hodgins, D. C., & Ronksley, P. (2015). The efficacy of motivational interviewing for disordered gambling: Systematic review and meta-analysis. *Addictive Behavior, 43,* 72–82.

Yeh, H. C., Lorenz, F. O., Wickrama, K. A. S., Conger, R. D., & Elder, G. H., Jr. (2006). Relationships among sexual satisfaction, marital quality, and marital instability at midlife. *Journal of Family Psychology, 20*(2), 339–343.

Yoshimura, K. (2017). Current status of HIV/AIDS in the ART era. *Journal of Infection and Chemotherapy, 23*(1), 12–16. https://doi.org/10.1016/j.jiac.2016.10.002

Yovetich, N. A., & Rusbult, C. E. (1994). Accommodative behavior in close relationships: Exploring transformation of motivation. *Journal of Experimental Social Psychology, 30*(2), 138–164.

Yucel, D., & Gassanov, M. A. (2010). Exploring actor and partner correlates of sexual satisfaction among married couples. *Social Science Research, 39*(5), 725–738.

Yus, F. (1999). Misunderstandings and explicit/implicit communication. *Pragmatics, 9*(4), 487–517.

Zrenchik, K. (2015). Two appreciations: A couples therapy intervention to enhance intimacy and relational satisfaction. *Journal of Family Psychotherapy, 26*(1), 74–80.

Zuckoff, A., & Dew, M. A. (2012). Research on MI in equipoise: The case of living organ donation. *Motivational Interviewing: Training, Research, Implementation, Practice, 1*(1), 39–41.

For the benefit of digital users, indexed terms that span two pages (e.g., 52–53) may, on occasion, appear on only one of those pages.

Tables, figures, and boxes are indicated by an *t*, *f*, and *b* following the page number.